CHRISTO
Universit
and Nortl

Further p

'Based on
to take its
ship of th
Revolutioi

'This judi
driven "w;
the Syrian
Ian Black,

D1423650

CHRISTOPHER PHILLIPS

THE BATTLE FOR SYRIA

INTERNATIONAL RIVALRY IN
THE NEW MIDDLE EAST

YALE UNIVERSITY PRESS
NEW HAVEN AND LONDON

For information about this and other Yale University Press publications, please contact:
U.S. Office: sales.press@yale.edu   yalebooks.com
Europe Office: sales@yaleup.co.uk   yalebooks.co.uk

Typeset in Minion Pro by IDSUK (DataConnection) Ltd
Printed in Great Britain by Hobbs the Printers, Totton, Hampshire

Library of Congress Control Number: 2017956653

ISBN 978-0-300-21717-9 (cloth)
ISBN 978-0-300-23461-9 (pbk)

10 9 8 7 6 5 4 3 2 1

Contents

Preface to the paperback edition

It has been eighteen months since I finished writing *The Battle for Syria* and, sadly, the war still rages. The conflict is now more international than ever, with Russia and Iran deeply embedded alongside the forces of Syrian president Bashar al-Assad, while the United States controls the skies over eastern Syria and has special forces on the ground in its fight against the Islamic State of Iraq and al-Sham (ISIS). Meanwhile, Turkey now directly occupies a strip of northern Syria, while Saudi Arabia, Qatar and others continue to sponsor the anti-Assad rebels in some form. This book, which explains why and how these external actors became involved in Syria's uprising and civil war and how they have helped shape its character and longevity, continues to be relevant for our understanding of how we got here.

That said, inevitably, events on the ground have developed since the book was published. The Vienna Peace Process of 2016, which closed the hardback edition, has fallen apart and Assad now looks likely to triumph in some form over the armed rebels. At the same time, ISIS, once so fearsome in the east, is retreating, largely to the benefit of the Kurdish-led Syrian Democratic Forces (SDF) whose presence has expanded far beyond its traditional hinterland. In many ways, these developments vindicate *The Battle for Syria*'s central argument – that international factors have been key in shaping the conflict – as each of these developments was prompted by external shifts. Assad's successes, including the capture of eastern Aleppo in December 2016, came after increased Russian and Iranian backing on the one hand, and the withdrawal of Turkish support for the rebels (after an agreement with Moscow) on the other. The weakening of the rebels more broadly has been largely due to the withdrawal of Turkish and American support and the Turkish–Iranian–Russian-led Astana Peace Process that heavily favours Assad. Meanwhile the collapse of ISIS and the empowerment of the SDF has come about after considerable American armament, training and support. As ever, domestic factors have interacted with these external forces, and no Syrian on the ground should be considered a puppet of an outside power, but these international components have certainly shaped developments.

I have taken the opportunity of this new paperback edition to update the text to include these key events. The main addition is an eleventh chapter, which covers the final year of Barack Obama's presidency – including the fall of Aleppo and the Turkey–Russia rapprochement – before considering how President Donald Trump's administration has fared on Syria. Some changes have also been made to the Introduction and Conclusion, to better reflect how events have unfolded. However, the vast majority of the text remains as it was: an account of how and why international rivalries have tragically played out on the bloody battlegrounds of Syria.

Queen Mary, University of London, September 2017

Acknowledgements

This book is the result of five years of research on the international relations of the Syrian civil war. It has taken me to fourteen different countries, from ministries to refugee camps, where countless people have gone out of their way to assist me. I am extremely grateful to all of those who have helped and encouraged me along the way. I want to particularly thank those who have asked not to be named. A work such as this is dependent on the willingness of those with intimate knowledge of the conflict – whether policymakers, government officials or those caught in the fighting – to speak frankly and openly about their experiences and observations. To the dozens who have shared their insights but understandably prefer to remain anonymous, my sincerest thanks.

My deepest thanks also to everyone at Yale University Press for supporting this work and making it a reality: to Heather McCallum for helping channel my broad ideas into a workable volume; to Rachael Lonsdale for answering my endless, no doubt tedious, queries; and to Melissa Bond and Beth Humphries for their sharp editorial work.

The School of Politics and International Relations at Queen Mary, University of London, has been my professional home throughout this project, and I am most appreciative of the wide-ranging support it has offered. Multiple research trips have been generously funded, as has a sabbatical. I am grateful to all my colleagues for helping create such a friendly and stimulating environment to work in, but particular thanks must go to Adam Fagan, a hugely encouraging Head of School, and to Lee Jones, Bryan Mabee and Eleanor Bindman, who kindly read over draft chapters and papers. My second home during this time has been Chatham House, where I am an associate fellow in the Middle East and North Africa Programme and where I helped found the Syria and its Neighbours Policy Initiative. This initiative has allowed me access to many key policymakers in the conflict, which proved invaluable to this book. The Chatham House team and other associate fellows, past and present, have been incredibly supportive of my work, including involving me in informative research trips and workshops. Special thanks are due to Abdullah Ali, Sara Bazoobandi, Doris Carrion, Kristian Coates Ulrichsen, Tim Eaton, Hassan Hassan, Jane Kinninmont, Neil Quilliam, Claire Spencer and Helen Twist.

Away from London, I must thank the three institutions that kindly hosted me while I conducted field research: the Georgetown Center for Contemporary Arab studies in Washington, DC; the Orient Institut in Beirut; and the King Faisal Center for Research and Islamic Studies in Riyadh. I am also extremely grateful to the following, who, in many different ways, supported, helped and facilitated my research: Dania Akkad, Malik al-Abdeh, the Arab Peace Center for Research and Policy Studies in Doha, Gokhan Bacik, Julien Barnes-Dacey, Abdul Hakim Bashar, Andrew Bowen, Lakhdar Brahimi, Alistair Burt, Glen Carey, Martin Chulov, Simon Collis, Roland Dannreuther, Ramazan Daurov, Toby Dodge, Chris Doyle, Filipo Dionigi, Abigail Fielding-Smith, Robert Ford, Alice Fordham, Jasmine Gani, the Genc family, Fawaz Gerges, Bryan Gibson, Haid Haid, Ibrahim Hamidi, Raymond Hinnebusch, Steven Heydemann, Fred Hof, Marwan Kabalan, Mehran Kamrava, Saban Kardas, Brian Katulis, Rania Kiblawi, Caroline Kinj, Kemal Kirisci, Bassma Kodmani, Andreas Krieg, Marc Lynch, Thomas McGee, Jihad Makdissi, Alexey Malashenko, Kevin Mazur, Elsy Melkonian, Vitaly Naumkin, Daniel Neep, Ahmed al-Omran, Soli Ozel, Jeremy Shapiro, Steven Simon, Randa Slim, Ken Sofer, Andrew Tabler, Gonul Tol, Ilhan Uzgel, Steven Walt, Becca Wasser, Katherine Wilkins, Jon Wilks, Steven Wright, Paul Wood and Irina Zvyagelskaya.

I must express special thanks to David Lesch, David Butter and the anonymous reviewers who kindly looked over early drafts of the manuscript, offering valuable recommendations and feedback. Finally, I must thank my family, friends and loved ones, without whose support this book could not have been written.

This book is dedicated to the people of Syria, on all sides of this vicious and tragic conflict, who deserve better from the world.

Key actors and abbreviations

The Assad regime and its allies

'The regime'

Bashar al-Assad, Syrian President 2000–

Hafez al-Assad, Syrian President 1971–2000

Asma al-Assad (née Akhras), Syria's First Lady 2000–

Maher al-Assad, brother of Bashar al-Assad, Commander of Republican Guard and 4th Armoured Division

Anisa Makhlouf, mother of Bashar al-Assad

Assif Shawkat, brother-in-law of Bashar al-Assad, head of military intelligence 2005–9, deputy minister of defence 2011–12

Rami Makhlouf, cousin of Bashar al-Assad, wealthy businessman

Manaf Tlass, Republican Guard General, defected 2012

Farouk al-Sharaa, First Vice President of Syria 2006–

Walid al-Muallem, Foreign Minister 2006–

Bouthaina Shabaan, political and media adviser to the Syrian President 2008–

Ba'ath – Arab Socialist Ba'ath Party, the ruling party of Syria since 1963

Mukhabarat – Set of notorious regime intelligence agencies

Shabiha – Gangs of irregular pro-regime thugs

NDF – National Defence Force, formed 2013

Russia

Vladimir Putin, Russian President 2000–8, 2012–, Russian Prime Minister 2008–12

Dmitri Medvedev, Russian President 2008–12, Russian Prime Minister 2012–

Sergei Lavrov, Foreign Minister 2004–

Mikhail Bogdanov, Deputy Foreign Minister 2011–

Iran

Ayatollah Ali Khamenei, Supreme Leader of Iran 1989–

Mahmoud Ahmadinejad, Iranian President 2005–13
Hassan Rouhani, Iranian President 2013–
Ali Akbar Salehi, Foreign Minister 2010–13
Mohammad Javad Zarif, Foreign Minister 2013–
Qassem Suleimani, Commander of the Quds Force 1998–

IRGC – Islamic Revolutionary Guard Corps
Quds Force – Special forces unit of IRGC

Hezbollah
Hassan Nasrallah, Hezbollah Secretary General 1992–

The Assad regime's opponents

'The opposition'

Political

SNC – Syrian National Council, formed 2011
SOC – The National Coalition for Syrian Revolutionary and Opposition Forces, formed 2012
LCCs – Local Coordination Committees (*tansiqiyat*), formed 2011
MB – The Muslim Brotherhood, Syrian branch formed 1940
NCB – National Coordination Body for Democratic Change, formed 2011
HNC – Higher Negotiations Committee, formed 2015

Burhan Ghalioun, President of SNC 2011–12
Ahmed Moaz al-Khatib, President of SOC 2012–13
Riad Seif, Vice President of SOC 2012–17, President of SOC 2017–
Suhair Atassi, Vice President of SOC 2012–13
Ghassan Hitto, Prime Minister of SOC, March–September 2013
Ahmed Jarba, President of SOC 2013–14
Hadi al-Bahra, President of SOC 2014–15
Khaled Koja, President of SOC 2015–16
Anas al-Abdeh, President of SOC 2016–17
Michel Kilo, veteran oppositionist affiliated with Damascus Declaration, SNC and SOC
Haytham Manna, leftist veteran oppositionist, joint founder of NCB
Mahmoud Farouq Tayfour, MB's Second Deputy
Riad Hijab, head of HNC 2015–

Armed

FSA – Free Syrian Army, formed 2011
FSA–SMC – Free Syrian Army Supreme Military Council, formed 2012

SILF – Syrian Islamic Liberation Front, active 2012–13
SIF – Syrian Islamic Front, active 2012–13
Islamic Front, active 2013–15
The Southern Front, formed 2014
Jaysh al-Fateh (Army of Conquest), formed 2015

Riad al-Asaad, founder and commander of FSA 2011–12
Selim Idriss, commander of FSA–SMC 2012–14
Hassan Abboud, founder of Ahrar al-Sham, active 2011–14
Zahran Alloush, founder of Jaysh al-Islam, active 2011–15

Leading jihadists

ISIS
ISIS – Islamic State of Iraq and al-Sham (Greater Syria), also known as Islamic State, ISIL, Da'ash, adopted name 2013
ISI – Islamic State in Iraq, ISIS forerunner, active 2006–13
AQI – al-Qaeda in Iraq, ISI forerunner, active 2004–6

Abu Bakr al-Baghdadi, leader of ISIS and its predecessors 2010–

Jabhat al-Nusra
Jabhat al-Nusra, active 2011–16
Jabhat Fateh al-Sham, rebranded name for Nusra 2016–17
HTS, Hay'at Tahrir al-Sham, new coalition dominated by Nusra, formed 2017

Abu-Mohammad al-Jolani, founder and leader of Nusra 2011–

Kurdish forces

KNC – Kurdish National Council
PYD – Democratic Union Party (Partiya Yekîtiya Demokrat)
YPG – People's Protection Units (Yekîneyên Parastina Gel), the PYD's militia
SDF – Syrian Democratic Forces, mixed Arab/Kurdish fighting group aligned with PYD
KRG – Kurdistan Regional Government, mostly Kurdish autonomous region of northern Iraq
PKK – Kurdistan Workers Party (Partiya Karkerên Kurdistanê), Turkish Kurdish militant group
Abdel Hakim Bashar, chairman of KNC 2011–, Vice President of SOC 2013–
Salih Muslim, chairman of PYD 2010–
Massoud Barzani, President of KRG 2005–

United States and Western allies

United States

Barack Obama, US President 2009–16

Joe Biden, US Vice President 2009–16

Hillary Clinton, US Secretary of State 2009–13

John Kerry, US Secretary of State 2013–17

Robert Gates, Defense Secretary 2006–11

Chuck Hagel, Defense Secretary 2013–15

Ash Carter, Defense Secretary 2015–16

Samantha Power, Special Assistant to the President, National Security Council 2009–13, Ambassador to the UN 2013–16

Susan Rice, Ambassador to the UN 2009–13, National Security Advisor 2013–16

Thomas Donilon, National Security Advisor 2010–13

Denis McDonough, Deputy National Security Advisor 2010–13, White House Chief of Staff 2013–16

Ben Rhodes, Assistant to the President and Deputy National Security Advisor for Strategic Communications and Speechwriting 2009–16

John Brennan, Homeland Security Advisor 2009–13, CIA Director 2013–16

Martin Dempsey, Chairman of the Joint Chiefs of Staff 2011–15

Tony Blinken, Deputy Assistant to the President and National Security Advisor to the Vice President 2009–13

Robert Ford, US Ambassador to Syria 2011–14

Donald Trump, US President 2017–

Mike Pence, US Vice President 2017–

Rex Tillerson, US Secretary of State 2017–

James Mattis, Defense Secretary 2017–

Nikki Haley, Ambassador to the UN 2017–

H.R. McMaster, National Security Advisor 2017–

Key Europeans

Nicolas Sarkozy, French President 2007–12

François Hollande, French President 2012–17

Eric Chevallier, French Ambassador to Syria, 2009–12

David Cameron, British Prime Minister 2010–16

William Hague, British Foreign Secretary 2010–14

Simon Collis, British Ambassador to Syria, 2007–12

Angela Merkel, German Chancellor 2005–

Saudi Arabia

Abdullah bin Abdulaziz, King of Saudi Arabia 2005–15

Salman bin Abdulaziz, King of Saudi Arabia 2015–

Nayef bin Abdulaziz, Interior Minister 1975–2012, Crown Prince 2011–12

Saud Al Faisal bin Abdulaziz, Foreign Minister 1975–2015

Mohammed bin Nayef bin Abdulaziz, Interior Minister 2012–17, Crown Prince 2015–17

Bandar bin Sultan bin Abdulaziz, Director General of the Saudi Arabian Intelligence Agency 2012–14

Mutaib bin Abdullah bin Abdulaziz, Chief of National Guard 2010–13, Minister of National Guard 2013–17

Muqrin bin Abdulaziz, Director General of Saudi Intelligence Agency 2005–12, Crown Prince January–April 2015

Mohammed bin Salman bin Abdulaziz, Minister of Defence 2015–, Deputy Crown Prince 2015–17, Crown Prince 2017–

Qatar

Hamad bin Khalifa al Thani, Emir of Qatar 1995–13

Tamim bin Hamad al Thani, Emir of Qatar 2013–

Hamad bin Jassim al-Thani, Foreign Minister 1992–2013, Prime Minister 2007–13

Yusuf Qaradawi, al-Jazeera presenter affiliated with the Muslim Brotherhood

Turkey

Recep Tayyip Erdoğan, Turkish Prime Minister 2003–14, Turkish President 2014–

Ahmet Davutoğlu, Foreign Minister 2009–14, Turkish Prime Minister 2014–16

Hakan Fidan, head of MİT 2010–

AKP – Justice and Development Party (Adalet ve Kalkınma Partisi)

MİT – National Intelligence Organisation (Milli İstihbarat Teşkilatı)

The United Nations

UNSMIS – United Nations Supervision Mission in Syria, April–August 2012

UNHCR – United Nations High Commissioner for Refugees

Ban Ki-Moon, UN Secretary General 2007–16

Kofi Annan, Joint United Nations and Arab League Envoy to Syria, February–August 2012

Lakhdar Brahimi, Joint United Nations and Arab League Envoy to Syria, 2012–14

Staffan de Mistura, Joint United Nations and Arab League Envoy to Syria, 2014–

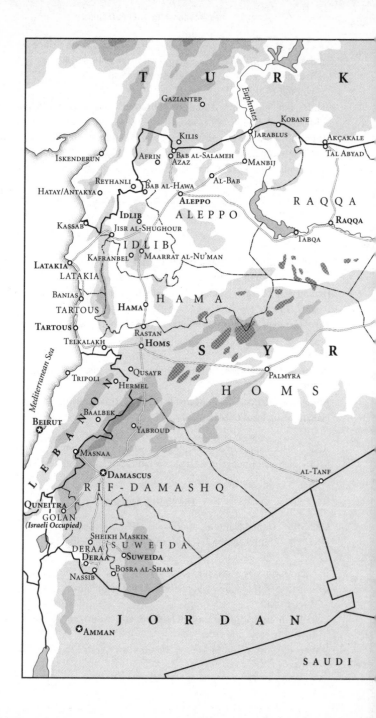

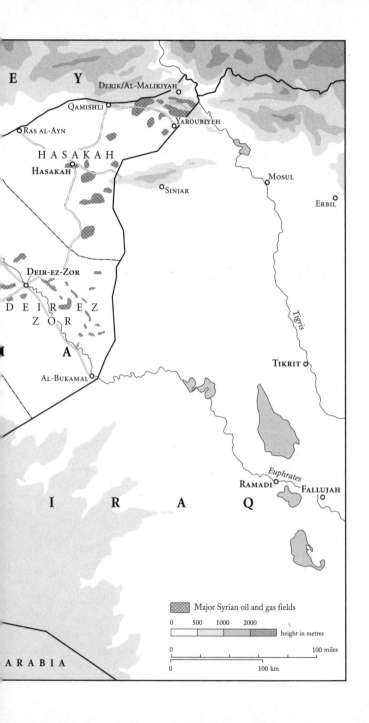

Introduction

[I]t is as a mirror of rival interests on an international scale that [Syria] deserves special attention. Indeed, her internal affairs are almost meaningless unless related to the wider context, first of her Arab neighbours and then other interested powers.

Patrick Seale, *The Struggle for Syria*, 1965[1]

The Syrian civil war is the greatest human disaster of the twenty-first century. Since conflict broke out in 2011, it is estimated that over 470,000 have been killed and 1.9 million wounded. Over 4.8 million have fled the country and 6.6 million more are internally displaced, more than half the pre-war population of 21 million. A United Nations report estimated that by the end of 2013 Syria had already regressed forty years in its human development. Two years later, half of its public hospitals had been closed, barely half of its children were attending school and over 80 per cent of Syrians were living in poverty, a third in abject poverty. Thousands of cases of long-absent diseases like typhoid and measles returned due to a lack of vaccination. Large parts of Syria's cities were rubble. The economy was in ruins. Hundreds of the country's precious cultural heritage locations, including five of its six UNESCO World Heritage Sites, had been damaged or destroyed. The average life expectancy of a Syrian dropped from seventy to fifty-five in four years.[2]

Over the course of its conflict Syria has been fragmented. The regime of President Bashar al-Assad concentrated its efforts on retaining a heavily populated strip of land stretching from Suwaida in the south to the capital Damascus, the central cities of Homs, Hama and the coast. Yet he lost control of large swathes of the east, north and south, and only slowly clawed some of this back. Where regime forces withdrew, a patchwork of different opponents claimed authority, often challenging each other as much as the regime. Along the northern border, Syrian Kurdish forces ruled three self-proclaimed cantons, while the sinister ISIS, a jihadist organisation originating in neighbouring Iraq, captured much of the east. In the south and north different opposition militia ruled local fiefdoms, some secular but many Islamist, often radically so. Attempts to end the war through negotiation have struggled, with neither Assad nor the rebels willing to make significant compromises. At the time of writing, Syria looks likely to remain unstable for years: even were the Assad regime to proclaim victory, suddenly fall or reach some tentative compromise peace, violence looks likely to continue in Syria for long afterwards.

How did this happen? When peaceful protests broke out in the southern town of Deraa in March 2011 few could have imagined the horror to come. The protesters initially called for reform rather than regime change, inspired by similar demonstrations that had toppled the leaders of Tunisia and Egypt. When the authorities replied with force, killing several in Deraa, the protests snowballed, spreading to other cities where they were also met by regime violence. Opposition grew rapidly, particularly in poorer regions, now demanding Assad's fall. The prosperous urban centres of Damascus and the commercial capital, Aleppo, remained comparatively quiet, and large orchestrated pro-Assad counter-demonstrations were held. The regime deployed cynical and brutal tactics. Agents provocateurs were placed among peaceful protesters to fire at regime troops, justifying them in replying with lethal force. In some cases the regime's secret police, the Mukhabarat, were placed within military and security units to threaten execution if soldiers refused to fire on civilians. False reports were delivered to Syria's religious minority groups, claiming that the protesters, who were mostly from the 65 per cent of the population who were Sunni Muslim Arabs, were Islamist radicals determined to slaughter them, which scared many into backing Assad. Tens of thousands were arrested and tortured, while female protesters reported sexual assault by regime thugs, the *shabiha*.

Facing such violence and brutality, segments of the opposition, which emerged as a localised, largely leaderless movement, fought back. Initially, local militia were formed to protect protests, but as thousands defected from Assad's military in disgust these groups swelled and began to challenge the regime head on. By late summer 2011 skirmishes between the regime and rebels were commonplace, and a civil war developed. Yet the decentralised nature of the opposition, which had allowed it to survive multiple arrests, proved a hindrance to waging a military campaign. The rebels formed more than 1,000 independent militias, often centred on a particular individual, region or ideology, hindering subsequent efforts to coordinate them under a single command structure. Personal and ideological differences, particularly over the role of Islam and jihadism, only grew as the conflict dragged on. The failure to land a decisive blow on

Assad contributed to rebel recrimination and the growing appeal of emerging radical groups such as ISIS.

Most narratives of the conflict focus primarily on internal dynamics.[3] The brutality of the Assad regime, combined with the incompetence and disunity of the opposition, led to a violent and intractable civil war. The role of international actors tends to be presented as secondary: they are sucked in once the war has begun, pursing their own regional or global agendas. This book offers a different interpretation, giving international factors a more central role in the narrative. It does not deny agency to either Assad or his opponents, and certainly does not indulge conspiracy theories that either acted as an agent of a foreign power from the beginning. Indeed, it recognises the complexity of the Syrian conflict and the multiple factors driving and shaping it. However, it argues that from the start, external factors have been essential in enabling and facilitating both regime and opposition actions. The war's character, scale and scope have been greatly impacted by these factors.

As we shall see, the international dimension shaped the war in three crucial ways. Firstly, the international and regional environment in which Syria's uprising began was key to its transformation into a civil war. From the shifting regional balance of power through to the proliferation of weapons and transnational ideologies, this structural environment made the shift towards civil war more likely. Secondly, the decisions made by leading states in the year following Syria's first protests and Assad's repression played a major role in escalating the uprising into a civil war. Finally, once the war was under way, the policies pursued by regional and international actors shaped its character and, importantly, ensured that it continued. Indeed, it is a core contention of this book that the Syrian civil war cannot be explained without a detailed understanding of the international dimension. As a result, until the various external actors involved either have their goals sufficiently satisfied or cut their losses and leave the stage, the war is likely to continue in some form.

After the Pax Americana

The regional political environment has been a key factor in Syria's civil war. On the eve of conflict, the Middle East was undergoing profound change. The perceived Pax Americana of US dominance over the region after the Cold War was coming undone. The failures of the 2003–11 occupation of Iraq, the decreasing importance of Gulf oil, economic and military retrenchment following the 2008 financial crisis, and the election of Barack Obama who criticised his predecessor's military adventures, all prompted a reluctance in Washington to continue the active hegemony of the past. At the same time new regional powers were emerging. Iran, Turkey and the Gulf states, previously peripheral players, all benefited from the fallout of the 2003 Iraq war and a hydrocarbons boom to increase their regional activism. Russia also took advantage of the favourable geopolitical and economic climate to strengthen its ties to the region after several decades' absence. In parallel, traditional regional powers weakened. Iraq was consumed by civil war and, like Egypt and Syria after 2011, was transformed from being a 'player' in regional politics into a 'prize' for other powers to fight over.[4] Israel remained largely unaffected by these changes, but with its peace process making no progress, its ability to project influence in the region was limited.

The significance of these changes to the regional political system has been debated. Numerous scholars and commentators have claimed that US power was in decline globally. What was a 'unipolar' post-Cold-War international order, dominated by the United States, became a 'multipolar' one with China, Russia and possibly the EU, India and Brazil challenging US hegemony.[5] In the Middle East, what Fawaz Gerges calls 'America's moment' was over, and multiple regional powers moved to fill the vacuum.[6] The weakening of states like Iraq and the growth of transnational actors such as Hezbollah, the PKK (Kurdistan Workers' Party) and al-Qaeda are other features of this new multipolar order.[7] Another set of scholars agree that change has occurred, but rather than a multipolar order American hegemony has given way to a bipolar system based around two blocs led by Saudi Arabia and Iran.[8] Sectarian differences between Sunni Saudi Arabia and Shia Iran play a factor in what Gregory Gause calls a 'New Middle East Cold War'.

In contrast, many have argued that US dominance is not over. Globally, by the 2000s the US was weakened, but no emerging power was even close to matching the US' military strength, and international institutions remain those designed and dominated by Washington. Many have predicted US decline in the past, such as in the 1980s, and been proven wrong.[9] These voices, dominated by those in the US' national security establishment, are 'still committed to trying to run the world'.[10] The Middle East, they argue, reflects the global situation. The US may have stepped back somewhat, but this is a temporary political move rather than a structural shift away from US hegemony. They had hoped that when the anti-interventionist Obama left office, there would be a reversion to dominance.[11] Yet no regional power or group of powers is in a strong enough position to fill the vacuum and, indeed, key regional powers like Turkey, Saudi Arabia and Israel remain reliant on a sizeable US presence.[12]

While the debate over US decline globally will continue to rage, it will be made clear in the pages that follow that the US no longer dominates the Middle East as it was once believed to. Indeed, some argue that stepping back in the Middle East is a way of preventing US decline elsewhere.[13] This does not mean, however, that a new system has yet replaced it, whether multipolar or bipolar. The regional order is currently in flux. The US is still the most powerful actor, and has played a pronounced role in regional politics, pursuing initiatives such as trying to revive the Israel–Palestine peace process and reaching an international agreement on Iran's nuclear programme. However, it no longer enjoys the perceived hegemony of the 1990s and 2000s, and regional actors and Russia have vied to increase their influence. Yet the breakdown of an old system and the emergence of a new one does not happen overnight, and the years before and after 2011 have witnessed each actor, including the US, probing what is possible. Importantly, the US has still been perceived by many Middle Eastern actors to be hegemonic, while Washington has understandably not sought to promote the reality that it is less dominant than before. This misperception has impacted some states' policies, with allies such as Saudi Arabia repeatedly urging the US to be more active, and growing disillusioned with Washington when it refused.

Of the three options, a multipolar Middle East appears the most accurate description of the changes under way, with a Saudi-Iranian Cold War a component of it rather than the defining feature. That said, future US leaders less reticent than Barack Obama might yet attempt to reassert US hegemony, albeit with difficulty. What matters for the analysis of the Syrian civil war that follows is that it took place in an era of regional uncertainty as the perception of US hegemony was slowly coming undone: a post-American Middle East.[14] Not only was the Syrian civil war shaped and driven by this regional environment, but it in turn reinforced the trend towards multipolarity and an end of US dominance.

The battle for Syria

In his classic 1965 work, Patrick Seale argued that from 1945 to 1958 a 'Struggle for Syria' took place. The leading Arab states of the day, Iraq and Egypt, along with the Western powers and the Soviet Union each influenced Damascus' weak political system in the hope of 'winning' Syria and with it regional clout. The rise to power of Hafez al-Assad in 1970 marked an end to most external interference as he transformed Syria into a stronger albeit autocratic state.[15] The challenge to power faced by his son and successor,

Bashar, in 2011 marked the struggle's return. Syria's civil war echoes the regional and international struggle highlighted by Seale in the post-war period. Yet while in the 1940s and 1950s Syria had an (albeit flawed) participatory political system in which to contain these rivalries, today they are played out on the battlefield. Though the methods are different, as in the post-war period, several powers see victory in Syria as part of a wider regional goal: Syria is a battleground in the struggles emerging within the post-American Middle East.

Studies of the Syrian civil war thus far have focused more on the domestic than the international dimensions of the conflict. This is perhaps understandable given how little known Syria was to Western audiences when the war broke out, reflecting a general blind spot by policymakers and commentators.[16] These studies have focused on a domestic struggle that sucked in international and regional actors, but this book argues that international factors play a central role in any analysis of the conflict. This is a question not just of the agency of the various actors involved, although leaders' decisions were crucial, but also of the structure of the international environment. Domestic factors should not be overlooked and any discussion of the Syrian conflict must be multidimensional. Indeed, as Seale noted, there is interaction between internal and external actors and Syrians are not simply 'passive victim[s] of other people's quarrels'.[17] However, given how important international forces have been in facilitating and shaping the conflict, and how relatively underexplored these have been in accounts of the war thus far, within this book's combined analysis the external dimension will receive the greater emphasis.

Past scholarship on how international actors impact civil wars proves useful for understanding two key ways that the internal and external have interacted in the Syria conflict. Firstly, numerous studies have examined how external forces can escalate domestic conflicts. Foreign material support such as weapons and finance and even the expectation of it by domestic actors encourages military solutions to disputes.[18] This occurred in Syria where, from the beginning Assad and his enemies expected and received outside support. Yet external factors are also important when there is the likelihood of a domestic dispute turning into civil war.[19] As well as the general stability of the region, involving the recent occurrence of conflict nearby and the (related) ease of access to arms, past studies have shown that transnational factors such as the number of ethnic groups shared with neighbouring states, the scarcity of democratic governments in the region, and the lack of regional economic integration all increase the likelihood of civil war. Syria was surrounded by three recently warring states (Lebanon, Iraq and the Kurdish regions of Turkey), was poorly economically integrated, shared tribal, sectarian and ethnic ties with numerous neighbours, and was surrounded by largely non-democratic governments. Add to this the regional changes brought about by receding US hegemony and there was evidently a combustible mix.

Secondly, conflict studies also show how external actors can prolong civil wars once begun. Involvement by a foreign state on one side can shorten civil wars by increasing the chances that the state's ally will win or force its enemy to negotiate. However, 'balanced interventions', when multiple actors become involved on both sides, lengthen wars by creating a stalemate.[20] Involvement by external parties is likely to extend a civil conflict if they suffer relatively low costs in blood and treasure, as they have little incentive to negotiate.[21] Moreover, the more external actors involved, the longer civil war is likely to last, as they are unlikely to cease their involvement until their agendas are met and the more actors in play, the more difficult for any resolution to satisfy all agendas. For many years, Syria's conflict was 'balanced' in this way. Both the regime and its opponents received external support from multiple sources but not sufficient for either to achieve military victory or force the other side to negotiate. Similarly, the many actors involved have divergent agendas that have changed as the circumstances of the war have evolved. Any explanation of Syria's civil war must therefore explore why and how these actors became so involved.

There have been six main external state protagonists in Syria whose independent and often conflicting agendas have helped escalate and prolong the civil war: the US, Russia, Iran, Saudi Arabia, Turkey and Qatar. Other state actors have played a role, most notably the UK, France, China, UAE, Lebanon, Israel, Jordan, Iraq and Egypt, but none has had sufficient leverage detached from one of these main players to impact the conflict independently. Similarly, several non-state foreign actors have also influenced the war, notably Hezbollah, the PKK and ISIS, with the latter two largely operating independently of state patrons. These actors will also be analysed, alongside the six state players that have impacted the conflict from the beginning. Given the prominent role of these six, understanding their actions, the structural pressures they face and the politics and personalities of their rulers is key. The changing regional environment that contributed to the civil war has been exacerbated by misinterpretations, mistakes and overambitious regional agendas that often don't match up to actors' capacity to deliver.

The forces at play: An outline

This book is not intended as a history of Syria's civil war. Others will doubtless produce such a volume once the conflict is in the past and sufficient and reliable documentation and data have been gathered. Instead, this is a study in international relations, which utilises broader approaches from that discipline to increase our understanding of the origins, expansion and continuance of Syria's conflict. It offers a broad narrative that emphasises the interaction of internal and external forces. There is plenty of scope for further studies of each of the six actors' policies towards Syria and their impact on the ground in greater detail in the future.

The book draws on a combination of first-hand interviews and secondary open source material. Over five years, dozens of interviews have been conducted with Syrians and officials from each of the main protagonist states and other international institutions, although many wished to remain anonymous. Gaining reliable data from secondary sources to corroborate these interviews has been hindered by the highly political nature of reporting on this conflict. A 'war of narratives' has been under way from the beginning, with both sides seeking to manipulate the media and international bodies to present their view.[22] This has been compounded by the political preferences of some journalists sympathetic to either Assad or his opponents. As much as possible this work has sort to parse these biases to present a balanced picture, but inevitably not all data utilised can be definitively corroborated.

The book is organised into eleven further chapters and a Conclusion. The chapters are thematic, focusing on the different tools deployed by the six main actors to influence the Syrian crisis, such as diplomatic pressure, arming the rebels, supporting Assad's regime or directly intervening. The themes are loosely ordered chronologically, offering an analytical narrative of the conflict. Chapter 1 sets the historical context for the book. It sketches out the international relations of the Middle East on the eve of the Syrian civil war, considering how the perception of US hegemony impacted the Middle East and how that began to change after the 2003 Iraq war. The main goals and outlook of the six principal actors on the eve of the crisis will also be explored.

Chapters 2, 3 and 4 explore the early months of the crisis: the key period in setting Syria on a path to civil war. Chapter 2 considers the circumstances in which unrest began in Syria, profiling Bashar al-Assad's regime and explaining the logic behind its repressive strategy. Chapter 3 discusses the positions of the main actors over the course of May–August 2011. It charts how loose stances on Assad evolved into two camps for and against him, with Turkey's sudden turn on its former ally particularly profiled. Chapter 4 explores the early multilateral efforts to pressure Assad, such as economic sanctions and the peace plans of the Arab League and the United Nations, and the reasons for their failure. It particularly notes the role that Russia played in defending Assad.

Chapters 5, 6 and 7 consider why the six players backed different groups once civil war was under way and how this protracted and stalemated the conflict. Chapter 5 discusses the anti-Assad states' support for political opposition groups. It outlines the evolution of the Syrian opposition and charts how the main external supporters contributed to its weakness, with Saudi Arabia's role highlighted. Chapter 6 explores the other side of this support, that given to the different fighting opposition groups within Syria, with a pronounced profile of Qatar's role. Chapter 7 looks at Assad's allies, particularly Iran, and their support for the regime.

Chapters 8, 9, 10 and 11 explore the direct intervention by foreign militaries. Chapter 8 examines the question of Western intervention and why no state deployed its military to bring about regime change in Syria, particularly looking at the United States' position. Chapter 9 then looks at why the US and other states did choose to intervene in eastern Syria after 2014 following the rise of ISIS, which is profiled here. It explores the fragmentation of Syria and considers how other regional events shifted actors' calculations. Chapter 10 discusses Russia's decision to send its air force to directly support Assad in late summer 2015, what motivated this dramatic mobilisation and what impact it had on the conflict. Finally, Chapter 11 considers what changes to US policy were brought about by the election of a new president, Donald Trump, in 2017. While Trump positioned himself as anti-Obama, including launching direct US strikes against Assad for the first time, did this actually represent a radical departure or was it more style over substance? The Conclusion draws together the main arguments of the book and emphasises how the absence of regional consensus has been a key cause of Syria's tragedy.

CHAPTER ONE

Syria and the Middle East on the eve of civil war

As the First World War made painfully clear, when politicians and generals lead nations into war, they almost invariably assume swift victory, and have a remarkably enduring tendency not to foresee problems that, in hindsight, seem obvious.

Adam Hochschild[1]

Syria in the Middle East

Young country in an ancient land

Syria is a young country in an ancient land. While it boasts two of the oldest continuously inhabited cities on earth, Damascus and Aleppo, the modern state of Syria gained its independence only in 1945. In the 1920s, the territory was created and ruled over by France, the Arab territories of the Ottoman Empire having been divided between France and Britain after the First World War. As elsewhere in the Middle East, and in other colonised states, arbitrary borders drawn up in London and Paris took little account of either the will of the local populace or their pre-existing political, economic and cultural ties. Ancient trade routes from Mosul to Aleppo and Antioch were now divided between the new states of Iraq, Syria and Turkey. Damascus' main port, Beirut, was now the capital of Lebanon. Tribes in the south were cut off from their kin in Jordan, and in the east from Iraq. The new state was far from homogenous, with its ethnic make-up reflecting the ebbing and flowing of peoples and religions in the region. Ninety per cent of the population were Arabic-speakers, but the 10 per cent who spoke Kurdish had been separated from their co-linguists in Iraq, Turkey and Iran. Tiny pockets of Turkmen and Aramaic speakers also remained, while Armenian and Circassian communities had recently arrived as refugees from Anatolia and Russia. The people newly labelled 'Syrians' practised different religions and belonged to different confessions. Under the previous Ottoman rulers the Sunni Muslim majority had periodically persecuted the non-Sunni Muslim sects, often leading to their concentration in remote, defensible areas. Alawis dominated the coastal western mountains, while Druze clustered around a mountain in the south. A small number of other Shia sects, such as Ismailis and Twelvers, were concentrated in isolated villages.[2] Syria's (mostly Orthodox) Christians had a second-class status under the Ottomans, but were largely free from persecution and came to thrive in certain trades and businesses in the urban centres.

Syria was not the first, nor the last, post-colonial state to gain independence within borders imposed by outside powers. Like many such post-colonial states, it faced an uphill battle to bind its disparate population to the idea of a nation state. While an authentic sense of Syrian identity did develop over time, it came alongside a pronounced sense of insecurity and a rise in the popularity of revisionist transnational ideologies.[3] Arab nationalism, the call to unite all the Arabs in one state, found a receptive audience, as did Greater Syrian nationalism, which called for Syria to be united with neighbouring Lebanon, Jordan and Palestine. Political Islam also gained traction among some Sunnis. Meanwhile Kurdish nationalism grew in popularity among Kurds as Syria's Arabs increasingly denied them cultural rights.

These weak building blocks contributed to Syria's emergence as a fragile and unstable state after independence. The French left a weak parliamentary system and a powerful military that swiftly undermined it. Between 1949 and 1970 there were eight successful coups. These domestic struggles were greatly influenced by regional politics, as Syria's weakness made it a ripe political battleground for the regional rivals of the day. In 1958 Syria joined into a political union with Egypt as the United Arab Republic (UAR), which saw the Egyptian government introduce new authoritarian structures that remained even after Syria left the UAR in 1961.[4] In 1963 Syria's most prominent Arab nationalists, the socialist Ba'ath Party, seized power. The radical left wing of the party then launched an internal coup in 1966, initiating accelerated land reform and adopting a provocative line with Israel that contributed to the disastrous Six Day War of 1967 and the loss of the Golan Heights. The Syrian political scene was chaotic and unstable, weakened further by the machinations of external actors.

Assad takes over

This changed after November 1970 when Hafez al-Assad, the Ba'athist Defence Minister, seized power in a final coup and began to build a regime that survived long after his death in 2000. Hafez expanded the reach of the state, building institutions to ensure the support of everyday Syrians. He wooed the peasantry and workers with a heavily controlled economy that provided jobs and subsidies, and pursued ambitious infrastructural projects such as the electrification of Syria's villages.[5] He rolled back some of the radical socialism pursued in the 1960s, winning support from much of the merchant class. Hafez proved a savvy politician, patronising key tribal leaders and co-opting trade unions. At the same time, the President sought to protect his regime from the destabilising coups of the past. He restructured the security forces, packing key positions with relatives and Alawis, the sect from which he hailed, believing they would see his regime as protection against any return to the Sunni persecution of the Ottoman era. He disproportionately favoured Druze and Christians for the same reason, all the while ensuring that certain Sunnis remained in key positions, such as that of Prime Minister. A complex set of intelligence agencies was established to spy on regime insiders to prevent plotting, as well as on the population at large. While not as habitually bloody as Saddam Hussein, Hafez was still willing to use ruthless force when necessary, notably slaughtering up to 10,000 in 1982 when the banned Muslim Brotherhood tried to seize control of the city of Hama. For those not persuaded by the material benefits and stability of the regime, a wall of fear was built to keep them in line.

Hafez was a cannier leader than those before him, but he was also helped by three shifts in the regional environment. The first was the oil boom of the late 1970s. Whilst Syria had only modest oil reserves of its own, with exports from the eastern fields beginning in the 1980s, it shared in the region's increased wealth. This included remittances from Syrians working in the Gulf and generous funding from the newly rich Gulf states for its 'steadfastness' against Israel. Hafez eventually became a master of using changing political developments to obtain financial support from wealthy regional actors. The second shift in the 1970s was to an era of Arab cooperation. After Syria, Egypt and Jordan were defeated by Israel in the 1967 Six Day War, the previously feuding Arab states agreed at a summit in Khartoum to respect each other's state sovereignty and no longer interfere in each other's affairs. While this continued to be flouted in certain cases, notably Lebanon, it ensured that there was less appetite among potential regional rivals to stir up trouble for Assad at home, sparing Syria the machinations of the past. Finally, Cold War dynamics stabilised the region. During the 1950s, the Cold War powers held the region at arm's length, only signing closer alliances in the 1960s. After the 1973 October War nearly brought the US and USSR to war, Syria was effectively protected by its Soviet patron and there was little question of any external interference in Syrian affairs. As Richard Murphy, US ambassador to Syria 1974–78 remarked years later, 'the United States was little concerned with Assad's repressive domestic policies'.[6]

This combination of regional factors and Hafez' regime consolidation prompted Syria's transformation from an arena of competition to a projector of influence. Hafez took a leading role in Lebanon's civil war (1975–90), deploying his own troops there from 1976, and establishing a web of client relationships with multiple political actors and militia. Elsewhere he deployed the tactic of supporting non-state militias, with the Turkish Kurdish separatists, the PKK, given safe haven in Lebanon and Syria by Hafez from 1979 to 1998 as a means to pressure his northern neighbour, Turkey. A sign of Syria's new clout was its alliance with Revolutionary Iran from 1979 against shared enemies in Israel and Saddam Hussein's Iraq. Though he spoke the language of an Arab nationalist socialist at home, abroad Hafez was ever the pragmatist. This was seen in 1990–91 when, following the retreat and later collapse of his Soviet patron, Syria nimbly courted US support by backing the Western-led coalition to liberate Kuwait from Saddam Hussein. Though backing a Western power seemed an abandonment of Arab nationalism, it dealt a blow to his long-term personal enemy, Saddam, and by incurring American gratitude gained numerous rewards. One was Washington's endorsement of Syrian suzerainty over post-war Lebanon. Another was the invitation to engage in a US-led peace process with Israel over the 1990s that, while ultimately failing, allowed Syria to improve its image internationally. Bridges with other Arab states were rebuilt, notably with Kuwait and Saudi Arabia, who offered new loans and grants just as Syria's economy was suffering from the Soviet collapse, all the while quietly maintaining Syria's ties to Tehran.

Change and continuity under Bashar

Hafez' health declined in the late 1990s and he died of a heart attack on 10 June 2000, aged sixty-nine. Over thirty years he had ended decades of instability, building a strong autocratic regime that survived military defeat in 1973, the Muslim Brotherhood uprising, an attempted coup by his own brother, and the collapse of his Soviet ally. Hafez had groomed his eldest son, Bassel, to succeed him. When Bassel died in a car crash in 1994, his second son, Bashar, an ophthalmologist training in London at the time, was recalled home and rapidly promoted through Syria's military. Against the muted objections of a few old regime hands who believed dynastic succession should have no place in a socialist republic, key security and political figures endorsed

Hafez' plan and the way to the presidency was cleared. Bashar was elected in an unopposed referendum and became president on 17 July 2000, aged 34.

While many Syrian and international observers hoped that the young, partly Western-educated new president would abandon his father's ruthlessness at home and abroad, most were soon disappointed. At home, a short-lived liberal reform movement, the 'Damascus Spring' was snuffed out by autumn 2001.[7] Abroad, Assad's first decade in power would be defined by a confrontation with the neo-conservative administration of US President George W. Bush.[8] Though the US initially courted Damascus after 9/11, leading to some intelligence cooperation, Assad's staunch opposition to the planned invasion of Iraq in 2003 prompted confrontation, with then Undersecretary of State John Bolton adding Syria to a second tier of Bush's famous 'axis of evil'. Assad feared that successful regime change in Iraq would create a pro-Western state on his eastern flank, strengthening US and, by extension, Israeli regional power, and might embolden Bush to try the same in Damascus. Assad therefore revived his father's tactics of backing non-state militia to undermine his enemies, facilitating the flow of jihadists into Iraq to undermine the US occupation.[9]

The Bush administration hit back where it hurt: Syria's control over Lebanon. The Syria Accountability and Lebanese Sovereignty Restoration Act, which Bush signed into law on 12 December 2003, linked Syria's subversion in Iraq to its continued presence in Lebanon for the first time. Banning all US trade with Syria, aside from food and medicine, it demanded both 'an end to its occupation of Lebanon', and to all 'illegal shipments of weapons and other military items to Iraq'.[10] In September 2004, the US then co-sponsored with France UN Resolution 1559, which called for all 'foreign forces' to withdraw from Lebanon – code for the 14,000 Syrian troops and intelligence agents who had remained after the civil war.[11] Assad ignored the UN calls, but on 14 February 2005 a massive bomb in Beirut killed former Lebanese Prime Minister, Rafic Hariri, a popular supporter of UN1559, and fingers immediately pointed at Damascus. Huge anti-Syrian demonstrations broke out in Beirut, demanding Syrian withdrawal. Counter-demonstrations led by Hezbollah, the militia built during the Lebanese civil war by Syria's ally, Iran, did little to ease the pressure. Even Syria's traditional ally, Russia, and key Arab states such as Saudi Arabia, joined Western calls for Assad to comply with UN1559 and, on 9–10 April, the last Syrian troops were finally withdrawn.

But the showdown was far from over. As the flow of fighters into Iraq sporadically continued, Bush, who withdrew the US ambassador from Damascus immediately after the Hariri assassination, urged the international community to diplomatically boycott Syria. Facing isolation, Assad drew closer to Iran, also ostracised by Bush. Damascus promoted the idea that, far from an axis of evil they – Iran, Hezbollah and the Palestinian Islamist group Hamas – were an 'Axis of Resistance' against US and Israeli domination of the Middle East. Israel's inability to defeat Hezbollah in the summer war of 2006 greatly enhanced the Axis' popularity on the Arab street, even if it frustrated pro-US Arab governments such as Egypt and Saudi Arabia, and seemed to turn the tide against Bush. While the US continued to oppose Assad, including sending a special forces raid to capture an al-Qaeda operative near the eastern Syrian town of Al-Bukamal in 2008, its attempts to isolate the regime had failed. As well as strengthening ties to Iran, Assad courted Russia, Turkey and Qatar, all of whom helped bring Syria back in from the cold. In July 2008 France became the first Western state to end the boycott by inviting Assad to Paris for Bastille Day.

After a trial by fire, Assad emerged at the end of the Bush era in a confident position.[12] The new US president, Barack Obama, was talking engagement and in 2010 approved the return of the US ambassador; former regional enemies such as Saudi Arabia were humbly following suit and improving ties; while a series of underhand tactics had ensured that Syria's allies, led by Hezbollah, held sway again in Lebanon. However, the regional shifts caused by the Bush era actually meant that Assad's position was not as strong as he and others assumed.

The Middle East and American hegemony

While Hafez made the most of the shift in regional circumstances marked by the end of the Cold War, Bashar conversely suffered from the gradual end of US regional hegemony. In order to understand the full effects of this shift, and how it played a major role in Syria's descent into civil war, the nature and extent of that dominance needs to be considered.

America's 'moment'?

The collapse of the Soviet Union in 1991 marked the end of the Cold War and the bipolar international system that had defined global politics since 1945. In its place came an era of unrivalled American dominance, a 'unipolar' order, in which the United States was the only world superpower. Politics in the Middle East seemed to reflect these global trends. While Cold War rivalries had made direct intervention by either Moscow or Washington difficult, the Soviet collapse enabled George H.W. Bush's campaign against

Saddam Hussein in Kuwait in 1991. The swift success of Operation Desert Storm, which had included the key regional states of Egypt, Syria, Saudi Arabia and Turkey in the anti-Saddam coalition, suggested George H.W. Bush's vision of an American-led 'New World Order' was at hand. Diplomatically, former Soviet allies either sought accommodation with the United States, such as Syria and South Yemen (the latter via unification with the pro-Western north), or faced isolation, such as Iraq or Libya. The US-led Middle East peace process drew Jordan, Israel and the Palestinians into peace agreements, and nearly added Syria (and by extension, Lebanon) too. US trade to the region steadily increased, benefiting from neo-liberal reforms and the opening up of economies, which caused US trade to nearly double in a decade, from $33.67 billion in 1990 to $63.38 billion in 2000.[13] In terms of security, new US military bases opened in Kuwait, Saudi Arabia, Bahrain and Qatar, while operations against Iraq and Sudan in 1998, along-side those further afield in Somalia (1993), Bosnia (1995) and Kosovo (1999), emphasised this new unchallenged US military dominance.

However, the impact of US hegemony on the region should not be overstated. Recent scholarship on the Cold War era questions to what extent the superpowers were actually able to get their way in the Middle East. The 'globalist' tendency to view the Middle East, and the Third World as a whole, as merely a region upon which the struggle between the US and USSR was projected has been challenged.[14] 'Regionalists' have instead emphasised the agency of local governments, often acting against the interests of the superpowers. Egypt and Syria's attack on Israel in 1973, against the wishes of their Soviet ally, and Israel's invasion of Lebanon in 1982, despite objections from the Reagan administration, are examples. Unlike in Europe, the region did not always divide into neat binary camps but displayed complexity, of which Cold War politics was but one dynamic. Saudi Arabia and Israel, for example, were both close US allies, but each other's enemies. The Iranian revolution in 1979, similarly, created a threat unrelated to the Cold War that impacted US and Soviet allies alike. As Barry Buzan and Ole Waever argue, 'superpower intervention neither controlled the Middle East nor played more than a marginal role in shaping the powerful military–political security dynamics at the regional level'.[15] While the Cold War was therefore an important context for understanding the evolution of the region's politics, it was characterised more as an inter-action between the global superpowers and the regional actors than as a mere reflection of bipolar rivalry.[16]

So as America's 'moment' in the Middle East began in 1991, few regional governments had actually subordinated their foreign policy to a superpower patron in the way that most European states had, and many of the intra-regional rivalries were unaffected by the changing global dynamics. Even so, both the George H.W. Bush and the Clinton administrations actively pursued, 'maintaining U.S. predominance' as policy and saw the Middle East as one such arena for dominance.[17] However, when it came to Middle East policy, the influential voices in each administration tended to be former cold warrior globalists, while the regionalists who knew the region well were sidelined or ignored.[18] Whether overestimating the transformative nature of the Cold War's end and the continued ascendancy of globalists in Washington contributed to US failure in the 1990s is unclear, but fail it did. There was no 'New World Order', as American pressure and diplomacy proved unable to persuade or cajole allies and enemies into action – as signified by the failed Arab–Israeli Peace Process. Despite increased economic penetration, only Israel and Turkey developed beyond a level of crony capitalism. The autocratic systems of government that both the US and Soviets had tacitly supported before 1991 remained in place. We should therefore be wary of overstating US dominance after 1991. The US was militarily unchallenged and certainly extended its footprint in the region. However Pax Americana was limited and struggled to transform the region's politics.[19]

An important caveat should be added. While in hindsight Washington's difficulty in translating military dominance into diplomatic and political transformation is clearer, that wasn't the case for either the regional governments or the emerging hegemon at the time. Not only did the United States government believe that such transformations were possible, but the regional leaders and their populations *perceived* American power to be the future of the region.[20] This explains why states such as Syria felt the need to engage with the US-led peace process. Moreover, though US military power was not able to translate into political transformation, regional media and regime propaganda repeatedly emphasised its ability to do so. In states such as Iraq and Iran, and later Syria when Bashar clashed with Bush, the US was portrayed as all-powerful, thereby reiterating the impressiveness, and therefore legitimacy, of regimes able to resist and thwart the US regional agenda. This reinforced the *idea* of US hegemony and power, meaning that when the Syrian civil war began, there lingered an expectation from leaders and populations alike, built over decades, that US military power *could* transform the region's politics.

Limited though US hegemony was, the post-1991 era had established a relatively balanced regional order in the Middle East. Iran and Iraq were effectively neutralised by dual containment; Gulf security was guaranteed by a heavy US military presence; Turkey had begun a limited re-engagement with its southern neighbours, mostly to subdue Kurdish militants; and Israel and its neighbours, Jordan, Egypt, Syria, Lebanon and the Palestinian Territories, were engaged in an imperfect peace process that at least was diminishing the chances of renewed conflict. While we should be wary of attaching too much importance to a single event, and much of what follows was the consequence of long-term trends as well as short-term triggers, the 2003 Iraq war was still an important turning point. It unleashed three inter-related trends in particular that would have a major impact on the Syrian civil war: the breakdown of the post-1991 order and the re-emergence of regional competition; the regional proliferation of sectarianism, jihadism and Kurdish nationalism; and the weakening of the US.

Shifting the balance of power: The 2003 Iraq war

The destruction of the Saddam Hussein regime in 2003 and the occupation of Iraq by US-led forces shifted the regional balance of power. The major beneficiary was Iran. As one of the region's largest states, Iran had long sought to expand its influence, an ambition that was amplified and infused by Islamist revolutionary rhetoric after the 1979 revolution. In the modern era Iraq had acted as a barrier to this expansion. Saddam was particularly combative, launching the gruelling 1980–88 Iran–Iraq war that effectively ended Ayatollah Khomeini's ambitions of exporting the revolution – although the two regional successes he had, founding Hezbollah and forging an alliance with Syria, would be long-lasting. The death of Khomeini in 1989 and the rise of more moderate politicians, a need to focus internally after the long war, and a faltering economy hindered by US sanctions implemented as part of the Clinton administration's 'dual containment' policy put a further brake on Tehran's aspirations. Then, just as the US was deposing their bête noire Saddam, internal changes in Iran increased the appetite to take advantage of this opportunity. Firstly the economy grew dramatically, seeing a near fourfold increase from 2000 to 2010.[21] Secondly, a more radical and regionally expansionist set of politicians closely identi-fied with the Islamic Revolutionary Guard Corps (IRGC) came to power in Tehran, affirmed by the election of President Mahmoud Ahmadinejad in August 2005.

In Saddam's Iraq the regime had disproportionately favoured Sunni Arabs to the detriment of the majority Shia Arabs. Many Shia leaders, partic-ularly those of an Islamist persuasion, had been persecuted and sought refuge in Shia Iran, where they forged close ties with the regime and elements of the IRGC. This meant that after 2003 when these Iraqi Shia leaders returned and were eventually elected to power, Iran had deep and broad ties to a whole generation of Iraqi leaders. Iraqi Prime Minister Nouri al-Maliki (2006–14), for example, lived in Iran for eight years and pursued strongly pro-Tehran policies while in office. Encouraged by its increased presence in Iraq, Iran bolstered its political ties to actors in Yemen, the Palestinian Territories and Lebanon while growing ever closer to the Syrian government. Moreover, it actively courted regional public opinion. Echoing the Arab nationalist Egyptian President Gamal Abdul Nasser in the 1950s, Ahmadinejad's populist slogans against Israel and pro-US Arab rulers were well received on the Arab street, notably during the Lebanon war of 2006 and the Gaza war of 2008–09.

If Iran's increased influence was one post-2003 regional shift, Saudi Arabia's reaction to that rise was another. Saudi Arabia perceived both a military and an ideational threat from Iran. Militarily, Saudi Arabia's lucrative oilfields in the Persian Gulf have long been vulnerable to the emergence of a regional hegemon, whether Iraq or Iran. Dual containment had restricted both rivals, so its end with the fall of Saddam exacerbated Riyadh's fears of increased Iranian activism. The large US military presence in the Gulf guarded against any military attack, but the ideational threat was far greater, both at home and abroad. Up to 15 per cent of Saudi Arabia's population were Shia and faced discrimination, as in Saddam's Iraq. Riyadh's leaders, who are prone to a sectarian outlook, feared that increased Iranian regional power would embolden their own Shia to demand greater rights or even rise up – a particularly damaging prospect given that they form a majority in the Eastern Province, home to Saudi Arabia's oilfields. Beyond this, ever since the 1979 Revolution Riyadh had feared the alternative model of governance Tehran offers. The House of Saud based the legitimacy of their autocratic monarchical rule on Islam: their alliance with Wahhabi clerics and their custodianship of the holy places of Mecca and Medina. After 1979 Iran presented another, more participatory model of Islamic government that Saudi Arabia feared could inspire its own population.

The ideational threat abroad was newer. The Saudi leadership historically preferred to use their financial clout to steer and balance diplomacy from behind the scenes, leaving leadership to other Arab states. However, with Iraq slipping into the Iranian orbit, and Egypt diminishing in regional influence, Saudi Arabia found itself in the unfamiliar position of leading efforts to counter Iran.[22] In a foretaste of what was to come after 2011, certain arenas emerged as low-level proxy conflicts between the Saudi-led pro-US bloc and the Iranian-led 'Resistance Axis'. Many scholars labelled this a new 'Cold War', further weakening the creaking Khartoum consensus of non-interference in Arab states' internal politics.[23] Lebanon was one such arena, where Saudi Arabia led regional support for the anti-Syrian forces, while Iran and Syria's ally Hezbollah formed their main opponents. Saudi Arabia also reluctantly stepped into Iraqi politics, backing certain Sunni parties in an ultimately forlorn attempt to halt the pro-Iranian tide.[24] In Yemen too, Saudi Arabia poured money into the regime of President Saleh, who was battling Shia Houthi rebels, that Riyadh claimed were armed by Iran, and eventually launched its own military campaign against them in 2009–10. Conscious that it was losing the Arab street in this ideational battle, Riyadh and its allies stepped up their own ideational weapons. The al-Arabiya news channel was set up to offer a more pro-Saudi-Arabia perspective in contrast to the popular Qatar-owned pro-Resistance (though not necessarily pro-Iran) al-Jazeera.

The rise of the Saudi–Iranian rivalry was perhaps the most dramatic regional shift caused by the Iraq war, but other changes were facilitated too. Turkey became more active in the Middle East. The US invasion led to the establishment of the Kurdish Regional Government (KRG), prompting greater Turkish interest both in terms of the security threat this might pose regarding its own Kurds, and also in the commercial opportunities it provided. The 2003 war highlighted the growing divergence in view between the moderately Islamist AKP government in Turkey and Bush's neo-conservatives. Turkey increasingly adopted an independent Middle Eastern policy, often opposing its American ally. Like Iran, Turkey's leadership saw an opportunity to fill the regional vacuum created by the fall of Saddam. Qatar also saw opportunities. A wealthy gas state and long-term US ally, Qatar directly benefited not from the Iraq war but from its aftermath. The increased rivalry between Saudi Arabia and Iran provided space for Qatar to take on Saudi Arabia's previous role as regional moderator, raising its profile with mediations in Gaza and Lebanon. Like Iran, Qatar's economy skyrocketed following huge leaps in fuel prices, enabling it to pay for this increased activism. It was also greatly helped by its sponsorship of al-Jazeera which, via its populist anti-US, anti-Israel coverage, also raised Qatar's standing in the growing arena of competition, the Arab street.

The rise of sectarianism, jihadism and Kurdish nationalism

Three pre-existing transnational forces were greatly exacerbated and gained region-wide significance as a result of the Iraq war: sectarianism, jihadism and Kurdish nationalism. Sectarianism, the politicisation of differences between sects within a religion, often leading to discrimination, hate or

tension, has a long history the world over.[25] The Middle East is no exception, with divisions between Sunni and Shia Muslims well documented
since the coming of Islam in the seventh century. However the 'Sunni–Shia'
divide had not been the defining, perennial struggle within Middle Eastern
communities that some contemporary commentators argue.[26] In multi-sect
states such as Lebanon, Syria and Iraq, communities had lived side by side
for generations, often intermarrying, and frequently seeing commonalities,
such as a shared religion or Arab ethnicity, rather than divisions. Indeed,
contrary to many Iranian expectations, Iraqi Shia mostly sided with their
fellow Arab and Iraqi Sunnis against Shia Iran in the Iran–Iraq war. It
was modern political developments, in the case of Iraq, Saddam's systemic
discrimination and then brutal oppression of Shia in revolt in 1991, rather
than ancient unceasing hatreds that gave rise to sectarian politics.[27]

The rise in importance of Sunni and Shia identities during the 1990s,
which increased as Saddam's state retreated under international sanctions
and sect-based support networks grew, contributed to sectarian conflict
in Iraq after 2003.[28] Tens of thousands were killed by rival sectarian
militia, up to four million were displaced as neighbourhoods were force-
fully homogenised, and rival mosques were attacked. With the Middle East
increasingly culturally integrated by satellite television, this Shia–Sunni
violence was widely publicised, supported by the horror stories told
by refugees flooding into Syria and Jordan. Certain voices in the pro-
Saudi-Arabia camp risked exacerbating matters by framing Iran's increased
prominence as part of a Shia takeover of the region. In 2004 King Abdullah
of Jordan, an ally of the US and Saudi Arabia, spoke of a potential 'Shia
Crescent' spreading from Lebanon to Syria, Iraq and Iran. In Saudi Arabia
a group of thirty-eight *ulema* (religious leaders) signed an anti-Shia fatwa
offering support to Iraq's Sunnis and calling on Riyadh to do more.[29] While
this exaggerated the sectarian nature of Iran's allies in Lebanon and Syria at
that time, Tehran did back Shia sectarian forces in Iraq, such as the Badr
organisation and Prime Minister Maliki. Interestingly, however, neither
Iran's support for sectarian groups, nor Saudi Arabian warnings seemed to
resonate with the Arab street. In 2008, at the peak of the Iraq violence, in
a poll of 4,000 Arabs from Egypt, UAE, Saudi Arabia, Morocco, Lebanon
and Jordan – all of which are Sunni-majority except for Lebanon – the three
most popular leaders were Hassan Nasrallah of Hezbollah, Mahmoud
Ahmadinejad and Bashar al-Assad, two Shia and an Alawi (a Shia deriva-
tive).[30] However, a regional sectarian narrative had now been established
and, to an extent, normalised. The Syrian civil war would provide it with a
more receptive audience.

Jihadism was also transformed into a major regional current by the Iraq war. Prior to 2003, adherents of Sayyid Qutb's 'offensive jihad' were in relative decline. Organic militant Islamists such as Hezbollah and Hamas had moderated to an extent, while others, such as the Syrian Muslim Brotherhood, Egypt's al-Gama'a al-Islamiyya and Algeria's GIA (Group Islamique Armée), were suppressed. Al-Qaeda, formed primarily from Arabs who had fought in Afghanistan, had failed to attract substantive support in the Middle East in the 1990s, hence its retreat to Taleban-ruled Kabul.[31] That said, though the ideology had limited support, it had been far from discredited. It is a tragic irony that the US invasion of Iraq, ostensibly to defeat al-Qaeda and prevent it from acquiring Weapons of Mass Destruction, proved a massive recruiter for regional jihadism. Not only did the occupation act initially as a rallying point for radicals to flood into, or inspire jihad elsewhere such as Saudi Arabia, but American-run Iraqi prisons soon served as a further breeding ground.[32] The subsequent civil war served to add a more explicit sectarian dimension to Sunni jihadist ideology. One of the main forces to emerge in this conflict, al-Qaeda in Iraq (AQI), was the parent to two of the Syrian civil war's most prominent jihadist forces: Jabhat al-Nusra and ISIS.

Lastly, Kurdish nationalism was greatly impacted by the Iraq war. The creation of the KRG created a self-ruled Kurdish territory for the first time, an inspiration for Kurdish nationalists in neighbouring Syria, Turkey and Iran. More importantly, it transformed the Iraqi Kurdish lands from an arena of regional competition to a projector of regional influence. In the 1990s internal rivalry between the two main Iraqi forces, Jalal Talabani's PUK and Massoud Barzani's KDP had attracted attention from Turkey, Iran and Saddam's Iraq, as well as the Turkish PKK. However, a deal after 2003 that made Talabani president of Iraq and Barzani leader of the regional KRG government, along with the economic boom brought by northern Iraq's oil reserves, stabilised this proto-state. This gave Barzani a platform to later influence Syria's Kurds during the civil war. The second development was the PKK's reaction to the change in regional climate. The rise of Barzani, as opposed to its traditional ally Talabani, and Turkey's later alliance with the KRG squeezed the Turkish Kurdish separatists who had always seen them-selves as the leaders of region-wide Kurdish nationalism. The PKK too would come to see Syria as an arena where it could recover lost influence.

Ending America's moment?

Finally, the Iraq war and its consequences shifted US power in the Middle East, both perceptions of it by regional actors, and its own leaders' views of what it could achieve. The rapid defeat of Saddam's regime in 2003 appeared to confirm the unchallenged dominance of the US over the region that had emerged in the 1990s. The fact that Bashar al-Assad allowed jihadis into Iraq from Syria, although they were his sworn enemies, illustrates how seriously the US' regional opponents perceived America's military threat. Similarly, the willingness of allies such as Egypt and Saudi Arabia to acquiesce to Bush's pressure to hold (albeit restricted) elections in 2005 as part of his post-Iraq 'agenda for freedom' suggests they too perceived America's moment to be at hand. Indeed, that Bush attempted to remake the region off the back of his success, whether pressuring Assad over Lebanon, or supporting democracy in Egypt, Saudi Arabia and the Palestinian territories, suggests that he and his administration believed that they could translate overwhelming military power into a region-wide political transformation.

Such goals were soon shown to be hubristic, however. The freedom agenda was quietly abandoned when undesired Islamists made electoral gains in Egypt in 2005 and the Palestinian Authority in 2006. Wider regional goals were shattered after Israel failed to defeat Hezbollah in the 2006 Lebanon war – illustrating the limitations of military force while providing Syria and Iran with a victory. Meanwhile Iraq, the original success story, was descending into a violent insurgency costing American lives. At the same time a sectarian civil war was undermining any hope that Iraq would become a model pluralist democracy, while the rise of pro-Iranian Shia politicians suggested it would not become the new US regional ally originally hoped for. A troop surge in 2007 and the accompanying alliance with Sunni Iraqi tribes, known as the Awakening councils, helped end the insurgency, opening the door for eventual US withdrawal in 2011, but Bush's military adventurism was ultimately a failure.

Added to Bush's failures were three related factors that shifted the US approach to the Middle East. The first was the 2008 financial crisis, which in the short term focused political attention internally, and in the long term led to cuts in military spending. Second, there was public fatigue with deploying troops and money abroad, particularly in the Middle East. After losing nearly 5,000 killed and 45,000 injured in Iraq, and with priorities on the economy, in 2009 US public opinion temporarily favoured international isolation for the first time since the Cold War.[33] Thirdly, in January 2009 and in relation to this, was the coming to power of Barack Obama as president, who had opposed the Iraq war and approached US regional policy with a different worldview. Though committed to continuing Bush's counter-terrorism policies in his first term – increasing drone warfare and ordering the killing of Osama bin Laden in 2011 – Obama stepped back US activity in the Middle

East, culminating in the withdrawal from Iraq. According to former CIA analyst Kenneth Pollack in his conversations with Obama's team, there was a belief that the US had consistently over-invested in the Middle East in recent years, that its importance to the US was exaggerated and that energy would be better deployed elsewhere in the world, notably Asia.[34]

There are broadly two schools of thought as to what caused this post-2009 retrenchment. One attributes the shift to agency, mostly the choices of the Obama administration. The other attributes it to structural changes in both the Middle East and the wider world, to which Obama had to react. These two arguments warrant further exploration as they will prove key when it comes to questions over Obama's Syria policy – whether his reluctance to become involved was really a choice or a realistic assessment of US capacity to affect the situation. Those favouring agency see Obama's drawdown from the Middle East as a result of his choices. Obama is viewed as a *declinist* who wrongly believed that the United States' post- Cold-War global dominance was ending. His preference for multilateralism and offshore balancing – backing regional allies to police the region rather than deploy US troops – was based on learning the wrong lessons from the Iraq war. As Pollack argues, while Bush overstretched, Obama swung the pendulum too far the other way. These anti-declinists, or *supremacists*, who tend to be Obama's critics in the US foreign policy establishment, argue that an assertive United States in both the Middle East and beyond is good for both the US and the world, sustaining the post-1991 unipolar order. Importantly, they argue, the US will only lose this global position if its leaders allow it to.[35]

The counter-argument is that Obama's retrenchment is a reaction to unstoppable structural changes. Globally, academics such as Christopher Layne argue, the Bush era oversaw the end of unipolarity. The financial crisis and the rise of China and the 'Beijing model' of state-led capitalism, undermining the post-Cold-War 'Washington Consensus' of free markets, challenged uncontested US economic power. The failure in Iraq exposed the limitations of military power alone, while it made the US wildly unpopular, costing it dearly in 'soft power'.[36] In the Middle East, Fawaz Gerges concurs, arguing that the new multipolar globalised world order has provided space for and 'awakened the ambitions of other regional and international powers'.[37] Through this reading, versions of which are usually voiced by Obama's domestic supporters, the President's policies of disengagement and regional balancing should be seen as managing America's transition into a new role brought on by structural changes beyond his control.

To an extent, both sides overstate their case. As discussed, even during the era of hegemony after 1991, military and economic dominance did not mean that the US was able to achieve all its goals in the Middle East, with regional actors continuing the Cold War trend of bucking superpower direction. Even if post-2009 the structural shifts against US power were exaggerated, a more engaged Obama would still have been likely to face the same obstacles as Clinton in pursuing his agenda. On the other hand, while it is clear that the global and regional structure was less favourable to US dominance in 2009 than in 2003, Obama's personal views cannot be dismissed. The new president was not simply a product of his time but someone who actively opposed deeper involvement in the Middle East. In all probability, after the misadventures of Bush, structural factors would have required a major reassertion of US activity in the region to repair the damage to the perception of US hegemony in the Middle East after 2009, but Barack Obama's approach certainly accelerated its decline. Importantly, whether US regional retreat was due to Obama's choices or structural shifts, it was something that was increasingly perceived to be the case by the region's actors. As Gerges notes, after the Iraq debacle and Obama's retrenchment, 'The US is no longer seen as omnipotent and invincible.'[38]

After America: A shift in power

The Middle East in 2011 was a region in transition. The perceived dominance of the United States, already more limited than assumed, was ebbing after 2009 and a nascent multipolar regional order was emerging. The Syrian civil war must be understood within the context of these regional shifts, as both a symptom and a subsequent reinforcer of them. The US was still the most powerful, but now other powers were independently asserting or reasserting their influence. This book focusses on the five that, alongside the US, would go on to shape the Syria conflict: Russia, Iran, Saudi Arabia, Turkey and Qatar.

The six players were not of equal power or influence in Syria, yet each was sizeable enough to impact the conflict, often independently of the others. Due to this variation in power, different players deployed a variety of tools at different times whether military, economic or diplomatic, sometimes overtly, but more often covertly. Each actor was constrained by structural forces, whether international or domestic, but the agency of their leaders should not be discounted, with personal decisions having major consequences. Importantly, these actors all had interests beyond just Syria, and developments elsewhere as well as inside Syria affected their policies. The remainder of this chapter assesses their regional positions on the eve of the crisis.

The view from the United States

Barack Obama had an ambivalent approach to foreign policy. On the one hand, he had little foreign policy experience, having a background in domestic campaigns and a preference to focus on an economy in crisis.[39] On the other hand, in his election campaign he made much of his opposition to the unpopular Iraq war, distinguishing himself from both his predecessor Bush and his main Democrat rival, Hillary Clinton. He came to office with a clear idea of how US foreign affairs should be conducted differently and, with the public disillusioned with foreign adventures, had a mandate to do it. Some observers claim that he transformed from a foreign policy idealist into a realist once in office, but even on the campaign trail Obama had praised the realism of George H.W. Bush. Similarly, in a 2007 speech he critiqued humanitarian intervention.[40] In office, while liberal interventionists as Samantha Power and Susan Rice were drafted into his administration, Obama's most influential foreign policy advisers, such as national-security adviser Thomas Donilon, and deputy national-security adviser Denis McDonough, later to become White House Chief of Staff, were realists. Clinton was appointed Secretary of State but often found herself marginalised on key decisions. That said, insiders insist that there was plenty of scope for debate in the Oval Office, with the president keen to understand the complexities of foreign policy decisions, especially on the Middle East. As it had with all US presidents, internal pressures impacted foreign policy, not only in terms of public opinion – with Obama's team particularly sensitive to opinion polls – but also the rival views of government institutions such as the State Department, military and intelligence branches.[41] His detractors argued that Obama was inconsistent and lacked grand strategy, but supporters replied that a single 'one size fits all' approach is a Cold War relic incompatible with today's complexities. Obama's non-ideological approach instead allowed him to deal with issues on a case-by-case basis to best protect American interests.[42]

When the Arab Spring began in December 2010, Obama had been in office nearly two years and his priorities in the Middle East were relatively clear.[43] Firstly, he wanted to reduce the US physical presence. He announced in December 2009 that US troops would be removed from Iraq and Afghanistan by the end of his first term, although he later extended the Afghanistan deadline. Secondly, he wanted to rebuild America's reputation in the Middle East and wider Islamic world. He made two high-profile speeches in Ankara and Cairo in 2009, rolling back on Bush's interventionism, stating, 'America does not presume to know what is best for everyone.' This signalled a retreat from democracy proselytising, although investment in grass-roots civil society activism quietly continued.[44] An attempt was made as part of this to relaunch the Israel–Palestinian peace process, but this was put on the back burner when it became clear that Israeli Premier Benjamin Netanyahu was determined to act as spoiler.[45] Thirdly, he had sought to reach out to the US' enemies, most notably Iran and Russia. After repeated tensions between former Russian President Putin and Bush, Obama pushed the idea of relations being 'reset' with new President Dmitri Medvedev. Similarly, in a video message to the Iranian public on 20 March 2009, he addressed 'the people and leaders of the Islamic Republic of Iran'.[46] While this agenda was somewhat derailed by the Iranian regime's crushing of unrest in 2009, Obama's comparative silence was interpreted as a sign of rapprochement. At the same time, Obama was committed to nuclear non-proliferation, and stepped up the pressure on Tehran to abandon its programme. After the 2009 crackdown, the White House backed a new round of UN sanctions in June 2010.

A shift in approach to Syria was part of Obama's new agenda. The administration cautiously retreated from Bush's isolation of Assad, nominating an ambassador, Robert Ford, to Damascus for the first time in five years in February 2010. Re-engagement with Assad was a means to several other ends: to help stabilise Iraq in order to enable US withdrawal by 2012 and ensure that Damascus didn't reactivate its flow of jihadi fighters eastward; and to increase pressure on Iran by pursuing a long-hoped-for Saudi Arabian goal of 'flipping' Syria into the pro-Western orbit. However, US officials noted in private how low a priority Syria was prior to 2011.[47] Re-engagement efforts were led by individuals such as Ford and Clinton's adviser Fred Hof, but there was little coordination between them, the State Department or the White House. After five years of isolating Assad, knowledge of his regime, and interest in it, was limited. Moreover, outside the State Department, Syria was viewed primarily through the lens of relations to Israel. The pro-Israeli American Israeli Public Affairs Committee (AIPAC) briefed Congressmen on Syria, offering certain biases, which contributed to an anti-engagement atmosphere on the Capitol. Indeed, such views stalled Ford's confirmation, meaning that he only arrived in Damascus in January 2011.

France and Britain – Washington's closest Western allies, when it came to the Middle East – were more up to date on Syria, having retained a diplomatic presence in Damascus. France, as Syria's former colonial master, believed itself particularly well placed. The new French President, Nicolas Sarkozy, had taken the lead in bringing Damascus in from the cold – a departure from the policy of his predecessor, Jacques Chirac, who as a close friend of Rafiq Hariri led international outrage at Assad after the 2005 assassination. Sarkozy became the first Western leader to break the Bush boycott and visit Damascus in September 2008. French diplomats cautiously briefed that a separation of Syria from Iran was possible, while intelligence cooperation had reportedly never stopped.[48]

Like the US, Britain was prioritising internal matters, weary after a decade of war in Iraq and Afghanistan and implementing a strict post-financial crisis austerity programme that was cutting deep into the defence budget. Traditionally more aligned with US regional policy than France, it too had improved ties with Syria in the wake of the new direction from Washington. The new government of 2010 under Premier David Cameron continued this, and seemed to favour a commerce-led realist approach – both the UK and France significantly increased their economic and related diplomatic ties with the Gulf. When Foreign Secretary William Hague met with Assad in Damascus in January 2011, he met business leaders as well as civil society activists and spoke about openness to investment, as well as political pluralism.[49] Both Britain and France would go on to play an important role supporting and augmenting US efforts in Syria once the crisis began a few months later.

Russia: Putin's evolving view

America's Cold War rival had seen its position in the Middle East quietly transformed during the 2000s. Once of similar regional prestige to the US with a rival number of allies and bases, diplomatic and military defeats in the 1970s and '80s, followed by the collapse of the USSR and internal chaos under President Boris Yeltsin in the 1990s, left Moscow peripheral. However, Yeltsin's successor, Vladimir Putin, slowly reasserted Russia's clout. A former KGB officer from St Petersburg, Putin has often been portrayed by Western commentators as ruthless, autocratic and expansionist, seeking a return to Russia's power under the Soviet era – whose collapse he remarked in 2005 was 'the greatest geopolitical catastrophe' of the twentieth century. However, Russian Middle East policy under Putin was more nuanced than this simple caricature allows.

Firstly, Putin's worldview was far from fixed and appears to have evolved. Up until 2003 balance-of-power realists such as former Prime Minister Yevgeny Primakov had Putin's ear, while afterwards he was more inclined towards nationalists.[50] Secondly, despite autocratic tendencies, Putin was a populist and public opinion mattered. In his first term (2000–04) the average Russian saw a 26 per cent increase in their annual income.[51] Benefiting from the increase in oil and gas prices, the Russian economy grew fivefold between 2000 and 2010. This allowed Putin to modernise his military, boosting Russian prestige and, consequently, the support of an increasingly nationalist public. However, it also meant economics became a core pillar of foreign policy. Thirdly, Putin was opportunistic and reactive. While he opposed the US' invasion of Iraq publicly, he only began to step up his rhetoric when Bush's wars started going badly, and global (and Russian) public opinion turned against them. In his 2006 annual state of the nation speech, the Russian President compared the US to a hungry wolf that 'eats and listens to no one'.[52] Relations sank even lower when Russia launched an attack on America's ally Georgia in 2008. By this point Putin's protégé, Dmitri Medvedev had taken over as President, with the Russian constitution forbidding more than two terms in office. While most assumed that Putin, who was appointed Prime Minister, remained the power behind the throne, the Obama administration hoped that the change of leader might allow space for its 'reset' agenda.

As 2010 ended, the Kremlin looked at the Middle East through three lenses.[53] First was the domestic security lens. Moscow feared the long ties between Middle Eastern Islamists and secessionists in its Muslim north Caucasus region, having fought a long war in Chechnya and suffered numerous terrorist attacks by Islamists in the 2000s. Second was the regional economic lens. As part of his economy-anchored foreign policy, Putin had greatly expanded Russian trade with the Middle East. Gas was sold to energy-poor states such as Turkey while opportunities for arms sales greatly increased.[54] The third lens was geopolitical. Putin and his nationalists mostly saw the Middle East through a zero-sum perspective, seeing each diplomatic or economic gain for Russia there as a defeat for the US, and vice versa.[55] Therefore, as US popularity decreased under Bush, a major effort was made to improve Russia's image. Israel, to which almost a million Russian Jews emigrated after 1990, was consciously courted. Putin was the first Russian President to visit, in 2005, visa-free agreements were made between the states in 2008, and trade increased considerably – more than with any Arab country.[56] Russia also sought to soften its image with Arab and Muslim states, obtaining observer status at the Organisation of the Islamic Conference in 2007. Russia did not simply align with the anti-US 'resistance axis' of Iran and Syria, but rather courted both US enemies and allies, promoting itself as a third force in the region. A sign of this was Moscow's endorsement of the 2010 UN sanctions on Iran.

As for Syria, Damascus may have been a close Soviet ally, but in the 1990s that connection had largely lapsed. Tartous hosted Russia's only Mediterranean naval installation, but it was not dredged and revived until 2007, and even then hosted barely fifty personnel.[57] Eight thousand

Russians lived in Syria, but far more lived in Israel. Assad had purchased a considerable amount of Russian weaponry before 2011, including sophisticated anti-aircraft weaponry, but more had been sold to other Arab states and Putin had had to agree to write off most of Syria's $13 billion Cold War debt with Russia in 2005 to enable the purchase. Assad had courted Putin, especially during his years of isolation, notably endorsing Russia's 2008 invasion of Georgia, but Syria was afforded no special place in Russian strategic thinking. Putin did not personally like Assad, quipping once that he spent more time in Paris than Moscow. As will be discussed in the coming chapters, Moscow's ultimate backing of the Assad regime once the crisis began owed much to the events of 2011.

Iran: Competing powers

Another state with a more complex leadership than often characterised was Iran. Though no liberal democracy in the Western sense, the post-1979 Islamic Republic is far more participatory than most of its Arab autocratic neighbours. Moreover it has various competing centres of power that influence its regional policy. The most powerful figure is Ayatollah Ali Khamenei, who succeeded Ruhollah Khomeini as Iran's Supreme Leader in 1989. According to Carnegie's Karim Sadjadpour, Khamenei's worldview was shaped by four priorities: to resist the US' and, by extension Israel's, plans to dominate the region and Iran; to maintain support for the Palestinians (and Lebanese) in their struggle against Israel; to pursue nuclear power as a route to Iranian independence and regional prestige; and to be a key player, even *the* key player within the Islamic world.[58] However, while these views guided Iranian strategy, the Supreme Leader was no absolute dictator and other currents operated below him influencing how these policies, and others, were pursued.[59] Several factions emerged in the early 2000s, the most powerful of which, the radicals dominated by the IRGC, reached the peak of power with the election of Ahmadinejad as President 2005–13.[60] As discussed above, this prompted a more aggressive anti-American, anti-Israel line of rhetoric, a more assertive regional policy and accelerated the pursuit of nuclear power. Importantly, Ahmadinejad was but one figure in the IRGC establishment whose political and economic power was growing. Yet this was far from unchallenged and three other factions, the Reformists, the Traditionalist Conservatives and the Conservative Pragmatists each retained a power base and differing levels of popular and elite support.[61]

While Iran had emerged as the big winner of the 2003 Iraq war and its aftermath, on the eve of the Syria crisis Tehran's confidence had been somewhat checked. The 'Green Revolution' anti-Ahmadinejad protests of 2009, led by Reformists who claimed that the President had fraudulently claimed re-election, damaged Iran's regional reputation. Having spent much of the preceding four years berating the region's pro-Western Arab autocrats and winning a reputation in the Arab street as a man of the people, the sight of Iranian security forces brutally suppressing unarmed protesters broadcast widely on al-Jazeera made Ahmadinejad seem a hypocrite. Khamenei damaged his own domestic reputation by endorsing the disputed election result, and Ahmadinejad soon lost his crown as hero of the Arab street to Turkey's populist Prime Minister, Recep Tayyip Erdoğan. The protests also made it difficult for Obama to continue with his hoped-for rapprochement, though it is questionable how receptive Iran ever was. It was also easier for its enemies, notably Israel's Netanyahu, to present Iran as a repressive autocracy in his campaign to highlight Tehran's continued nuclear enrichment, ultimately leading to the 2010 sanctions. Even so, the regional gains of the 2000s were far from lost. Iran consolidated its alliances with Iraq, Syria, Hezbollah and Hamas and a growing relationship with Yemen's Houthis. Moreover, it had developed a strong diplomatic and trade relationship with Turkey, who, with Brazil, had led calls against the UN sanctions. However, its IRGC leaders were increasingly feeling paranoid and encircled by enemies determined to prevent Iran emerging as a leading regional power.[62]

On the eve of the 2011 crisis Syria remained a key pillar of Iran's regional policy. While the fall of Saddam meant that Iraq was now its greatest strategic priority, Revolutionary Iran's oldest regional ally was still of great value. Immediately after the 2006 war, Hezbollah began preparing for the next possible round with Israel, and Syria was a key land bridge via which Iran seat its Lebanese ally weapons, money and training. As both states were isolated by the Bush administration, Iranian trade with Syria grew steadily, with a fourfold increase from 2006 to 2011, though it remained small compared to that of other states.[63] While grand infrastructural projects were announced, such as a $10 billion proposed Iran–Iraq–Syria–Lebanon gas pipeline in July 2011, some analysts doubted they would ever come about, as Syria's value to Iran was primarily political rather than economic.[64] The 'Resistance Axis' had given both regimes domestic and regional legitimacy and the alliance continued to flourish. In February 2010 Assad frustrated the many Western and Arab diplomats trying to 'flip' him from Iran by hosting a lavish dinner for Ahmadinejad and Hassan Nasrallah in Damascus, announcing, 'There is no separating Iran and Syria.'[65] That said, it would be wrong to see Assad as subservient to Iran on the eve of the crisis and he continued to pursue independent policies.

Unfamiliar ground for Saudi Arabia

Saudi Arabia was among the biggest losers of the 2003 Iraq war. King Abdullah, then Crown Prince, had urged the Bush administration against the invasion in vain. The regional fluctuations that followed, particularly the rise of Iran, forced Saudi Arabia away from its preferred quiet diplomacy towards greater activism. However, this unfamiliar shift did not come easily, and numerous internal concerns proved a distraction. First among these were questions over generational change in Saudi Arabia's leadership. Since Ibn Saud founded the kingdom in 1932, his successors had been drawn from his legitimate sons. Yet this pool was ageing and questions arose over which of the hundreds of grandsons would ultimately succeed, with competing factions accumulating power to press their claims. Abdullah, who turned eighty-seven in 2011 and was in ill health, promoted himself as a reformer, improving women's rights for example, and so promoted princes whom he believed would continue this legacy, notably his son, Mutaib, and half-brother, Muqrin. In opposition to these reforms, was another half-brother; the more hard-line conservative Interior Minister Prince Nayef. He led the main competing royal faction to Abdullah's: 'the Sudairi clan', a powerful group of seven of Ibn Saud's sons who shared the same mother, and their sons.[66]

Alongside and often related to these dynastic manoeuvres, Abdullah faced other domestic concerns. First was his relationship with the powerful Wahhabi clerical establishment, a strict ultra-conservative form of Islam that Ibn Saud had aligned with in a mutually supportive pact that continued to define the religious and political nature of the kingdom. Far from controlled by the regime, many Wahhabi *ulema* proved a constant source of pressure on Abdullah to be more conservative at home and abroad, particularly targeting the Shia. Nayef and the Sudairis enjoyed close ties to these *ulema*. Second was the threat of domestic jihadist terrorism. After encouraging jihad abroad against the Soviets in Afghanistan in the 1980s, Riyadh was surprised when its citizens, among them Osama bin Laden, returned radicalised and determined to wage jihad at home. Fifteen of the nineteen hijackers on 9/11 were Saudi Arabian citizens. From 2003 to 2006 Riyadh had to battle with the newly formed al-Qaeda in the Arabian Peninsula (AQAP) , ultimately crushing them and forcing them into neighbouring Yemen. While the *ulema* officially urged loyalty to the kingdom, there remained a strong potential for domestic radicalisation. This related to a final concern: the economy. Saudi Arabia is blessed with 16 per cent of the world's petroleum reserves and oil dominates the economy, in 2015 making up roughly 80 per cent of budget revenues, 45 per cent of GDP, and 90 per cent of export earnings.[67] Unlike smaller Gulf

States, however, Saudi Arabia had a large population of close to 30 million whose continued loyalty to the state appeared to be determined by the continuation of royal patronage. This made its domestic sector sensitive to fluctuations in the oil market and therefore encouraged a desire for regional stability. Fears remained that an unsatisfied domestic population might challenge Saudi Arabian rule and be more susceptible to Islamic radicalisation.

Despite these internal concerns there was broad consensus among Saudi Arabia's elite after 2003 that the threat from Iran was the number one regional issue, especially Tehran's accelerated nuclear programme. As enrichment intensified, Saudi Arabia poured money into its military, benefiting from high oil prices. Arms imports from the US were nine times greater in 2008–11 than in 2004–07.[68] Saudi Arabia's leaders became increasingly paranoid. Riyadh perceived Yemen's Houthis as Tehran's proxy, yet there is scant evidence its involvement was any more than superficial before 2011.[69] International relations were diversified, improving ties with China, from whom it purchased a long-range missile system, but the US remained by far its most important ally. The Iranian question was causing tension, however. Abdullah had urged the Bush administration to attack Iran to end its nuclear programme, to 'cut off the head of the snake', as the king reportedly told US General David Petraeus in April 2008.[70] The accession of Obama in January 2009, with his desire to increasingly disengage from the Middle East and even pursue detente with Iran, worsened matters. Obama and Abdullah's first meeting, in Riyadh in 2009, was an hour-long lecture from the king on the dangers of Iran.[71] Obama's contrasting style to Bush didn't help. While Bush's amiable character fitted well with the Saudi Arabian personal approach to politics, including issuing numerous invitations to his ranch in Crawford, Texas, Obama's more detached professionalism left Abdullah cold. At the same time Saudi Arabian commentators criticised Riyadh's naïvety, and especially its diplomatic staff in Washington, for being too slow to adjust to Obama's new foreign policy team.[72] The end result was a distinct cooling in US–Saudi ties on the eve of the Syrian civil war.

Fear of Iran partly motivated Saudi Arabia's own detente with Syria. In 2009–10 Assad visited Saudi Arabia three times, and Abdullah paid one return visit to Damascus.[73] The Syrian President had reacted personally to the Saudi-Arabia-led regional diplomatic boycott after 2005, publicly calling Abdullah and other pro-Western leaders 'half men' for not supporting Hezbollah against Israel in the 2006 war. This was the latest in a long line of strained Saudi Arabia–Syria ties. They had different patrons during the

Cold War, and the Syrian–Iranian alliance of 1979 worsened matters. Ideologically, the Assads' socialist Arab nationalism clashed with the conservative Islamic monarchy of the Sauds, while their Alawite sect seemed a natural enemy to the self-declared guardians of Sunnism in Riyadh. However, the relationship was far from static, with neither ideology nor religion truly defining it. In bad times Saudi Arabia tended to back opposition to Assad, whether Sunni politicians in Lebanon or the Muslim Brotherhood in Syria, many of whom were welcomed in Saudi Arabia after their defeat in 1982. However, in 1973 and 1990 the regimes formed a military alliance in the face of a common enemy, Israel and Iraq respectively, and Saudi Arabia expelled members of the pro-Saddam Syrian Muslim Brotherhood during the latter conflict. Riyadh's 2009–10 detente was therefore typical of a fluctuating relationship, not an anomaly. Given the animosity to follow after 2011, this temporary reconciliation suggests a realism in Riyadh's thinking: driven primarily by a desire to contain Iran but not seeing Assad's sect or professed ideology as an obstacle to courting his support.

Turkey's return to the Middle East

Historically Turkey had limited its engagement with the Middle East, propelled by founding father Mustafa Kemal Atatürk's desire to face Westwards and a lingering perception that the Arabs betrayed the Ottoman Turks in the First World War.[74] Three factors shifted that position in the 2000s. First, the aftermath of the Iraq war created dangers and opportunities. The danger was the militant Islamism, sectarianism and Kurdish separatism described earlier. This necessitated greater cooperation with fellow southern neighbours Syria and Iran, and later on the KRG, in search of stability.[75] The opportunity came from the regional power vacuum left after the fall of Saddam and the entanglement of the US in the subsequent quagmire. Like Iran, Turkey's ambitious leadership saw its chance. Secondly, Turkey's export-driven economy was growing rapidly. Particularly successful were the 'Anatolian Tigers' – southern industrial cities, such as Gaziantep, that produced medium-level manufactured goods ideal for the developing economies of the Middle East. These business leaders, distinct from the old economic elites of Istanbul and Ankara, were strong supporters of the Adalet ve Kalkınma Partisi (Justice and Development Party, or AKP) that came to power in 2002. As a result, the pursuit of new markets, particularly in the Middle East, became a key tenet of foreign policy.

The third factor was the election of the mildly Islamist AKP and its ambitious founder, Recep Tayyip Erdoğan. Prime Minister from 2003 to 2014 and President thereafter, Erdoğan departed from Atatürk's legacy

(Kemalism). At home he challenged the traditional elite's quasi-autocratic secularism, curbing the power of the Kemalist military and judiciary in the name of democracy, though ultimately adopting autocratic tendencies himself. As part of a cultural war over Turkish identity between secularists and religious conservatives, Erdoğan sought to rehabilitate the Ottoman Empire, moving it away from the negative Kemalist historical view, proudly referring to himself and his supporters as *Osmanlı torunu* (descendant of the Ottomans). A more active foreign policy in the former Ottoman lands of the Middle East, 'neo-Ottomanism' became a feature of this.[76] Ahmet Davutoğlu, a professor of international relations, Erdoğan's foreign policy adviser, Foreign Minister 2009–14 and Prime Minister 2014–16, was instrumental in this. Davutoğlu rejected the 'neo-Ottomanism' tag, instead formulating his foreign policy as pursuing 'strategic depth' in foreign relations and seeking 'zero problems with neighbours' in order for Turkey to become a 'central country' in the Middle East and beyond.[77] With trade at its centre, ties were improved with Syria, Iran, Libya, Egypt and the Gulf while, initially at least, military cooperation with Israel, begun in the 1990s, continued. The Arab world in particular was courted, in an attempt to improve Turkey's (historically maligned) regional image. Much was made of the popularity of Turkish soap operas dubbed into Syrian Arabic, increasing Turkey's soft power, while Erdoğan's growing vehemence against Bush's policies and Israel's repression of the Palestinians increased his popularity on the Arab street.

However, despite the rhetoric of 'zero problems' there was a mismatch between Turkey's regional ambitions and its capacity to bring them about. The US ambassador to Ankara, James Jeffrey, noted in 2010 that Turkey had 'Rolls Royce ambitions but Rover resources'.[78] Having spent most of its history facing Westward, it lacked both the institutional depth and the material resources to suddenly become a Middle Eastern power. Moreover, already by 2010 foreign policy was becoming personalised under Erdoğan. Turkey had far more developed institutions than its Middle Eastern neighbours, notably the military and foreign service, but both were dominated by the AKP's Kemalist rivals and so Erdoğan and Davutoğlu increasingly bypassed or subordinated them. This concentration of power allowed for sudden shifts in policy to be announced based on Erdoğan's whims – seen most dramatically when he walked out of a Davos meeting with Israeli leaders during the 2008–09 Gaza war, prompting a sudden and unplanned break in Turkish–Israeli ties.

Moreover, despite presenting their regional approach as new, the AKP retained two core Kemalist policies. First was the steadfast rejection of

Kurdish secession from Turkey. While the AKP would propose concessions to Turkey's long-suffering Kurds, it remained committed to preserving Turkey's borders and the post-First World War regional settlement. Any factor that could threaten that, notably the growth of pro-secessionist groups in Syria, Iraq or Iran, was viewed as a threat. Second, it remained committed to Turkey's long alliance with the US and NATO. Erdoğan built a regional image as an anti-US voice: criticising Bush after the Iraq war, clashing with the US over Israel, and also frustrating Obama with his last-minute opposition to the Iran sanctions in 2010. However, at the same time Bush pressured the EU to welcome Turkey as a model of Muslim moderation, while Obama hoped a close alliance with Turkey, referred to by Deputy Secretary of State Nicholas Burns in 2012 as 'an important model of success', would allow for US regional retrenchment.[79] The ultimate importance of this tie was seen in September 2011 when Turkey agreed to host NATO's missile defence radar on its territory – 435 miles from Iran – despite Iranian objections.[80]

Syria was the 'poster child' of the zero problems policy, having overcome historical enmity to forge a close relationship by 2010.[81] Sharing Turkey's longest border, 910 kilometres, Syria had been on the opposite side of the Cold War, claimed the right to the Turkish province of Hatay, demanded greater access to Euphrates water that Turkey dammed upstream, and supported the PKK in its struggle with Ankara. The states almost went to war in 1998 over the latter. However, with goodwill from new leadership on both sides, long-running issues were swiftly settled. Hafez had already expelled the PKK in 1998 to avoid Turkish invasion, but Bashar al-Assad accelerated the rapprochement, becoming the first Syrian leader to visit Ankara in 2004, deliberately sidelining the Hatay issue in 2005, and reaching agreement on Euphrates water in 2008. This enabled an ever-deepening economic, diplomatic and cultural relationship. A free trade agreement, initiated in 2007, and a visa-free travel arrangement in 2009 saw trade flourish. Syria's exports to Turkey more than tripled from $187 million in 2006 to $662 million in 2010, while Turkish exports to Syria grew from $609 million to $1.85 billion in the same period.[82] Syrian visitors to Turkey increased more than sevenfold between 2002 and 2011 to just under a million a year.[83] In a sign of the personalisation of Turkish foreign policy, Erdoğan and Assad formed a friendship, even holidaying together. Both benefited from these public ties: Assad ended his diplomatic isolation, while Erdoğan enhanced his anti-US credentials on the Arab street by associating with a 'Resistance Axis' leader. Few would have expected Turkey to emerge soon as a leading sponsor of the anti-Assad opposition.

Qatar: The ambitious emirate

The same could be said of Qatar, which had grown close to Assad in the late 2000s. The emirate boasted three significant assets for the activist foreign policy it would pursue after 2011: a tiny population, enormous wealth, and, like Turkey and Iran, an ambitious leadership. The fossil fuel boom of 2002–08, aided by sensible reforms to its Liquefied Natural Gas (LNG) sector, and a diversification in its economy saw an explosion in Qatar's wealth, from a GDP of $25 billion in 2001, to $100 billion in 2010, and $200 billion in 2013.[84] This attracted a wave of migrants to the peninsular state, increasing the population from under 700,000 in 2002 to 1.7 million in 2010 and 2.3 million in 2015. Yet of these, only 300,000 were citizens, giving Qatar by far the highest per capita income in the world, resulting in considerable largesse from the state.[85] The Qatari leadership could therefore conduct foreign policy largely unrestrained by domestic concerns. However, unlike small states in similar positions, such as Singapore, Qatar's emir had grand ambitions.

Having seized power from his father in a bloodless coup in 1995, Emir Hamad bin Khalifa al Thani utilised Qatar's vast gas wealth to set it on the path to rapid economic growth. While under his father Qatar had followed Saudi Arabian leadership alongside the other Gulf states, Hamad was determined to pursue an independent path. This was seen almost immediately when he permitted al-Jazeera to be founded in Doha in 1996 by a group of mostly anti-Saudi Arab journalists.[86] This distinction from Saudi Arabia was a key trait of Hamad's foreign policy, including more amiable ties with Iran, with whom Qatar shared the vast South Pars / North Field gas field. Hamad was autocratic and ran his country in a highly personalised way, making his foreign policy somewhat idiosyncratic and unpredictable.[87] While this meant a lack of institutional depth and a weak bureaucracy, it allowed for swift decision-making and rapid policy shifts.[88] Alongside Hamad was a small circle of decision-makers, most importantly Sheikh Hamad bin Jassim al-Thani (HBJ), Foreign Minister from 1992 to 2013, and Prime Minister as well from 2007–13.

On the eve of the Syrian civil war, Qatar was in the process of greatly expanding its regional and international influence.[89] Its security was guaranteed after the US agreed to relocate its air force from Saudi Arabia to the purpose-built Al Udeid base in Qatar in 2003. Rather like Turkey, this deep alliance with Washington should always be recalled even when Doha pursued seemingly anti-American policies. Further to this, it aimed to manage its relationship with Iran. It was seemingly on course with this too, aligning itself more with the 'Resistance Axis' in the late 2000s by improving ties with Assad's Syria and promoting an anti-Western agenda on al-Jazeera. Secondly, it sought to expand its regional influence, particularly distinguishing itself from Saudi Arabia. This was done in two stages. Firstly via al-Jazeera's dramatic rise, which boosted the tiny emirate's profile and increased its popularity on the Arab street. Secondly, after 2006 it took on Saudi Arabia's traditional role as mediator in regional disputes, sponsoring mediation after the Gaza war in January 2009 and brokering the 2008 Doha Agreement in Lebanon. A third stage, financial and armed support for opposition groups, would follow in 2011. A final, related, aim was to boost Qatar's international 'brand', by spending much of its wealth on high profile projects at home and abroad, such as sponsoring football clubs or buying London department stores – certainly helped by the 2007 financial crisis, which resulted in assets being offered abroad at comparatively low prices. This branding reached its apex in 2010 when Qatar was awarded the FIFA World Cup for 2022.

Qatar's improved ties with Syria thus should be seen as part of its bid to boost its regional influence. As with Erdoğan, there was kudos on the Arab street to be won for Hamad by associating with the then-popular Assad, but there were other advantages. Helping the diplomatic boycott of Assad to fail represented a defeat for Saudi Arabia. Indeed, it was Qatar that facilitated French President Nicolas Sarkozy's rapprochement with Damascus. Similarly, Hamad had helped effectively reverse Saudi Arabian gains in Lebanon at Syria and Iran's expense after the 2005 Cedar Revolution by brokering the 2008 Doha Agreement that helped consolidate Hezbollah, Syria and Iran's power there. As with Erdoğan, Hamad's ties to Assad were personal, with the Syrian leader also forming a close bond with the Emir's son and heir, Tamim. As a further sign of friendship Doha announced up to $12 billion in investments from 2006 to 2010, a huge amount for Syria, although many remained unrealised.[90] That said, Assad did refuse a Qatari proposal in 2009 to build a gas pipeline over Syrian territory to Europe via Turkey. Some later claimed this was to protect Russian and possible future Iranian dominance of the European market – seemingly confirmed when the Iran–Iraq–Syria–Lebanon pipeline was announced soon afterwards.[91] As with Iran, Syria's main value to Qatar was the political rather than economic, with the platform it lent Doha. Such ties, however, were expedient and, as was soon to be seen during the 2011 crisis, ultimately proved shallow and expendable.

On the eve of civil war, Syria and the Middle East appeared deceptively stable. Regionally, Barack Obama's proposed engagement with former enemies Iran, Russia and Syria suggested a less militaristic approach to the region than that of his predecessor. However, the Bush administration's policies, particularly the 2003 Iraq war and its aftermath, had already set about transforming the regional order. The previous balance of power was upset to the advantage of Iran, in turn provoking more active policies from Saudi Arabia and creating opportunities for ambitious states such as Turkey, Qatar and Russia. Three previously more marginal transnational forces – sectarianism, jihadism and Kurdish nationalism – were exacerbated and saw their reach considerably widened, while the non-state actors promoting them proliferated. Moreover, this prompted a reassessment of US power in the region, both in Washington and among America's regional allies and enemies. Whether due to changing global structural forces such as the financial crisis, globalisation and the rise of China, or due to policy choices, the US was increasingly seen as in decline and questions over the extent of US hegemony, already overstated, were being raised.

Against this backdrop in Syria President Bashar al-Assad had come through an uneasy first decade in power. He had survived confrontation and isolation with the West and its regional allies, all of whom were now seeking detente with Damascus. However, this foreign policy victory couldn't mask the array of problems below the surface that Assad faced at home. As shall be discussed in the next chapter, he failed to adapt the autocratic regime he inherited from his father to new and pre-existing economic, political and social challenges, often making matters considerably worse.

CHAPTER TWO

The Arab Spring comes to Syria

Syria is not isolated from what is happening in the Arab world. We are part of this region. We influence and are influenced by it, but at the same time we are not a copy of other countries.
Bashar al-Assad speech to the People's Assembly, 30 March 2011

Syria's Presidential Palace towers over Damascus. Built by Hafez al-Assad, its imposing white marble walls stand alone on Mount Mezzeh in the west of the capital like a modern-day castle, leaving the Syrians below with no doubt who is in charge. Yet Hafez' son and successor, Bashar al-Assad, used this looming fortress only for official functions, and opted instead to live with his family in a modest apartment in the nearby upper middle-class neighbourhood of Malki. Living among the people, surrounded by minimal security and even driving his own car were important components of an image that Assad and his supporters carefully crafted. Contrasting himself to his father and other Middle Eastern dictators, Syria's President was presented as approachable, modern and popular. It was therefore sitting on a leather sofa in his home rather than in the cold empty palace that Assad gave an interview to the *Wall Street Journal* on 31 January 2011. He spoke of his confidence that the wave of unrest spreading across the Arab world at that moment, soon dubbed 'the Arab Spring', would not spread to Syria. In what would prove to be a hubristic gloat, he claimed, 'We have more difficult circumstances than most of the Arab countries but in spite of that Syria is stable.'[1]

Six weeks earlier a frustrated youth in far off Tunisia had unexpectedly set the Middle East aflame. On 17 December 2010, Mohamed Bouazizi a 26-year-old street vendor, self-immolated in frustration at the latest in a long line of humiliations meted out to him by the authorities. Within hours protests erupted in his home town of Sidi Bouzid in the poor Tunisian interior. Opposition swelled and spread to the capital, Tunis. On 14 January, under popular pressure Tunisia's military ended the twenty-four-year autocratic rule of Zine al-Abidine Ben Ali, who fled by plane for exile in Saudi Arabia. Few expected events in Tunisia to reverberate elsewhere.[2] When Saddam was toppled in 2003 it had not led to the regional democratic awakening that the Bush administration had hoped for, so why should a small country on the Arab world's periphery be different? Western and regional governments had for decades discounted the importance of the Middle East's populations, dealing directly with autocratic rulers and with little thought to popular opinion. Yet the people power of the Tunisians inspired copycat protests across the Arab world where populations shared the frustrations and hardships of Mohamed Bouazazi. First came protests in neighbouring Algeria on 29 December 2010. Then, once Ben Ali fled, a wave of unrest erupted in Jordan on 14 January 2011, Oman on the 17th, Egypt on the 25th and Sudan on the 30th. Egypt, the most populous Arab state saw sustained, widespread and mostly peaceful public protest, with hundreds of thousands gathering for days in Cairo's Tahrir Square. Echoing events in Tunisia, on 10 February in the name of the people the military ousted Hosni Mubarak, who had ruled for thirty years. This in turn set off another wave of regional protest, hitting Iraq on 12 February, Bahrain on the 14th, Libya on the 17th, Kuwait on the 19th, Morocco on the 20th and even eastern Saudi Arabia on 11 March.

Yet on his leather sofa, Assad believed his dictatorship would somehow be immune. Unlike his Western-allied neighbours that were being toppled, Assad told the *Wall Street Journal* he was 'very closely linked to the beliefs of the people'. While acknowledging Syria's economic difficulties, stating, 'we do not have many of the basic needs for the people', he remained confident that his anti-US 'Resistance Axis' foreign policy was so in tune with popular opinion that it would compensate for shortcomings elsewhere. This confidence proved to be misplaced. On 6 March a group of teenagers were arrested in the southern Syrian town of Deraa for scrawling anti-regime graffiti, echoing the slogans shouted in Tahrir Square the previous month. It would prove to be Syria's own Mohamed Bouazizi moment.

By the end of the month Syrians too would be out on the street demanding change and, it would seem, Assad's boasts of Syria's difference were wrong. But were they? The question of Syria's similarity or difference to other states in the Arab Spring greatly impacted national and international reactions to the emerging unrest there. Initially foreign governments shared Assad's mistaken belief that Syria was different, and adopted a cautious line. Months later, many went too far the other way, believing Syria to be so similar to Tunisia and Egypt that the regime would soon collapse.

While the thinking behind those miscalculations will be discussed later, this chapter examines Syria's eruption into revolt to assess how similar or different it truly was. As shall be seen, Assad would tragically prove to be only half wrong. Below the façade of a modernising young ruler leading populist foreign polices, the same economic disparity, political disenfranchisement and social resentment existed as in other protesting Arab states. However, the structure of its ruling regime and the complexities of its relationship with society would mean that Syria would not mimic Tunisia and Egypt in the swift exit of their leaders. Assad was correct when he told his parliament on 30 March, 'Syria is not isolated from what is happening in the Arab world . . . but at the same time we are not a copy of other countries.' It was similar enough to be caught up in events, but different enough to have quite different, far bloodier, outcomes.

Syria's Troubles

The image: Assad's Syria

Like many autocratic states, on the surface Syria appeared stable. Assad apparently enjoyed a degree of genuine popularity prior to 2011, although the wall of fear ever present in dictatorships such as Syria made it difficult to truly assess. His brief spell studying in London and marriage to a glamorous British-raised Syrian, Asma Akhras, added to this modern, approachable image compared to his stern father. Many restaurants in the old cities of Damascus, Aleppo and Homs boasted pictures of Assad eating there when he had 'dropped in' unannounced. Hafez al-Assad's brash Soviet-style personality cult was replaced by an initially softer cult, with officials insisting that the pictures of Assad and family on cycling holidays plastered on market stalls and car windows indicated spontaneous adoration and was not officially 'encouraged'.[3] Even disgruntled elements in Syrian society tended to distinguish between Assad and his regime: the President was seen as held back in his desire to reform Syria by remnants of his father's era – the 'Old Guard'. While he won an absurdly inflated 97 per cent victory margin in unopposed re-election in 2007, many commentators believed he would have won a genuinely democratic poll had he allowed it.[4]

After he had spoken in surprisingly open terms in his inaugural presidential address in 2000, even criticising the old ways of his father, hopes of reform were raised both at home and abroad. Political reform was mooted but sidestepped and transforming the economy was prioritised. Socialism had been slowly abandoned under Hafez, but the economy remained heavily state-dominated and sluggish. Oil exports were diminishing, having previously provided vital foreign currency in the 1990s after the Soviet Union collapsed, bringing an end to its economic support. Meanwhile the forced withdrawal from Lebanon in 2005, which had been a useful source of black market income, and the sanctions inflicted by the George W. Bush White House, prompted an accelerated move towards a 'social market economy'. Under the leadership of Nibras al-Fadel and Abdullah Dardari, a Deputy Prime Minister (2005–11), a 10th 'Five Year Plan' was launched in 2006.[5] Private banks and a stock exchange opened. A marked increase in foreign direct investment, especially from the Gulf, prompted growth in luxury construction and tourism – the latter providing 12 per cent of GDP in 2010 – while trade flourished, particularly with post-Saddam Iraq.[6] GDP more than doubled in five years, from $27.9 billion in 2005 to $60.1 billion in 2010.[7]

The new tourists, mostly from the Gulf and Turkey, plus some Westerners, would see this positive visage of Assad's Syria. Parts of central Damascus and Aleppo were transformed: modern shopping centres and Western coffee shop chains appeared, old cities were smartened with new boutique hotels and Ottoman courtyard restaurants. Syria's 'mosaic' of diverse religious and sect communities peacefully coexisted, with large churches standing beside mosques – a sharp contrast to the persecution of Christians in neighbouring Iraq. Syrians were celebrated for their friendliness to visitors. They also seemingly approved of the regime's anti-US, anti-Israel 'resistance' foreign policy and rhetoric, and of Assad himself. Flanked by his popular glamorous wife, labelled by *Vogue* as 'the rose in the desert', Assad's confidence that Syria would be immune to the Arab Spring did not seem misplaced.

Beneath Assad's glamour: The murkier reality

Yet problems existed below the surface. Just like the protesters on the streets of Egypt and Tunisia demanding 'Freedom, Bread and Dignity', Syrians also had deep political, economic and social complaints. Politically, as in Tunisia, Egypt and elsewhere in the Arab world, power remained concentrated in the hands of a tiny elite. According to Raymond Hinnebusch, the autocracy built by his father and inherited by Assad was a hybrid of Leninism and Gaullist constitutionalism.[8] The 1973 constitution declared the Ba'ath Party the 'leader in state and society', and guaranteed it the majority of seats in parliament, the unicameral People's Assembly. Hafez packed allies and lieutenants into the party's two executive bodies, the National Command and the Regional Command, from which he would then appoint key administrative positions, including Prime Minister, cabinet and regional governors. At the same time, a parallel, informal power structure kept the regime secure. Hafez ensured that key security, military and intelligence institutions were packed with loyalists, dominated by members of his Alawi sect, the protectors of his regime and the holders of true power.

After coming to power, Bashar al-Assad gradually made changes to this ageing autocratic structure, what Hinnebusch calls 'authoritarian upgrading'. His efforts consolidated his own power, but they also narrowed his support base, excluding key constituencies. He retired old regime hands, notably Mustafa Tlass (Defence Minister 1972–2004), Abdul Halim Khaddam (Foreign Minister 1970–84 and Vice President 1984–2005) and, on his ascent to power, Hikmat al-Shihabi (Army Chief of Staff until 1998 when forcibly retired to prevent opposition to Assad's succession) – the 'Old Guard' seen by many as holding back reform. Yet these old hands had long established networks of supporters that were now also excluded.[9] Their replacements, moreover, were an even narrower clique of technocrats and Bashar loyalists, cynically labelled the 'New Guard' by some observers.[10] Assad promoted family members to prominent positions in the security structure, notably his brother Maher, brother-in-law Assif Shawkat, and cousin Hafez Makhlouf. He gave even more key security positions to members of the Alawi community than his father had, who had sought to promote prominent Sunni Arabs (the majority sect) like Khaddam and Tlass. Assad's attempts to shake up the Ba'ath Party largely failed. Though elections were opened up to attract young members and rejuvenate it, he simultaneously relegated the party's importance. After 2003 government appointments were no longer exclusively drawn from the party, with Dardari a high-profile non-Ba'athist, while funding was cut and the party's relevance declined. In rural areas local tribal and religious leaders emerged as power brokers in the way that local party bosses once had. The party ceased to be the tool of patronage and (relative) social advancement it had been under Hafez and, despite still counting 12 per cent of the population as members in 2010, was no longer the glue binding both society and political allies to the regime.[11]

Yet no wider political opening was pursued. One more loyalist party, the Syrian Social Nationalist Party, was permitted to join the Ba'ath Party-dominated National Progressive Front in parliament, and loyalist independent 'non-partisans' were allowed to stand for election to the powerless body, but that was the extent of political reform in ten years. All independent opposition remained forbidden. Membership of the Muslim Brotherhood remained punishable by death. Calls from liberals for Assad to lead reform were crushed, first the 'Damascus Spring' of 2000–01, and then the 2005 'Damascus Declaration' that followed uncertainty after the withdrawal from Lebanon. Many of the liberal leaders of these initiatives, such as Michel Kilo, Riad Seif and Samir Nashar ended up in prison.[12]

Such arrests typified a darker undertone that Assad showed little sign of curtailing. Syrians are known for their black humour and a popular joke even before 2011 was that life was so much better under Bashar than Hafez, because if you insulted the President, you disappeared. This was preferable to life under Hafez where the same offence would lead to you, your family, and every one of your friends disappearing. Emergency law (officially Decree No. 51) had been in place since 1963, ostensibly due to the continued state of war with Israel but in reality utilised to arbitrarily detain, try and sentence on the grounds of 'protecting the state'.[13] The regime's tool in this was the Mukhabarat, a ruthless set of intelligence agencies, comprising 50,000–70,000 security officers willing to utilise fear, torture and intimidation routinely. East Germany's notorious Stasi had originally provided much of the training of the Mukhabarat, including its many interrogation and torture techniques.[14] These agents went beyond repression, becoming a fixture of everyday life via widespread corruption.[15] Their visible presence increased under Assad, partly because the more benevolent arms of the state, such as peasant and worker unions, shrank from view after economic reforms cut their funding. This meant that in some areas the security services became the principal arm of the regime people interacted with. Also, the withdrawal from Lebanon in 2005 sent a swathe of agents that had previously spent their days harassing and fleecing the Lebanese back home.[16] When Syrians, like other Arab protesters, demanded 'dignity' the Mukhabarat was the primary target of their anger.

As in much of the Arab world, Assad's superficial economic successes masked the failure of benefits to be felt across Syrian society. These problems were partly structural, but also the result of policy. Changing demographics put the economy under severe strain. The population exploded under the Assads' rule, from 3.3 million in 1950 to 21 million in 2011.[17] Much of this came between the 1970s and 1990s, a combination of improved living conditions and a pro-natalist government policy, leading to a sizeable youth bulge: in 2010, 55 per cent of the population were under 24.[18] Compounding this was a growth in education, part of Hafez' socialist legacy. Up to a quarter of youths attended state-funded universities, but, like Mohamed Bouazizi in Tunisia, found no jobs suitable for their qualifications, falling back frustrated on menial employment or none at all. The regime acknowledged in 2006 that annual economic growth of 6 to 7 per cent minimum was necessary to find jobs for its increasing population, but the average growth of only 4.9 per cent in 2006–10 proved insufficient. The result was persistent unemployment and under-employment – officially averaging 10.1 per cent in 2003–11, but estimated to be closer to 20 per cent in reality, and much higher among youth.[19]

Unfortunately for Assad, his proscribed treatment proved worse than the illness. The shift to a social market economy prompted limited successes but it came at significant cost to society. The logic was to gradually adopt market-led economics without the brutal abandonment of the welfare state seen elsewhere. Yet, as David Lesch argues, the result was an ad hoc marketisation that didn't go far enough to actually produce the jobs needed but still 'diminished the social safety net to which many Syrians have become accustomed'.[20] There weren't massive lay-offs from state employment, which continued to employ 20–30 per cent of the population, although some manufacturing, especially in Aleppo, was hit by the availability of Turkish goods under the new free trade agreement. Long-standing subsidies were suddenly removed. The cost of diesel fuel, for example, more than tripled overnight in May 2008 from SYP7.3 ($0.15) to SYP25 ($0.53).[21] This, along with the loss of subsidies on fertilisers, hit the peasantry particularly hard, as they relied on fuel for heating, transporting produce and powering water pumps. Rural areas, previously a bastion of regime support, were already suffering from neglect as Assad directed investment in infrastructure towards the cities, and new land laws that took ownership and usage rights away from cooperative models of the past.[22]

This rural decline was greatly exacerbated by the drought that hit in 2006–10. Water resources had been mismanaged for over fifty years by successive Syrian governments, so when the drought hit it was not surprising that the regime did little to contain the impact. The north-eastern region (governorates of Aleppo, Deir ez-Zor, Hasakah, Idlib and Raqqa) was the worst hit, already home to 58.1 per cent of Syria's poor. The conjunction of the drought, the lack of regime response made worse by the endemic corruption of officials, and the economic impact of the social market reforms prompted a humanitarian crisis, ultimately leading to massive internal migration. The number working in agriculture dropped from 30 per cent in 2001 to 13.2 per cent in 2010.[23] Between 1.2 and 1.5 million migrated, settling in unofficial camps and shanty towns in Aleppo and Damascus, but also in smaller cities like Deraa or Suweida.[24] It was estimated that up to 20 per cent of Syrians lived in some sort of rural–urban migration slum by the late 2000s.[25] Indeed, the tent camp of Mzeirieb near Deraa swelled with drought victims from the north-east from 2008, adding to the pressures on the local economy and resentment of the regime in the city where Syria's uprising began. Many of the areas that would join elsewhere had also been impacted by the drought.[26]

Though it had been slower than Egypt to abandon socialism, Syria was beginning to mirror the largest Arab state in terms of wealth disparity. By 2010, 30 per cent of Syrians lived below the poverty line, 11 per cent below the subsistence level.[27] Yet as the slums of Aleppo and Damascus multiplied, the city centres thrived. Luxury housing and hotels boomed as provision of social housing proved wholly inadequate for the needs of the masses.[28] According to Bassem Haddad, Hafez had already transformed Syria in the 1990s, 'from a semi-socialist state into a crony capitalist state par excellence', enriching a select number of families tied to the regime.'[29] However, under Assad and his reforms, the level of wealth accumulated by these families became much more visible. The Assads themselves, but also the Shalish, al-Hassan, Najib, Hamsho, Hambouba, Shawkat and al-As'ad families all gained large stakes in the economy. The most notorious was Rami Makhlouf, Assad's cousin. Known as 'Mr 10 Per Cent', he owned controlling stakes in oil companies, duty-free trade zones, the largest mobile telephone network, Syriatel, and Cham Holding, a controlling company that was granted government monopolies and forced most businessmen to tie themselves to its fortunes to obtain any state contracts or licences.[30] Corruption and nepotism had long been rife in Syria, but never quite so blatant.

Closely related to the political and economic troubles were Syria's social divisions. Again, as with Egypt, Tunisia and other Arab Spring states, Syria had far deeper social divisions than its public narrative of a united 'mosaic' nation would suggest. Syria's diverse sect and ethnic make-up added further complexity to the usual dividing lines of class, geography and kinship found in most other affected Arab states. Both Assads privileged members of the Alawi sect (12 per cent of the population), which had historically been persecuted by rulers from the Sunni Arab majority (65 per cent). A sizeable section of this group improved their economic and social standing as a result of regime patronage, although there remained poor rural Alawi communities. Nevertheless, a combination of material benefit and fear of the alternative successfully bound most Alawis to the fate of the regime. Some Sunnis resented this perceived privilege and many, especially in Hama and Aleppo, supported the Muslim Brotherhood revolt of 1976–82, which deployed anti-Alawi sectarian rhetoric. While enough Sunnis backed Hafez for him to defeat the revolt, Sunni–Alawi tension remained and was exacerbated at times. Assad's sidelining of key Sunnis such as Tlass and Khaddam didn't help, nor did the visible wealth of prominent Alawis such as Makhlouf – even though there were many wealthy Sunni and Christian regime-cronies as well. This privilege was extended at a local level in some areas too. In Homs, for example, while the mostly Sunni peasantry were suffering in shanty towns hit by the drought, recent Alawi migrants were rewarded with government jobs.[31] A growth in the 2000s of conservative Salafism[32] among Sunnis exacerbated matters in some areas, facilitated by the increased provision of social services by Islamic charities as state services were cut.[33] While few Salafi sheikhs dared be either anti-Alawi or sectarian, the growth of religiosity and public observation created a more visible wedge between some Sunnis and other Syrians than existed before.

That said, the Alawi–Sunni division should not be overstated. While sectarian resentment existed among *some* Sunnis towards some Alawis, and some Alawis reciprocated, it would be inaccurate to say these feelings were widespread and prominent across both communities. As ever, in a closed state like Syria where such issues were deliberately repressed, the extent and depth of such divisions are difficult to assess but the lack of sectarian slogans in early protests suggests this wasn't initially the main source of frustration. The significance of the sect should not be diminished: clearly the Alawi–Sunni tension in particular played an important role in fuelling anti-Assad protest and directing the development of the civil war and its international dimension thereafter. However, neither should Syria's many problems prior to 2011 be reduced to simply one of long-festering sectarian resentment. Not all Alawis sided with the regime, not all Sunnis sided with the opposition, and not all Syrians were motivated by ethno-sectarian concerns. As shall be discussed, variations over space and time were considerable, and political, economic, geographical, tribal, ethnic and local motivations were to prove as divisive as sect.

Unrest begins

Despite these long- and short-term problems, it is quite possible that Syrians would have remained largely passive were it not for the trigger of the Arab Spring, which served as both an inspiration and a guide. Syrians had been encouraged to feel a sense of Arab identity for decades and so empathised far more with the 2011 protests than recent equivalents in Iran (2009), Ukraine (2005) and Georgia (2004).[34] The shared conditions of political, economic and social dispossession and such slogans as 'the people want the fall of the regime' resonated more when screamed in their own language. Technology helped facilitate protest. The proliferation of the Internet and satellite television, particularly the popular al-Jazeera, meant that Syrians were now informed of events immediately. It took days and weeks for Syrians and the world to learn about the Hama massacre in 1982, but in 2011 technology allowed instant information. Smartphones were now widespread and social media such as YouTube, Twitter, Skype and

Facebook allowed populations to interact largely under the radar of repressive regimes – something recognised by the US before 2011 when it exempted Skype from sanctions against Syria.[35] Syrians could now observe and mimic foreign protesters, and communicate with them to share techniques. The regime did not help itself in this regard. It had welcomed al-Jazeera's anti-US stories in the 2000s, and encouraged a wide viewership. Moreover, having previously recognised its subversive potential and blocked Facebook and YouTube in 2008, on 9 February 2011 these bans were rescinded. This might have been to make online monitoring by the Mukhabarat easier, or because Assad was convinced it posed no threat. Either way this seems a strange and ultimately damaging decision, given the evolving regional climate.

In early March a group of teenagers from Deraa had been arrested for scrawling on their school wall 'doctor, your turn next' – referring to Assad – and, 'down with the regime' – a phrase no doubt learned from watching Egypt's protests on al-Jazeera. They were taken to Damascus and tortured.[36] Such cruelty was not abnormal, but their families' response was. Having had all pleas for their children's release ignored, on 15 March they and hundreds of others protested outside Deraa's central Omari mosque. Security forces opened fire, killing four. The next day, at the funerals of those killed, thousands more took to the street, chanting anti-regime slogans and smashing up regime symbols: the offices of the Ba'ath Party and Rami Makhlouf's Syriatel. As protests continued, by 23 March security forces had launched a harsher crackdown and surrounded the city, cutting off electricity, water and mobile phone networks. But technology had already allowed the news to spread; Deraa was not to be another Hama.

The Deraa protests were not the first inspired by the Arab Spring. Online opposition groups had failed to get a significant turnout for a 'day of rage' on 4 February, while a spontaneous protest in Damascus' old city on 17 February had been dispersed after a personal appeal by the Minister of the Interior. Deraa itself saw minor protests on the same day.[37] On 12 March Kurds protested in Qamishli and Hasakah, while on 15–16 March, at the same time as the first Deraa unrest, several hundred liberals and human rights activists gathered in central Damascus only to be violently broken up. However, the Deraa unrest was different. Firstly, opposition was more united and concentrated. Deraa could identify with almost all of the grievances described above. It was poor and agrarian, having suffered from the effects of the drought and Assad's 'social market' reforms. It was homogenous, being mostly Sunni and tribal, while its Mukhabarat commander was an outsider, Assad's brutal cousin Atef Najib, an Alawi. When protesters were killed, tribal and family ties drew in even more protesters against what seemed like an outside, parasitic force. This contrasts to divided Qamishli and Hasakah, where only Kurds protested, and not Arabs, or cosmopolitan Damascus, where the protesters might have been seen as a liberal elite that struggled to connect to the masses. Secondly, the regime killed. Protesters were arrested in Damascus and Qamishli, but they were murdered in Deraa. An interesting contrast is what happened in neighbouring Jordan, which initially saw more protests than Syria in January and February. Despite some violence, the autocratic monarchy wished to avoid escalation, so ordered police to distribute water and juice cartons to protesters, giving the impression that it was benevolent and open to criticism. Whilst this ultimately proved false, it pacified some and halted the protesters' momentum.

The reverse was true in Syria. Once news spread about the murders in Deraa, so did protest. The 18th of March saw peaceful protests spread to Homs, Banias and parts of Damascus. By 8 April Latakia, Tartous, Idlib, Qamishli, Deir ez-Zor, Raqqa and Hama had been added to that list. Protesters shared outrage at events in Deraa, inspiration from the Arab Spring, and long-standing economic and political disenfranchisement. Yet from the beginning some motivations behind unrest were localised, with grievances specific to each area. In the conservative coastal Sunni town of Banias, recent secularising government laws that forbade *niqab* (face veils) on female teachers – a backlash against increased Salafism among Sunnis – drew ire, while in Homs it was the perceived privilege of Alawi migrants. In the Damascus suburbs, neighbourhoods dominated by recent arrivals from other centres of protest rose up, such as Kafr Susa and Shaghur – which hosted many from Deraa – while other areas remained quiet.[38]

These differences would prove key in determining the future shape of Syria's uprising and civil war. French anthropologist Fabrice Balanche has demonstrated that the regime had long treated Syria's regions in different ways for different political ends.[39] The protests were paradoxical from the beginning in sharing a sense of national outrage at the regime, but based on different local grievances. These local and national differences also contributed to the flip side of Syria's uprising – the fact that a very large number did not join the protests. To understand why this was, the Syrian regime and its support base requires greater analysis. Indeed, as shall be seen, it is the structure and behaviour of the regime that made Assad's comments about Syrian uniqueness half right. Syria did share the same social, economic and political misery as Egypt, Tunisia and other Arab Spring states, but its regime was a very different animal than those that quickly crumbled.

The regime fights back

Buy-ins and coup-proofing

In 2004, when drawing comparisons with the regime of Saddam Hussein, the International Crisis Group remarked, 'ironically, the Syrian regime has become far more embedded in the nation's social fabric than was its Iraqi counterpart because of its comparative limitations and weakness'. Unlike Saddam's regime, that ruled either through the financial largesse of its oil wealth, or the brutality of its security forces, the Assads' poorer regime had to deploy a more nuanced strategy to stay in power.[40] Certainly fear and brutality were ever-present, the Hama massacre serving as a lesson to all, but like contemporary dictatorships the regime constructed an autocratic bargain with its populace. Such bargains usually included economic growth and political stability. Yet the Assads' bargain was more complex than Saddam's or even those of Egypt and Tunisia. As seen by the sizeable chunk of Syrians that did not protest in 2011, one of the factors that made the Assad regime different was the multitude of reasons, or 'buy-ins', it had constructed for continuing support.

One buy-in was economic benefit. For all the impact on the working class and peasantry, middle-class Syrians benefited from Assad's reforms. Damascus' merchants had long backed the regime, but the more sceptical Aleppo bourgeoisie was consciously courted by Assad. These mostly Sunni merchants were partly wooed by both Assad and his brother Maher marrying into established Sunni families, but more by the economic bene-fits of infrastructural projects, greater trade and new private schools and universities for their children. Central Damascus and Aleppo were conse-quently relatively passive in 2011. Syria's many government workers simi-larly had reason to remain loyal, and if there was any doubt, the government announced a pay increase on 1 April. A related buy-in was patronage. In Syria's tribal east, political alignment during the uprising tended to be decided by whether the regime had backed the tribe in the past. Traditional tribes such as the Ageidat, Hadidiyin, and Beni Khalid were marginalised under Assad and transferred their support to the opposition, while the Baggara, who thrived under his rule, continued to back their patron.[41] Another buy-in was ideology. Even if Assad was wrong to assume that all Syrians were content because of the regime's foreign policy, a number were probably convinced by ideas of Western and Israeli-led conspiracies after decades of reinforcing propaganda.[42] Moreover, some no doubt clung to the fiction that Assad truly was a reformer, even after a decade of failure.

Sect was another source of buy-in. Some, but by no means all, Alawis had enjoyed material benefit from regime patronage, and a larger number were worried that after Assad might come a Sunni-led government determined to exact revenge. Other minorities, the Christians (8 per cent of the population), Druze (3 per cent), Ismailis (1 per cent) and other Shia sects (1 per cent) also feared what might follow. For all its brutality, the avowed secularism of the regime provided a degree of religious freedom not seen in many neighbouring countries, notably Iraq where the fall of Saddam in 2003 had seen the Christian population reduce from 3 per cent to 1 per cent.[43] Many secular Sunnis were also drawn in for this reason, seeing Assad as a bulwark against Islamism and jihadism. Finally was the appeal of stability. Older Syrians may have remembered the unstable pre-Hafez years, while younger ones would have been reminded by regime propaganda of the recent chaos in Iraq and Lebanon. These multiple buy-ins, partly based on Syria's pre-existing diversity, but also due to the regime's skilful manipulation and support building over many years, were enough to give many Syrians a reason not to join the opposition in 2011. This may not have amounted to supporting the regime, but neutrality was sufficient to prevent the massive waves of protest that engulfed central Cairo and Tunis, keeping early protests in the periphery and away from the centres of power.[44]

Another difference between the Syrian regime and those that fell in Egypt and Tunisia was the extent of coup-proofing.[45] Many Arab autocrats 'coup-proofed' their regimes to prevent their military or security services from toppling the regime. Ben Ali and Mubarak clearly failed on this front. Similarly, while Libyan dictator Mu'ammer Gaddafi's military didn't turn on him in the palace, whole battalions defected to the opposition. This did not occur in Syria. Soldiers and officers later deserted individually, but not in whole units, and the military as an institution remained loyal. In Egypt the military proved too independent, developing economic interests which they needed to sacrifice Hosni Mubarak to retain; and extensive ties to the US meant they listened when the Obama administration urged the President's ouster. No such independence existed in Syria. The officer corps had been packed with loyalists over the years, mostly Alawis, who were linked to or indebted to the Assads.[46] This was particularly the case in the elite divisions: the Republican Guard, the Third Corps and the Fourth Armoured Division. The latter was de facto commanded by Maher al-Assad and estimated to be 80 per cent Alawi. While much of the military actually was allowed to decline in the 2000s, when Assad invested instead in hi-tech defences, the best equipment and training was reserved for these elite units, deployed in strategic locations to protect the regime.

A further component of Hafez' coup-proofing was his use of the Mukhabarat within the regime. Rather than being a single body that might accumulate independent power, Hafez' Mukhabarat was composed of multiple different agencies, fifteen by 2011, that spied on each other and members of the regime as well as the population. The most important of these were Military Intelligence, Air Force Intelligence, General Intelligence and Political Security. Any regime insiders who might have been plotting against Assad therefore feared discovery. In the past high-ranking regime officials had been mysteriously killed, notably Interior Minister Ghazi Kanaan, found dead in 2005, with many speculating he was disposed of to prevent his exposing Assad's link to the Hariri assassination.[47] On numerous occasions after 2011, key officials would similarly disappear from public sight, suddenly retire, or be killed in suspicious circumstances. Though many 'disappearances' were rumour or exaggeration, they illustrated that Hafez and his son had constructed a climate of fear that existed within the regime as well. Mukhabarat threats extended to ordinary soldiers and security forces too. In the early days of the protests there were numerous reports of Mukhabarat officers assigned to security and army units to shoot soldiers if they refused to fire on civilians. The opposition body-count website, the Violations Documentation Center in Syria, attests that hundreds of regime soldiers were executed in this manner.[48] However it was achieved, the result was that while Egypt's soldiers in February 2011 refused to fire on protesters, precipitating the swift fall of Mubarak, Assad's coup-proofing ensured he could call on troops that showed no such reservations a month later.

Regime violence

As protests spread the regime claimed that peaceful demonstrators were, instead, 'armed gangs', to justify using force. In most cases, however, the only armed elements were regime agents provocateurs deliberately shooting at soldiers. Security forces and then loyal military units were deployed and casualties mounted, reaching a short-term peak on 22 April, when 109 people were killed in one day. A pattern emerged: demonstrators protested about earlier deaths, more were then killed, initiating larger protests the next day. One such example was on 18 April, when an estimated 10,000 gathered in the Clock Square of Homs, Syria's third city, to protest about the murder of protesters the day before. After tear gas failed to disperse them, security forces opening fire, killing seventeen people, as recorded by several activists on mobile phone YouTube footage and then sent around the country. Not surprisingly, Homs soon became an early centre of the 'revolution', as protesters began calling the anti-Assad movement.

The military and security forces' violence was supplemented by the Shabiha and Mukhabarat. The Shabiha were gangs of irregular thugs that had previously run smuggling rings and protection rackets – their name deriving either from the Arabic word for 'ghost' or alternatively from the distinctive Mercedes S600 they frequently drove, known as *Shabah*. Though characterised as poor Alawis from the coastal region, often fanatically pro-Assad and anti-Sunni, they drew from a range of poor unemployed, marginalised and urban subaltern young men from different backgrounds.[49] These groups performed a number of roles from intimidation through to alleged massacres and systematic rapes in opposition strongholds.[50] They operated with a degree of autonomy and were often privately funded by pro-regime individuals, giving the regime some plausible deniability.[51] The Mukhabarat arrested thousands in the early months of the uprising. Sometimes known opposition leaders were targeted, but often the arrests were deliberately arbitrary, to intimidate the population. The veteran *New York Times* journalist Anthony Shadid reported an example in May 2011, when 286 were rounded up in Saqba near Damascus, mostly men aged between 18 and 50.[52] Gratuitous torture in custody was widespread, such as the gruesome case of Hamza Ali al-Khateeb, a 13-year-old from Deraa whose body was returned to his family burned, shot and castrated – a clear message to deter potential protesters.

However, there was more to the regime's response than blunt thuggery. In what would prove a common theme of the uprising and civil war, there was considerable regional variation. While Deraa and Homs were hit hard, Hama and others were initially dealt with more lightly. Sometimes this was the personal choice of local commanders, governors and officials, some-times an apparent tactical decision. The authorities were keen to avoid a Tahrir Square-style centre for protesters in Damascus, for example.[53] Though shopkeepers hoping to join strikes in solidarity with the opposi-tion had their shutters forced open and there were plenty of detentions, there was no arbitrary gunning down in the street, which avoided begin-ning the pattern seen elsewhere. Importantly, the regime also responded in non-violent ways. It reached out to tribal leaders in the Houran and Suwaida, while it met with religious leaders and key businessmen as well.[54] There was an effort to appease conservative Muslims by repealing the ban on *niqab* for teachers, closing a controversial casino and allowing Syria's first Islamic television channel, Nour ash-Sham.[55] The price of *mazout* gas oil was lowered. Efforts were made to dissuade the long-oppressed Kurds from joining the unrest by offering citizenship to 200,000 '*bidoon*' who had been left stateless by previous policies and inviting leaders of their political parties to Damascus for the first time; however, this was refused.[56]

One high-ranking former official, who later defected, remarked how this behaviour seemed schizophrenic.[57] Why was Assad meeting with the families of the arrested teenagers and tribal leaders from Deraa at the same time as his tanks surrounded the city? There are several explanations. The first is that the regime was attempting to divide and rule. This was a tactic deployed successfully by Hafez during the Muslim Brotherhood revolt of 1976–82. In 2011 Assad tried this by tapping into the various buy-ins discussed above. On 30 March he made an underwhelming speech to the People's Assembly, where he fell back on nationalism. He blamed the unrest on foreign conspiracy, led by satellite TV stations, the United States and Israel. 'Deraa is on the frontline with the Israeli enemy!' he railed. This theme repeatedly appeared in regime propaganda thereafter. The fears of minorities and secularists were similarly manipulated, as the regime began to portray the rebellion as Sunni jihadist. On 18 April, the Interior Ministry announced that it was facing an 'armed insurrection under the motto of jihad to set up a Salafist state'.[58] Similarly, regime agents travelled to Alawi villages delivering sandbags, and falsely reported that neighbouring Sunnis were planning to attack, while signs appeared in Damascus warning citizens of sectarian strife.[59]

Assad also made some superficial concessions: the events in Deraa were to be investigated; several political prisoners were released; the long-serving government of Prime Minister Naji al-Otari was dissolved and, when a new cabinet was formed on 16 April, Assad announced that the emergency law was to be lifted. To Assad's opponents this was either disingenuous or too little too late, and his speech on 30 March prompted even more unrest. The repeal of the emergency law, for example, meant little when security forces remained immune from prosecution, and new laws to 'protect national security' granted them similar powers. However, for those still clinging to the notion of Assad the frustrated reformer, this sliver of reforms was enough – especially when the opposition offered little alternative. Indeed, these tended to resonate more with the older generation and there were instances of a generational divide within the middle classes: youth heading out to protests against the wishes of their loyalist parents. Assad's divide and rule practice was not as successful as his father's, excluding far too large a portion of the population. However, he did show sufficient adaptability to successfully tap into the buy-ins of his regime in March–April 2011 to retain enough key supporters.[60] Pro-regime counter-demonstrations involving tens of thousands were arranged in Damascus, Aleppo, Homs, Hama and Hasakah on 29 March to illustrate this.

The second reason for this early 'schizophrenia' was internal divisions within the regime hierarchy. The inner workings of the regime are notoriously opaque, so getting a clear sense of what took place is difficult. However, a combination of regime experts and high-level defectors, who obviously benefit from presenting a certain picture, have suggested shock and uncertainty from the regime. Assad's flawed character was an important dimension; he lacked the ruthless decisiveness of his father. One of his biographers, David Lesch, paints the Syrian President as someone who courted opinions from multiple sources.[61] Others noted how he frequently changed his mind, '20 times a day'.[62] Indeed, some insiders later suggested that Assad was hours away from delivering a reform-minded speech on 30 March, only to switch to his nationalist rant at the last minute.[63]

Assad was more 'chairman of the board' than the one-man dictatorship of his father, and the differences of opinion within his inner circle alongside his indecisiveness help explain the contradictions.[64] Reports suggest that from the beginning some were arguing for an even harder line. Assad's influential mother, Anisa Makhlouf, his sister Bushra, brother Maher, and cousin, Hafez Makhlouf, led those urging him to repeat Hafez's brutality in Hama, smashing the demonstrators with overwhelming force. Manaf Tlass, the former Defence Minister's son and friend of Bashar, who defected in 2012, says he and others urged greater compromise. As a Republican Guard General, Manaf Tlass initially reached local accommodations in the Damascus suburbs of Douma and Harasta to allow limited protests, but was soon overruled by hardliners.[65] Within the inner circle some urged Assad to address the nation and appeal for calm, while others advised the opposite.[66] Assad's close ally Iran, whose role will be discussed in the following chapters, urged a more nuanced approach, recommending replicating the Islamic Republic's own crackdown of 2009, targeting ringleaders with extreme violence but without unnecessary collateral damage that might alienate the wider population.

Events elsewhere in the Arab Spring also impacted regime thinking. Officials later noted that the quick fall of Ben Ali and Mubarak taught the regime *not* to respond immediately to demands for change, as the raft of concessions given emboldened protesters to demand more.[67] Indeed, when Assad made concessions in his speech of 30 March he claimed this was long planned and not a reaction to unrest. Lessons were no doubt learned from elsewhere too. On 14 March, the day before the Deraa protests, Saudi Arabia and the United Arab Emirates sent tanks into neighbouring Bahrain to crush protests there. International response was muted. Damascus was possibly alerted firstly that force can work to crush dissent and secondly that the international community could be selective in its outrage. This contrasts with events in Libya. On 17 March the United Nations approved Resolution 1973 to mandate NATO to intervene to protect anti-regime demonstrators that Gaddafi had threatened to crush. We cannot know, but this may have had a chastening effect on the hardliners, as Assad and others saw that all-out brutal force and threats to wipe out a population might prompt international intervention. Indeed, throughout the first year of the crisis the regime did not deploy all its forces at once but rather incrementally increased its levels of brutality. British diplomats reported back to London that the regime was engaging in a 'calculated escalation of violence'.[68]

Finally, the regime's mixed response can be explained by a degree of incompetence. Whether they favoured a hard line or compromise, it is clear that Assad and his inner circle underestimated both the receptiveness of Syrians to the Arab Spring, and the resilience of their protests. Those that knew Assad claim he genuinely believed what he said to the *Wall Street Journal* – that Syria would be immune. Even once the unrest began, Assad repeatedly misread or was in denial of what was happening.[69] It did not help that he was surrounded by sycophants who told him what he wanted to hear. Yet even the hardliners misread things. One Western diplomat based in Damascus at the time expressed amazement that the regime only rarely cut off the nation's Internet and phone networks, which were doing it so much damage.

The only option?

Could Assad have done things differently? Arguably there were two options open to him: those recommended by the hardliners and by the compromisers in his inner circle. In Morocco and Jordan, in the face of similar protests, the ruling monarchs offered limited reforms, more so in Morocco, and took a degree of ownership of the Arab Spring in their states. Could Assad have done something similar: a reform-lite? It would have been difficult. Even more sympathetic biographers such as Lesch acknowledge that Assad lacked the skill and vision to transform Syria from the autocracy he inherited.[70] Even if he had vague intentions to do so, ten years in power assimilated him into the dictatorial system. Many have questioned, moreover, whether he had any intention to do so in the first place.[71] Emile Hokayem adds that the regime's structure as a security state that saw repression as the first solution to any problem made it highly unlikely any other route would have been taken, regardless of Assad's personality.[72]

If that was the case, then why did Assad not go the other route and deploy even more lethal force? Circumstances were quite different to Hafez' crushing of the Muslim Brotherhood in Hama. Assad was not as decisive as his father, and there were divisions within his inner circle. Events in Deraa happened very quickly, unlike the Hama massacre, which was the culmination of a six–year campaign against the Muslim Brotherhood. In that time the population had been readied by anti-Brotherhood propaganda to the extent that enough seemed willing to accept events in Hama as a necessary evil. In contrast, such brutality in Deraa would have seemed disproportionate and might have alienated even more Syrians. Additionally, technology meant that containing news of such a massacre would be difficult both at home and abroad, and within days of the Deraa protests news had already spread beyond an easily containable area. The international dimension was also crucial. While events in Tunisia, Egypt and Bahrain may have shown the value of repression over compromise, the UN reaction to Libya also suggested that unrestricted violence would not go unpunished. How much the regime believed the UN or US alone would authorise such a strike will be discussed later, but it further limited repressive options for the regime. Launching the kind of air assaults and use of chemical weapons it showed itself willing to use later on was not an option in March 2011.

Syria's uprising therefore fell between three stools. Despite Assad's claims to the contrary, Syria actually shared many of the same political, economic and social problems as other states that rose up during the Arab Spring, and so the outburst of unrest in March 2011 was not that surprising. However, the regime was structured quite differently from those of Egypt and Tunisia that fell quickly. Through a combination of brutality, ethnic solidarity, economic benefit and ideology enough of the population had a buy-in to the regime's survival to remain neutral when parts of the periphery rose up. Moreover, the military and security forces had been sufficiently 'coup-proofed' not to turn on the regime or refuse orders to slaughter civilians. Yet the uprising was widespread enough not to be as easily contained by force as the uprising in Bahrain, and indecision by the regime hierarchy and fears of international intervention further deterred an immediate hardline option. Finally, the Morocco or Jordan option of reform in the face of protest never seemed likely, given the weakness of Assad's character and the security orientation of his regime.

With hindsight what emerged by the end of April 2011 already looked like a civil war in the making. The Assad regime had not been able to re-erect the wall of fear, and protest had spread beyond a containable extent. However, it *had* deployed enough signposts to its buy-ins to retain the loyalty, or at least neutrality, of a large segment of the population. Undoubtedly the incredible levels of violence deployed by the regime were the primary factor in lighting a fire that would lead to civil war in Syria. However, as shall be discussed, a significant amount of oxygen was provided by the reaction of external actors to the events taking place in Syria within a region already undergoing profound systemic changes.

CHAPTER THREE

Assad must stand aside? The international community's ambivalent response

We have consistently said that President Assad must lead a democratic transition or get out of the way. He has not led. For the sake of the Syrian people, the time has come for President Assad to step aside.

US President Barack Obama, 18 August 2011[1]

In Syria's north-west, the border with Turkey follows the snaking Orontes River for about 30 kilometres. That this is the border at all has long been a sore point for Damascus as the neighbouring Turkish province of Hatay was originally Syrian before being given away by France in the 1930s. This was one of many issues underpinning an uneasy relationship for most of these neighbours' modern history. In early 2011, however, such hostility had been consigned to the past. Signifying a recent flourishing of ties, on 6 February Turkish Prime Minister Recep Tayyip Erdoğan joined his Syrian counterpart, Muhammad Naji al-Otari, on the banks of the Orontes to lay the foundation stone for a new 'Friendship dam', a $28.5 million joint project. 'We want the whole region to prosper, together with Turkey,' Erdoğan told television cameras, 'we struggle not to walk all over each other but to help each other. And we have achieved this with Syria.'[2] Yet within months Syria would be engulfed in unrest and Turkish–Syrian relations would sink to their lowest ever ebb.[3]

Turkey, like most foreign leaders and analysts, had shared the Syrian President's presumption that his country would be immune from the unrest seen in Tunisia and Egypt. The international response, when it did come, was cautious and uncertain. Surprise was compounded by political calculation. Almost no government welcomed the Arab Spring spreading to Syria. Old allies, such as Russia and Iran, and new, such as Turkey and Qatar, had no desire to see Assad dispatched like Mubarak or Ben Ali after so much political investment. Even Assad's traditional enemies in the West and in Saudi Arabia had recently re-engaged with Damascus. Moreover, from early on most foreign actors recognised the potential combustibility of Syria with its diverse population and its location on multiple regional and international fault lines. On top of this, attentions were focused elsewhere. By the time of the Deraa demonstrations twelve other countries had seen substantial protests and there were serious crises in Egypt, Bahrain and Libya. Attention for Syria was limited and Assad was to be given a chance. Western leaders condemned the violence but alongside pleas for reform, while regional players urged compromise in private meetings.

However, with the violence escalating, patience with Assad expired, and it did so quickly. Over two crucial months, July–August 2011, Assad's allies Qatar and Turkey abandoned him, and several Western states, led by Barack Obama, called for him to stand aside. Similarly, in what would prove a key dividing line for the coming civil war, Russia and Iran, despite some early ambiguity, stood by Assad. The decision to turn on Assad by the West and regional actors would play a key role in the move towards civil war and will therefore be explored in this chapter. In particular it will be asked why these states, having been so conscious of the dangers of instability in Syria early on, adopted such a harsh line so suddenly, further escalating the situation. It will be seen that while moral considerations may have justified these policymakers' stances, a range of factors, including domestic concerns, personal opinion, ideology and regional ambition, actually drove their actions. Moreover, all of the states that would turn on Assad betrayed a lack of knowledge and understanding of the regime at this point, as illustrated in their mistaken analysis that the regime was close to falling.

The Arab Spring shakes the Middle East

To understand the international response to the Syrian crisis, the impact of the Arab Spring must be considered. The Deraa protests began in between two of the most important episodes of the Arab Spring: the crackdown in Bahrain and the UN vote to intervene in Libya. From the beginning then, no foreign-policy maker was ever dealing with Syria in isolation, but rather as yet another strand of what appeared a sudden and confusing regional transformation. Bureaucrats and leaders struggled to keep up, and developing any regional strategy proved next to impossible. This would have an important impact on their approach to Syria.

Egypt

Barack Obama came to power determined to lessen American involvement in the Middle East, so the Arab uprisings were somewhat undesired. Having abandoned Bush's democracy proselytising, the President now found himself under pressure to support the protesters. The Tunisian revolution had been fast and in a relatively peripheral country, but, when tens of thousands took to the streets in Egypt, the US' key Arab ally, the White House was dragged in. The US had influence with the military to which it provided $1.3 billion in annual military aid, but how should it be exercised? With media coverage constant, led by al-Jazeera, the White House and State Department scrambled to make difficult decisions with limited facts.[4] In her memoirs, Hillary Clinton notes how 'some of Obama's aides were swept up in the idealism of the moment', urging the President to call on Mubarak to stand down immediately, while she and other realists like Defense Secretary Robert Gates urged caution. They believed Mubarak should stand down, but in a gradual transition that guaranteed stability and didn't give the impression that Washington quickly abandons its allies.

At first Obama appeared to be swayed by Clinton but, as protests spread and Mubarak refused to make concessions, he came under increasing domestic pressure to call for the Egyptian leader to go. Frustrated, Obama tacked towards the idealists.[5] When Mubarak didn't resign as expected on 10 February, instead defiantly stating that 'I will not, nor will I ever, accept to hear foreign dictations' – a not-so-veiled message to Obama – Gates was drafted to call Egyptian Army Commander-in-Chief Field Marshal Mohamed Hussein Tantawi to deliver a swift message: Mubarak must go now. The next day, he was gone, but the cost to Obama was considerable. Events had sucked him back into the Middle East against his will. He was criticised for having stuck by Mubarak too long by idealists and for 'throwing him under the bus' too quickly by realists. These two poles were going to pull at the President throughout the Arab Spring.

The US proved to be the only external state with any real influence over Egypt, yet the remaining regional players' reactions were an indicator of the shifts in behaviour to come. Qatar, Turkey and Iran positioned themselves on the side of the people. Erdoğan and Iranian Foreign Minister Ali Akbar Salehi spoke in support of 'freedom' in early February, while al-Jazeera's near constant coverage of the revolution implied Qatari approval. Seeing potential geopolitical advantage, Iran falsely gloated that events in Tunisia and Egypt were both 'Islamic' and 'anti-Western', and Ayatollah Khamenei tweeted that the Egyptian Revolution marked an end of superpowers.[6] Pressing the point, Tehran sent two ships – both apparently unarmed – to Syria on 18 February, believed to be the first time Iranian vessels had been allowed to use Egypt's Suez Canal since 1979.

Even before such Iranian provocations, Saudi Arabia was greatly alarmed by Mubarak's fall. Of the six regional players in the Syria crisis, Saudi Arabia was the only one directly threatened by the contagion effect of the Arab Spring, and so most feared its spread. It publicly condemned the uprisings in Tunisia and Egypt, providing refuge for Ben Ali and offering the Egyptian military £4 million in aid the day after Mubarak's ouster, allegedly in exchange for not bringing the former President to justice.[7] With a substantial segment of its own population, among the most avid Twitter and Facebook users in the world, showing support for the Egyptian protesters, Riyadh turned its immediate attention internally and it's Gulf neighbours. However, it was livid at Obama for what it saw as his Egyptian betrayal.

Bahrain

Riyadh's fears were realised almost immediately when protests broke out in neighbouring Bahrain three days after Mubarak's departure. The largely peaceful protesters called for democratic reform, but included a sectarian dimension. Most were drawn from the under-represented Shia who made up 65–75 per cent of Bahraini citizens, while the ruling elite including the royal family was Sunni. With 100,000–150,000 joining the crowds, the government requested help from fellow Gulf Cooperation Council (GCC) monarchies and on 14 March 1,000 Saudi and 500 Emirati troops crossed into the island kingdom to help crush the unrest.

This proved an important turning point for the regional actors. Firstly, it revealed the selective nature of international support for the Arab Spring. Qatar, happy for protests in faraway Egypt but not in a neighbouring fellow GCC state, endorsed the invasion while al-Jazeera's Arabic channel offered no coverage. Turkey similarly was silent. The United States, which had voiced concerns about Bahrain, kept quiet. The kingdom had important strategic value: it was home to the US' Fifth Fleet, and Washington was concerned about Iran's influence over the Shia protesters – something claimed by the Bahraini and Saudi Arabian governments, but later disproved by Bahrain's own independent report into the unrest.[8] Moreover, the US was trying to secure GCC support for NATO action in Libya, and Hillary Clinton later admitted that she compromised on Bahrain to ensure their participation.[9]

Secondly, Saudi Arabia, which led the Bahrain operation, positioned itself as the leading counter-revolutionary force against the Arab Spring.[10] Alongside military activity in Bahrain, it donated generous grants to Bahrain and the governments of Oman and Jordan, which had also suffered unrest, in an attempt to stem the tide of protest. It also took a leading role in trying to manage the growing instability in Yemen. Following its anger after Egypt, Saudi Arabia moved into Bahrain without informing the US, illustrating a growing independence.[11] Obama would seek to patch up the relationship, sending Gates and then Donilon to meet with King Abdullah in April, when the Bahrain intervention was not discussed and hence implicitly endorsed. However, this did not sufficiently persuade the Saudi Arabian leadership that this administration could be counted on.

Libya

The first major protests in Libya began on 15 February, a day after those in Bahrain, but produced a very different international reaction. The ruling dictator Muammar Gaddafi refused protesters' calls to stand down, instead calling them 'cockroaches' and 'rats', and threatening to 'cleanse Libya house by house'.[12] The regime's violent response prompted rebel militia to form and on 27 February a National Transitional Council (NTC) to act as a de facto rebel government based in the eastern city of Benghazi from which Gaddafi's forces had withdrawn. Civil war broke out and initial rebel gains were soon repelled as loyalist forces headed towards Benghazi, amplifying opposition calls for a protective no-fly zone. In an example of how earlier episodes of the Arab Spring impacted later ones, France, embarrassed by its offer to help Ben Ali restore order in Tunisia in January, was determined to be on 'the right side of history' this time and was the first to call for Gaddafi's ouster on 25 February. Britain's David Cameron likewise saw an opportunity to get ahead of events and called for a no-fly zone three days later.

The White House, under pressure from its European allies and members of the Senate, experienced the same idealist–realist divisions as on Egypt. Gates and Vice President Joe Biden counselled caution, warning that Gaddafi's downfall might bring chaos in which al-Qaeda would thrive.[13] Samantha Power and Susan Rice, long advocates of the Responsibility to Protect (R2P) doctrine supported intervention. Clinton, cautious on Egypt, now argued that as France and Britain were determined to intervene it would be better for the US to 'drive' efforts and ensure a favourable result.[14] Persuaded away from his initial caution once more, Obama supported UN1973, proposed by Britain, France and Lebanon (representing the Arab League) on 17 March. However, insiders later argued that Obama had been 'goaded' into action, with some US officials calling the operation France's 'shitty little war'.[15] The campaign took longer than anticipated and Libya still descended into the chaos that Gates and Biden feared, impacting Obama's view on military intervention – a lesson that would later shape his Syria policy. Ironically, US support for UN1973 led regional actors to a different conclusion: the Libya model of external intervention in support of armed resistance prompted new thinking among Syria's opposition and its regional allies. Observers wrongly believed that this was a return to American regional hegemony, and not an exception to Obama's preferred retrenchment.

Other regional responses varied. Saudi Arabia supported UN1973, but unlike UAE, Jordan and Qatar sent no material support. Turkey, revealing the limitations to its newfound support for the people, questioned the no-fly zone, claiming it was motivated by Western desires for Libyan oil. Commentators noted, however, that Turkey enjoyed $2.6 billion in annual trade with Gaddafi's Libya and had $15 billion in pre-existing construction contracts.[16] Eventually Erdoğan was persuaded, as was Russia, which abstained from the UN Security Council vote on 17 March. Quite what Moscow believed it was implicitly endorsing would later be debated and have consequences for Syria.

Qatar's role in Libya would also reverberate in Syria. The Arab League's support for a no-fly zone, announced on 12 March, was primarily due to Doha's efforts. Qatar was the first Arab state to recognise the NTC as the legitimate government of Libya. Qatar saw multiple advantages: to boost its regional profile, increase popularity on the Arab street, and strengthen its value to Western allies. This proved the first stage of a more activist regional policy after the Arab Spring. As the conflict progressed, Qatar would send six combat fighter jets, forge close relations with Islamist fighters and politicians on the ground – notably Abdelhakim Belhadj and the al-Salibi brothers – send weaponry to the rebels and, it was later revealed, dispatch its own special forces.[17] The eventual success of the campaign, with Gaddafi defeated and killed on 20 October, greatly boosted Qatari confidence in its regional ventures, again to be seen in Syria.[18]

Syria

When the first protests erupted in Deraa the international community was therefore poorly placed to respond. Western diplomats talked about a lack of 'bandwidth': the limited number of simultaneous crises they could handle at once. One British official noted that 'we had Tunisia and Egypt, Yemen, then Libya, Bahrain, so from the point of the Foreign Office, by the time you got to Syria we were so steeped in daily, hourly even, issues to do with the Middle East'.[19] With limited capacity, certain crises took precedence. Egypt, as a key US ally and the largest Arab state, was the greater priority. State Department officials worked 24–hour shifts through the Egypt crisis.[20] The military campaign in Libya also understandably took precedence and a

British official remarked that only when Libya was nearing its conclusion in September was sufficient energy directed towards Syria.[21]

Regional actors also suffered from a lack of bandwidth. In March and April, Saudi Arabia's attention was focused internally and in the Gulf. Qatar was primarily concentrating on Libya. Importantly, regional actors were disinclined to draw attention to Syria at this stage. Russia and Iran were solid Assad allies. Qatar and Turkey, also close to Assad, kept quiet – it was almost two weeks before al-Jazeera started covering the crisis.[22] Riyadh too initially offered Assad support, with King Abdullah telephoning him on 28 March.[23] Moreover, the governor of the Saudi Arabian Monetary Agency, Muhammad al-Jasser, announced in mid-March that the kingdom was offering Syria $140 million in loans.[24]

Nor did Western states immediately adopt a confrontational tone. On 27 March Clinton told CBS, 'Many of the members of Congress of both parties who have gone to Syria in recent months have said they believe he [Assad]'s a reformer.' This comment was apparently unplanned and alarmed members of the State Department, but it reflected the West's preference for urging Assad to reform while condemning the violence. In statements on 8 and 22 April, Obama reiterated this line. He demanded that 'this outrageous use of violence to quell protests must come to an end now', but still called on Assad 'to change course now'.[25] Behind the scenes, European diplomats expanded this line. In Damascus the Western embassies of the US, UK, France, Germany, Canada, Japan, Denmark and the Netherlands, among others, reached out to protesters, offering support and forging connections. Yet at the same time, they met frequently with Syrian officials such as Foreign Minister Walid al-Muallem, Bouthaina Shaaban and Mohammad Nassif Kherbei (a confidant of Assad) to urge engagement with the opposition and offer EU support for reform efforts. Meetings were held in Brussels to discuss how the EU might support the regime were it to take the reform path.[26] Despite the genuine outrage at the regime's violence, there was no rush to call for Assad's removal – quite the contrary. A combination of stretched capacity due to events elsewhere and political choices to persist with the engagement of recent years meant that international reaction to the Syria crisis was initially muted.

Syria: Protests and violence increase

This became increasingly untenable in the late spring and summer of 2011. Protests continued in the rebellious cities of Homs, Deraa and Banias, while dozens of smaller, provincial towns such as Idlib, Telkalakh, Rastan and

Tafas, joined in. That summer, the uprising was probably at its most pluralist. Syria's Kurdish north-east saw some protests, as did parts of the Alawite-dominated coastal city of Latakia and the more tribal eastern city of Deir ez-Zor. Nor was this just a peasants' revolt: a large segment of Syria's middle-class youth took a prominent role, with wealthy Damascenes travelling out to unfamiliar poor suburbs to join in.[27] Indeed, in the relatively quiet second city of Aleppo, students led what few demonstrations there were.

In response, the regime continued its violent crackdown: a UN report revealed that up to 1,900 protesters had been killed by mid-July.[28] Rebellious centres were targeted: Deraa saw numerous sieges, as did Homs, Banias, Telkalakh, Tafas and Rastan among others. Troops and security forces, often supported by tanks, were deployed widely and rapidly in an attempt to deprive demonstrators of either a Tahrir Square-esque central location, or a Benghazi-esque liberated region that might act as a launch pad for foreign intervention. To this end massive military assaults using helicopter gunships were made in June on the towns of Jisr al-Shughour and Maarrat al-Nu'man in Idlib province. These operations also led to the first wave of Syrian refugees fleeing into neighbouring Turkey. They would be the first of many. Meanwhile the Mukhabarat and Shabiha's terror continued: 8,000 were detained by the end of July.[29] Vicious examples were made, such as Ibrahim Qashoush, a Hama fireman who had written and sung a popular anti-Assad song to protesters, found floating in the Orontes in July with his throat slit and vocal cords cut out.[30]

Yet the regime persisted with its two central narratives: that it was facing an uprising led by armed gangs, criminals and sectarian jihadists, supported by outside powers; and that Assad was persisting with his own reform programme. In his third major public address of the crisis, on 20 June, Assad spoke at Damascus University, noting how the protesters were akin to 'germs', leaving Syria open to 'foreign intervention'. Yet he also detailed more reforms, including a new electoral law and the possibility of a national dialogue. As after previous speeches tens of thousands gathered in orchestrated shows of support for Assad the next day. As an indication of the divisions taking hold of Syrian society, these rallies took place not just in Damascus and Aleppo, but in areas experiencing unrest: Homs, Hama and Deir ez-Zor.[31] In contrast, oppositionists dismissed Assad's 'reforms', given the simultaneous violent crackdown. These reforms, including a new law on 26 July that theoretically allowed non-Ba'ath-aligned political parties, would have been seismic before 2011, but by now it was too late. Many oppositionists boycotted the promised 'National Dialogue' when it convened on 10 July under the supervision of Vice President Farouk al-Sharaa. Indeed, the hollowness of the event was underlined when several of the activists who might have attended were rounded up by the Mukhabarat beforehand.[32]

Ramadan 2011, which began on 1 August, proved something of a turning point. Conscious that the holy month might galvanise the (mostly Sunni) protesters, the regime launched a new crackdown on 31 July on Hama, Deir ez-Zor, Al-Bukamal and other centres of protest. Up to 136 people were reported killed in one day. The Hama assault was particularly brutal. The regime's approach to Hama thus far had been more hands-off than in the case of other rebellious cities. The city had been surrounded with troops and tanks, but they had not moved in. Buoyed by the presence of the audacious American and French ambassadors who visited protesters on 6 July, two days later 500,000 gathered in the city's al-Assy Square for the uprising's largest protest. It is unclear whether the regime's reluctance to immediately crush such displays was due to the discretion of local commanders, sensitivities about Hama's past as the centre of the 1982 massacre, the military's preoccupation with events elsewhere, or all three. Either way, this initial reluctance only amplified the crackdown when it came, enraging the opposition and international opinion alike. Between 31 July and 4 August, 200 were estimated to have been killed. Days later the military also entered Homs and Deir ez-Zor, followed by Latakia. As always, the gratuitousness of this violence was captured on mobile phone cameras and broadcast around the world. With such brutality seemingly exposing the hollowness of his attempts at reform and dialogue, Western states, Saudi Arabia, Qatar and Turkey finally lost patience with Assad and undertook a dramatic shift in stance.

Iran, Russia, Qatar and Saudi Arabia: The world turns to Syria

As the world's attention belatedly turned to Syria, regional powers settled into the positions they would occupy for the coming years. According to Iran expert Jubin Goodarzi, Tehran faced Hobson's choice: stick by its long-term ally and appear hypocritical after nearly a decade of championing the Arab street, or let events play out and hope that if Assad fell his successors would be friendly.[33] There was some ambiguity. On 25 August President Ahmadinejad criticised the regime, stating, 'they must sit down together to reach a solution, away from violence'. Similarly two days later Foreign Minister Salehi said protesters had 'legitimate demands'.[34] Later on, in November, Syria's opposition claimed that Iran had reached out to some of them to see what their position would be on key Iranian security interests such as Israel, Lebanon and the US.

However, public statements and outreach came alongside support offered in private, and may have been primarily about maintaining Iran's regional image. Salehi made numerous trips to Damascus to reassure Assad. Mistakenly seeing the unrest through the lens of their own Green Revolution uprising, a brief surge that would pass quickly, the Iranians offered the expertise learned in 2009. Riot equipment was donated and hundreds from the IRGC Quds Force were dispatched to offer security advice. Tehran also suggested countering the opposition's messaging. Key technical assistance and training in cyber warfare to combat social media was provided, along with $1 million worth of equipment and training from Lebanese Shia broadcasters.[35] In its Hobson's choice Tehran opted to stick by Assad at the cost of regional credibility.

Like Iran, Russia hinted at public criticism when it joined a statement at the UN Security Council on 3 August condemning the regime's human rights violations. However this was an exception and Russia mostly offered support from the beginning. In May and June Moscow blocked Britain and France's draft UNSC resolutions condemning Assad's use of force. Similarly when the UN Human Rights Council voted on 22 August to launch an investigation into crimes against humanity possibly committed by Assad, Russia joined China in strongly objecting. The two also released a joint statement two days later urging the international community to stay out of Syria's 'internal affairs'. Playing along with the regime's narrative of attempting reforms in the face of an externally led conspiracy, deputy Foreign Minister Mikhail Bogdanov visited Damascus and endorsed Assad's reforms on 29 August.

Riyadh's approach was driven as much by external developments as those within Syria. The Saudi Arabia regime had two primary concerns: to contain the Arab Spring to ensure its own safety and to counter Iran. In the late spring and early summer, the first goal drove policy. Institutionally slow and conservative in its foreign policy making and distracted by events in its immediate neighbourhood, Riyadh shared the view that sticking with Assad, perhaps after a few cosmetic reforms, was the best way to halt the Arab Spring's momentum. Privately King Abdullah sent his son, Prince Abdulaziz bin Abdullah, to Damascus three times to persuade Assad to end his crackdown.[36] Each time, the prince was rebuffed, which personally offended Abdullah. By this point however the immediate domestic threat presented by the Arab Spring had passed. Abdullah had shored up his own position with $37 billion of welfare measures, contained the protests in

Bahrain and lavished grants on Oman, Bahrain and Jordan. If anything, Abdullah's silence on Syria was becoming a risk as the outrage of Saudi Arabia's social media savvy population at the continued Syrian violence grew, supported by religious leaders. It also was becoming clear that the opposition to Assad was not as easily containable as in Bahrain.

As the reasons for standing by Assad rapidly diminished, Saudi Arabia's second goal, restricting Iran, came to the fore. Were Assad to fall it would be a blow to Riyadh's regional nemesis, just as it seemed that Tehran was going to be the big beneficiary of the Arab Spring. On 8 August Abdullah finally broke his silence, stating, 'What is happening in Syria is not acceptable for Saudi Arabia', and urging Assad to stop his, 'killing machine'. [37] At the same time Saudi Arabia withdrew its ambassador to Damascus, a move copied by its close allies Kuwait and Bahrain.

Qatar transformed itself from Syrian ally to leading anti-Assad state in a few months. As the crackdowns stepped up al-Jazeera abandoned its caution, covering the crisis extensively and encouraging citizen journalism. However, subsequent research has shown that it sometimes broadcast, 'inaccurate reports and unverified or fake footage', which actually undermined the opposition by giving credence to Assad's claims of foreign conspiracy.[38] Al-Jazeera journalists insisted they were not acting at the behest of the Doha government but did admit to top-down pressure on certain politically sensitive issues, such as not covering protests in Bahrain. A Syrian regime defector even claimed that at one meeting in Doha Emir Hamad told Walid al-Muallem he could reverse the channel's position in favour of Assad if Damascus accepted reforms.[39] As the crisis continued the station essentially became an anti-Assad vehicle, with the Muslim Brotherhood ideologue Yusuf Qaradawi using his regular slot to rail against Damascus.

As al-Jazeera was unleashed Doha simultaneously sought to persuade Assad to cease the violence. Like Abdullah, Emir Hamad dispatched his son, Tamim, who counted Assad a friend, to Damascus. Tamim later recalled urging Assad to end the violence and promising him support if he reformed.[40] Syrian defectors suggest that, privately, these 'reforms' entailed power-sharing with a rehabilitated Syrian Muslim Brotherhood, tied closely to Doha. Yet Assad refused, and the repression continued. Qatar by this point viewed the Arab Spring as an opportunity to boost its regional influence, and was confident after the Libya campaign. Having found it had no leverage, Doha changed tack. In July it became the first Arab state to freeze relations with Syria. Officially this was a reaction to anti-al-Jazeera protests outside its Damascus embassy, but in reality it was the first step in a new strategy of opposing Assad.

Turkey's U-turn

For Turkey too, the summer saw a sharp shift. Even more than Doha and Riyadh, Ankara believed that Assad could be talked round and, when its friend ignored frequent pleas, reacted angrily. Turkey's transformation from ally to enemy was a far greater blow to Assad than losing Qatar, or the return to enmity of the West or Saudi Arabia. The Turkish frontier was to be the main entry point and supply line for the armed opposition and Ankara's acquiescence would play a major role in shaping the civil war. It is worth therefore examining in some depth why Turkey turned on Assad over the summer of 2011.

Revolution in Turkey's foreign policy

In 2003 Professor Philip Robins, a Turkey expert at St Antony's College, Oxford, noted that Ankara's foreign policy was directed by the government of the day, with input from the indirectly elected President, the Foreign Ministry (MFA) and the security establishment, but 'the high priests of Kemalism' determined grand strategy.[41] These senior military officers, bureaucrats and top diplomats were part of a wider Kemalist 'Deep State' that had been willing to overthrow elected governments in 1960, 1971, 1980 and 1997 to preserve what they saw as the vision of Turkey's founder, Mustafa Kemal Atatürk. When it came to foreign affairs, Atatürk's famous maxim, 'peace at home, peace in the world', led these 'high priests' to pursue a cautious approach, particularly in the turbulent Middle East, which they sought to keep at arm's length.

However, the coming to power of the AKP in 2002 revolutionised Turkish domestic politics and, consequently, transformed foreign policy. Erdoğan was determined to curb the power of the Kemalist establishment, particularly the military. This was primarily political: before he founded the AKP his two previous Islamist parties had been banned and he wanted to avoid the same fate. There was also a personal aspect as he had been sent to prison for ten months (though served four) in 1999 for 'inciting religious hatred'. A series of challenges to the secular establishment were launched, such as lifting a ban on headscarves in universities. More significantly, two high-profile trials – Ergenekon (after 2008) and Sledgehammer (2010) – saw hundreds of military figures and journalists accused of plotting against the state, and over 500 formally charged. In less than ten years Erdoğan overturned decades of military dominance. This was partly down to divisions within the Kemalists, as many opposed the Deep State's undemocratic practices, even if they shared their secular outlook. Yet it was also the result of Erdoğan's remarkable political skill. He was charismatic, populist and savvy, forging a wide alliance with businesses, conservatives, democrats and, importantly, the religious Gülen Movement that found support in the press, police and parts of the judiciary. Repeated success at the ballot box, increasing his share of the vote in 2007 from 34 per cent to 46 per cent, gave him a popular mandate to press on with reforms.

Though more democratic, the sidelining of the Deep State weakened the independence of Turkey's institutions, making foreign policy far more personalised around Erdoğan and Ahmet Davutoğlu. They shared similar characteristics: both were self-assured, stubborn and high-minded. Neither was known for seeking a wide range of advice and opinions, and both were criticised for making political decisions for personal reasons. Davutoğlu was greatly influential in foreign policy, masterminding the highly successful 'zero problems' and 'strategic depth' approaches of the late 2000s and encouraging deeper engagement with the Middle East. Yet this was as much directed by the Foreign Minister's worldview as by pragmatism. Though recognising the benefits of seeking EU entry, Davutoğlu argued in his academic work that a degree of 'irreconcilability' existed between the cultures of the West and the Islamic world.[42] There was ambivalence to his relationship with the West, as he was greatly influenced by five years working at the International Islamic University of Malaysia and sceptical of the Westernisation that underpinned Kemalism.[43] Crucially, the AKP's foreign policy ideologue saw Turkey not as a bridge between East and West but as a central country that should project influence, and saw the Islamic world and the Middle East as a key route to this.

Assad stands firm

A lot was at stake for Turkey in Syria. Instability was a threat to security as the PKK might take advantage of it to use a weakened Syria as a base, plus there was the growing number of refugees crossing the border. The economy might also suffer. Syria was a trading partner and an even more important overland trade route south. Politically, Ankara did not want to be seen siding with a murderous tyrant, either by its own population or by the Arab street. Erdoğan assumed that political investment in Syria would translate into influence so when unrest broke out Turkish officials informed the US 'not to worry' about Assad.[44] However, as violence went on Erdoğan became ever more embarrassed and angry.

Ankara adopted a dual strategy. Erdoğan ramped up the condemnatory tone of his statements and support for the Syrian opposition was gradually increased, with Assad's opponents permitted to hold conferences in Turkey in May and June – although to show balance Ankara also invited the Syrian government.[45] Meanwhile armed opposition groups formed in Hatay in July. At the same time, private diplomacy with the regime remained the main policy until late August. Numerous envoys were sent between Damascus and Ankara, while Erdoğan spoke on the phone with Assad frequently, urging restraint. On 15 June, when Syria's envoy, Hassan Turkmani, claimed that reports of Syrian abuses were fabrications, Erdoğan rebuffed him, saying that he had seen the YouTube videos with his own eyes and believed them.[46] Days later Erdoğan sent his own envoy to Syria, demanding that Assad fire his brother Maher, the 'thug in chief'. At the centre of Turkey's approach was a belief in Assad's image as a frustrated reformer surrounded by bad influences. As one MFA official stated, 'We knew that the people around Bashar were evil, like the Makhloufs and the wider Assad family, but we thought that Assad himself was not a bad man.'[47] Assad was urged to stand in fair elections, which Turkey believed he could win. However, a Syrian official present at some of these talks disputes this, suggesting that Turkey actually agreed with Qatar on favouring a power-sharing deal with the Muslim Brotherhood.[48] This is plausible, given the close affinity between the Muslim Brotherhood and the AKP. Another Syrian official claimed that this was something Erdoğan had been urging Assad for years. However, whether Ankara was insisting on the return of the Muslim Brotherhood or free elections, it betrayed a profound misunderstanding of the regime: both represented far too great a concession to have been seriously countenanced.

The 2011 Ramadan assaults proved the breaking point for Ankara. Frustratingly, Assad had implied he was considering Turkey's advice, buying time, only for the violence to continue. As the assault on Hama raged, on 9 August Davutoğlu spent hours in Damascus. The next day tanks were withdrawn and Erdoğan told the press it was a sign that 'our initiative is producing results' – desperately trying to prove that his influence was worth something. Yet within hours the tanks returned and Erdoğan was enraged. He had long seen himself as the senior figure in his relationship with Assad and felt personally betrayed by the dictator's duplicity.[49] Ties were not cut until 21 September, and only in November did Erdoğan formally call for Assad to go, in a speech where he compared him to Hitler, but the die was cast in August 2011. On 23 August the opposition Syrian National Council was formed in Istanbul, dominated by the Muslim Brotherhood and with Ankara's blessing. Turkey had turned on Assad.

Miscalculations

Why was Ankara unable to persuade Assad? Turkey's leaders greatly overestimated their influence over and their understanding of Syria. The alliance was built on three components: economic, soft power and personal relationships. The first two proved of little value when trying to pressure an autocratic regime. The mass popularity of Turkish soap operas and Erdoğan's politics were of little consequence while Syria's economy was far from dependent on or integrated with Turkey's and its crony capitalists had far more to lose by abandoning the regime. The personal ties were genuine but Erdoğan mistakenly believed they were stronger than Assad's other relationships. Assad met as frequently with the Iranians as with the Turks, who offered support without condition and represented a deeper and older alliance. He and his inner circle, moreover, were proud nationalists and unlikely to respond well to angry Turkish demands.

Turkey greatly mistook the nature of Assad's regime. It is perhaps forgivable to be deceived by a leader believed to be an ally, but there were clear gaps in Turkish knowledge and intelligence. In a sign of the mismatch between the AKP's regional ambition and its capacity to achieve them, discussed in Chapter 1, Turkey had little institutional expertise on Syria. The MFA had faced westwards for decades and had only recently begun looking south. Only 6 of the 135 Turkish diplomats working in the Arab world in 2011 spoke Arabic.[50] Many MFA officials on the Syria desk had never visited the country. Critics argue that Turkey's interaction with Syria centred on a specific unrepresentative group, dominated by Aleppo's Sunni merchants and the Muslim Brotherhood in exile, and too little effort was made to understand the country's complexities. Erdoğan and Davutoğlu's critics argue they were arrogant, assuming they knew Syria due to a shared Islamic culture that would somehow compensate for the knowledge gap.[51] Soli Özel, a columnist for the Turkish daily *Haberturk*, argues this led to wishful thinking and a failure to understand that reform for the Syrian regime was a matter of life and death.[52]

Yet the reasons for Turkey's failure to influence Assad do not explain its dramatic volte-face. Exasperation is one thing, but why U-turn so dramatically to demanding Assad's resignation and backing his enemies? Erdoğan, Davutoğlu and other officials understandably emphasised the moral case. However, while their outrage may have been genuine, Turkey's silence on Bahrain, and its concerns over its Libyan contracts, illustrated that its morality could be flexible. There are wider reasons why Assad was turned on. Many of the structural conditions that had originally pushed Turkey to embrace Assad had recently lessened in importance, and the costs of abandoning him with them. Economically, Syria was now only Turkey's seventh largest regional market and Turkish business offered little significant pressure to stand by Assad.[53] Geopolitically, northern Iraq had stabilised and become a booming market for Turkish goods, reducing Assad's diplomatic and economic value. Finally, having acquired hero status on the Arab street, Erdoğan no longer needed Assad to boost Turkey's soft power. Indeed, as the Arab uprisings broke out, his association with Assad was damaging.

In the shorter term, the successful conclusion of parliamentary elections in June 2011, in which the AKP gained 49 per cent of the vote, placed fewer domestic constraints on Erdoğan's actions. However, it was regional calculations that were the main driver. The Arab Spring elsewhere was turning to Turkey's advantage. As transitional governments formed in Egypt and Tunisia, the AKP was touted in both the Arab world and the West as a 'model' to follow, striking the right balance between Islamism and democracy. Erdoğan saw his popularity in the Arab world reach even greater heights, as he was hailed as the 'saviour of Islam' at Cairo airport when he visited in September.[54] Keen to preserve this reputation, Turkey wanted to make sure that it remained on 'the right side of history' regarding Assad as well. Like Western leaders, Turkey shared the miscalculation that Syria's regime would soon crumble – a former minister later claimed Erdoğan said the crisis would be over within six months.[55] This was further infused by an ideological component: Turkey's leaders drew parallels between the Arab Spring and the AKP's own earlier struggles with the Kemalist Deep State and, like the AKP, their victory was considered inevitable.[56] While they had hoped Assad could be part of the solution, now he was in history's path.

Erdoğan also saw the Arab Spring as an opportunity to promote a new regional order in Turkey's favour. Though enjoying strong trade links with both Iran and Saudi Arabia, Davutoğlu and Erdoğan believed Turkey was a more suitable 'third force' regional hegemon with its popular Islamic democracy, strong diverse economy and Ottoman heritage. After his June 2011 re-election, Erdoğan's victory speech revealed these ambitions: 'Beirut has won as much as İzmir. West Bank, Gaza, Ramallah, Jerusalem have won as much as Diyarbakir. The Middle East, the Caucasus and the Balkans have won, just as Turkey has won.'[57] Zero problems had been the first phase of expanding Turkish regional influence, and the Arab Spring – which at that point seemed likely to bring to power like-minded popular moderate Islamist governments – could be the next step. As Davutoğlu stated, Turkey 'will lead the winds of change in the Middle East.'[58] In the same way as Syria under Assad had proven a key gateway to expanding Turkish regional influence in the 2000s, if he could be toppled quickly a new democratic Syria, preferably dominated by the Muslim Brotherhood, could play the same role in the new Turkish-orientated Middle East.

Did Turkey have a choice?

Erdoğan's defenders argue that Turkey had little choice but to U-turn on Syria, given Assad's repeated duplicity.[59] In contrast, while few of his detractors reproach the condemnation of Assad's violence, Erdoğan's rush to support the opposition, cut ties and call for Assad's departure is criticised. Ilhan Uzgel, for example, argues that Ankara narrowed its options too soon.[60] Robins similarly argues that Erdoğan could have proceeded more cautiously, possibly using his relationship with Assad to offer Turkey up as a mediator.[61] Turkey's regional success in the 2000s had partly come from acting as a neutral arbiter, but taking such a decisive side in what increasingly became a regional war cost it this reputation. On the one hand, with the benefit of hindsight it is easy to condemn a strategy based on a swift Assad departure that never came. Erdoğan and Davutoğlu were wrong but, as will be discussed below, they were far from alone. Perhaps Turkey deserves particular criticism for not having better understanding of its neighbour, especially given its boasts to have superior relations with the state, but others were also taken in by Assad's image as a reformer.

More concerning is *why* the decisions were made. Clearly a personal dimension was in play. Erdoğan and Davutoğlu were already prone to impulsiveness, and the sense of personal betrayal added to this, possibly ahead of a long-term strategy. Similarly there was an ideological dimension. The belief that the regime would fall swiftly was partly based on a view of the Arab Spring as the inevitable triumph of the masses struggling against military autocrats. Moreover, the desire to utilise the Arab Spring to further regional ambitions greatly affected the decision not only to abandon Assad, for fear of the negative regional connotations of standing by him, but also to immediately switch to the opposition in the hope of a quick transition that Turkey could dominate. While Erdoğan's critics point to his Islamism as his main ideological crutch, Turkish nationalism was as important.

'Assad must step aside'

Turkey's U-turn to support Assad's opponents was one of two major international developments in the late summer of 2011 that edged Syria closer to civil war. The second was the coordinated announcement by the US, Britain, France, Germany and Canada on 18 August demanding that Assad stand down. At the time this appeared the logical next step in a gradual increase in condemnation. However, Western leaders, not least in the White House, greatly underestimated the impact of this statement in Syria and the region. To

Assad's enemies and his allies, regime change in Syria was now official Western policy and, with the campaign in Libya still under way, many wondered whether an assault on Syria might be next. It hardened Russia and Iran's resolve to stand by Assad, reviving their fears of American imperial projects. Conversely, it raised expectations in Qatar, Turkey and Saudi Arabia that the US was committed to toppling Assad and might eventually offer whatever resources were needed. Syria's oppositionists and emerging rebel fighter groups also had their hopes raised. Ultimately, the announcement acted as a conflict escalator. Yet this was not its purpose and was viewed differently in Western capitals. Moreover, Western leaders, especially the Obama administration, based it on a flawed assessment of the Syrian situation.

It is worth recalling two points about the US approach. Firstly, in 2011 intelligence and expertise on Syria was limited. American penetration of Syria had long been constrained, it being a hostile, pro-Soviet opaque regime. This deteriorated further after a decade of disengagement under George W. Bush, with officials noting that in 2009 the State Department's Syria desk consisted of one person only.[62] Even with Obama's engagement, Syria remained low down the priority list, with the focus on Assad's external dealings, not internal matters. The multiple crises of spring 2011 meant further delay in channelling resources towards compensating for this knowledge gap, despite the efforts of Ambassador Robert Ford and others. American understanding of Syria was thus quite unlike that of Egypt, where calling for the President to stand down had eventually worked. While Washington had over thirty years to build up intelligence and leverage over Egypt's rulers, Syria was out of its sphere of influence and a more unknown quantity.

Secondly, Obama ran a highly centralised foreign policy.[63] Numerous observers and former officials noted that there was a 'cabal' of advisers holding the greatest influence with the most important in 2011 being Biden, Rice, McDonough, Power, Special Assistant Ben Rhodes, CIA Director John Brennan and Deputy Assistant Tony Blinken. While the President sought advice from government bureaucracy, according to Fred Hof, Obama was comfortable taking decisions without it, and others have expressed frustration at a frequent lack of inter-agency process.[64] When he did consult, Obama preferred the Department of Defense to the State Department, but the former had less interest in Syria than in long-term allies Egypt and Saudi Arabia. The State Department offered some input, but the White House and Obama's small group of advisers primarily drove Syria policy. In addition to this it is worth recalling Obama's domestic pressures. He was up for re-election in November 2012 and his team, many of whom had more domestic than international experience, remained conscious of foreign messaging. Vali Nasr, a former Obama staffer cynically suggested that how Middle East policy played out in the nightly news directed strategy.[65]

The 'escalator of pressure'

Early attempts to urge Assad to reform failed. Despite Ankara's insistence that it could sway Damascus, Western leaders shifted from carrot to stick. They found themselves on what one Western official called an 'escalator of pressure' with Assad.[66] A diplomatic punishment was announced and, when it did not change behaviour, a harsher one was adopted a few weeks later, gradually ratcheting up. On 29 April, Obama signed executive order 13572 imposing targeted sanctions on individuals deemed complicit in the killing, including Maher al-Assad and Iran's IRGC Quds force. The EU created its own list of thirteen sanctioned regime individuals on 9 May and instigated an arms embargo forbidding EU companies from selling Syria weaponry. Assad himself was not sanctioned until 23 May, five days after the US had also added him to its list. These lists would steadily grow, with the EU alone initiating over twenty rounds, freezing the foreign assets of 180 regime individuals and 54 Syrian institutions by the end of 2012.[67]

Alongside sanctions Britain and France led activity against the regime at the UN, but efforts to push through critical statements at the Security Council were blocked by Russia and China in May and June. Anti-Assad rhetoric was also escalated. On 19 May Obama reiterated that Assad must, 'lead ... transition, or get out of the way'. Hillary Clinton said on 3 June that Assad was about to lose legitimacy, on 1 July that he was 'running out of time', and finally, after pro-Assad gangs attacked the US embassy in Damascus on 11 July, that he had now 'lost legitimacy'. In the same speech, she stated, 'President Assad is not indispensable and we have absolutely nothing invested in him remaining in power.' This is a curious statement as it implies far more leverage than the US actually had. It suggests that Syria was viewed through the same lens as Egypt: pressure and rhetoric from the US would be sufficient to collapse the regime. Indeed, most Western officials interviewed concur that policy was driven by the belief that the regime would be the latest falling 'domino' in the Arab Spring. However, as discussed, the structure of the regime was quite different to that of Egypt, being far better coup-proofed and insulated from outside influence. This was a regime that had survived long periods of international isolation and sanctions in the past, notably in the 1980s and 2000s, and also had Iranian advice on 'sanction-busting'. As Bouthaina Shaaban commented in May, 'this is a weapon used against us many times'.[68]

This mischaracterisation of the regime as close to collapse was one of the key flaws of the 'escalator of pressure'. The second was that it was an escalator: something that had to keep moving up. The logic of escalation was rarely questioned. Western leaders became prisoners of their own rhetoric and, in conjunction with the rapidity of events elsewhere in the region, calling for Assad's removal appeared the next obvious move.

Our guys in Damascus

In fact, there were leading Western officials cautioning that Assad was not about to fall: the ambassadors in Syria. The demand for on the ground intelligence in Western capitals understandably increased, and embassy staff were vital in parsing the media hype. Syria's Western diplomatic corps, already close given their small number, cooperated tightly, particularly the ambassadors of the US (Robert Ford), France (Eric Chevallier), and Britain (Simon Collis).[69] These three would meet regularly, sometimes with other ambassadors, notably Danish ambassador Christina Markus Lassen, to swap notes, helping to create a united 'Western' approach. Each engaged with the regime while simultaneously expanding contact with protesters. Given travel restrictions this was mostly limited to Damascus, although the British led a visit to Homs in late April, while Ford and Chevallier famously visited oppositionists in Hama in July (Collis was visiting the UK at the time). This trio expressed sympathy for the uprising from early on. Collis' reports to London refer to the uprising as a 'Revolution' as early as May, while in early July after the US embassy was attacked, Ford referred, on its Facebook page to the pro-Assad mob as 'mnhebaks' (we love yous) – a derogatory term used by the opposition.[70] This reflected their governments' polices, irrespective of their personal views. The trip to Hama and, later in September, the attendance by many Western ambassadors at a vigil for Ghiyath Mata, a murdered activist, were encouraged by Western capitals. Indeed Ford found his visit to Hama widely praised in the US, especially by the anti-Assad Republicans who had delayed his confirmation the year before.[71]

Yet any personal sympathy that the ambassadors had with the opposition did not sway their analysis, and all three bucked against the notion that Assad's fall was imminent. Collis, who had been in Damascus the longest, since 2007, wrote to London that several tipping points were required for the regime to fall: major unrest in Damascus, Aleppo and the Kurdish regions; a collapse in the cohesion and effectiveness of the army and security forces; and weakness in the regime's inner core. In their current absence, the regime could hold on.[72] He wrote on 19 July that despite middle-ground

Syrians being appalled at the violence, 'Assad can still probably count on the support of some 30–40 per cent of the population (Alawite and Christian minorities alone account for about half of this).' Moreover, arguing that the regime's weakness was the economy, he claimed it could take eighteen months to two years for any sanctions to prompt regime collapse, not the imminent fall expected in Western capitals. Chevallier also counselled caution, noting to Paris that Assad was not about to fall and that regime change would take time and be more difficult than the hawkish French press was then suggesting.[73] Ford also opposed calling for Assad's departure, arguing that the US would not be able to bring it about.[74]

This counsel was overruled. Chevallier was reportedly involved in a verbal 'brawl' at the Quai d' Orsay with Sarkozy's diplomatic adviser, Nicolas Galey, in early August. Galey, a subscriber to the domino theory that Assad's fall was inevitable, dismissed Chevallier's caution. 'Your information does not interest us,' he reportedly said, 'Bashar al-Assad must fall and he will fall.'[75] British officials note that Paris, buoyed by its success in Libya and also feeling especially betrayed after Sarkozy had helped bring Assad in from the cold, was particularly impatient. However, ultimately Paris and London both followed Obama in the decision to call for his departure. As one diplomat in Damascus at the time noted, 'The White House made the decision to call for Assad to go, and so Britain, France and the rest followed. That's why it happened against our advice.'[76]

Decision from DC: Assad must go

On 18 August, President Obama announced:

> The future of Syria must be determined by its people, but President Bashar al-Assad is standing in their way. His calls for dialogue and reform have rung hollow while he is imprisoning, torturing, and slaughtering his own people. We have consistently said that President Assad must lead a democratic transition or get out of the way. He has not led. For the sake of the Syrian people, the time has come for President Assad to step aside.[77]

At the same time David Cameron, Sarkozy and German Chancellor Angela Merkel released a joint statement saying, 'We call on him [Assad] to face the reality of the complete rejection of his regime by the Syrian people and to step aside in the best interests of Syria and the unity of its people.'[78] Calling for Assad to go was not a decision taken lightly, and Obama, ever cautious, had resisted for months. He was determined that the Syrian people should 'own' their revolution and not be seen to be influenced by the

US, especially after Assad's claims of a foreign conspiracy. However, as with Egypt and Libya, several developments persuaded him.

Firstly, by August Obama's team were increasingly convinced that Assad was finished. In the debates between Arab Spring idealists and realists within the administration, summer 2011 was the high-water mark of the former's influence. While officials were at pains throughout the Syria crisis to insist on the individuality of each Arab case, reflecting Obama's preferred caution and lack of a one-size-fits-all strategy, the idealists saw the Arab Spring as an unstoppable historical force that would eventually sweep aside Assad as it had Mubarak. The considerable differences between the Egyptian and Syrian regimes were glossed over. In fairness, this view was dominant among US allies in Turkey, Britain and France, intelligence reports were briefing that Assad's fall was nigh, as were Syrian exiles in Washington who argued that a strong statement by the US would prompt an anti-Assad coup. The views of Ford and others warning that Assad might last longer were discounted. Importantly, it was believed that rhetoric and sanctions would be sufficient to push the regime over the edge and certainly nothing like the military commitment of the Libya operation. Indeed, after his statement Obama's National Security Committee (NSC) did not advise the President to seek military contingency plans from the Pentagon.[79]

Secondly, the domestic cost of not calling for Assad's departure was perceived as getting too high. The press took an increasingly critical line and Obama's team were sensitive to a series of op-eds in the *Washington Post*. On 22 April US inaction was branded 'shameful', while on 1 August Obama was attacked for speaking publicly on the matter only twice since the crisis began. The same piece asked pointedly, 'Is it any wonder that Mr Assad thinks he can slaughter the people of Hama with impunity?'[80] Echoing this belief that the US has the power to influence and shape wherever it wishes, Congressmen challenged the administration to do more. In July, Republican Representative Steve Chabot asked the House Foreign Affairs Subcommittee in Syria, 'How many must die before we have the courage to stand up and say that Assad is illegitimate and he must go?'[81] With an eye on the upcoming election in 2012, Obama's advisers questioned being left open to such attacks when Assad was going to fall anyway. The need to be on the 'right side of history' again was raised, and some feared embarrassment should Assad fall *before* Obama called for his departure. The legacy of Egypt was again being felt. The White House was not alone in the impression that a longer wait was unpalatable. Then British Deputy Foreign Minister Alistair Burt remarked, 'We reached a point where you either said something about this or in some way you were implying that he [Assad] could be dealt with even though the killing was mounting up.'[82] Though Burt insists media pressure did not influence this decision, British diplomats note how David Cameron demanded more from the Foreign Office after advocacy groups such as Amnesty International and editorials in *The Economist* urged action.[83] While Western leaders were no doubt genuinely outraged by Assad's actions, domestic considerations along with the mistaken belief in Assad's inevitable fall substantially contributed to the joint statement in August 2011.

Obama's statement immediately raised concerns in the State Department: he had declared it was US policy to pursue regime change in Syria, but without a clear strategy to achieve this. Possibilities and scenarios had not been discussed with experts beforehand. Moreover, he made the announcement hours before leaving for a ten-day vacation in Martha's Vineyard, at a time when Western policymakers were holidaying, so how to proceed was not discussed in the inter-agency for weeks. Clinton and Leon Panetta, Gates' replacement as Secretary of Defense from July, had previously warned that should rhetoric prove insufficient to prompt Assad's departure, Obama would need to back up his statement with action. Following on from this, State Department Syria experts such as Fred Hof began preparing written strategies suggesting how regime change might be achieved, yet found the White House uninterested.[84] As the crisis continued, it would increasingly be those voices that had initially warned that Assad would last longer than expected who pushed for greater American involvement to achieve Obama's stated goal while the President and his team demurred. Having got on to the escalator of pressure they assumed that calling for Assad to go would be the end point. When he did not fall, they were alarmed to find the escalator still rising and with it the expectation that the US would use military means to achieve its now stated goal.

Had the Obama administration's assessment proved accurate, and Assad's fall followed soon after, it would have proven a relatively cost-free diplomatic victory. However, given the US' significant historical knowledge gap on Syria, the fact that the best informed voices, such as Ford, urged caution but were discounted, and that urgency in pressing for the statement was driven more by internal factors than by what was happening in Syria, it is not surprising that this analysis proved wanting. Even if the idealists' urging of this course of action might be explained by the heady optimism of the Arab Spring, the administration's unwillingness to explore contingency plans and possible follow-up actions are more inexcusable.

This mistake had a considerable bearing on the shape of Syria's civil war. The White House was very cautious in the wording of Obama's statement, reportedly consulting lawyers to ensure that calling for Assad to 'stand aside' did not constitute a legal intent, but such detail mattered little to outside observers.[85] Russian and Iranian policymakers now saw the US weighing in against their ally and redoubled their determination to stand by him. Qatar, Saudi Arabia and Turkey felt their own hostile stances to Assad vindicated, and proceeded on the expectation that Washington was committed to regime change. Syria's opposition greeted the news with joy. *The Guardian* reported the hopes raised:

> One veteran dissident in Damascus said: 'I am jubilant. This came at the right time for the street.' He said protesters were telling him they wanted to dance in the streets. A middle-aged woman in Homs said: 'More protesters will go out now.'[86]

When considering the impact of Obama's statement it is worth recalling Chapter 1's discussion about the perception of US power in the Middle East. Most Syrians, and indeed Middle Easterners, had long been encouraged to believe the US to be an all-powerful state that can achieve whatever it sets its mind to. The failures in Iraq may have caused some to question this, yet the campaign in Libya revived the image. As the President had come out in open opposition to Assad, it was not unreasonable for the Syrian opposition and their regional supporters to rejoice and expect future help. Paradoxically, the White House may have expected this power projection to be sufficient to cow Assad or scare those around him into a coup. When it failed to do so, the White House was in a dilemma. As shall be seen, Obama had little intention of following up with military action, but to admit that would represent an unacceptable loss of regional prestige. However, in the absence of such communication, Qatar, Turkey and Saudi Arabia would proceed to act in Syria on the assumption that eventually the US would step up.[87] Yet this regional dimension does not seem to have been taken into sufficient consideration.

By the end of summer 2011, the different regional actors had formed into the pro- and anti-Assad camps that would come to define the Syrian civil war. Iran and Russia on one side, Turkey, Saudi Arabia, Qatar and the West on the other. Yet much was based on limited knowledge or capacity to follow through on powerful rhetoric, such as Obama's demand for Assad's departure, without the intent to enforce it. Yet such positioning served to escalate the divisions within Syria, with each side believing their external patrons were behind them. Rather than act to deter conflict, external actors helped to fan the flames of war.

CHAPTER FOUR

International institutions and the slide to war

Syria can still be saved from the worst calamity – if the international community can show the courage and leadership necessary to compromise on their partial interests for the sake of the Syrian people.

Kofi Annan, speaking as he resigned as UN–Arab League joint special envoy to Syria, 2 August 2012

When does a civil war begin? When the first shots are fired or when the protagonists and outside observers assert that such a conflict is under way? Interstate wars have the convenient marker of governments declaring war, but civil wars, especially those like Syria's without secessionist territories that might make such a declaration, tend to emerge over time rather than suddenly break out. It is usually the historians who determine the specific date civil war begins, but the contemporary populations rarely share that assessment. Who knows whether a skirmish will be an isolated incident or the first of years of conflict? 'Civil war' is itself a loaded term. For a long time Syria's oppositionists rejected it, arguing that what was happening was state oppression of peaceful protesters, rather than two sides engaged in violent conflict. Similarly, on 27 June 2012, when President Assad finally acknowledged that 'we live in a state of war', he was careful not to use the word 'civil' as that might convey a sense of equality and therefore legitimacy on his opponents.

At some point, Syria's uprising became a civil war. The regime's security forces, military, Mukhabarat and Shabiha had used lethal force right away, but when did the opposition start shooting back? Protests were initially peaceful and while there were some instances of anti-regime violence from the beginning, not enough to be considered civil war.[1] Similarly, even after anti-regime militia formed and engaged in sizeable battles, peaceful demonstrations continued. Indeed, many of the militia initially aimed not to fight the regime directly, but to defend the protesters from attacks. The evolution from uprising to civil war was not neat, with both protests and reciprocal violence occurring at the same time in different parts of Syria. A widely used definition of civil war is when a combined total of 1,000 people a year from each side has been killed in combat (i.e. not civilians). According to the opposition-run Violations Documentation Centre (VDC) the regime had lost over 500 combatants by the end of August 2011, while the opposition, who did not begin to form units that could be defined as 'non-civilians' until summer 2011, lost the same by the end of January 2012.[2] Between this time period the first battles took place between regime forces and organised militia, many loosely under the banner of the 'Free Syria Army' (FSA). It was also when Navi Pillay, UN High Commissioner for Human Rights, first characterised the crisis as 'civil war' on 1 December 2011. This book will therefore regard the war as beginning some time between August 2011 and January 2012.

However, though future historians will no doubt debate these dates further, contemporary observers were fully aware of the civil war threat looming. The question this chapter seeks to answer is why the international institutions charged with upholding international order proved unable to prevent it. Two serious attempts at early mediation took place, firstly the Arab League plan of winter 2011–12, and then the diplomacy of Kofi Annan, the joint Arab League–UN envoy, in the first half of 2012. This chapter considers whether such attempts were doomed from the beginning and, if so, why?

Civil war

The autumn and winter of 2011–12 in Syria saw momentum towards civil war rapidly grow, coinciding with an internationalisation of the crisis. Obama's call for Assad to step aside in August and the recent military successes in Libya prompted a reciprocal shift from the oppositionists to court foreign support. Since the uprising's beginning, each Friday – usually the largest day of protest – was given a special name, voted for online beforehand.[3] Initially these had a domestic focus, often aimed at appealing to sections of Syrian society yet to join the rebellion, such as 'The Friday of the Tribes' or 'The Friday of Saleh al-Ali' (an Alawi Syrian nationalist hero from the 1920s). Yet from the autumn titles increasingly appealed to external actors, including requests for military intervention. 'The Friday of International Protection' on 9 September was followed by 'No Fly Zone' on 28 October, and 'The Buffer Zone is our demand' on 2 December. International organisations engaging with the crisis were likewise lobbied. The Arab League's peace plan was dismissed on 16 December with the title,

'The Arab League is killing us' while, later on, the UN–Arab League's Annan plan was attacked on 13 July 2012 with 'The Friday of Toppling Annan, the Servant of Assad and Iran'.[4]

Pro-Assad crowds reflected this internationalisation too. US Ambassador Robert Ford was mobbed while visiting an opposition figure on 29 September and forced to leave Syria for several months. Later, in reaction to new sanctions and the Arab League's decision to freeze Syria's membership, crowds attacked the Saudi Arabian embassy in Damascus and the French and Turkish consulates in Latakia on 12 November. The next day, Western media outlets reported 'hundreds of thousands' marching in support of Assad across Syria, particularly in Damascus, Aleppo, Tartous and Latakia.[5] Large crowds gathered for pro-regime demonstrations on 7 October and again on 24 December, the latter following a twin bomb attack on security buildings in Damascus that had killed forty-four. Central Damascus and Aleppo remained relatively free of protests and an opposition nationwide strike in early December failed in the two largest cities – though the Mukhabarat reportedly threatened anyone considering joining, to make sure. Assad persisted with his 'reforms', announcing new parliamentary elections in November. Then on 26 February 2012 a new constitution was put to a referendum that removed the Ba'ath Party's monopoly on power and limited the president's term in office to two seven–year terms. Though largely a cosmetic change and doing little to open up the political system, it was approved by 89.4 per cent on a 57.4 per cent turnout. With international observers absent, it cannot be known whether the 7.49 million voters the regime claimed actually supported the changes, but the rallies and strike failure do suggest that Assad retained some support. The multiple buy-ins mentioned in Chapter 2, including fear, still held for a sizeable segment of Syrian society despite the pressures of the crisis. Such social division made civil war ever more likely as violence increased.

And violence was increasing. The regime persisted with what David Lesch termed a 'whack-a-mole' approach: deploying security and military forces to the centres of protest in force, hitting the protesters hard, then moving on.[6] However, by autumn 2011 the opposition was fighting back. The FSA was founded in late July in Turkey by a small group of former regime army officers that had defected, but gained momentum in late September when it joined with another collection of defectors, the Free Officer Movement. As will be discussed in Chapter 6, the FSA acted more as a loose umbrella than a tight top-down organisation.[7] Even so, a steady stream of Assad's troops began to defect and many formed or joined militias (*katiba*) under the FSA banner. Early battles were often ad hoc, with the first major regime–FSA clash in Rastan (27 September–1 October) coming after defectors spontaneously attacked the military with RPGs and booby traps before being forced to retreat.[8] Similar episodes occurred in opposition strongholds the following months, with rebel fighters adopting guerrilla tactics, targeting regime checkpoints with ambushes before hastily retreating.

Homs, Syria's third city and labelled the 'capital of the Revolution' saw much of the early fighting. Its demographics made it particularly susceptible to the emerging divisions: a sizeable, recently emigrated Alawi population who had benefited from government largesse; and a Sunni majority, some resentful of Alawi privilege, swelled by recent rural–urban migration, sympathetic to the opposition. Patterns of protest reflected these demographics: the poorer, Sunni neighbourhoods of the north and south-west, such as Baba Amr and al-Khaldiyeh saw daily unrest, while wealthier and/or Alawi-dominated areas remained quiet.[9] The city eventually saw some of the civil war's worst sectarian bloodletting, with reciprocal acts of violence and kidnappings between Alawi and Sunni neighbourhoods becoming a frequent occurrence. The city's mostly Alawi Shabiha was accused of systematically raping Sunni women.[10] The regime frequently assaulted Homs' rebellious neighbourhoods throughout the autumn, with FSA *katibas* forming to defend the protesters. YouTube videos of protesting men dancing in rows shouting anti-Assad slogans suggested that Homs might yet become Syria's Benghazi.[11] Determined to prevent this, the regime launched a massive assault on Baba Amr in February 2012, with the FSA defenders eventually retreating on 1 March. This could be seen as the end of the beginning of the civil war. The fighting cost 700–1,000 lives, a dramatically increased rate compared with the 7,000 killed in total since March 2011.[12]

The international response: Economic sanctions

Having called for Assad's departure, in autumn 2011 the anti-Assad states considered what tools they were willing to deploy to achieve their goal. Military intervention was debated, as was political, financial and military support for the armed opposition – discussed further in Chapters 5, 6 and 8. Initially, however, most looked to multilateral institutions. The EU and Arab League, along with the US, Turkey, Canada and Australia introduced or expanded economic sanctions. The EU and US worked closely to ratchet up 'smart sanctions' that targeted individuals and institutions. On 2 September 2011 the EU echoed the US' decision the previous month to ban the import of Syrian oil. Turkey imposed an arms embargo on 23 September, and on 30 November suspended all relations with Syria's Central Bank and froze Syrian government assets.[13] Days earlier the Arab League, led by Qatar, announced economic sanctions that froze business with the Central Bank and government, imposed travel bans on regime officials, suspended infrastructure spending, and banned private and commercial flights to Syria.[14]

The impact upon the Syrian economy was substantial, but ultimately failed to either change the regime's behaviour or induce its fall. The EU oil sanctions were felt hardest. Before the crisis, Syria produced 385,000 barrels per day (b/d) of oil in 2010, exporting about 150,000 b/d, almost entirely to EU states, mostly Italy and Germany. Revenue from these sales made up roughly 20 per cent of total budget revenue in 2005–10, so its loss was costly when the regime struggled to find alternative buyers, though this became moot within a few years as the regime lost control of most oilfields.[15] A report by the Syrian Center for Policy Research estimates that 28.3 per cent ($6.8 billion) of Syria's total GDP loss in 2011–12 was due to sanctions and over half of this ($3.9 billion) was from the oil sector. It also estimates that Arab League sanctions caused Syria's exports to Arab states to more than halve.[16] Though this was partly tempered by Iraq and Lebanon, allies of Iran that refused to join the trade embargo, the end of Arab trade contributed to the slow collapse of the pre-war Syrian economy.[17]

The failure is not surprising. Most academic analysis concurs that economic sanctions rarely achieve their official objective.[18] Having imposed the disastrous sanctions regime on Saddam Hussein from 1991 to 2003 that impoverished Iraq but failed to topple the dictator, Western and regional officials were surely aware of the limited chances of success in Syria. So why pursue them? Sanctions served three purposes. First was the optimistic hope they would persuade Syria's business elite to oust Assad. Still believing that Assad's fall was inevitable, the White House, particularly Tom Donilon, took the lead, and European officials note that the administration pressed the EU to adopt oil sanctions.[19] It was believed that the 'smart' sanctions could push the regime over the edge while avoiding the poverty seen in Iraq. However, this strategy was based both on the exaggerated fragility of the regime and on the view that Syria's economy would behave in a certain way. As Simon Collis explained in October 2011, 'This is not an economy susceptible to normal analysis.'[20] While the business elite did have some influence over the regime, for example forcing a U-turn on new import duties introduced in reaction to the sanctions, too many of their fates were tied to the regime's to abandon it. Similarly, as it was a relatively isolated economy, the loss of international markets was not as fatal to businesses as it would be elsewhere. It was also later revealed that several Syrian businesses linked to the regime found ways around the sanctions by using shell companies in the Seychelles.[21]

The sanctions did impact society however, especially the increased cost of fuel. It was estimated that of the 3.1 million Syrians who fell into poverty in 2011–12, 877,000 did so as a result of sanctions.[22]

A second more realistic purpose was to increase the cost of violence for the regime. As Robert Ford told the Senate Committee on Foreign Relations in March 2012, sanctions aimed at making 'it harder for the government to pay for its repression, to pay for its military and security forces.'[23] However, as will be discussed in Chapter 7, the willingness of Russia and Iran to make up for any regime shortfalls was underestimated. Thirdly, sanctions had a symbolic importance. Even once it became clear that Assad might not be as vulnerable as first assumed, the 'escalator of pressure' and the domestic need to be seen to be doing something made sanctions an obvious route for Western policymakers. For regional powers, such as Saudi Arabia, Qatar and Turkey, sanctions had a different symbolic value: acting as a stepping-stone to legitimise more hawkish moves. It was barely three months between the first application of Arab League sanctions and the first public calls, by the Emir of Qatar, to arm the Syrian rebels. This was far too short a time for sanctions to have any effect. Yet as with the Arab League Peace Plan, discussed below, sanctions were approached more as a necessary step to take to justify escalating involvement. No doubt they hoped sanctions would work, but Doha, Ankara and Riyadh were too impatient to see the emerging civil war's conclusion and Assad's fall to wait to see if this tool alone could be effective.

The Arab League plan

Despite being over sixty-five years old, the Arab League has always struggled to exercise serious authority over its twenty-two member states. The proliferation of dictatorial governments, a lack of economic integration and an unwillingness to pool sovereignty has not helped. Occasional, sometimes dramatic, symbolic gestures have been made, notably expelling Egypt for making peace with Israel in 1979, but eventually it was the League, not Cairo that backed down. Unsurprisingly, then, the League's approach to the Syria crisis ultimately proved ineffective. However, its involvement saw the League at its most assertive in years, and the peace plan it proposed in late 2011 was the first concerted effort to mediate the conflict.

With several of its members enveloped in chaos and others fearing contagion, the Arab League was initially mute on Syria, only condemning the crackdown for the first time on 14 June. As violence increased, so did the League's involvement. On 27 August, it counselled restraint. Secretary General Nabil El-Araby travelled to Damascus to urge reform in early

September, later announcing that 'a deal has been agreed', only to discover, like Davutoğlu before him, that Assad's deals were rarely worth the paper. El-Araby led another delegation in late October, and on 2 November the government accepted the plan, which included commitments to end the violence, withdraw tanks from the streets, release political prisoners and enter into dialogue with the opposition. Within days, however, the League claimed that Damascus had breached terms, prompting a threat to suspend Syria, something urged by protesters on 11 November with 'the Friday of Freezing Syria's Arab League Membership'. On 16 November the League acted on its threat, followed soon by economic sanctions.

The League's persistence was led by the Gulf States, particularly Qatar, which held the rotating presidency. After failing to persuade Assad privately, and boosted by success in Libya, Doha sought to utilise the League once again in Syria. In fact the presidency was due to pass to Iraq in February 2011, but Doha used the Libya crisis to successfully lobby for a one-year extension. It utilised the League as a cover for its increased regional activism, with members complaining that Qatar stifled debate and forced through policies during closed-door sessions.[24] It helped Qatar that the Arab Spring had weakened some of the Arab League's stronger voices, notably Egypt, Libya and Syria. When another, Algeria, raised doubts about the move to suspend Syria, the Qatari Prime Minister Hamad Bin Jassim (HBJ) reportedly threatened its Foreign Minister Mourad Medelci that, 'your turn will come'.[25] Eventually Algeria was cajoled, and only Yemen and Lebanon opposed the move – the former facing unrest of its own, and the latter partly governed by Hezbollah. Iraq, Iran's other regional ally, abstained.

Damascus eventually agreed to a revised Arab League Peace Plan on 12 December, under pressure from Russia.[26] This plan, hashed out in Doha, included deploying a team of Arab League monitors to ensure regime compliance. On 22 December the first monitors arrived in Damascus, followed two days later by the mission's head, Sudanese General Mohammed Ahmed Mustafa al-Dabi. By the end of December over one hundred monitors were in Syria.

However, the mission was beset by difficulties from the start. Reflecting the League's historic weakness, the monitors lacked experience, were poorly equipped and too few. By contrast, a comparable European mission to Kosovo in 1998 had fourteen times as many monitors (1,400) for a territory seventeen times smaller than Syria.[27] Jonathan Litell, a French journalist embedded with rebels in Homs, recalled the monitors' weakness. FSA fighters told him that the five to eight unarmed monitors took two days to cross the front line into rebel-held territory. Once there, rather than monitor as they were mandated to do, they urged the militias to negotiate with the army.[28] Few had confidence in the mission. Within days of his arrival protesters demanded Dabi's removal, claiming his record as Sudan's head of military intelligence during the alleged genocide in Darfur naturally placed him on the side of authoritarianism. Dabi's comments to a BBC news interviewer on 31 December that no observers saw snipers in Deraa, despite an amateur video showing an observer telling activists just that, seemed to justify allegations of his pro-regime bias.[29] The opposition SNC leader Burhan Ghalioun argued that the regime was just using the mission to buy time. Criticism also emerged from within the Arab League. Barely a week after Dabi's arrival, the Arab Parliament, a powerless consultative Arab League forum, called for the mission's withdrawal. A few days later, the mission's architect, Qatar's HBJ also publicly criticised it. Even within the team doubts were raised, with one Algerian monitor resigning on 11 January saying the mission was 'a farce'.[30]

This criticism was primarily a reaction to the glaring breaches by the regime. It deliberately escalated the crackdown before the monitors arrived, with over 200 reported killed in two days on 19–20 December. After the mission's arrival, regime agents had learned from their experiences with the International Atomic Energy Agency (IAEA) how to restrict and misdirect international monitors and were more than a match for the inexperienced Arab League team.[31] Some concessions were made, such as the release of over 3,000 prisoners, the delivery of humanitarian aid to embattled regions, and the temporary withdrawal of tanks from hotspot areas like Homs. However, as soon as the small team moved on, assaults restarted. It was clear that neither the regime nor the embryonic rebel militias took the plan seriously.

Unsurprisingly, the mission swiftly broke down. Both Dabi and El-Araby publicly defended the monitors' work, and the League agreed to extend its mandate first on 8 January, and then again on 19 January. However, a death blow was delivered three days later when Saudi Arabia announced that the mission had failed and withdrew its funding and observers. That same day a new Arab League plan was revealed by HBJ that required Assad to stand down in favour of his Vice President, Farouk al-Sharaa, who would form a national unity government after dialogue with the opposition, similar to that being attempted at the time in Yemen. HBJ later called for an Arab peacekeeping force, ironically modelled on the Syria-led Arab Deterrent Force dispatched to Lebanon in 1976. Not surprisingly, the Syrian government immediately rejected this new plan and, in response, on 24 January the remaining Gulf states withdrew their support for the monitor mission. Four days later, the Arab League announced the withdrawal of the mission.

While officially this was due to the increased violence levels, it would have been hard to continue without Gulf support.

So why did this first attempt at mediation fail, and why so quickly? Emile Hokayem argues that the plan was undone by 'the ineffectiveness of its monitoring mission, the duplicity of Assad over dialogue and the Syrian opposition's divisions and contradictions'.[32] This is certainly true, particularly the lack of commitment by both the regime and the opposition. Indeed, the violence meted out by the regime during December and January suggests Assad's only interest was to take advantage of the plan to better his military position. Yet the opposition also clearly had no faith, with Ghalioun calling for an externally imposed 'safety zone', rather than considering mediation a realistic option.

Two further factors help explain the lack of success. Firstly, the failure of the Arab League to manage expectations. Within Syria protesters seemed to expect this underequipped, inexperienced mission of one hundred to end the conflict. On 27 December, on hearing that the monitors were nearby, protesters in Homs rushed into the central square to demonstrate, then were surprised when the regime repressed them. The next day groups gathered in Hama chanting, 'Where are the Arab League monitors?' Similarly the League's own members clearly saw the mission as a 'magic bullet' to end the conflict, causing them to quickly turn on the mission when it did not have this desired, but unrealistic, outcome. Of course, it is not unsurprising that this weak institution proved as incapable of managing messages as it did of putting together a mission with any chance of success. That it even attempted to do so was more a reflection of the enthusiastic zeal of its Qatari president than any newfound institutional competence.

The second factor was the Gulf States' own lack of commitment to the mission. The GCC, led by Saudi Arabia, withdrew support for the mission less than a month after it began. Were they naïve, believing the mission would succeed against the odds or were they cynical? Qatar and Saudi Arabia had determined by this point that Assad had to go, so their support for mediation was primarily to gain consensus from sceptical League members like Algeria. The speed with which they revealed a new plan that included Assad's departure on 22 January 2012, the same day that Riyadh declared the mission a failure, suggests they were waiting for the Peace Plan to fail rather than subsequently reacting. Hassan Hassan argues that Riyadh had no interest in the mission, but saw it as a necessary stepping-stone to the Libya-style military intervention in Syria.[33] Qatar too, by this point already covertly sending limited weaponry to the rebels, seemed decided on a military solution to the conflict. The fact that the Qatari-led Arab League referred the matter to the UNSC on 24 January, as soon as the Gulf states had withdrawn support, but before the mission was declared over, shows the impatience to push the matter up the UN's agenda in the hope of a mandated intervention. As with the use of sanctions, Qatar and Saudi Arabia saw the importance of being seen to deploy both stick and carrot with Assad, but impatiently believed the stick was the only real option.

Russia and the United Nations: Stalemate

The Arab League's referral to the UNSC quickly failed when, on 4 February, Russia (along with China) vetoed a resolution in which the UN would demand Syrian compliance with the Arab League plans. In an attempt to gain Moscow's endorsement, all explicit mentions of Assad's departure were removed and there was no mention of military intervention. However, its support for the 22 January Arab League plan that called for a 'Syrian-led political transition', including Assad's removal in favour of al-Sharaa, was too much for Moscow. Russia and China had already vetoed a previous UNSC resolution on 4 October 2011 that condemned the regime's violence. Another resolution threatening Article 41 (non-violent) sanctions suffered a similar fate on 19 July 2012, as did a later proposal on 22 May 2014 to refer the regime to the International Criminal Court (ICC). Moscow also frequently defended the regime, often supported by China, in other UN institutions, such as its Human Rights Council.

However, Russia's diplomacy was not completely obstinate. Having backed the first Arab League Peace Plan, it then endorsed the follow-up Annan plan in March 2012, and the June 2012 UN Action Group for Syria's 'Geneva Communiqué' that called for a negotiated solution. Later on it would co-sponsor an agreement to disarm Assad's chemical weapons with the US in September 2013 and a resolution supporting the Vienna Peace Process in December 2015. Along with China it endorsed the regime's alleged reform efforts, and urged dialogue. Indeed, both governments proposed draft UN resolutions in 2011 calling for all sides to engage, but baulked at Western insistence on placing all the blame on Assad. Far from shying away from the Syria crisis, Russia sought to play a leading role. However, at the heart of its strategy was opposition to anything that might seriously weaken Assad or lead to direct military intervention. The reasons are complex and warrant further consideration.

The limits of the UN: 'Responsibility to Protect' (R2P)

Before looking at Russia, it is first worth noting that the UN is greatly limited when it comes to violent crises such as Syria's. This might seem a strange statement given that in the same month as Syria's uprising broke out, the UNSC authorised military intervention in Libya. However, this was the first time direct military action had been authorised under Chapter Seven of the UN Charter against the wishes of a sovereign state.[34] Though many commentators and politicians used the Libya example to call for a similar resolution on Syria, the UN is structured in such a way as to make any such intervention difficult. Unfortunately many failed to recognise that the Libyan case was exceptional.

Advocates of R2P base the concept on a reformed interpretation of sovereignty to include responsibility, arguing that states can sacrifice sovereignty if they fail to protect the welfare of their citizens or prevent human suffering from spreading over their borders. The UN codified R2P in several stages, but the most important was the Outcome Document of the 2005 World Summit in New York, endorsed by the UNSC, including Russia, and the General Assembly. It called for collective action when 'national authorities manifestly fail to protect their populations from genocide, war crimes, ethnic cleansing and crimes against humanity'.[35] However, this codification actually made direct military intervention more difficult. It limited the accepted causes of intervention to four highly contentious concepts: 'genocide, war crimes, ethnic cleansing and crimes against humanity'. It also determined that R2P actions would be decided at the UNSC, effectively permitting the five permanent UNSC members (P5) to veto any action against their allies or themselves.[36]

UN1973, the resolution authorising intervention in Libya, echoed much of the Outcome Document's language. It reiterated 'the responsibility of the Libyan authorities to protect the Libyan population', and stated that Gaddafi's 'widespread and systematic attacks . . . may amount to crimes against humanity' – one of the four crimes to which R2P was resolved to respond. However, even then there was no actual mention of R2P in the resolution. Obama's National Security Adviser and R2P advocate Susan Rice claimed UN1973 was 'inspired by R2P', but both the US and Britain justified their actions in terms of national interests rather than responsibility.[37]

The Libya episode thus illustrated the weakness of the UN's legal commitment to R2P. Even when R2P's numerous restrictions were overcome, in the exceptional circumstances of the Libya crisis, R2P was still not officially invoked. The reluctance by the US and others to explicitly refer to R2P implies recognition of its controversy, especially by Russia and China. The Libya case was a rare occasion when the national interests of the P5 aligned with R2P, and even then, as shall be discussed, Russia felt it was signing up for (or abstaining from) something more modest. The Syria case, however, like examples in Darfur or Sri Lanka before it, was far from any such P5 consensus. The codification of R2P actually gave Russia a legal basis for supporting Assad. This meant that as long as Russia stood by Assad at the UN, the only means for external actors to intervene in the conflict would be covertly or if they were willing to break international law.

Why did Russia support Assad?

Given repeated Russian obstruction, why did Assad's international oppo-nents keep returning to the UN? It should be recalled that in 2011–12 Western leaders retained hopes that Obama's 'Reset Agenda' with Russia could still deliver, boosted by Moscow's tacit support for UN1973. Indeed, disagreement over Syria was a major factor in derailing Western–Russian ties. Before then Western diplomats hoped that Moscow could be persuaded. Before the February 2012 veto Hillary Clinton noted in her memoirs her efforts to personally lobby Russian Foreign Minister Sergei Lavrov. Clinton insisted that, 'if we did not begin a peace process, the endgame would be grim indeed'.[38] The problem for Russia was that Western ideas of a 'peace process' involved Assad's removal. Insiders in Moscow admit privately that the Kremlin never intended to concede to Western demands that might open the way for Assad's departure, but made a show of cooperation and deliberation.[39] This duped the West enough to persist with lobbying, playing into Moscow's desire to remain centre stage. As then British deputy Foreign Minister Alistair Burt later conceded, 'As long as we had the Russians saying, "yeah, we'll think about it", we kept hoping they would shift their view.'[40]

Western belief that Russia could be persuaded contained two miscalcu-lations. Firstly, that Moscow's primary interest in Syria was material and strategic: Russia's only Mediterranean naval installation was in Tartous, while Damascus was a valued customer for arms. Clinton believed that 'Assad's regime was too strategically important to them.'[41] Based on this assumption the Obama administration reassured Russian diplomats these interests would be safeguarded in a post-Assad Syria.[42] However, as discussed in Chapter 1, the base in 2011 was small and primarily symbolic, while arms exports accounted for only 5 per cent of Russian arms deliveries abroad, less than those sold to Assad's enemies in Israel and Turkey – who also had a better record of payment.[43] Even so, the Russians might still have questioned how exactly the US proposed to make such guarantees in an uncertain post-Assad Syria.

The second miscalculation concerned the changing power dynamics of Russia's leadership. Much of the Reset Agenda had focused on President

Dmitri Medvedev, seemingly more liberal-minded and amenable to the West than his Prime Minister and predecessor, Vladimir Putin. It was Medvedev who supported UN1973, echoing Western condemnation of Gaddafi by calling him a 'political corpse'.[44] Putin was presumed to be the power behind Medvedev's throne and expected to return to the presidency after his protégé's term ended. But the young President had struck out on his own in some areas, attempting to diversify Russia's resource-based economy and entertaining Obama's overtures, and some speculated that he might seek a second term in 2012. He even criticised Assad, telling Russian television in October 2011, 'If the Syrian leadership is incapable of conducting such reforms, it will have to go.'[45] Yet his stance on Libya shocked Putin, prompting an unprecedented internal debate. The Prime Minister argued that UN1973 was 'deficient and flawed', that it allowed 'anyone to do anything they want – to take any actions against a sovereign state,' and that Medvedev should have vetoed it.[46] Putin's hard line eventually gained the ascendancy, ending any hopes of a second Medvedev term, with Putin announcing in September 2011 he would stand again. Externally, with NATO interpreting UN1973 as a mandate to pursue regime change rather than the humanitarian mission presumed by Russia, Putin believed Moscow had been betrayed and felt vindicated. He concluded that 'we must not allow the "Libyan scenario" to be attempted to be reproduced in Syria.'[47] Rather than the Libya crisis representing a new era of Russian–Western cooperation that could be transferred to Syria as Westerners hoped, it actually helped swing power back toward Putin and reinforced his instinctive suspicions of 'humanitarian' intervention.

Analysts of Russian Syria policy concur that all major decisions come from Putin.[48] While Boris Yeltsin consulted experts, Putin's critics in Moscow complain that there were no Middle East specialists in his Kremlin. The Ministry of Foreign Affairs (MFA) is largely reduced to implementer, with only Lavrov regularly heard.[49] As such, to understand why Russia stood by Assad it is important to understand Putin's approach. There is an ideational component. Though his views evolved in power, Putin had an instinctively nationalist and anti-Western worldview. He was also an orientalist, sharing the view of many Russian analysts that the Middle East was not ready for democracy. As he stated in 2013, 'Some people from outside believe that if the region were to be bought into compliance with a certain idea – an idea that some call democracy – then peace and stability would ensue. That's not how it works. You can't ignore the region's history, traditions and religious beliefs, and you can't just interfere.'[50] He saw the Arab Spring as primarily Islamic rather than democratic and believed that multi-ethnic societies as Syria were fragile and could easily fall apart without a strong regime.[51]

In Chapter 1, it was noted that Russia viewed the Middle East through three lenses: geostrategic, domestic and regional economic. Geostrategically, as global attention fell on Syria, Putin viewed condemnation of Assad as another attempt at regime change. Despite Qatar, Saudi Arabia and Turkey's leading roles against Assad, Russia saw the US as chief instigator. After the Libya 'humiliation', and Iraq before it, Putin was determined to prevent any more Western-led regime changes. As Lavrov stated bluntly in November 2011, 'I don't think we will allow anything of that sort to be repeated'.[52] This acknowledgement that it is within Russia's power as a veto-holding member of the UNSC to 'allow' direct military intervention, or not, reiterates how legal action is contingent on the will of the P5. Moscow frequently promoted itself as a defender of state sovereignty, although its invasion of Georgia in 2008 and interference in Ukraine after 2014 illustrated a highly selective interpretation of this. Even so, there remained a fear that, should regime change elsewhere establish itself as legitimate, Moscow might eventually become a target. This gave extra significance to Obama's call for Assad to stand aside. From Russia's perspective, this made Syrian regime change official US policy, ruling out any chance of cooperation at the UN that might further this goal.[53]

In Putin's view of the world, denying the US in Syria was an important motivation for backing Assad. As one insider remarked privately, 'the key word for Moscow is not "Assad" but "intervention".'[54] Some suspected Putin would have no problem with an internal coup against Assad, as long as it was not interpreted as a Western victory. At the same time, there was pragmatism in Putin's strategy. Early on, Moscow made two accurate assessments about the crisis: that Assad was far more secure than many predicted and that there was not much appetite from the West to go into Syria.[55] Importantly, unlike in Iraq or even Libya, Russia had the tools to derail the Western agenda without too great a cost.

Domestic factors were also important. Moscow was rocked by popular unrest in December 2011 against Putin's planned return to power and contesting the victory of his United Russia party in recent parliamentary elections. Though it had little direct impact, such unrest was rare and helped turn the Kremlin even more against the Arab Spring for fear it would inspire more domestic protest. Conversely, among Putin's core constituency, his strong line on Syria was popular. The nationalist public and pro-United Russia media reacted badly to Medvedev's abstention on Libya, while in general Putin, who was sensitive to opinion polls, saw his popularity spike when confronting the West. Related to this was a religious dimension.[56] Under Putin the Russian Orthodox Church was increasingly influential and, according to Carnegie's Dmitri Trenin, became a centrepiece of national identity and foreign policy.[57] Religious leaders pressed Moscow to ensure the safety of Syria's Christians, 8 per cent of the population, who were mostly Orthodox, largely backed Assad and faced increasing persecution by the more radical Islamist elements of the opposition.

A final and important domestic concern was jihadism. Fourteen per cent of Russia's population is Muslim and the Kremlin feared Syrian radicals might inspire domestic Islamist violence, not only in north Caucasian trouble spots but also among the Russian and Central Asian Muslim migrants of Moscow.[58] Russia had suffered numerous Islamist terrorist attacks during the 2000s, notably the 2002 Moscow Theatre crisis that left 130 civilians dead and, more recently, a suicide bombing in Moscow's Domodedovo international airport that killed 37 in January 2011. Russia perceived the FSA as largely Islamist and susceptible to infiltration by al-Qaeda and also noted with alarm the number of Russian-speaking Islamists heading to Syria to join the rebels. Having fought what was characterised as an Islamist insurgency in Chechnya at the beginning of his presidency Putin was determined to maintain his reputation as someone who could keep jihadism at bay.

Finally, wider regional and related economic factors played a role, though mostly nuancing details rather than setting the agenda. Putin was willing to risk the ire of Assad's regional enemies for his pro-regime stance. Gulf states cancelled economic deals in 2012, while in July of that year the Russian ambassador to Qatar was beaten up at Doha airport. Public support for Russia fell to below 20 per cent in Jordan and Egypt, while Yusuf Qaradawi called on Muslims to boycott Russian products on al-Jazeera.[59] Yet at the same time, Putin was careful to maintain economic ties in spite of emerging political differences. Trade with Turkey continued to thrive. Putin travelled to Istanbul to sign trade deals with Erdoğan in December 2012, barely two months after expressing public outrage at Turkey's forcing down a Syrian airliner on suspicion of carrying Russian weapons.[60] Likewise, despite Qatar's hostility, Doha maintained important trading ties with Russia's state-owned giant, Gazprom, including a substantial LPG deal in December 2012.[61] Nor was Putin completely insensitive to some regional concerns. Israeli objections prompted Moscow to cancel supplying Syria with S-300 missiles in 2013–14, for example.[62]

Russia's influence

Russia's consistent backing for Assad, especially its UN vetoes, were predictably condemned by Western diplomats, with Clinton calling the February veto 'despicable'. Yet Russia, clinging to its view that the opposition was as much to blame as the regime, saw its support as no more incongruous than repeated Washington's UN vetoes in defence of Israel, most recently in February 2011.

Did this support translate into influence over Damascus? Dmitri Trenin points out the paradox of the Kremlin's relationship with the Assad regime. On the one hand Moscow's polite pleas to actually implement some of Damascus' touted reforms largely fell on deaf ears, and Putin repeatedly stated that he had little leverage over Assad. At the same time, Moscow claimed credit for the few concessions that the regime did make, such as acquiescing to the first Arab League plan, the Annan plan, the Geneva Communiqué and the 2013 chemical weapons deal.[63] In a 2013 report, Trenin argued that Moscow did have leverage over Assad that it was not using. It had good intelligence on the regime after appointing the MFA's knowledgeable Arabist Mikhail L. Bogdanov as special envoy to Syria, who made frequent trips to Damascus. Assad also relied on financial support and the steady supply of Russian arms – 'defensive' weapons that Moscow insisted it was delivering to a legitimate sovereign government, having successfully made it so by preventing any UN-sanctioned arms boycotts.[64] Even though the regime was opaque and closed, including to its Russian ally, Putin could have squeezed these pressure points to wring out more concessions. Vitaly Naumkin offers a different perspective. He suggests that once the civil war expanded in 2012, Moscow feared that withdrawing its support would lead to rapid regime collapse. Assad played on this fear, knowing Moscow saw this as a worst case scenario that would deliver the dreaded Western-led regime change, effectively removing any Russian manoeuvrability.[65]

The truth is likely somewhere in between. In the early years of the civil war Moscow clearly had some leverage over Assad, able to nudge his regime towards at least playing along with processes such as the Arab League plan that did not pose a direct threat to its power, yet not enough to make it take them seriously. While Trenin is correct that Putin could have attached more conditions to support had he been inclined, Naumkin is also correct that once the war expanded withdrawing of support was risky. In addition, the changing international circumstances, notably the clash with the West over Ukraine from late 2013 and subsequent sanctions on Russia, made Putin even less motivated to push Assad. Moreover, as shall be discussed in Chapter 7, at that point Iran had emerged as Assad's principal external backer and it is questionable whether a withdrawal only of Russian support would have had the desired effect. This might expose Putin's diminished influence over Assad, risking his hard-fought-for perceived international relevance for very little gain. Indeed, as we shall see in Chapter 10, eventually Putin opted to expand support by deploying the Russian air force in September 2015, partly as a means to increase his influence and leverage over Assad.

Kofi Annan's diplomacy

The Annan plan and the Geneva Communiqué

After the failure of the Arab League Peace Initiative and the deadlock at the UN, two final efforts were made to pull Syria back from the brink under the stewardship of former UN Secretary Kofi Annan, who was appointed joint Arab League–UN envoy to Syria on 23 February 2012. The first of these was a six-point plan, backed by both Russia and China in a unanimous UNSC Presidential Statement on 21 March, pressuring the Assad regime to acquiesce six days later. The plan called for a 'sustained cessation of armed violence in all its forms by all parties with an effective United Nations supervision mechanism'; provision of humanitarian assistance to all areas; freedom of movement for journalists; the right to demonstrate peacefully; accelerated release of prisoners; and a commitment to 'an inclusive Syrian-led political process to address the legitimate aspirations and concerns of the Syrian people'.[66] Importantly it steered well away from Russia's red lines of demanding Assad's departure or threatening military intervention. It was put together rapidly, in only three weeks, and was designed primarily to reduce tensions and de-escalate the crisis in lieu of a long-term solution.[67]

A ceasefire was agreed by the regime and opposition on 12 April and after the successful deployment of an advanced team a larger United Nations Supervision Mission in Syria (UNSMIS) of 300 was dispatched on 21 April. Teams of unarmed monitors spread over eight sites – Damascus, Aleppo, Deir ez-Zor, Hama, Homs, Idlib, Deraa and Tartous – to monitor and report on the plan's implementation. UNSMIS immediately reported difficulties, however. Access to key locations was sometimes restricted, mostly by regime forces but also by the opposition. As with the Arab League monitors before them, civilians came to expect the UN forces to protect them and, when they proved unable, grew critical. After about two weeks the fragile ceasefire began to break down. On 1 May, Hervé Ladsous, the UN's Under-Secretary-General for Peacekeeping Operations, stated that both sides had violated the agreement. UNSMIS reported thereafter major efforts by the regime to reclaim urban centres of resistance, and a corresponding increase in opposition military activity.[68]

On 25 May shocking videos emerged of a massacre by Shabiha of civilians in the village of Houla near Homs.[69] The next day UNSMIS observers arrived to confirm that 108 had been slaughtered. A string of other alleged regime massacres followed, including up to 55 reportedly killed in the village of al-Qubeir near Hama on 6 June. Five days earlier, the FSA had announced it was resuming all 'defensive operations'. Meanwhile the small UNSMIS teams were increasingly facing danger. UN Secretary General Ban Ki-moon claimed that heavy weapons had been used against the monitors, while on 12 June outside the village of al-Haffah UNSMIS vehicles were attacked by a crowd and then fired upon by unknown assailants. This proved too much, and three days later the mission suspended normal operations, and remained confined to its bases. Despite attempts to safely resume, UNSMIS could no longer continue, and its mandate was ended on 16 August.

As Annan scrambled to rescue his plan he received little support. As with the Arab League Peace Initiative, Assad seemed to be paying lip service. Russia may have pressured Damascus to accept the plan, but its support went no further, and it circled the wagons around Assad after the Houla massacre story broke, echoing the regime's lines that opposition extremists were responsible.[70] On the other side the opposition wasn't united enough to completely abide by the cessation and as the regime began to violate the ceasefire, the weak FSA central leadership came under insurmountable pressure to do likewise. Not that the opposition's external backers disapproved. Turkey, Qatar and Saudi Arabia, who by this point were all lending some form of support to armed opposition groups were critical of Annan from the beginning for not including a mechanism to oust the Syrian dictator. Saudi Arabia effectively shunned Annan and criticised his engagement with Assad.[71] Annan even found critics in his own team, with many agreeing with the Gulf position of pressing harder for Assad's departure.[72] Likewise, he came up against Western diplomats who seemed to believe his mandate was to engineer Assad's departure not, as Annan himself believed, create a framework for peace.

As his six-point plan faltered, Annan changed tack. He authorised his deputy, Nasser al-Kidwa to pursue an ultimately unsuccessful second track process to bring the various strands of the Syrian opposition around one united platform. More significantly, he pursued a second international initiative, what became the Geneva Communiqué. Correctly identifying that the crisis could now only be solved with consensus among the Syrian factions' external backers, Annan proposed establishing a Syria contact group, not unlike that formed during the Bosnia crisis in 1994, which eventually helped mediate a solution. However, his insistence that Iran be included was swiftly rejected by Britain and the US.[73] Instead, on 30 June

Annan gathered a new 'Action Group for Syria' in Geneva composed of the secretaries general of the UN and Arab League, the EU's High Representative for Foreign and Security Policy and the foreign ministers of the US, UK, France, China, Russia, Turkey, Kuwait, Iraq and Qatar (the latter three fulfilling Arab League functions). Neither Saudi Arabia nor Iran nor any Syrians were invited. All present signed up to a new communiqué that reiterated support for the six-point plan and agreed on a set of 'Principles and Guidelines on a Syrian-led transition'. Crucially, it called for the 'establishment of a transitional governing body which . . . could include members of the government and opposition and other groups and should be formed on the basis of mutual consent'.[74] In addition, the 'continuity of governmental institutions and qualified staff' in transition Syria was assured. This was a lesson learned after the occupation of Iraq when regime institutions were dismantled, accelerating state collapse.

As with his six-point plan, Annan had avoided any mention of Assad's departure to ensure Russian and Chinese cooperation. However, that is not how Western diplomats interpreted it. Hillary Clinton later remarked that she had backed Annan's neutral language in the interests of obtaining consensus, but that she saw the communiqué as 'a blueprint for Assad's departure'.[75] This, of course, was not the Russian view: Assad himself could be one of the 'members of the government' to remain in place. Lavrov and Clinton clashed at Geneva on this issue. To press their point Western diplomats, led by Britain, France and the US, immediately prepared a Chapter VII UN Resolution that would enforce Article 41 (non-violent) sanctions on Syria if it did not fully implement the Annan plan. China and Russia again vetoed on 19 July, and whatever international consensus appeared to have been established at Geneva quickly evaporated. A frustrated Annan resigned on 2 August.

Why did Annan fail?

A few weeks after his resignation, Annan told American broadcaster NPR that his failure was due to, 'first of all, the government and its intransigence, and its refusal to implement faithfully the six-point plan. And the opposition, which eventually also gave up and decided to accelerate its military actions'.[76] Having lamented the 'finger-pointing and name-calling in the security council' in his resignation speech, in this interview he specifically criticised Russia and China for vetoing the Geneva Communiqué UN resolution on 19 July.[77] Annan saw clearly the key sticking point, stating, 'Assad will have to go . . . No leader can retain legitimacy after this. The question is how he goes, and when he goes.'

Annan's apportion of blame is broadly correct. As with the Arab League plan before it, neither the regime nor the opposition seemed to take the six-point plan seriously, with both using the ceasefire to rearm and consolidate rather than de-escalate. J. Michael Greig notes that in past civil wars sides only seriously engaged with mediation once both had reached a 'hurting stalemate' with unacceptably painful conflict costs and a perception that they cannot win. In the first half of 2012 Syria's civil conflict was still in its infancy, fluid and far from reaching this point. Indeed, civil war literature suggests a stalemate-induced mediation is likely to succeed only after an average of 130 months' fighting and over 33,000 battle deaths – a point Syria had not reached when Annan launched his plan.[78]

Moreover, as Annan complained, the international and regional actors offered too little external pressure to compensate for the absence of internal pressure to compromise. Russian and Chinese protection at the UN coupled with a steady supply of Russian and Iranian weaponry and finance did little to dispel the Assad regime's belief that it would ultimately triumph. Similarly, Qatari, Saudi Arabian and Turkish material support for the armed rebels was on an upward trend from spring 2012. Encouraged by the clear contempt that Saudi Arabia had for the Annan plan, and the misguided belief that eventually NATO would launch a Libya-style no-fly zone that its regional allies did little to dispel, the opposition felt it had the momentum and was also given little incentive to compromise.

Indeed, the Annan mediations established a pattern that would be repeated throughout the civil war: external powers being unwilling to prioritise ending the conflict over their own wider geopolitical agendas. The refusal to invite Iran to Geneva, for example, reflected Western and Gulf strategic desires to isolate Tehran, even though it was clearly already a key player in the Syria crisis. Similarly, one day after Annan's appointment as joint UN–Arab League envoy, Saudi Arabia and Qatar declared that the rebels should be armed at the inaugural 'Friends of Syria' international meeting – hardly an expression of faith in his mediated solution. The West and Gulf showed absolutely no willingness to back down from demanding Assad's departure as a precondition, while Russia showed equal determination to avoid this. At Geneva, Qatar, Turkey, the US, UK, France and Russia all signed Section 8 of the communiqué stating that they were 'opposed to any further militarization of the conflict', yet in reality their actions served to make Annan's de-escalation next to impossible.

For all its failures, Annan's diplomacy did have a handful of positives. Like the Arab League monitors before them, UNSMIS' presence helped to shine a light on the conflict and to document atrocities. Though UN Human Rights

Chief Navi Pillay was unsuccessful in referring the regime to the ICC, it is hoped that when the war eventually ends the evidence gathered by UNSMIS will play a key role in prosecuting human rights violations. Similarly, though it had no immediate success, the Geneva Communiqué remained the basis for subsequent negotiations, forming the starting point for Geneva peace talks in 2014, 2016 and 2017, even though interpretation continued to be contested. Finally, for all their criticism, the Annan plan actually contributed to a momentary decrease in violence. During the 59 days when UNSMIS was active, 16 April–14 June 2012, 3,991 deaths were reported, fewer than the 4,290 documented in the same period before their arrival (17 February–15 April), and much lower than the figure of 9,251 deaths recorded in the 59 days after operations were suspended (14 June–12 August).[79] As with the Arab League peace plan, it remains an unknown whether a larger contingent of monitors with sufficient international support would have made a greater difference. It might not have prevented the war, but it might have had a better chance of containing it and reducing the violence.

With belligerents on both sides, particularly the regime, seeing violence as the only route to achieve their goals, it would have been very difficult for international actors to prevent Syria's uprising from descending into a civil war. However, none of the major players involved really committed to that goal, undermining the various attempts by international organisations to halt the slide to conflict. The Arab League plan received little support either materially or politically, with Saudi Arabia and Qatar as impatient for quick results as they had been with economic sanctions. The Annan plan that followed it was similarly undermined by Russia, Iran, Saudi Arabia, Qatar and Turkey who continued to provide arms and other forms of support for the regime and opposition fighters, discouraging either from taking the proposed ceasefires seriously. Likewise at the Geneva conference in summer 2012, neither the US nor Russia was willing to prioritise the prevention of conflict over their positions on Assad's future.

That no foreign government was willing to encourage mediation owed much to miscalculations, changing regional dynamics and misperceptions of power. Despite lacking the capacity to topple Assad themselves, Qatar, Saudi Arabia and Turkey were convinced both that Assad was close to falling and that eventually the US would intervene as it had in Libya, and so saw no need to compromise. The US, though not inclined to intervene, having wrongly expected Assad's swift departure now believed that Russia could be persuaded to discard him. Yet Moscow, recognising that Washington's hand was far weaker in Syria than either it or its regional anti-Assad allies believed, saw no reason to abandon the regime, which furthered its regional and domestic interests. While any of the proposed plans, or at least an international contact group such as that agreed on over Bosnia in the mid-1990s, might have helped de-escalate if not completely resolve the crisis, none of the actors was willing to compromise its interests. The result was, unsurprisingly, that the rapid march towards civil war continued unchecked. Yet as Assad himself had noted in October, the impact would be felt far beyond Syria's borders. He menacingly threatened, 'Any problem in Syria will burn the whole region.'[80]

A legitimate representative? Supporting and subverting Syria's political opposition

The Syrian coalition is for Syrians and when there are regional hands interfering and making decisions inside the country, it means the people inside have lost their ability to decide their own fate.

Moaz al-Khatib, former President of the National Coalition for Syrian Revolutionary and Opposition Forces, speaking to al-Jazeera International, 11 May 2013[1]

Underestimating the Assad regime's durability was a costly error by its international opponents, but just as damaging was the overestimation of Syria's opposition and its ability to form a united and effective force. All of the international actors' strategies against Assad, whether to negotiate a transition via the Geneva Communiqué process, or to topple the regime militarily, required a viable opposition. Yet this was a huge challenge. Since 1963 the Ba'ath regime forbade independent opposition, outlawing or co-opting independent institutions such as trade unions, the press and political parties. Civil society was curbed. Serious political opposition, notably the Muslim Brotherhood and the secular liberals and leftists of the 2001 Damascus Spring and the 2005 Damascus Declaration, had been crushed. As a result, in 2011 the traditional opposition to Assad was weak and fragmented, divided along multiple fault lines including between insiders and exiles and between Islamists and secularists. Few had played a role in the spontaneous unrest and so were unprepared and often unsuited to the task of leadership. Unlike successful resistance groups elsewhere like the FLN or IRA, from the beginning the opposition reacted to events rather than led them. Recognising the scale of the task, international allies sought to advise and assist to better their chances of bringing about Assad's fall. However, as this chapter will show, foreign states' pursuit of their own agendas combined with a frequent lack of ability actually helped to keep the opposition fragmented and ineffective.

Demands for a leader: The Syrian National Council

At first, the uprising was essentially leaderless. The protests in Deraa, Homs and elsewhere were organised locally by individuals with few connections to the traditional opponents of Assad. Activists, some of whom had first come together at the Damascus demonstrations of 16 March, formed *tansiqiyat* or Local Coordination Committees (LCCs) to coordinate their local activities and to link up with protesters elsewhere in the country.[2] Lacking national leaders, the LCCs could withstand the mass detentions of its activists. Had it been more centrally organised the regime might have been able to decapitate it and halt momentum yet, ironically, the decentralisation that enabled the uprising's early survival also proved a major obstacle to uniting the opposition later.[3]

As the protests spread the demand for a single opposition body grew. Like so much in the early stages of the conflict, the shadow of the simultaneous Libya war loomed large. There, an opposition National Transition Council (NTC) had quickly formed, gained international recognition and successfully lobbied the UN to back a NATO campaign against Gaddafi. Many Syrians and their external supporters, though initially less enthusiastic about military intervention, believed that a similar Syrian body was necessary, prompting a series of conferences in Turkey in summer 2011. Eventually the Syrian National Council (SNC) was announced in Istanbul in August then relaunched in October, bringing together the Muslim Brotherhood, figures from the Damascus Declaration and representatives from the LCCs. Electing a secular Paris-based academic, Burhan Ghalioun as its chairman, its stated goal was 'the overthrow of the regime, its symbols and its head'. However, it soon became clear that the SNC was no NTC. The Libyan opposition already controlled Benghazi and much of eastern Libya even before the NTC was formed, Gaddafi had less domestic and external support than Assad and the international appetite to intervene was far greater than in Syria. While Gaddafi fell relatively quickly before the divisions within the Libyan opposition could emerge, the SNC had no such momentum. It soon became clear that the council had multiple flaws and was not the viable alternative to Assad that many hoped.

Activists and exiles

Among several weaknesses that the SNC never overcame was the gap between the exile-led SNC and the opposition on the ground. LCC representatives were included in the council and initially there was some enthusiasm among activists, seen when 7 October 2011 was named the 'Friday of The National Council Represents Me'.[4] However, with the LCCs being decentralised, inevitably some protesters were more enthusiastic than others. The domination of long-term or recent exiles linked to earlier anti-Assad political movements but who had played little role in the 'Revolution' meant the SNC began with a credibility gap. This only widened with time as it proved unable to meet the various demands of different activists, including international intervention, weaponry and humanitarian support.[5] As well as disappointing the activists, the SNC proved unable or unwilling to work with other internal opposition groups. Few Kurdish groups joined. The SNC distanced itself from the National Coordination Body for Democratic Change (NCB), formed in June 2011 by leftist veterans Hassan Abdul Azim and Haytham Manna, because the NCB advocated dialogue with Assad and was adamantly opposed to external intervention.[6] Similarly Louay Hussein, a high-profile Alawi dissident, kept his Building the Syrian State group out of the SNC, also over external support and dialogue with the regime.[7] Ideological divisions were not helped by personal rivalries and a lack of political experience. One Western diplomat noted how the very skills that had allowed oppositionists to survive in Assad's Syria – stubbornness and a principled refusal to compromise – now proved problematic.[8] Another, who worked closely with the SNC, described them as like 'newly released hostages', unprepared for the task ahead and, after decades of regime propaganda, paranoid and suspicious of all, especially the West.[9]

The opposition's international supporters, though conscious of an exile–activist divide, contributed to it. At the inaugural 'Friends of Syria' meeting in Tunis on 24 February 2012 the SNC was recognised as 'a legitimate representative of Syrians seeking peaceful democratic change' by over sixty countries, including the US, UK, France, Qatar, Saudi Arabia and Turkey.[10] However, this was a long way from the recognition most had granted to the NTC as 'the sole legitimate representative of Libya' the previous year and reflected concerns over the SNC's abilities and internal support. While this made sense to foreign diplomats who weren't convinced, the failure to win significant foreign support only reinforced the perception of SNC weakness within Syria.

Foreign governments also pursed often-conflicting policies to the SNC, and each other. Few states knew much about the opposition and scrambled in spring 2011 to make connections. Qatar and Turkey had the strongest tie to one group, the Muslim Brotherhood (MB), but this made them less willing to explore others or press the SNC to improve its internal links once the MB had secured a leading role in the council. Several former SNC figures believe this helped contribute to factionalism within the SNC and the wider Syrian opposition. Among them, former spokeswoman Bassma Kodmani noted how 'outside governments "captured" factions

within the council, to prioritize their agenda over what might be best for
the SNC as a whole.[11] When the conflict became militarised Qatar and
Turkey, and to a lesser extent Saudi Arabia, worked directly with armed
groups, effectively undermining SNC efforts to become a logistical hub for
the rebels.[12]

The US and EU states, having taken a back seat in the SNC's formation
to avoid it appearing a Western tool – which opened space for Turkey and
Qatar – thereafter pressed it to improve internal links. Robert Ford, who
effectively acted as US liaison with the Syrian opposition after the US
embassy was closed in February 2012, was particularly wary of diaspora-
dominated oppositions following the US' disastrous sponsorship of Iraqi
exiles after the 2003 war. Like other Syria-based diplomats, Ford forged ties
with activists on the ground when the uprising began and was critical of the
SNC for not sufficiently representing them.[13] These ties, often with local
LCCs, were utilised to offer Western support to the opposition, in the form
of non-violent training programmes in Turkey.[14] Once the regime withdrew from territory in 2012, many LCCs morphed into local councils that
attempted to combine activism and relief work with governance, prompting
increased Western support and training in civil administration.[15] However,
these programmes were only loosely coordinated between different foreign
states and often had a limited or no role for the SNC. Western diplomats
correctly complained that the SNC lacked the organisation and ability to
handle such tasks, but it meant that foreign aid worsened rather than
improved ties between the internal activists and external opposition.

The controversial role of the Muslim Brotherhood

Controversy over the role of the Muslim Brotherhood within the SNC also
contributed to its weakness. Liberal and leftist critics claimed that the MB
was afforded too large a role, consequently scaring away potential
supporters, notably Alawis, Christians, Kurds and Sunni Muslim secularists. Supporters of the SNC deny both charges. Yet debates over the MB's
role did play a major part in the SNC's divisions, and ultimately contributed
to its demise. That the MB ended up playing any leading role in the opposition was a remarkable turnaround. After its brutal defeat in Hama in 1982
the surviving leadership squabbled in exile while its grass-roots support
diminished, assisted by the regime's Law No. 49 that made MB membership
punishable by death. A misguided, though short-lived, opposition alliance
in 2006 with former Vice President Abdul Halim Khaddam, an exiled crony
of Hafez al-Assad, discredited the MB further, as did the bitterly fought
leadership battle of 2010.[16] There is no evidence that the MB played any role

in the early stages of the uprising and it seemed to catch them totally unaware; the MB only offered public support after six weeks.[17]

Yet the MB was well placed to take advantage of the uprising. It was one of few opposition groups with 'brand recognition' and a historic anti-Assad reputation, and was helped by the post-revolutionary success of MB branches in Tunisia and Egypt. Though Syria's activists were not explicitly Islamist at first, most were poor, Sunni and religious, gathering at mosques to demonstrate on Fridays and shouting 'Allah Akhbar' as a protest slogan, making them a demographic potentially sympathetic to the MB. The leadership also adapted quickly. The new leader, Mohammad Riyadh al-Suqfah built bridges with his rivals. Old networks inside Syria were reactivated, especially in Jisr al-Shughour, Homs and Hama. Also important were the networks of exiles. These included financial contributors and lobbyists, especially in Turkey and Qatar, and Western-based publicists such as Obaida Nahas of the Levant Institute in London. The administrator of the 'Syria Revolution 2011' Facebook page that determined the title of the Fridays of protest was reportedly leader of Sweden's MB chapter.[18]

Raphaël Lefèvre, a Muslim Brotherhood expert, argues that despite its limited presence inside Syria the MB was welcomed into the SNC because 'their ideological influence, history of unyielding opposition to the Ba'ath, significant financial resources and organisational capacities would nonetheless make them an essential future component of any post-Assad settlement'.[19] Yet as important was the patronage of Qatar and Turkey. Qatar had a long-standing relationship with the MB across the region, not just the Syrian branch. These ties were primarily personal and practical rather than ideological.[20] Since the 1990s Doha built a web of relationships to leading MB figures, often via the much-feted Egyptian Brotherhood public ideologue Yusuf Qaradawi, who had his own show on al-Jazeera and was appointed Dean of Qatar University's faculty of Islamic Studies. Doha saw in the Brotherhood a means to increase its regional capacity. The MB already had a wide international network, meaning that if Qatar supported its leadership it could project influence without needing to build a large foreign service.[21] After 2011 Doha firmly believed that the MB was the future and that helping it to power in Syria would make the new regime in Damascus beholden to Qatar.[22] It pursued a similar approach in Egypt and Libya. Turkey's ruling AKP also had historical ties to the Brotherhood, having lobbied Assad throughout the 2000s to rehabilitate them. As discussed in Chapter 3, though Ankara had a practical justification – an MB-led Syria would be friendly to Turkey – Erdoğan and Davutoğlu were idealistic too, seeing in the MB the Arab equivalent of the AKP.

Qatari and Turkish support facilitated the MB's dominance of the SNC. Officially, roles in the council were balanced. The MB was one of the two largest blocs, along with the Damascus Declaration, but the large number of independents meant that it had fewer than 20 per cent of the seats.[23] Moreover, to show its commitment to cooperation and pluralism, the MB deliberately chose not to enter a candidate for the chairmanship. However, the unparalleled unity of the MB, in contrast to the feuding Damascus Declaration, made its 20 per cent a powerful voice.[24] The MB also dominated two of the SNC's key offices, covering military affairs and development, which gave them millions of dollars of donations to build their own support networks in Syria.[25] Western diplomats who worked closely with the SNC admit that Qatari and Turkish support for the MB added far greater weight to its voice than would be expected from its official representation.[26] Qatar ensured that the Brotherhood was given the best media access on al-Jazeera.[27] Qatar also effectively bankrolled the SNC. Of its $40 million budget announced in November 2012, $20 million came from Libya – which at that point was a staunch Qatari ally – while $15 million came from Qatar itself.[28] Turkey, meanwhile, hosted the council in Istanbul and controlled its access to Syria via the long border, meaning the SNC would have struggled to ignore Ankara's preferences.[29]

Struggling with the Kurds

A further SNC weakness was its inability to bring political representatives of Syria's Kurds into its fold. The Kurds had long been marginalised by the Ba'ath regime, enjoying no cultural or political autonomy and occasionally facing violent oppression, most recently in the Qamishli riots of March 2004 when at least thirty were killed. Yet this instinctively anti-Assad constituency proved unwilling to join the opposition movement due to internal developments among Syria's Kurds, the policies of the opposition and influence from external forces.

Historically Syria's Kurds (10 per cent of the population) were less pronounced Kurdish nationalists than in neighbouring Iraq and Turkey. Syria had three Kurdish-majority regions – the Jazeera (around Qamishli) in the east, Kobane and Afrin in the north – but many lived for generations in cities elsewhere and had become more assimilated within a Syrian identity.[30] A Kurdish identity did develop, especially in response to aggressive government policies such as forbidding teaching in Kurdish or the deliberate settlement of Arabs in Kurdish areas, but activists favoured cultural autonomy over political independence.[31] Moreover, through a combination of regime manipulation, personal and ideological rivalries and a generational divide, on the eve of the uprising Kurdish political groups were weak.

Traditional leaders therefore did not immediately respond to the March 2011 uprising. Young Kurds took to the streets like young Arabs but the organised parties did not mobilise or demand the fall of the regime for the first five months.[32] Eventually recognising the opportunity, in May 2011 the 'Kurdish National Movement' brought together seventeen different political parties, including the PYD, Syria's affiliate branch of the Turkish Kurdish separatist PKK.[33] This soon broke down over the PYD's demands for a directly elected congress. A more successful bloc was formed in Qamishli in October, the Kurdish National Council (KNC), but this initially included only ten of the original seventeen, and the PYD declined to join.[34]

Uniting these long-feuding parties into the durable KNC was impressive, but the KNC's emerging rivalry with the PYD pointed to new Kurdish divisions. The PYD's position was boosted after Assad's forces began withdrawing from Kurdish areas in 2012 and the PYD's militia, the YPG, took its place. The regime initially withdrew from the regions with the strongest PYD sympathies, Afrin and Kobane, and the YPG were by far the best armed among Syrian Kurds, trained by the PKK. Given the regime's alliance with PKK up until 1998, something it reactivated after Turkey turned on it in 2011, and the regime's voluntary withdrawal under no military pressure, many in the KNC, the Arab opposition groups and the Turkish government accused the PYD of being in league with Assad, something its leaders strongly denied.[35]

The Syrian National Council faced an uphill task in trying to woo two conflicting Kurdish actors, but did a poor job of it nevertheless. The PYD was dismissed as pro-Assad early on, plus it was already a founding member of the rival NCB. The KNC was more amenable but the SNC repeatedly did too little to reassure the Kurds. Two powerful opposition strands were reluctant to embrace the Kurds: firstly older nationalists who were often Arab nationalists at heart and feared Kurdish secession ambitions, and secondly Islamists, who disliked the largely secular Kurdish Sunnis. At an early meeting in Istanbul in July 2011, opposition leaders refused a request to drop the word 'Arab' from the 'Syrian Arab Republic' and offered Kurds no leadership seats, prompting Kurdish delegates to walk out. When the SNC's first incarnation was created that August, the persistence in defining Syria as an Arab state meant only one Kurdish party leader, the youth leader Meshaal Tammo was willing to join the executive board. His assassination on 7 October, possibly by regime agents or Kurdish rivals, left no prominent Kurds within the SNC.[36] Statements by SNC leaders exacerbated matters. Samir Nashar, a member of the executive committee, accused the Kurdish parties of 'not effectively participating in the Syrian revolution' in August 2011, and even threatened 'consequences after the fall of the regime'.

Similarly, though Ghalioun publicly reached out to Kurds, along with Alawis and Christians, in Tunis in February 2012, months later he outraged Kurds by saying, 'there is no such thing as Syrian Kurdistan.' The unwillingness to guarantee that a post-Assad Syria would improve Kurdish cultural and political rights ensured that, when the KNC was formed, it declared itself committed to opposing the regime but separate from the SNC. While later attempts by the SNC to woo the Kurds with a National Charter on the Kurdish Issue in April 2012 did prompt some KNC members to consider a closer alliance, partly to counter the rise of the PYD, the two bodies remained officially estranged.[37]

Western actors pressed the SNC on the issue. Yet other international actors played a less benign role. Turkey, though encouraging the SNC to include some Kurds, was adamantly opposed to any PYD role in the SNC, seeing it as an extension of the PKK and an ally of Assad. In 2012, possibly with Assad's encouragement, the PKK increased its terrorist attacks within Turkey, notably a bombing in Gaziantep in August that killed nine civilians. While the PYD did enter into a limited dialogue with the Turkish government, in private Davutoğlu briefed against it.[38] Conversely Turkey's closeness to the SNC helped deter the KNC. Its leaders were conscious of Ankara's historic repression of Kurds and also feared the AKP's preference for the Muslim Brotherhood, which sat uneasily with the largely secular Kurds.[39]

The other major external influence was Massoud Barzani, President of Iraq's KRG. The success of the KRG since 2003 provided Barzani with an array of new tools to project influence: economic power from oil wealth; military power in his well organised Peshmerga armed forces; and the soft power of the KRG becoming a model for other Kurdish nationalists to emulate. Barzani now rivalled the PKK, previously the leading pan-Kurdish voice. This rivalry was ideological, Barzani was tribal and conservative compared to the socialist PKK, geopolitical, the KRG allied with the PKK's enemies in Ankara, and personal, the PKK had historically backed Barzani's Iraqi Kurdish rival, Jalal Talabani. In this context, Barzani saw developments in Syria as an opportunity to expand his regional power and block the advance of the PKK via the PYD. He was instrumental in forming the KNC in October 2011, sponsoring the Qamishli conference. Similarly in July 2012 he sought to mediate the growing tensions between the PYD and KNC, organising the 'Erbil Agreement'. This accord agreed that Syria's Kurdish regions would be jointly administered in a KNC–PYD Supreme Kurdish Committee and a joint popular defence force, but the PYD with its military advantage often proved unwilling to share power and frequently acted unilaterally.[40] The agreement ultimately failed to settle either the

KNC–PYD divide or the Barzani–PKK Kurdish regional power struggle influencing it.

Debate over armed force as violence rises

Alongside the structural weaknesses of the SNC, issues of policy proved highly divisive, particularly the debate over armed resistance and the possibility of external intervention. An early opposition conference in Antalya, Turkey, in June 2011, committed to a 'peaceful revolution' and a rejection of Western military intervention.[41] As the violence increased, however, pressure grew within the SNC to review its stance. Again, external actors influenced this. Western diplomats repeated two messages to the opposition in 2011: to remain peaceful, and not to expect Western military intervention.[42] Even so, high-ranking members of the SNC increasingly saw Western intervention as the least bad option. Ghalioun, despite being known for his pacifism, called for a no-fly zone in December 2011, while the next month, the council's spokesperson Bassma Kodmani said that intervention was better than the alternative of greater militarisation.[43] Robert Ford claims that many actually expected Western intervention from an early stage, ignoring his insistence to the contrary. He recalled later, 'At one meeting [in Damascus] they said to me, "You're wrong Robert, the Americans will come." I said, "I'm the American ambassador, I really think I understand them better than you do!"'

However, in the wake of the Libya intervention and their turning on Assad, Qatar, Saudi Arabia and Turkey began to deliver a different message on both intervention and an armed strategy. Indeed, the first 'Friends of Syria' meeting in February 2012 ended in public disagreement when the Saudi Arabian and Qatari foreign ministers both advocated arming the emerging rebel groups on the ground, a strategy not endorsed by their Western allies. With Saudi Arabian, Qatari and Turkish encouragement and the rapid escalation on the ground, the hawkish elements within the SNC – particularly the MB – challenged the council to endorse a military strategy.[44] This again reflected the insider–outsider divide as members were aware that the armed rebel groups were developing their own networks that would leave the SNC even more marginalised – even though many peaceful activists and LCCs rejected the militarisation of the conflict.[45] After a series of heated meetings, the doves were overruled and the SNC had abandoned its non-violent policy by March 2012. Attempts were made to link the SNC to the fighting groups, particularly the FSA. On 1 March an SNC military body to oversee the rebels was announced by Ghalioun, to 'be like a defence ministry'.[46] In a sign of foreign influence, soon afterwards Saudi Arabia,

Qatar and UAE announced a $100 million fund for the military body to distribute salaries to the FSA. However, almost immediately Colonel Asaad, the nominal head of the FSA but with limited influence over the rebel fighters himself, announced that the SNC had not consulted him. Moreover, the $100 million never arrived and the SNC, as it feared, became ever more irrelevant to the fighting groups.[47]

The National Coalition and Saudi Arabia's takeover

A new hope?

It soon became clear that the SNC could not surmount its weaknesses. As early as February 2012 Haytham al-Maleh, a veteran Islamist activist, complained that the council was doing too little to help the FSA, and formed the breakaway Syrian Patriotic Group with over twenty secular and Islamist SNC members. Ghalioun was criticised for his poor management, lack of charisma, and for staying as leader beyond a pre-agreed three-month term.[48] When he did eventually resign in May 2012, his successors, Abdulbaset Sida and then George Sabra, were also weak, elected more to woo Syrian minorities than for their abilities – Sida was a Kurd, Sabra a Christian. Several other members, including Kodmani in August 2012, followed Maleh in resigning, variously citing personal rivalries, the lack of support for the FSA, a disconnect from actors on the ground, and the domination of the MB.

Crucially, external powers lost faith. As they came to realise that Assad's fall might not be as quick as initially hoped – prompted by the failure of Annan's diplomacy, the increased fighting inside Syria, and Russia and China's 19 July 2012 UN veto – the weaknesses of the SNC came into sharper focus. Western leaders were aware that regional rivals were dividing the opposition and on the suggestion of Lakhdar Brahimi, Annan's replacement as UN–Arab League Special Representative, in early 2013 Britain's Foreign Secretary William Hague reduced the Friends of Syria to a more manageable 'London 11' – the UK, US, France, Germany, Saudi Arabia, Qatar, Turkey, UAE, Italy, Egypt and Jordan. However, as Jon Wilks, Britain's envoy to the opposition later admitted, 'Maybe we contained their [Qatar, Saudi Arabia and Turkey's] differences, but we never overcame them and delivered a unified message to the opposition.'[49] At the same time as trying, in vain, to reconcile external differences, the idea to restructure the opposition gained ground. In October 2012 Riad Seif, a leading Damascus Declaration dissident and one of the few founding SNC members to be based in Syria and thus removed from the council's Istanbul machinations, proposed a new, broader organisation. Soon afterwards Hillary Clinton, echoing Ford's long-held misgivings about the exile-dominated SNC, effectively endorsed Seif's plan by calling for an opposition representing 'those who are on the front lines', not 'by people who have many good attributes, but have, in many instances, not been inside Syria for 20, 30 or 40 years'.[50]

Taking Seif's proposal as a basis, in early November Syria's main oppositionists, including the SNC, were jointly welcomed in Doha by Clinton and Hamad bin Jassem al-Thani, alongside diplomats from the main anti-Assad states, to thrash out a new agreement. The result was announced on 12 November 2012: the National Coalition for Syrian Revolutionary and Opposition Forces (SOC). A significant effort was made to avoid the mistakes of the SNC. After Turkish and Qatari pressure the SNC agreed to be absorbed into the new alliance, and was allocated twenty-two out of sixty-three General Assembly seats, aimed at diluting the influence of the MB, which was subject to particular ire at the Doha conference. The new alliance also worked more closely with activists on the ground and with the numerous military councils that had recently formed inside Syria – a formal arrangement with a reorganised FSA was agreed the following month. To ensure a balance between secularists and Islamists, Ahmed Moaz al-Khatib, a popular and respected Damascene imam, became President with Seif and another secularist, Suheir Atassi, as vice presidents. An Assistance Coordination Unit (ACU) was established to coordinate humanitarian aid in opposition-held territory that, with support from friendly governments and NGOs, attempted to strengthen SOC support on the ground via service provision. The Kurds were also courted and, while the PYD immediately rejected overtures, the KNC voted to join in December 2012, although they faced subsequent internal opposition.[51] Eventually, after diplomatic effort from Ford and his team, the KNC formally joined in August 2013, with Abdel Hakim Bashar made a vice president.[52] However, this actually reflected how much the KNC had been eclipsed by the PYD on the ground by this point.

Despite these efforts the SOC soon proved little better as a viable opposition than the SNC and, once again, this owed much to its international backers. Competition between Qatar and Saudi Arabia would ultimately lead to a complete transformation in the SOC's leadership midway through 2013 but international disagreement surfaced from the Coalition's inception. The US wanted to reorganise the opposition, but was unwilling to pay for a conference so Qatar, at the height of its activist regional policy, stepped forward. Yet as Ford lamented later on, 'that meant we lost control of the agenda and, most importantly, we lost control of the guest list'.[53] According to Ford, Western diplomats gave the Qataris a list of their LCC partners inside Syria, but 'they didn't invite any of them. They just invited the people from Istanbul and some of their cronies.' Other Western diplomats noted they were prevented from entering some meetings in Doha.[54] The key was money. As one diplomat remarked, 'all the money came from Saudi Arabia or Qatar, but mostly Qatar, and this really limited our leverage'.[55] Indeed, for a while Doha's hotels were reportedly packed with Syrian (and Libyan) activists, flown in and accommodated at Qatar's expense for conferences and meetings. As a result, though publicly welcoming the SOC, privately the US was frustrated. It did not copy the Gulf states in instantly recognising the Coalition as 'the legitimate representative of the Syrian people'. Though Obama eventually made this recognition a month later at a Friends of Syria conference in Morocco where over a hundred countries did likewise, it was not his preference. On 13 November France, possibly incentivised by Qatar, had gone back on an agreement with the US not to recognise the SOC until it had sufficient ties on the ground.[56] Britain and most other EU states followed days later, effectively forcing the US to do likewise. Yet like the SNC before them, the SOC was learning that retaining international support was a greater priority than building grass-roots legitimacy.

The story of Khatib's short-lived presidency illustrates the problems caused by external powers. Khatib was correctly identified as a more realistic president-in-waiting than Ghalioun, possessing considerable charm and enjoying the respect of secularists and Islamists. He was determined to show his independence, suspicious of the Americans and keen to avoid the label of Qatari or Turkish client, even visiting rebel-held parts of Syria to meet opposition fighters. On 30 January 2013 he surprisingly announced via Facebook that he was willing to 'sit down directly with representatives of the Syrian regime in Cairo, Tunis or Istanbul', in certain conditions. This was his own initiative, welcomed as a 'breakthrough' by Lakhdar Brahimi and even led to informal talks with Iranian Foreign Minister, Ali Akbar Salehi, in February.[57] However, though he received tentative backing within the Coalition, the MB-dominated SNC faction and the Qatar-aligned SOC secretary general, Mustafa Sabbagh, loudly rejected it. In response, the SNC faction pushed to elect an SOC provisional government, aimed at administering Syria's 'liberated areas' but also at weakening Khatib, who opposed the move.[58] The election on 18 March 2013 proved highly fractious, with Qatar and Saudi Arabia's various SOC allies championing different candidates for Prime Minister. The SNC's preferred Premier, Ghassan Hitto, a US-based businessman, triumphed but it prompted a return to the old accusations of MB and Qatari dominance and twelve members of the General Assembly suspended their membership in protest. Six days later

Khatib himself resigned, feeling his hands tied by external influence, although he remained in office until 21 April. A month later, he lamented the external interference of 'two or more' regional governments to an al-Jazeera interviewer. When the interviewer asked him to specifically name Saudi Arabia and Qatar he replied, 'Why are you asking about something that is well known?'[59]

Khatib's resignation, barely five months after the formation of the SOC, would prove a difficult blow to surmount. None of his successors had the same charisma or independence, with all ultimately seen as the clients of Qatar or Saudi Arabia, while the dispute over Hitto's election reawakened the divisions that the opposition had temporarily overcome in Doha. Khatib's departure was initially cushioned by the formation of a provisional government and the decision to offer the SOC Syria's seat at the Arab League in late March. However, with regional events exacerbating the growing rivalry between Saudi Arabia and Qatar, it was not long before divisions resurfaced.

The view from Riyadh

The summer of 2013 represented a significant shift for the political opposition. By its end the long-running feud between Saudi Arabia and Qatar had come into the open and Riyadh had manoeuvred to supplant Doha as the leading regional backer of the SOC. To understand how and why this came about, Saudi Arabia's view of the Syria crisis needs to be considered. Riyadh viewed Syria as part of a wider set of regional concerns that closely overlapped and interacted with perceived domestic threats. Most prominent among these concerns were: leading a regional counter-revolution to roll back the Arab Spring, confronting Iran, stemming the rise of the Muslim Brotherhood, and opposing jihadism. All of these were visible in Syria, though their importance to Riyadh varied over time. Importantly, this came amid domestic uncertainty over the successors to the ageing King Abdullah in a kingdom where policy is highly personalised.

Riyadh's immediate concern in spring 2011 was that the popular unrest might spread. King Abdullah's first instinct was to lead the counter-revolution, combining repression and patronage at home and abroad. Troops were sent to Bahrain, and grants to fellow monarchs under fire in Jordan and Oman.[60] New laws restricted domestic freedom of expression, 160 Saudis were arrested in February and March 2011, while $130 billion was allocated for increasing subsidies, public sector pay rises, 500,000 new low-income housing units and 60,000 new jobs.[61] When Abdullah turned on Assad in August, the immediate revolutionary threat appeared to be contained, allowing Riyadh space to renew its anti-Iranian agenda. It also faced increased public criticism for its silence. However, Saudi Arabia never abandoned its broad hostility to the Arab Spring and sponsored Syrian opposition elements that would help it achieve its regional goals with little regard to any commitment to popular democracy.

'Flipping' Syria from Iran's orbit had been a goal before 2011, and Riyadh believed that replacing Assad with a friendly Sunni-dominated government that it had helped put in power would achieve this. Cutting the land route to Hezbollah would also hit Iran's position in Lebanon, so both Damascus and Beirut could drift into the Saudi Arabian orbit. This might help compensate for the perceived loss of Iraq, for which Abdullah had faced considerable domestic criticism after 2003.[62]

The Iranian threat was also felt domestically. The limited unrest that had spread to Saudi Arabia in spring 2011 took place in Qatif in the Shia-majority Eastern Province.[63] Riyadh has long assumed that any unrest among its Shia must be encouraged by Tehran rather than due to its long oppression of the minority, among the state's poorest. The sect's predominance in Saudi Arabia's most oil-rich regions has long made Riyadh fearful of Iranian-inspired Shia secessionism.[64] Beyond the security threat, domestic religious elements pressured Abdullah to strike against Iran in Syria. This was partly a problem of the al-Sauds' own making. Since its foundation the Sauds had a long alliance with the deeply religious and conservative Wahhabi Sunni leaders. After Salafist radicals captured the Grand Mosque in Mecca in 1979, prompting a bloody siege, the government encouraged even greater public religiosity, believing that a more pious population would shun ideas of a militant uprising or revolution.[65] As a result, the clerical establishment was given greater power in exchange for emphasising loyalty to the regime. Wahhabis had always viewed Shia as heretics, but thereafter anti-Shia zeal became more widespread. When the Syria fighting broke out anti-Shia clerics and lay folk framed it as part of a wider civilisational Sunni–Shia clash, as they had the Iraqi civil war in the 2000s. With Assad's Shia Alawi nature highlighted along with the Shi'ism of his Iranian allies, pressure increased on Abdullah to show his religious credentials as the defender of Sunnism.[66]

The pursuit of Saudi Arabia's goals in Syria was complicated by its simultaneous desire to prevent two forces among the anti-Assad groups from triumphing: the Muslim Brotherhood and the jihadists. Saudi Arabia had a mixed history with the Muslim Brotherhood, described in 2002 by Interior Minister Prince Nayef as the 'source of all problems'. In the 1950s and '60s persecuted Egyptian Brotherhood members found refuge in the kingdom, as did the Syrian MB in the 1980s, and the Egyptians intellectually cross-pollinated with some Saudi Wahhabists to develop the Salafist al-Sahwa al-Islamiyya (Islamic Awakening) or Sahwa. Yet the MB's support for Saddam Hussein's invasion of Kuwait in 1990 and a rising fear of its populist Islamism prompted a crackdown. Thereafter, with a few exceptions Riyadh opposed the MB abroad while restricting and sometimes co-opting the Sahwa at home. However, in 2011 key Saudi Islamists such as Salman al-'Awda, who had his own television show on MBC, and the conservative Nasir al-'Umar, vocally supported the anti-Mubarak revolution in Egypt.[67] Moreover, Saudi public opinion on Twitter and social media sided with the protesters, criticising Saudi Arabia's support for the old regimes.[68] When the MB then became a major political force in post-revolutionary Egypt, Tunisia and Libya, Saudi Arabian leaders, already worried that the Arab Spring might infect it, also feared it might revive the Sahwa.

The resultant Saudi Arabian hostility to the MB drew it into conflict with Qatar, and to a lesser extent Turkey, particularly in Egypt. Following interim military rule, the Egyptian MB emerged victorious first in parliamentary elections and then, in June 2012, its candidate, Mohamed Morsi, was narrowly elected President. Despite being Egypt's first democratically elected leader, Morsi was criticised for his overbearing style of rule. On the first anniversary of his accession huge protests began and, after he refused a military ultimatum, the army removed Morsi in a coup on 3 July 2013. Qatar and Turkey were outraged at the move, which saw a new autocratic regime established under the leadership of army chief General Abdel Fatteh el-Sisi, the arrest of Morsi, and a violent crackdown on the MB. Yet Saudi Arabia, which had originally supported Morsi's 2012 election rival Ahmed Shafiq, immediately welcomed the new Sisi government, as did the UAE and Kuwait and pledged $12 billion in unconditional aid within days.[69] Leaked tapes later implied that UAE officials had conspired with the Egyptian army – its Crown Prince, Mohammed bin Zayed, being strongly anti-MB – and many suspected Saudi Arabian collusion as well.[70]

The 2013 Egyptian coup highlighted the widening gap between Riyadh and Washington. Though Obama notably refused to use the word 'coup', he immediately expressed his 'concern' and threatened to 'review' Washington's $1.3 billion in annual military aid if democratic government wasn't restored. Riyadh replied that it would replace any withdrawn US military aid in addition to the $12 billion Gulf fund, undermining any US bargaining power with Sisi.[71] This snub came after repeated Saudi Arabian frustrations with its ally, notably the abandonment of Mubarak, unwillingness to intervene in Syria, tacit support for Morsi, and the growing prospect of a US–Iranian nuclear deal.[72] The alliance was already diminishing, due to economic factors, with the US less reliant on Saudi Arabian oil and Riyadh necessarily diversifying its international ties to Asia, especially China.[73] The relationship was far from broken: defence links remained vital, while Washington relied on Saudi Arabian largesse for many regional initiatives – what one US official referred to as 'the Gulf ATM'.[74] However, Riyadh was increasingly assertive and independent in its regional policy, with moves such as supporting the Sisi regime, like the Bahrain crackdown before it, being taken without prior notification of Washington.

Finally, Saudi Arabia feared the rise of jihadism. The Sauds' legitimacy rested on religion and, as discussed above regarding Iran and the Shia, they frequently instrumentalised Sunni conservatism. Indeed, as in 1979, in response to the Arab Spring Interior Minister Prince Nayef increased financial support for Saudi Arabia's religious organisations, hoping that increased piety and the empowering of loyal clerics would stem the revolutionary tide.[75] However, after encouraging jihad in Afghanistan in the 1980s only for returning combatants to bring the fight to Riyadh, the government knew it had to walk a fine line. As violence in Syria raged, its demands of clerics were very specific: endorse Saudi Arabia's policy against Assad, but discourage jihad. Not surprisingly, a handful of *ulema* were unwilling to be so proscribed and urged congregations to donate to militants and even travel to Syria to fight – something the same clerics had earlier called for in Iraq.[76] Over 1,000 Saudis did so, prompting the authorities in 2012 to ban certain preachers and then forbidding young men to travel to Syria in 2014.[77] Unlike Qatar, which feared no such domestic blowback, Riyadh was therefore concerned to limit the presence of jihadists in Syria's opposition.

Within Saudi Arabia's ruling elite there was consensus on these broad regional policies but in a state where policy remains highly personalised, the leading personalities had an impact too. King Abdullah had long had ties to Syria, and was genuinely concerned with its fate. One of his wives was Syrian, the sister of a wife of Bashar al-Assad's rebellious uncle, Rifaat, to whom the king became close during the 1980s.[78] There was also personal animosity towards Assad, initiated when the Syrian President denounced Abdullah as a 'half man' in 2006 and then, after a slight thaw, reawakened in 2011 when his son Abdulaziz was rudely ignored in his mission to Damascus. Alongside his own conviction, Abdullah was conscious of dynastic concerns. He was eighty-seven in 2011 and there were questions over which of Ibn Saud's grandsons would eventually take over when his last remaining sons died. This became more pronounced when Abdullah's immediate heirs died (of old age), Prince Sultan in October 2011 and Interior Minister

Prince Nayef in June 2012. Abdullah named his brother Muqrin second in line in 2013 but also promoted his own son, Mutaib, to Minister of the National Guard, prompting speculation that the latter was being favoured among the younger generation of princes. At the same time, alternative young leaders emerged from another wing of the royal family, the Sudairi princes. Previously led by Nayef, the Sudairi faction became dominated by the new first-in-line, Abdullah's brother Salman, and the new Interior Minister, Nayef's son Mohammed bin Nayef, who was popular among US leaders for his campaign against al-Qaeda in the Arabian Peninsula (AQAP) in the 2000s. Traditionally more conservative and closer to the clerical establishment than Abdullah, the Sudairis commanded a large security apparatus and religious groups controlling religious education, religious police and the judiciary.[79] Already labelled as soft by some of these forces, Abdullah would have been conscious that any perceived weakness over Syria might strengthen the hand of his internal rivals over long-term succession plans.

However, Saudi Arabia seemed to lack capacity to be overly dynamic. Abdullah was in ill health, having back operations in 2011 and 2012, and reportedly only able to work for a few hours a day in his final years. At times he made erratic decisions, such as suddenly turning down a much-coveted seat on the UNSC in 2014 in protest at US inaction in Syria. Yet all major foreign policy decisions went through the king. Ministries were fiefdoms held by leading royal family branches for decades: Abdullah's having the National Guard, Nayef's the Interior Ministry, Prince Saud bin Faisal the Foreign Ministry, Sultan having the Defence Ministry, until 2011 when it passed to Salman, and so on. Communication between ministries was often poor and policies lacked integration. Saudi Arabia had an extensive bureaucracy, but more for job creation than to produce innovative institutions.[80] So when the Syria crisis came round, decisions were made and implemented slowly and Saudi Arabia was lacking in knowledge and contacts. Indeed, as had been the case for Riyadh's ties with Yemen and Lebanon for decades, when the crisis broke Saudi leaders immediately turned to personal contacts and tribal ties in the absence of strong institutional relationships.[81]

Saudi Arabia takes charge

Despite its many interests in the Syrian conflict, for a long time Saudi Arabia delegated the international leadership of the opposition to Qatar and Turkey. This was partly a continuation of its traditional preference to lead from behind, but also due to distractions in its near abroad as well as Doha's superior capacity to act quickly. This actually frustrated some oppositionists who wanted greater Saudi Arabian involvement. At times during 2012, aside from formal conferences, Riyadh declined requests for meetings with SNC members who believed Saudi Arabia would be better than Qatar at persuading the US to send weapons to the rebels.[82] Saudi Arabia observers sympathetic to the government believe it always retained a 'veto right' over external relations with the opposition, yet that suggests more control than Saudi Arabia actually had and doesn't explain the evident dissatisfaction that prompted its 'takeover' in summer 2013.[83] It seems more likely that, like its misjudgement of Assad's fragility, Saudi leaders overestimated the opposition's strength and, on realising this was damaging its goals in Syria, eventually stepped in.

The first sign of a greater engagement came in July 2012 when Prince Bandar bin Sultan was appointed Director General of the Saudi Arabian Intelligence Agency, simultaneously taking over the 'Syria file' from Abdullah's son Abdulaziz. Saudi Arabia observers claim that Bandar, having been ambassador to the US from 1983 to 2005, persuaded Abdullah that he could successfully lobby the White House to play a more active role – although he was to find the Obama administration a very different beast to that of George W. Bush, his personal friend.[84] More surreptitiously, Bandar had played a key role channelling Saudi Arabian finance and support for the CIA's arming of mujahideen in Afghanistan in the 1980s, and was possibly brought in to explore similar clandestine operations in Syria.[85] Bandar gradually improved links with FSA fighters, built around his personal contacts, but soon saw the need for better ties between fighters on the ground and the political opposition.[86]

To this end Saudi Arabia had supported the Seif plan and acquiesced in Qatari dominance over the SOC immediately following the Doha conference. However, the MB continued to dominate and frustrate, as seen in the election of Hitto. The debacle over Khatib's resignation and the repeated failure for the SOC to create ties inside Syria frustrated the US too, which began to press Qatar to hand over leadership to Saudi Arabia. In early May 2013 a twelve–member delegation of the SOC visited Riyadh for the first time, where the Saudi Arabian leadership urged them to restructure the SOC leadership in order to dilute the MB and include more minorities, a particular American concern. Foreign Minister Saud bin Faisal also surprisingly met with Mahmoud Farouq Tayfour, the Syrian MB's Second Deputy, in a step towards improving ties and mollifying MB opposition.[87] Consequently, at the end of May the SOC spent a week holding stormy meetings in Istanbul and, on 31 May, eventually announced 54 new members (added to its previous 63) – almost all Saudi Arabia's allies. The FSA was given 15 seats, all to be chosen by Selim Idriss, the new chief of the FSA since

December 2012 and a Bandar ally. He also had effective veto over a further 14 seats representing 'the Revolutionary Movement' inside each of Syria's 14 governorates. Saudi Arabia ally Michel Kilo, a prominent Christian oppositionist, was also given 13 seats for his secular 'Democratic list' grouping. In contrast the SNC were given just three new seats.[88] There were suggestions that the MB-dominated General Assembly was strong-armed into agreement under pressure from Gulf and Western diplomats and a threat from Idriss to form a separate FSA political wing if the reforms were not made.[89]

The Istanbul meeting laid the groundwork for Saudi Arabia's takeover of the SOC, although this was not cemented until July 2013. Qatar found its position weakened, first by Emir Hamad's unexpected decision to abdicate in favour of his son, Tamim, on 25 June, and then by the deposing of Morsi in Egypt on 3 July. Days later, on 6 July, in Istanbul the reordered SOC membership elected a new pro-Saudi executive, replacing the temporary President, SNC leader George Sabra who had succeeded Khatib. The new President was Ahmed Jarba, a leader of the powerful Shammar tribe that stretches through Syria, Iraq and Saudi Arabia, connecting him to King Abdullah, whose mother was Shammar. Again this showed the importance of personal rather than institutional ties in Saudi Arabian foreign policy. Behind closed doors Jarba was nicknamed 'the man of Bandar bin Sultan', for his pro-Saudi leanings.[90] Interestingly, Tayfour was elected as vice president. However, rather than representing a shift in Saudi Arabia's relationship to the MB, this actually weakened Tayfour's stance within the MB as he boosted ties to non-MB Saudi Arabian allies in the Coalition. Qatar's ally Sabbagh lost his position as secretary general and then, on 8 July, Doha's other ally, Hitto, resigned as interim prime minister, to be replaced in September by the pro-Saudi Ahmad Tu'mah.

The reforms of summer 2013 were primarily driven by external factors and made the SOC little more effective as an opposition. Like the SNC before it, the new coalition had failed to win enough internal support from either activists or, as shall be seen in the following chapter, with fighters on the ground. Much of this was due to the failings of the opposition leaders themselves who, after decades of political repression by the Assad regime, were ill equipped for the task ahead. However, rather than assist and compensate for this gap in skill, external actors exacerbated and entrenched divisions. Western powers made high demands of the opposition, including that it be inclusive and democratic, but were unable or unwilling to offer the level of financial or logistical support provided by Saudi Arabia, Qatar and Turkey. This meant the latter played the dominant role even after Western capitals came to regret their earlier hands-off approach.

Yet the regional powers prioritised their own agendas ahead of helping to forge a united and effective opposition grouping. The Saudi Arabian–Qatari rivalry was particularly damaging, promoting factionalism in the SNC and contributing to the resignation of Moaz al-Khatib as leader of SOC, a popular figure who just might have been able to claw some credibility on the ground for the new coalition. Instead, the body eventually became dominated by figures loyal to Saudi Arabia, more united but unable to overcome its huge credibility gap to appear a realistic alternative to Assad, to either Syrians or external powers. The political opposition may have started with a bad hand, but their external allies made it worse, and all played their cards badly.

CHAPTER SIX

'Arm the rebels!' Backing the armed opposition

I am very much against excluding anyone at this stage, or bracketing them as terrorists, or bracketing them as al-Qaeda. What we are doing is only creating a sleeping monster, and this is wrong. We should bring them all together, we should treat them all equally, and we should work on them to change their ideology.

Khalid bin Mohammad al-Attiyah, Minister of State for Foreign Affairs for Qatar speaking about Syria's armed rebels in Manama, Bahrain, 8 December 2012[1]

The failures of foreign governments with the political opposition were nothing compared to their disastrous approach to the armed rebels. The results were more far reaching, helping to fuel the war's development, ensure its prolongation, and facilitate the successes of militant jihadist groups that would ultimately extend far beyond Syria. Iran and Russia's support for Assad's war were vital in this, and will be discussed in Chapter 7, but the external backers of the armed rebels share considerable responsibility. In different ways the key regional anti-Assad powers of Qatar, Saudi Arabia and Turkey came to actively support the armed rebellion within months of calling for the Syrian President's departure and eventually supplied a range of arms, finance and non-lethal assistance. Moreover, for a long time they did little to discourage private support for the rebels originating in their countries. These were audacious moves, given the limited capacity of each state. As discussed, despite their claims to the contrary, none had detailed knowledge of Syria. Nor were they experienced in supporting armed insurgencies in foreign countries. Saudi Arabia had financed fighters in Afghanistan in the 1980s, but logistics were primarily led by Pakistan and the CIA, while Qatar had recent experience supporting rebels in Libya, but the long-term success of that operation was far from clear. The willingness of such inexperienced governments to embrace the armed insurgency was initially based on two misjudgements. Firstly that Assad was close to collapse and that backing an armed rebellion would prompt his overthrow, and secondly that, as in Libya, the US was more likely to intervene if a viable military opposition was already on the ground.

However, despite a string of defections, Assad's military held together enough to retain a fighting capability and it started with vastly superior weaponry, including uncontested air power, before receiving greater material support from its allies. The two developments that might have tipped the balance – significant defections of whole military units with their equipment and Western aerial intervention (discussed in Chapter 8) – did not occur. Yet the regional powers were trapped by their previous policies and saw escalation as the only solution. However, each had a separate agenda within their desire to topple Assad, prompting them to back rival groups, exacerbating divisions among the rebels and facilitating the rise of jihadists. This further discouraged Western states which, though unwilling to launch direct military action, gradually backed a select set of rebels, albeit with deep ambivalence. The end result was a fractured rebel force that, despite some gains, proved unable to defeat the regime. This chapter examines the reasons behind this, looking first at the main rebel actors – the Free Syrian Army plus Islamist, Salafist, jihadist and Kurdish forces – and the role that outside forces played in shaping their character, exacerbating their divisions and contributing to their failure.

The Free Syrian Army

In the early months of the conflict, the 'Free Syrian Army' (FSA) became a byword for any armed rebel militia but the reality was more complex. On 29 July 2011 a group of recently defected Syrian army officers, led by a Colonel Riad al-Asaad, released a video clip filmed in Turkey declaring 'the formation of the Free Syrian Army to work hand in hand with the people to achieve freedom and dignity to bring this regime down'.[2] They called on soldiers, 'to stand on the side of the people and their revolution and abandon their military units'. Soon, various militias or *katibas* declared themselves part of the FSA. Defections that followed were frequently advertised via YouTube with soldiers and officers in their Syrian army uniform, holding their ID cards as verification, declaring their allegiance to the FSA. From late 2011 these videos usually featured the three red starred 'Istiqlal' flag, Syria's pre-Ba'ath flag of 1932–58 and 1961–63, which was incorporated into the FSA regalia.

However despite attempts to make the FSA appear a well-organised military with the goal of enticing more defections and foreign support, the reality was very different. Most *katibas* formed spontaneously to defend protesters in their area and, like the uprising itself, were highly localised. *Katibas* varied greatly. Some were highly idealistic, while others were based around former smuggling gangs and criminal elements. Some were centred on powerful individuals, local strongmen or new figures who had proven themselves as good leaders. Some merged into larger brigades with wider reach, mobility and better (often foreign) funding, while others remained highly concentrated companies, rarely straying beyond their locality.[3] In mid-2012, a US intelligence report noted that there were over a thousand different militias in Syria, while a year later the Carter Center identified 1,050 brigades and 3,250 smaller companies.[4] By way of contrast, at the height of Lebanon's fifteen-year civil war, the number of militias was in the thirties.

As with the formation of the political opposition, the decentralised origins of the *katibas* proved difficult to overcome and the kind of command and control enjoyed by successful insurgent groups such as the FLN or IRA was never achieved. One commentator drew a parallel with France's loosely structured wartime Resistance.[5] *Katibas* affiliated with the FSA expected it to secure much-needed weaponry from foreign sources and grew frustrated at its impotence, as they did with the SNC and later SOC for the same reason. The scarcity of arms and the wide range of *katibas* led to the formation of regional Military Councils to coordinate strategy and distribute weapons and funds, with mixed results.[6] A 'Higher Military Council' was then formed to nominally coordinate these bodies and in March 2012 the FSA merged with it. However, this was the FSA adapting to developments on the ground rather than leading the way as it hoped.

Other frustrations emerged. Defected soldiers were unimpressed by the poor military discipline of civilian militiamen, while idealistic (and often Islamist) *katibas* railed at the former's cautious military tactics.[7] As officers defected they expected to be given a comparable rank in their new militia, yet those who had been fighting Assad longer contested this. The rebels initially lacked strategy. While some fighters relied on conspiracy theory to explain Assad's survival, most commanders knew from the beginning that they could not defeat the regime without either massive military defections or Western military intervention, or both.[8] The absence of a Plan B, in case defections and intervention did not come, left the rebels exposed.

The myriad rebel forces enjoyed few successes until spring 2012, when two shifts helped. The first was an increase in weaponry after rebels captured more regime bases and their arsenals and as foreign allies established better distribution networks, especially after the opposition captured numerous border crossings.[9] The second was a new strategy after the defeat at Baba Amr, possibly encouraged by Turkish and Western intelligence. Rather than trying to capture large urban areas in the hope of provoking either a national uprising or international intervention, the regime's isolated rural military bases were targeted to lessen Assad's military grip on distant regions and create a 'liberated area'.[10] This proved remarkably successful and in summer 2012 the regime was forced to prioritise its resources. Following Iranian advice it retreated from rural areas in the east and north to concentrate on the more densely populated west and its strategically important gas fields.[11] For the first time the regime looked seriously shaken. In July the rebels launched their first major assaults on Damascus and Aleppo, and on 18 July a bomb, claimed by rebel forces (though this was subsequently contested) assassinated four top officials, including Assad's brother-in-law Assif Shawkat.[12]

However, sudden momentum couldn't paper over the rebels' weaknesses, exposed in the debacle over Aleppo. Syria's second city and commercial hub had been relatively passive for the first year of the uprising. Students at the university held protests that were sometimes met with force, but there was notable restraint by Aleppo's rulers compared with their equivalents in Homs or Deraa. Aleppo's sizeable middle class was broadly pro-regime, having thrived under Assad, and haughtily distrusted the local rebels, who mostly came from Aleppo's poor surrounding countryside. Having enjoyed success in the spring, these units swelled with confidence and, seemingly forgetting the lessons of Baba Amr, launched a sudden attempt to capture the city on 19 July.

In a sign of how uncoordinated the rebels were, the assault was launched by a militia, Liwa al-Tawheed (the Monotheism Brigade) that had only formed the day before. A collection of militia, some affiliated with the FSA and many with ties to the Muslim Brotherhood, created Tawheed specifically to 'liberate' Aleppo. The idea was to create a rebel-controlled corridor from Aleppo to the Turkish border, with the Bab al-Salameh border crossing also captured. Yet it attacked without coordinating with other groups. Presented with a fait accompli other rebels in Aleppo countryside and the Aleppo Military Council felt compelled to join, but the operation was beset by poor coordination and planning, stretched supply lines, ammunition shortages and even competition between the rebel groups.[13] The assault soon stalled and regime forces were reinforced. A stalemate emerged, with the regime entrenched in the city's wealthy west and the rebels finding succour in the poorer east. The Kurdish PYD militia took advantage of the chaos to capture Aleppo's handful of Kurdish districts. The poorly planned assault was disastrous for Aleppo, reducing much of the city centre to rubble and prompting a vicious war of attrition between the west and east that lasted for years. It also impacted the rebel cause more broadly, halting the growing momentum and exposing limitations.

Failures such as Aleppo highlighted the costs of rebel disunity. Major reorganisations came at the year's end under foreign pressure in conjunction with the creation of the SOC. On 7 December 2012, less than a month after the SOC was formed, up to 500 representatives of Syrian militia met in Antalya, Turkey, to elect a new thirty-man 'Supreme Military Command' (SMC) for the FSA. Colonel Asaad, who exercised little real authority, was retained as nominal head but true power was invested in the Chief of Staff, Selim Idriss. Idriss, a general in the regime's military until his relatively late defection in July 2012, was viewed as a better politician than Asaad, boasting close ties with Qatar and later Saudi Arabia. The SMC was designed to offer greater structure to the rebel groups, acting as a platform for coordination and to better channel foreign funds and weaponry. Indeed, representatives of US, French, British, Turkish, Jordanian, Saudi Arabian, Qatari and Emirati intelligence were all present in Antalya. However, as will be discussed, the role that external patrons had already played in bypassing formal structures had caused deep divisions that the SMC proved unable to surmount. Moreover, the rapid rise of radical Islamists on the ground, such as Ahrar al-Sham and Jabhat al-Nusra, neither of which were invited to Antalya, meant that FSA-SMC militia were already becoming marginalised.

Islamist, jihadist and Kurdish militias

The rise of the radical Islamists

The Islamist and jihadist presence within the armed rebellion was complex. The FSA was never explicitly secular and, despite a spine of laic nationalist former military figures in its leadership, boasted a large number of Islamist militias within its fold. This was unsurprising. Many of the rebels were already pious Sunnis and the life and death experience of combat further increased religiosity. Moreover, the search for external funds and weaponry offered further incentives to adopt Islamist identities. 'Islamism' is a vague term and does not adequately describe the range of militias inspired by religion. On the one hand, some groups' Islamism stretched no further than image: they were Islamic in appearance and name only; while others were fighting for the establishment of theocratic rule. Many militias were fluid in their composition and professed ideology, made easier by their local and personalised nature. Whole *katibas* might suddenly change identity. The loyalty of fighters also proved changeable: sometimes due to individual radicalisation, sometimes because they were drawn to more successful, better armed and better financed groups. However, while there was an Islamist presence from the start, its influence and power grew substantially as the conflict progressed. By mid-2012 only half of the active militias had sworn allegiance to the FSA, and by the end of that year many disillusioned former FSA brigades had broken off to form independent bodies, mostly with an Islamist bent.[14] By mid-2013 radicals who rejected the FSA controlled large swathes of Syrian territory. Who were the radical Islamists and why did they eclipse the FSA?

Given the national and regional context in which the Syrian civil war broke out it was unsurprising that Islamism emerged as a powerful force. Nationally, like Arabs elsewhere, Syrian Sunnis had become increasingly pious since the 1980s and the Assad regime had encouraged greater social religiosity permitting several formally banned preachers and organisations to return. Joshua Landis argues that under Assad religious education was paradoxically structured to undermine the regime's officially espoused secularism by promoting a sense of Sunni superiority.[15] This in no way guaranteed that all pious Sunnis would turn on Assad, indeed several Sunni groups such as the women's social organisation the Qubaysiat remained publicly loyal, but it did mean that many of the disaffected would be more receptive to Islamist groups. Regionally, as described in Chapter 1, the 2003 Iraq war had greatly boosted jihadists in the Arab world. Militarily, jihadists from Iraq crossed into Syria once war began and, due to the Assad regime's previous collaboration, already had established networks with Syrians.[16] Ideologically, it revived the appeal, first promoted in Afghanistan in the 1980s, of foreigners travelling to wage transnational jihad, making it less difficult for ideologues to switch destinations from Iraq to Syria. The rise of violent sectarianism in Iraq also helped reinforce the pre-existing narrative of regional Sunni oppression for radicals to tap into. The capture of four border posts by rebels in summer 2012 made it easier for foreigners to enter Syria and by late 2015 over 30,000 had come to fight jihad, swelling the numbers of the radicals.[17]

Some authors such as Christian Chesnot and Georges Malbrunot argue that radicals were present in the rebellion from very early on, but were deliberately erased from view by journalists and politicians sympathetic to the anti-Assad camp. Radical clerics such as Ibn Abdallah al-Hosni urged sectarian violence as early as August 2011, while sectarian chanting was reportedly heard in Homs and Banias protests in spring 2011.[18] Hassan Hassan and Michael Weiss argue that the Assad regime deliberately sought to radicalise an instinctively moderate opposition. After the uprising began Assad claimed that he was the only alternative to jihadism, telling the *Sunday Telegraph*, 'Do you want to see another Afghanistan, or tens of Afghanistans?'[19] Hassan and Weiss cite numerous regime machinations to achieve this. Sunnis were verbally, psychologically and corporally abused, with Shabiha purposely mocking Sunni belief with slogans such as 'There is no God but Bashar'. Moreover, much-vaunted amnesties were cynically used to release radical Islamists – including Hassan Abboud (founder of Ahrar al-Sham), Zahran Alloush (founder of Jaysh al-Islam) and Ahmad Issa al-Sheikh (founder of Suqour al-Sham) – so that they might radicalise the opposition.[20] The extent of regime collusion with jihadists will be discussed in more depth in Chapter 9, but at the minimum the regime was content to see the opposition radicalise.

Two other factors explain the success of the Islamists. Firstly were the failures of the FSA. Along with their inability to acquire adequate foreign weaponry, foreign intervention or sufficient progress on the battlefield, more ideologically moderate *katibas* sullied their reputations by excessive looting. Following capture of territory, local populations and many militiamen were appalled at the blatant warlordism of some rebel groups, with some reports of whole factories in north and eastern Aleppo being disassembled and sold off to Turkish businesses. This increased the appeal of radicals, who boasted superior discipline. The final factor, discussed in depth below, was the role of foreign actors in promoting radicals, whether by swelling their numbers from abroad, providing finance, weapons or ideological legitimacy – all of which dwarfed that provided to the more moderate *katibas*.

Many ideologies: Key Islamist militias

As the number and power of Islamist and jihadist militia grew, outside observers struggled to make sense of their varying ideologies. Islamism has many variants, the full range of which seemed to have some presence in Syria. However, ideological affinity did not always translate into alliance on the ground, with personal animosities and different external sponsors often obstructing cooperation. While there was fluidity, broadly there were three different strands of Islamist: moderate, Salafist and jihadist.

'Moderate' is a very subjective term and is here used to describe the broad group less radical than either the Salafists or jihadists. These ranged from those advocating social conservatism but a separation of religion and politics, such as Kata'ib al Farouq (The Farouq Brigades, named after the second caliph, Umar), to those calling for religious rule, but governed by civilians and protective of minorities, such as Tawheed.[21] Many of these groups, including both Tawheed and Farouq, found a natural ideological partner early on in the conflict in the Muslim Brotherhood (MB), who supported them financially via the military committee of the SNC. Similarly many either fought directly for the FSA–SMC or at least recognised its leadership. In September 2012 Tawheed and Farouq, who for a while were among the most powerful militias, helped form the Syrian Islamic Liberation Front (SILF), a loose alliance of mostly moderate *katibas* (though including Ahmad Issa al-Sheikh's Salafist Suqour al-Sham, indicating that ideological affinity did not always direct alliance formations), which fought for the FSA–SMC. These groups either radicalised or lost popularity over time and in November 2013 both Tawheed and Suqour left the SILF to join the newly formed Salafist-dominated Islamic Front alliance. Meanwhile the once powerful Farouq splintered and declined.[22]

Salafism as an ideology within Islamism is ultra conservative, taking its name from 'the pious forefathers' (*salaf as-salih*), Prophet Muhammad and his early followers, whose lives they wish to emulate. Unlike the moderates, all of Syria's Salafist militia were committed to establishing a religious state in Syria and frequently used the language of jihad. However, unlike jihadists, they confined their ambitions to Syria and did not profess transnational goals. Among the most successful was Ahrar al-Sham.[23] It was led by Hassan Abboud, who had been imprisoned for fighting in Iraq, and then conspicuously released from the notorious Sednaya prison by the regime in 2011.[24] Originating in Idlib, Ahrar absorbed several Islamist militias across northern Syria, earning a reputation for discipline, lack of looting, and military effectiveness. Having not been invited to the FSA–SMC formation, Ahrar refused to recognise its authority.[25] Instead it formed the Syrian Islamic Front (SIF) along with several other Salafists (though also with the FSA affiliate Liwa al-Haqq [The Truth Brigade] once again showing the blurred nature of ideological alliances). The SIF, which was a social as well as a military organisation, was initially willing to fight alongside both FSA–SMC militia and jihadists, notably Jabhat al-Nusra.[26] However, in November 2013 it voluntarily dissolved itself to form the Islamic Front, which refused to invite Nusra and ISIS but did welcome 'brothers who supported us in jihad' in its charter.[27]

Though most Islamists claimed to be waging 'jihad' against Assad, two groups – Nusra and ISIS – are here labelled 'jihadists' for their pursuit of a global jihad beyond Syria and association with al-Qaeda. Jabhat al-Nusra li-ahli ash-Sham (The Support Front for the People of Greater Syria) announced its formation in January 2012 but had older roots. In late summer 2011 Islamic State in Iraq (ISI), the descendant of al-Qaeda in Iraq (AQI), sent a small group into Syria. They were led by Abu-Mohammad al-Jolani, a Syrian jihadist who had previously been imprisoned by US forces in Camp Bucca in Iraq.[28] In Syria, Jolani spent months building a jihadist network that would eventually form Nusra, which ISI would partly fund, the rest coming from pre-existing al-Qaeda private donors from the Gulf.[29] However, Jolani hid his al-Qaeda ties and presented Nusra as an organic, Syrian group. The group launched several bombing attacks followed by successful armed assaults on regime positions. Jihadism expert Charles Lister argues that a string of Nusra victories from summer 2012 to March 2013 transformed it into one of the most powerful insurgent groups.[30] In March 2013, in alliance with Ahrar, they captured the eastern city of Raqqa, the first provincial capital to fall to the rebels. Many in the opposition believed them to be an Islamist militia like any other and, when the US designated Nusra a terrorist organisation on 11 December 2012 (its officials claiming to have known it was al-Qaeda from day one) opposition-ists protested.[31] The truth only emerged in April 2013 when the leader of ISI, Abu Bakr al-Baghdadi claimed that Nusra had formed on his orders and would now be merging with his own organisation to form the Islamic State of Iraq and al-Sham (ISIS). Jolani, unwilling to subordinate himself, denied the merger yet did reveal his identity for the first time by pledging allegiance to al-Qaeda leader Ayman al-Zawahiri. This paved the way for a major split between Nusra and ISIS, eventually leading to violent clashes between the two groups and ISIS' capture of Raqqa. In a sign of the radi-calisation of the rebellion, even after Nusra's declared al-Qaeda affiliation, most rebels fought alongside it at some point.[32]

Kurdish militias

As Syria's various Arab rebels took shape, Kurdish leaders tried to keep the war away from Kurdish areas. Yet they remained divided between the Kurdish National Council (KNC) and the PKK-aligned Democratic Union Party (Partiya Yekîtiya Demokrat – PYD). As Syria's uprising devolved into a civil war, the PYD was quick to declare its own militia, the People's Protection Units (Yekîneyên Parastina Gel – YPG), which commanders subsequently said had existed since 2004.[33] The YPG, well trained and armed with PKK assistance, gave the PYD a massive advantage over the KNC, many of whose members remained committed to non-violence. Indeed, the spectre of intra-Kurdish violence was raised in May–June 2012 when YPG forces clashed with KNC irregulars.[34]

The PYD actually came to dominate without needing to violently chal-lenge the KNC. As Assad's forces withdrew from much of eastern and northern Syria in the summer of 2012, the YPG quickly filled the vacuum in Kurdish areas and by 29 July claimed it had 'liberated' Kobane, Afrin and eight other towns, along with the Kurdish-dominated Ashrafieh and Sheikh

Maqsoud districts of Aleppo.[35] The rapidity of the takeover prompted the KNC's external patron, Massoud Barzani, to broker the Erbil Agreement in July between Syria's two Kurdish factions. The PYD agreed to jointly administer the liberated areas with the KNC, but in reality it entrenched control, erecting its own checkpoints, establishing local councils, distributing food and fuel and often refusing entry to KNC fighters. An attempt by Barzani to salvage the Erbil Agreement in September 2012 did little to halt this trend. By February 2013, the PYD claimed to be in control of 80 per cent of Syria's three Kurdish regions and in November it declared that Afrin, Kobane and Jazeera, were now cantons in 'Rojava' (Rojavayê Kurdistanê – Western Kurdistan) an autonomous region of Syria. The KNC, thoroughly outflanked and now based in northern Iraq, voted a month later to cease its recognition of the joint council agreed in July 2012.[36]

The triumph of the PYD on the ground added another layer of division to Syria's rebellion. While the KNC were eventually more receptive to the SNC and the FSA, partly due to the efforts of Barzani who was close to both Turkey and the US, the PYD was hostile. The historical ties between the PKK and Assad, along with the fact that the regime withdrew unchallenged from Kurdish areas and continued to provide services in PYD-held areas led many in the FSA to claim the PYD was collaborating with Damascus.[37] The PYD retorted that its enemy, Turkey, controlled the FSA. After the YPG units captured Afrin and Kobane the SNC demanded they be handed over to the FSA, a demand that, unsurprisingly, was refused. In October 2012 violent clashes erupted between FSA and YPG forces in Aleppo when FSA militias pushed into Ashrafieh despite pledging not to. The YPG clashed with Nusra in Ras al-Ayn the following month.[38] Truces were soon brokered (via the FSA) and for much of 2012–13 there was a degree of coexistence.[39] However, the continued rise of the jihadists brought the PYD back into conflict with the Arab rebels, as groups such as Nusra and ISIS sought to expand into Kurdish areas and the PYD sought to consolidate and expand Rojava. On 16 July 2013 the YPG attacked and defeated Nusra units in Ras al-Ayn, on the Turkish border between Jazeera and Kobane, initiating a new Kurdish–jihadist conflict within the Syrian civil war.

Foreign hands intervene

The remainder of this chapter will focus on the various ways in which foreign actors contributed to the division, radicalisation and failures described above. Initially, the most important players were Saudi Arabia, Qatar and Turkey, although private donors were also key, as was the West's ambivalence.

Before this, Qatar's view of the Syria crisis will be considered, completing the regional trio, given that Turkey and Saudi Arabia were profiled in Chapters 3 and 5 respectively.

Qatar's war of choice

Qatar was in the forefront of early international efforts to back the armed rebels, in parallel with its leading role with the political opposition. In January 2012, Emir Hamad became the first major leader to call for military intervention against Assad, and the following month Hamad bin Jassim al-Thani (HBJ) publicly advocated an Arab League force to create humanitarian corridors.[40] Qatar was not alone, but Doha proved itself both more effective and less cautious than others, notably Riyadh, and consequently shaped the early stages of the conflict more than any other anti-Assad state. However, more than other powers, Qatar's military involvement was a war of choice: no security or ideational threats came from the conflict like those concerning Turkey and Saudi Arabia. While Qatar's leaders insisted they were motivated by humanitarian concerns, these were largely peripheral compared to the personal grudges and opportunism that lay at the heart of Doha's activism.[41]

Like Turkey, Qatar had invested political and financial capital in Assad and its leaders were affronted that this delivered little influence. Sheikh Tamim was cold-shouldered when he visited Damascus to counsel restraint in spring 2011, while his sister's emails urging her friend Asma al-Assad to persuade her husband to flee were ignored.[42] Yet at the same time Qatar's friendship proved to be conditional, as its small decision-making circle opportunistically adapted to the new regional environment created by the Arab Spring. The campaign in Libya, in which Qatar had led international support against Gaddafi, had swelled Doha's sense of regional influence – boosting its popularity across the Arab world and among Western leaders. Insiders speak of a sense of triumphalism in Doha after the fall of Gaddafi and an increased belief from Hamad that something similar could be achieved in Syria.[43]

But Doha made a series of miscalculations. Firstly, Hamad overestimated Western willingness to repeat its Libya intervention in Syria and Doha's ability to persuade them. Like other Gulf States, Qatar had invested heavily in Western economies after the 2008 economic crash and enjoyed a close defence relationship with the US, which based its regional air force at Qatar's Al-Udeid base, France, which provided 80 per cent of Qatar's weaponry, and Britain, which trained its special forces.[44] After leading Arab support for UN1973, Western leaders were vocal in their praise, inflating Doha's sense of influence.[45] Yet while Qatar's leadership convinced itself Syria would be as straightforward as Libya, Western leaders, especially Obama, recognised the complexities.

This was a second Qatari error: overestimating its understanding of Syria – something it shared with the US and most other regional players. Qatar lacked the foreign policy and intelligence infrastructure to gauge events on the ground or who the key players were. Instead Doha relied heavily on individuals with political biases: the Muslim Brotherhood, Syrian expatriates living in Qatar and a collection of foreign policy experts.[46] These advisers reinforced Hamad and HBJ's belief that events in Egypt, Tunisia and Libya pointed to the inevitable region-wide rise of populist Islamists like the MB, breeding overconfidence. Along with frustration at Western inaction, this likely accelerated Doha's shift towards increasingly unilateral and arbitrary activities after its presidency of the Arab League ended in March 2012.

A third, related, misjudgement was assuming Qatar had the capacity to successfully sponsor the rebels. Its only experience of proxy warfare was Libya, a war that concluded just months before the first Qatari funds began to arrive in Syria. Subsequent events would show that the intervention against Gaddafi was not as successful as first assumed, with Libya descending into civil war. Had this been known before, perhaps Doha would have been more cautious in Syria. Yet a feature of Qatari foreign policy was its lack of coherent political strategy.[47] Qatar's 2003 constitution shows this incomprehension, declaring,

> The foreign policy of the State is based on the principle of maintaining international peace and security by encouraging the settlement of international disputes by peaceful means, and supporting the people's right to self-determination and non-interference in internal affairs of the State.[48]

It glosses over the fact that 'supporting the people's right to self-determination' can often run counter to the principle of 'non-interference in internal affairs of the State'. More favourable analysts explain Qatar's contradictions as the pursuit of 'omni-balancing': trying to manage multiple opportunities and threats at once. However, while that may have been the case prior to 2011, after the Arab Spring, and particularly in Syria, its behaviour seemed more impulsive than planned or strategised.[49]

Doha thus approached Syria confident it could have a positive impact, but lacking the knowledge and capacity to deliver. The result was a scattergun approach to the armed rebels, with support distributed liberally. Not only would this greatly impact the unity, effectiveness and ideology of the rebels, it would come back to haunt Doha as it found its reputation tarnished.

Backing the rebels

Qatar joined other governments in supporting the rebels with three key commodities: arms, money and non-lethal aid. Facing a fully equipped army, the rebels were in serious need of weaponry, but it is uncertain exactly when arms were first sent via foreign regimes. Initially, FSA spokesmen insisted their arms came from captured regime arsenals and sympathetic Syrian exiles. Yet they pleaded for more and in March 2012 Colonel Asaad criticised foreign governments that had pledged assistance but been slow to deliver.[50] In time the foreign supply network grew, and by mid-2012 rebel fighters claimed that 15 per cent of their weaponry came from foreign sources.[51] In November 2011 *The Telegraph* reported secret talks between Syrian rebels and Libya's new government about the latter sending arms.[52] Similarly in February 2012 *The Independent* interviewed a rebel fighter who had travelled to Libya to acquire arms, though he refused to say where they were from.[53] Given the lack of historical ties between Syria and Libya, and the closeness of Qatar to the new Libyan government, many claimed these connections were facilitated by Doha, especially after Qatar's closest Libyan rebel ally, Abdelhakim Belhadj, travelled to the Syrian–Turkish border to meet with FSA leaders in November 2011.[54] In March 2012 it emerged that Qatar had made a $100 million 'donation' to the Syrian opposition via Tripoli.[55] At the same time, in February 2012 Saudi Arabia was reportedly using tribal allies in Iraq and Lebanon to send weapons on an ad hoc basis.

As the civil war escalated, the weapons supply networks from regional governments expanded. Turkey became the main route, although some also flowed through Iraq, northern Lebanon and later Jordan. A 2014 UN report investigating arms transfers from Libya noted that weapons came by air to Gaziantep, Ankara and Antakya and by sea to Mersin and Iskenderun before being taken by truck over the border.[56] Syrian oppositionists and foreign representatives based in Turkey claimed considerable Turkish complicity, though Turkish authorities repeatedly denied involvement.[57] However, several Western officials stated that as early as summer 2012 MİT (Milli İstihbarat Teşkilatı), Turkey's intelligence service, was organising the distribution of weapons purchased by Qatar and Saudi Arabia to approved armed groups.[58] The UN report noted that multiple sources, including Libyan officials and foreign agents based in Libya, alleged that Qatar was arranging military materiel to be flown from Libya to Qatar and then to Turkey. When cargo details for several flights between Libya, Qatar and Turkey were requested, Doha refused.[59] Saudi Arabia was slower to expand beyond limited deliveries via tribal contacts, but in December 2012 Riyadh reportedly arranged a large arms transfer of 'thousands of rifles and hundreds of machine guns' plus ammunition from Croatia to FSA forces in southern Syria.[60]

Money was a second vital form of foreign support. Though arms supplied directly by foreign governments increased, most were purchased by rebels via black market arms suppliers. Syria's neighbours in Iraq, Lebanon and Turkey already had ample weaponry from their own wars to sell, but new networks responded to the increased demand. Northern Lebanon, which had a weak central government and a large number of Sunni Arabs sympathetic to the rebels, was an early source. Turkey soon eclipsed it and Ankara likely turned a blind eye to increased smuggling. Financial support helped rebels in other ways. Militias were expected to pay their fighters, who had to support their families. Similarly, they needed to win local support by providing aid and services. Unsurprisingly, wealthy Qatar and Saudi Arabia, in public at least, surpassed other state donors, announcing numerous schemes to fund the FSA such as $100 million to pay soldiers' salaries in April 2012. The non-FSA-aligned SIF, meanwhile, claimed to receive aid from the Qatar Charity and Turkey's İHH, both NGOs reportedly close to the Doha and Ankara governments.[61] The true extent of foreign donations, however, remains unknown. Moreover, as discussed in Chapter 5, public declarations did not always translate into deliveries.

The third key area of foreign support to the rebels was non-lethal assistance. Uniforms, medical supplies and communication equipment were provided by a range of foreign supporters, but 'non-lethal equipment' also included war materiel essential to fight. Vehicles in particular were key, with 4x4 pick-up trucks much sought after as welding a heavy machine gun on to the back could easily weaponise them. Doha reportedly flew several batches of Land Cruiser pickups to Turkey for the rebels.[62] As well as equipment, assistance included providing a base of operations. Both Turkey and, to a lesser extent, Jordan provided a hinterland for rebel fighters to retreat to where they could recuperate and plan. As the conflict progressed, command rooms with representatives from the FSA and numerous foreign forces were created in Istanbul, Ankara and Amman to plan, direct and coordinate rebel activity.[63] Out of range of Assad's forces, these were essential to keep the war going, especially early on. Finally, foreign governments provided training and strategic guidance.

Which rebels?

However, this range of support was neither well-coordinated among donor states nor directed exclusively to one set of rebels. Indeed, despite sharing the goal of toppling Assad and backing the FSA (later the FSA–SMC) as the principal armed opposition grouping, the three major regional powers of Qatar, Saudi Arabia and Turkey simultaneously pursued independent approaches, which undermined attempts to achieve that goal.[64] As with the political opposition, Qatar was the most active until late 2012. US officials admit they were impressed by how quickly Qatar built distribution networks. However, they also criticised its scattergun approach: using multiple routes to support multiple groups. One was to support the FSA and FSA–SMC publicly and financially. Another was via its ally the Muslim Brotherhood, supporting their favoured militias such as Tawheed and Farouq, even if their goals were not always fully aligned with the FSA as seen in Tawheed's assault on Aleppo. A third was support for more radical groups. While Saudi Arabia and the West expressed concern early about the rise of jihadists, Qatar was less cautious. In December 2012, Dr Khalid bin Mohammad al Attiyah, Doha's Minister of State for Foreign Affairs at the time and 'point man' on Syria, stated, 'I am very much against excluding anyone at this stage, or bracketing them as terrorists, or bracketing them as al-Qaeda', and that 'we should work on them to change their ideology'.[65] Whether this was naïvety or an attempt to present Qatar's policy in language acceptable to its allies is unclear. Either way, several accounts suggest that Qatar supported Ahrar and even Nusra fighters. This reflected Qatar's lack of capacity. Qatar's resort to informal networks such as the MB, because of the limits of its own intelligence capability, meant that it found it hard subsequently to control its proxies.[66]

Saudi Arabia was initially more conservative yet still undermined the unity of the armed rebellion. As with the political opposition, Riyadh stepped up its engagement only in late 2012. More than Qatar it appeared ostensibly committed to the FSA, and channelled support to its militia. Indeed, given Riyadh's fear of jihadists, the FSA appealed due to its perceived make-up of defected soldiers who Saudi Arabia assumed would be more secular-minded.[67] Yet it frequently ignored the formal structures of the FSA, also preferring informal, tribal and personal relationships, such as those with links to Prince Bandar. For most of 2012, and possibly before, Saudi Arabia's liaison with the rebels was Okab Sakr, a Lebanese politician. Sakr was present in the Istanbul command room pushing Riyadh's agenda among the rebels, but reportedly only working with groups that Saudi Arabia approved of – not the MB.[68] However, Saudi Arabia also lacked intelligence capacity and often relied on local middlemen, sometimes of questionable loyalty and ability, meaning that arms often found their way to unintended destinations.[69] As one US official noted, Saudi Arabia didn't know how to do proxy warfare. The CIA reportedly had to help them arrange the Croatian arms delivery in late 2012.[70]

Saudi Arabia's animosity to what it saw as Qatar and the MB's regional agenda prompted it to favour not just certain groups but even battlefield arenas, stretching rebel resources rather than concentrating them on a single front. With Qatar and Turkey dominating the north, Saudi Arabia favoured attacking Assad in the south via Jordan. The Houran region around Deraa was closer to Damascus but was also tribal and shared family ties with northern Jordan, both of which appealed to Saudi Arabia. Indeed the Croatian arms were channelled to Hourani FSA. Jordan was far stricter than Turkey in monitoring fighters over its borders, meaning, on the one hand, that fewer radicals emerged, but it was also more difficult for sufficient weapons and support to reach the southern front.[71] Saudi Arabia eventually became involved further north too, as it sought to displace Qatar as the principal Arab supporter of the opposition in 2013. Hassan Hassan noted that the failed Battle of Qusayr in mid-2013 saw previously Qatari-aligned groups such as Tawheed following Saudi Arabian instruction for the first time.[72]

Although it allowed Syrian fighters to use its territory and facilitated Qatari and Saudi Arabia flows of support, Turkey was slower to build contacts with rebel groups. Western diplomats based in Ankara, possibly shielding their ally, suggested that Turkish involvement had increased initially as a means to better control what the Gulf states were doing.[73] Yet by mid-2012 Turkish intelligence (MİT) was actively involved, reportedly playing a major role both in the formation of Tawheed and in its assault on Aleppo.[74] Again, despite its formal support, Turkey undermined the FSA by bypassing its central structures. Like Qatar, Ankara favoured groups aligned with the MB, although as the conflict progressed and Turkey grew frustrated it became more willing to work with others that successfully fought Assad. Hakan Fidan, head of MİT and a loyal Erdoğan follower, took the lead in diversifying sponsorship, with many Turkish news outlets claiming increased closeness to Ahrar and even Nusra after 2013.[75] Yet Turkey was no more experienced at proxy warfare than Riyadh or Doha, and still favoured its own agenda over forging a united front. As one Turkish official later admitted, 'the rebels lacked strategy and they were open to outside suggestion, but everyone, including Turkey, was telling them something, often different things. We just weren't coordinated enough.'[76]

Competition, sectarianism and radicalisation

Alongside regional governments, a key source of foreign rebel support came from private donations by individuals and charities, especially from the Gulf and Libya. Public fundraising drives by organisations such as the

Popular Commission to Support the Syrian People (PCSSP), supported by the wealthy Kuwaiti Ajmi family, raised hundreds of millions of dollars. It was then dispatched via a complex distribution network of traditional *hawala* moneylenders and bags of cash crossing by boat to Turkey then Syria.[77] These funds were often sent to the more radical militias, such as Ahrar, which in 2012 publicly thanked the PCSSP for sending $400,000.[78] In Saudi Arabia, prominent Sahwa sheikhs such as Muhammad al-Arafi channelled funds towards the Syrian Islamic Liberation Front (SILF).[79] Social media was widely used by religious figures and politicians to raise money. Some such 'drivers' would explicitly note what the funds would buy, such as $800 for a rocket-propelled grenade.[80] The extent of government complicity in this is open to debate. Kuwait, which lacked any coherent anti-terror finance law until summer 2013, consequently emerged as the clearing house for most donations, although donors came from all over the Gulf Cooperation Council (GCC).[81] When it surfaced that some were making their way to radical groups in 2012, Saudi Arabia and Qatar clamped down on such activities at home but claimed it was difficult to prevent transfers to Kuwait, given how integrated their economies were and how many families overlap. However, they would likely have clamped down much harder had donors been sending money to Assad rather than the opposition. The fact that the funds flowed for so long suggests a degree of complicity.

Private donors combined with governments contributed to the growth of openly sectarian Syrian fighters. Reacting to the seemingly anti-Sunni war being waged by Assad, many fundraising groups and clerics were overtly sectarian, and favoured groups such as Ahrar that were explicitly anti-Shia and anti-Alawi. This dovetailed with the sectarian tone of some media outlets, religious sermons and social media. Although not quite at the level of ethnic hatred espoused by Radio Télévision Libre des Mille Collines that helped fuel the Rwandan genocide of 1994, some figures such as Adnan al-Arour on Saudi-owned station al-Wesal stirred up sectarianism, threatening to 'grind the flesh' of pro-regime Alawites.[82] Similarly al-Jazeera's resident Muslim Brotherhood firebrand, Yusuf al-Qaradawi, for example, went from advocating Shia–Sunni reconciliation before 2011, to ranting against Hezbollah and Iran in 2013. He stated, 'The leader of the party of the Satan [Hezbollah] comes to fight the Sunnis . . . Now we know what the Iranians want . . . They want continued massacres to kill Sunnis.'[83] A perceived shift in al-Jazeera's tone towards a more propagandistic endorsement of Qatar's regional policy prompted a wave of resignations from the channel after 2011.[84] Saudi Arabian media similarly adopted a consistent anti-Assad and anti-Iranian line. At home, many Saudi Arabian clerics were vocally anti-Alawite, anti-Shia and sectarian in their preaching about Syria.[85] This helped amplify the Shia threat of Saudi Arabia's regional rival Iran to ordinary Sunnis, and seemed to enhance Saudi Arabia's self-proclaimed position as guardian of the Sunnis. Of course, this message reached far beyond Saudi Arabia and Qatar's borders, persuading wealthier Gulf individuals and charities to fund sectarian militia and encouraging jihadists from other states to head to Syria to fight.[86] By December 2013, up to 11,000 people from more than seventy countries were fighting for the rebels; by late 2015 it was above 30,000.[87]

These private funds alongside the fluid support of governments divided the rebels further by promoting competition rather than collaboration. *Katibas* desperate for arms outbid one another to obtain the foreign support that would keep them in the field and prevent their soldiers from defecting to better-funded groups. The hunt for support prompted rebels to squabble in Kuwaiti *diwaniyas* (private gatherings) over who was more deserving of funding, and encouraged them to boost their media profile via YouTube in the belief that the more sensational their acts, the more support they would gain irrespective of their strategic importance.[88] Many authors claim this contributed to the radicalisation of the rebels as they adopted Islamic dress, names and practices in attempts to woo the support of conservative Gulf charities.[89] Emile Hokayem notes that 'Several groups have a multitude of funders and change identity accordingly.'[90] Yet fighters were far from passive and often cynically played different funders off against one another in the search for support. However, in a climate where external backers favoured Islamist and sectarian groups and one that structurally favoured competition over unity, it is unsurprising that the general trend saw the Islamists, Salafists and jihadists dominate.

Armed rebellion: Western ambivalence

The US, Britain and France were more ambivalent towards the armed rebellion. While they wanted to see Assad toppled and backed the political opposition, from the beginning there were doubts about the armed rebels. Firstly, reflecting the US' unwillingness to directly intervene (discussed in Chapter 8), Western leaders did not believe that the civil war could end militarily, hence their (albeit uncompromising) support for the Annan plan and the Geneva communiqué. Any support for the rebels would at minimum be a means to protect civilians from Assad's slaughter, and at most a way of pressuring the regime into negotiating a transition, but, as Robert Ford noted, 'the purpose was not to have a military parade down the streets of Damascus.'[91] Secondly, as with the political opposition, in 2011 Western intelligence services had little experience of Syria and did not know who the rebel fighters were, meaning they had to build relationships from scratch.[92] While Turkey, Qatar and Saudi Arabia all assumed that their limited contacts within Syria were sufficient, Western leaders, cautious about the prospect of weapons falling into the hands of extremists, were more reserved.

Yet despite this caution they endorsed the regional powers' support for the rebels. Western intelligence knew of regional arms transfers and financial support and, while they urged coordination, there were few efforts to stop them. Indeed, Clinton effectively gave the green light, admitting in her memoirs that at a meeting in Riyadh in March 2012 she acknowledged what was already happening: 'certain countries would increase their efforts to funnel arms, while others [i.e. the US] would focus on humanitarian needs'.[93] Yet far from standing by, the CIA and other Western intelligence services allegedly facilitated many of these operations.[94] From spring 2012 CIA operatives were reported in southern Turkey helping to coordinate the distribution of arms, while some Western officials claim they were active as early as late 2011.[95] Likewise the CIA reportedly encouraged the command centres in Istanbul, Ankara and Amman and Western intelligence officials were present. The logic was to monitor the distribution of arms. However, given the perceived American power in the region, this will also have appeared an endorsement by Western leaders of the rebels, and raised expectations that further support was coming.

As the conflict escalated and political solutions like the Annan plan made little headway, rebel calls for Western assistance grew, as did their supporters. In July 2012 Hillary Clinton developed a plan with then CIA director David Petraeus to vet, train and equip a force of moderate Syrian rebels who 'could be trusted with American weapons'.[96] Though she recognised the risk and that such efforts had struggled in Afghanistan and Iraq, she argued it was the 'least bad option', hoping it would give a psychological boost to the rebels, deter Assad's backers, placate America's frustrated regional allies and allow the US to better shape events in Syria, diminishing the role of radicals.[97] Having discussed the idea with Turkey, and secured approval from France, Britain and Germany, Clinton and Petraeus presented the plan to Obama in August. According to Clinton, Obama asked many questions, including whether there were examples of the US having successfully armed an insurgency in the past, conscious that backing the mujahideen in Afghanistan in the 1980s had spawned al-Qaeda. He also noted that the numbers suggested in the plan, which explicitly excluded the rebels' demand for anti-aircraft weaponry, were insufficient to tip the balance against Assad. A debate ensued within the administration with Defense

Secretary Leon Panetta and the usually cautious Joint Chief of Staff Martin Dempsey, later telling Congress they supported the plan. Others, such as Ben Rhodes, remained unconvinced that weapons wouldn't end up in extremists' hands and warned that this might suck the US into another Middle Eastern quagmire. Ultimately Obama opted to continue with the current policy of caution. The plans were revisited that October, but again rejected and shelved.[98]

Yet as was the pattern, as the conflict worsened, Western leaders felt compelled on their 'escalator of pressure' to do more. Having promised logistical support to the rebels in May 2012, the US increased this to medical aid and food in February 2013 and $123 million worth of non-lethal battlefield equipment like body armour in April.[99] Similarly Britain and France increased their non-lethal aid, with London supplying £20 million worth by the end of 2013.[100] In May 2013 the two states controversially forced the EU to end its two-year embargo on sending arms to Syria, despite the opposition of all twenty-five other EU members. Domestic developments, discussed in Chapter 8, prevented Britain from then sending arms, although officials interviewed believe the embargo was lifted with this in mind.[101] The US, meanwhile, announced on 13 June that it would be sending arms to the rebels after all, following allegations that Assad had utilised chemical weapons. However, this CIA programme, 'Timber Sycamore', proved to be limited, with handfuls of vetted Syrians trained by the US' Saudi Arabian and Jordanian allies.[102] Ultimately the number deemed trustworthy was far fewer than the growing powers of Ahrar, Nusra and ISIS, and proved unable to compete.

Many of Obama's critics have subsequently argued that he made a major error by rejecting the Clinton–Petraeus plan and should have armed the rebels sooner.[103] These critics echo Clinton's original arguments: that Western arms to the rebels would have firstly deterred Assad and his allies and forced him to compromise, and secondly boosted moderate forces to the detriment of the radicals. Yet, as Obama saw at the time, these arguments are dubious. A CIA review commissioned by the President soon afterwards concluded that historically the agency failed when it backed indigenous forces without Americans on the ground working alongside them.[104] Moreover, in this instance arming the rebels was unlikely to convince Assad to change his stance. As will be discussed in the next chapter, for every rebel gain, the regime received greater support from Russia, Iran and Hezbollah. Within hours of the EU embargo being lifted, for example, Russia announced it would deliver S-300 anti-aircraft missiles to Syria (later cancelled following Israeli objections). As long as the regime retained its own foreign supporters, who appeared far more committed to Assad's survival than Western states were to his removal, it is unlikely that a limited number of Western arms would force any compromise.

It is also questionable whether Western arms would truly have boosted the moderate forces. Jihadist success was due not only to more arms but to better organisation and eschewing the corruption that plagued FSA militia. Jihadists and radical Islamists had pre-existing roots in Syria, immediately sought to take advantage of the uprising, and were actively facilitated in this endeavour by the regime. Even with Western arms, moderates would have faced a formidable rival for rebel loyalty and it is questionable they had the ability to overcome it. Moreover, Western leaders proved unable to deter their regional allies from backing radical groups, especially Qatar but also Turkey, and it would likely have taken a far greater commitment than just arming, possibly a full intervention, to persuade them otherwise. Even then, direct Western intervention in Libya proved insufficient to persuade Qatar to back a single set of moderate actors. In contrast, the risks to Obama when presented with the Clinton plan were very real. Weapons could have ended up in the wrong hands. Despite careful vetting there was no guarantee that fighters would not radicalise in the future. The fluidity of allegiance among the rebels, described above, in fact suggested it was quite likely. Indeed, soon after Saudi Arabia's first major shipment of Croatian arms to FSA forces in the south, some made their way to Ahrar and Nusra, having been shared or sold by the original recipients.[105] Similarly, there was the possibility that jihadists would simply steal the weapons from the US' allies. This in fact occurred later in the war with US-backed anti-ISIS militia attacked and robbed by Nusra.

The sad irony is that, despite the vast sums provided, no foreign state proved able to gain serious leverage over the fighting rebels.[106] Even more than with the political opposition, Saudi Arabia, Qatar and Turkey's pursuit of their own agendas, including a willingness to turn a blind eye to multiple private sources of support, trumped the desire to foster a united and effective armed resistance. Instead they helped produce a rebel marketplace that saw militia compete for resources rather than unite. Moreover, the unchecked radicalism of private donors alongside officially endorsed sectarianism from the Gulf states created, in conjunction with the Assad regime's brutality, an environment in which Salafists and jihadists thrived at the expense of secular and moderate Islamist forces.

Some have blamed the US for not backing more moderate rebels sooner. However, there is little evidence to suggest the limited package proposed by Clinton and Petraeus in 2012 would have been sufficient to tip the balance against Assad nor that it would have persuaded Saudi Arabia, Turkey, and especially Qatar and private donors, to stop undermining the FSA by backing groups unilaterally. The competitive marketplace would likely have continued, but with a US proxy sucking the Obama administration into the kind of Middle Eastern quagmire it had been determined to avoid. It would likely have taken the Libya-style intervention that Obama also wanted to avoid to convince the US' regional allies to channel all their resources through a single US-approved body, yet even in Libya Qatar proved independent minded, so there was again no guarantee. With so many risks and uncertainties at play, Obama's caution was understandable, though he could be criticised for not managing his allies and raising unrealistic expectations of greater US assistance from both the rebels and regional powers alike.

CHAPTER SEVEN

To the hilt: Assad's allies dig in

The Islamic Republic of Iran aims to strengthen its relations with Syria and will stand by it in facing all challenges ... The deep, strategic and historic relations between the people of Syria and Iran ... will not be shaken by any force in the world.

Newly elected Iranian President Hassan Rouhani,
Tehran, 5 August 2013[1]

For long stretches of 2013 there was only one area where residents of the divided city of Aleppo could pass between the rebel-held east and the regime-held west: Bustan al-Qasr checkpoint – nicknamed *ma'aber al-mout*, the Crossing of Death.[2] Two buses were stacked on top of each other across a boulevard to restrict passage to pedestrians, who would have to pay a hefty fee and then risk sniper fire to pass. Even so, one report estimated that from September 2013 to January 2014 up to 50,000 people crossed every day, carrying essential foodstuffs or to reach relatives on the other side. Young boys scratched out a meagre living making the trip on wealthier residents' behalf. As the Battle of Aleppo settled into a prolonged war of attrition, the two forces became entrenched.

A young smuggler from the east would leave behind a series of rebel-manned checkpoints, some aligned with Idriss' FSA–SMC, but increasingly dominated by the radicals like Tawheed and Nusra.[3] Passing into the regime-held west would reveal a different picture. The Syrian Arab Army soldiers on regime checkpoints sported new military fatigues, weaponry and vehicles. Alongside them and elsewhere in the city were paramilitary groups like the Ba'ath Brigades – a volunteer pro-regime local Sunni militia.[4] As half the city was out of its control, the visitor might wonder how the Assad regime had been able to survive this long. The answer was visible in the soldiers facing them. Their new equipment, training, salaries, reorganisation, and even some of the men doing the fighting, came from abroad.

This chapter examines how Assad's closest allies Russia and, particularly, Iran rallied behind Assad and gave his embattled regime the means to continue its war.

A friend in need

Assad maintained a veneer of calm and business as usual for over a year, persisting with his supposed reform agenda by holding parliamentary elections in May 2012 and appointing a new government the following month. However, this couldn't mask the regime's losses. Manaf Tlass, a general in the Republican Guard, close friend of Assad's and, crucially, the son of the former defence minister who had been a prominent Sunni in the regime, fled in July, denouncing the regime's 'criminal acts'. His was the most high profile in a string of regime defections that included high-ranking army officers, the newly appointed Prime Minister Riad Hijab, in August 2012, and the Foreign Ministry spokesman, Jihad Makdissi, in December 2012. More significant were high-level assassinations, such as the bombing of the National Security Headquarters on 18 July 2012 that killed four intelligence chiefs, including Assif Shawkat and Defence Minister Dawoud Rajiha; or the bombing of the Iman Mosque in Damascus on 21 March 2013 that killed forty-two people, including the respected cleric Mohamed Said Ramadan al-Bouti – the regime's 'last credible ally among the Sunni religious elite'.[5] These losses alongside rebel military successes gave the impression of a regime on the verge of collapse by late 2012.

The losses should not be overstated. Despite the embarrassment of the defections, none were power-wielding individuals – with the Prime Minister in Assad's Syria, for example, a manager not a leader, while Tlass was prominent but outside Assad's inner circle – and the regime avoided the high-level fractures suffered by Gaddafi.[6] Likewise, unlike in Libya, though many individual soldiers had defected, no whole units had gone over to the rebels with their equipment. Even the military losses were limited, with the rebels unable to capture any of Syria's fourteen regional capitals until March 2013, when the regime lost Raqqa, followed by Idlib in May 2015. However, it will not be known whether, unaided, the regime would have collapsed. As it was, significant economic, material and military support was provided by Russia and Iran to ensure Assad's medium term survival.

Russian diplomatic support and early Iranian help in media, cyber warfare and policing was discussed above. As the war expanded it became clear that more was needed, not least in the economic sphere. A combination of sanctions and the loss of trade and productivity, due to war, caused Syria's economy to contract more than 50 per cent in real terms between 2011 and mid-2015.[7] However, the regime needed money more than ever, to finance an increasingly expensive war and to continue to pay state salaries and provide services – essential in maintaining support.[8] Russia and Iran helped Syria cope with sanctions. When the EU forbade an Austrian bank from printing Syria's banknotes, Moscow delivered over 30 tonnes of new notes, ensuring salaries could be paid.[9] In 2013 $4.6 billion worth of loans was agreed with Iran while generous credit lines were similarly agreed with Moscow and Tehran for military equipment.

Weaponry and equipment was another key lifeline. Russia insisted that the weapons sold were for a legitimate government, that they were 'defensive', and that it was honouring contracts agreed with Damascus before the 2011 uprising. In terms of international law, Assad's was indeed still a 'legitimate government', but this was because Russia had made it so by preventing any UN arms boycotts. While deliveries of Yakhont anti-ship cruise missiles and SA-17 surface-to-air missiles might have been defensive, aimed at deterring any potential Western no-fly zone, delivering MiG fighter jets, short-range Pantsir-S missiles, tanks, small arms and sending engineers to repair Mi-24 helicopter gunships hardly fall into the same class.[10] Having used helicopters to raze whole villages in search of insurgents in Afghanistan in the 1980s, Moscow may have had a different interpretation of 'defensive'. Yet despite the Kremlin's denials, reports from Russia suggested that new contracts were agreed, as was confirmed by Assad himself in 2015.[11] Weapon deliveries also served a political purpose for Putin, often announced in response to Western anti-Assad measures. In December 2012, for example, NATO deployed Patriot missiles on the Turkish border following a request by Ankara, so within hours Moscow announced it had delivered its first shipment of Iskandar ballistic missiles. Similarly in September 2013, when it appeared that the US and its allies would strike Damascus, Russia again threatened to complete the controversial shipment of the S-300 air defence system. Using such 'delivery diplomacy' Putin assessed that this threat to Israel would help sway an already reluctant US to reconsider its position.[12]

Iran's weaponry was even more controversial, as from 2007 it was forbidden from exporting any arms by the UN as part of its nuclear-programme-related sanctions. Even so, Western officials claimed as early as 2012 that Iran was illegally supplying the regime with rockets, anti-tank missiles, RPGs and mortars by sending them on civilian aircraft and overland through Iraq, Turkey and Lebanon.[13] Tehran (and Baghdad) strenuously denied this, but Brown Moses, a UK-based blog monitoring the conflict, unearthed photographs of an Iranian rocket and a mortar shell crate found in Syria showing a manufacture date of 2012, adding credence to these allegations.[14]

Beyond weapons, the allies provided key advice and personnel. Moscow deployed its navy to Tartous on several occasions: in summer 2012, and again in January 2013 for its largest naval exercise since the fall of the USSR.[15] However, this was primarily a symbolic show of support. Until its dramatic intervention in summer 2015 Moscow had actually quietly withdrawn most of its military personnel, due to safety concerns in June 2013, although Russians employed by the regime as engineers and operators of Russian military equipment remained.[16]

Iran's contribution in the first few years of the war was far deeper. While it deployed a small number of IRGC advisers almost immediately, rebel gains from spring 2012 prompted several more substantial interventions. In May 2013 Hassan Nasrallah, leader of Iran's Shia Lebanese ally Hezbollah, admitted that his militiamen were fighting in Syria, but they were certainly there in some capacity before. Iran arranged for other foreign Shia militants to fight for the regime, mostly Iraqi militia until 2014 and from as far as Afghanistan and Pakistan after many Iraqis returned home to fight ISIS. These fighters helped compensate for the regime's manpower shortage. Defections, desertions and attrition reduced the regime's military from 325,000 in 2011 to an estimated 178,000 in 2013, and some claimed its active troops were as low as 70–80,000 by mid-2015.[17] Yet Iran (with Hezbollah) helped the regime make the most of the troops it did have, improving training and equipment and directing strategy and tactics. They spearheaded the creation of the National Defence Force, a collection of domestic local paramilitaries, more disciplined than the unruly Shabiha, to supplement the military by manning checkpoints and providing local security. How many IRGC troops were deployed remains contested. Syrian rebels claimed soldiers wore Syrian uniforms but spoke Farsi, and sometimes paraded captured Iranians, whom Tehran insisted were civilian pilgrims. Such was the extent of Iranian military involvement that by 2013 oppositionists claimed IRGC Quds Force commander Qassem Suleimani had more power in Syria than Assad.

How this altered the nature of the Iranian–Syrian relationship will be discussed below, but the assistance clearly had a dramatic impact on the war. After a gruelling set of defeats in late 2012–early 2013, when the regime incrementally lost ground in the Aleppo, Hama and Damascus countryside, as well as Raqqa city, the increased support began to show. The regime's new strategy, proposed by Iran and Hezbollah, was to give up trying to regain the whole country and instead consolidate its control of a defensible 'rump' of Syria from Suwaida in the south through Damascus, Homs, Hama and up to the coast, while defending remaining outposts like west Aleppo as best it could. In spring–summer 2013 regime offensives made advances in Idlib, captured the strategically important city of Qusayr in June and the rebellious Homs district of Khaldieh in July and repelled a rebel advance into Latakia in August. This was followed by a series of victories when trying to push the rebels out of Rump Syria, capturing areas such as Yabroud near Damascus on the Lebanese border in March 2014 and regaining the whole of Homs, once the 'capital of the revolution' that May. This did come at the expense of rebel gains in the periphery: establishing a presence along the Jordanian border in the south in autumn 2013, and capturing the last of the Deir ez-Zor oilfields that November, meaning the regime had to import all of its oil. However, the victories seriously weakened the rebel presence in rump Syria, and boosted Assad's confidence of survival. Continuing his 'reformist agenda' approach he held the constitutionally mandated presidential election in June 2014, in which opponents were permitted for the first time. In an election widely dismissed by Western commentators as a farce (though only observers from friendly countries were invited to attend), Assad won 88.7 per cent of the vote, easily defeating his two challengers, with a turnout of 73 per cent (11.6 million voters).

The view from Iran

Neighbourhood matters

Iran's policy in Syria was driven by a combination of domestic and external concerns. Despite accusations from its regional enemies, notably Saudi Arabia, that its agenda was expansionist, Tehran viewed the conflict primarily through a defensive lens. The great expansion in regional influence had actually come before, in the late 2000s when Iraq became a key ally, Hezbollah's position in Lebanon was increased, ties in Yemen and Palestine were strengthened, and its stature on the street as a regional anti-Western leader grew. The Syrian civil war pushed Iran into an unfamiliar role. Having spent decades trying to disrupt the established regional order, Iran was now seeking to consolidate and defend the post-2003 status quo. Meanwhile its great regional rival, conservative Saudi Arabia, was promoting change. Yet Iran in its foreign policy had long had a defensive mindset and its desire to expand its regional influence was, rather like Stalin's Soviet Union, considered protective. A fear of Western-led regime change had been a fixture of Iran's regional view since 1979 and what Tehran saw as Western sponsorship of Saddam Hussein's invasion the next year. Weakening the Western presence in its neighbourhood was long desired, including that of such key US allies as Israel and Saudi Arabia. While Riyadh's leaders played up the sectarian dimension of their rivalry, Tehran frequently emphasised Saudi Arabia's alliance with the US, presenting the House of Saud as the equivalent to Iran's Shah who had been deposed by the 1979 Revolution. Iran's pursuit of a nuclear programme also had a strong defensive component – possessing nuclear technology would deter potential attackers and also elevate its regional power projection to sway more states away from the Western camp. This defensive mentality fostered a sense of encirclement and paranoia, reinforced in the 1990s and 2000s by the increasing US military presence in Tehran's neighbourhood: the Gulf, Afghanistan and Iraq. The condemnation of the 2009 Green Revolution crackdown and the application of UN sanctions in 2010 only exacerbated this siege mentality.[18]

So what was Iran defending in Syria? The alliance had strategic value on several fronts. Firstly, the regime was a key bridge to deliver weapons to Hezbollah. Lebanon's fractious politics, with political groups often aligned with the West in government, blocked Tehran from sending arms directly to Beirut. This meant that deliveries by air (and occasionally ship and truck) to Syria for overland transfer to Hezbollah's strongholds in the Bekaa were an essential lifeline.[19] Hezbollah officials heading to Iran took the same route in reverse. Keeping Hezbollah powerful was a means of both pressuring Israel, and by extension the US, and maintaining the militia's political dominance over Lebanon, which it had asserted informally since 2008. Secondly, Iran utilised Syria's proximity to Israel and the occupied territories to strengthen its ties with Palestinian groups, notably Islamic Jihad (PIJ) and Hamas, the political wings of which were both headquartered in Damascus. Finally, with Iraq's post-2003 transformation from Tehran's traditional enemy into one of its closest friends and trade partners, Syria became an outer wall of defence for Iran's new asset.

Syria also held significant symbolic value. In the 2000s as Iran sought to improve its regional appeal, its enemies led by Saudi Arabia would seek to delegitimise its appeal to the Arab (mostly Sunni) masses by emphasising its Shia and Persian character.[20] Publicly aligning with Syria, a Sunni Arab majority country, despite its Alawi leadership, with a historic pan-Arab pedigree was a great legitimiser. Yet ironically, to defend this symbolic asset Tehran deployed tools that ruined its regional image. By supporting Assad in the first place, and then arranging for Hezbollah and other foreign Shia militias to fight for him, Iran reinforced the Saudi-led narrative of its Shia agenda against the Sunnis. Iran and Hezbollah always rejected this charge, attempting to present themselves as Muslims rather than Shia and carefully describing their Sunni enemies as 'Takfiris' (apostates) rather than using 'Sunni' in the pejorative way that their enemies used 'Shia'. Yet this couldn't mask the fact that Iran was almost exclusively importing foreign Shia militiamen to support what was presented as a Shia–Alawi regime. The cost to Tehran's regional standing was seen in early 2012 when Hamas' leader Khaled Meshaal, based in Damascus since 2001, relocated his politburo to Egypt and Qatar. Hamas was originally the Palestinian arm of the MB, had an entirely Sunni leadership and constituency and, with the regional climate seemingly shifting in favour of the MB, abandoning Assad seemed expedient. However, it further highlighted how sectarianised the regional fault lines of the conflict were becoming and dealt a considerable blow to Iran's claims to speak for all Muslims, whether Shia or Sunni.

While supporting Assad was battering Tehran's regional credibility and costing it financially, it is worth noting the wider regional context for Iran. Despite Syria's violence, for some time Tehran saw the Arab Spring as an opportunity. President Ahmadinejad particularly wooed President Morsi in Egypt, making a great show of his arrival in Tehran in August 2012 for a Non-Aligned Movement conference – the first Egyptian leader to visit Iran since 1979.[21] While Morsi caused shock by publicly criticising Iran's Syria policy, Ahmadinejad persisted in the relationship, visiting Cairo to rapturous welcome in February 2013. Iran also welcomed Morsi's proposal in 2012 for a set of Syria contact groups involving Egypt, Turkey, Russia, Iran and Saudi Arabia – only for Riyadh to refuse. However, whatever hopes Ahmadinejad may have had for improved Iranian–Egypt ties were ended by the coup of July 2013, which placed Cairo firmly back into the pro-Saudi camp.

Despite being on opposite sides of the Syria conflict, Iran also enjoyed mixed ties with Turkey. In a sign that Prime Minister Erdoğan was prioritising economic need over his fight with Assad, Turkey helped Iran bypass the 2010 sanctions that blocked Tehran's access to the global banking system by indirectly purchasing Iranian natural gas with gold. This earned Tehran up to $13 billion in 2012 and 2013, much of which could have been used to support Assad.[22] Similarly Qatar, with whom Iran shared the vital South Pars/ North Dome gas field, continued to trade with Iran despite rivalry over Syria and sanctions – Qatar Airways even took over 20 per cent of Iran's domestic airline in November 2011.[23] There was also some ambivalence towards Russia. Although Moscow was also a key supporter of Assad, for the first years of the conflict the two powers hardly acted in concert. Russia and Iran might be seen as 'frenemies' in the Middle East: as much rivals as friends. They shared a desire to reduce Western influence but saw themselves, not each other, as the beneficiary of a post-American Middle East. Historically Iran has been suspicious of Russia, which had invaded alongside its Western allies during the Second World War and sought to manipulate thereafter. Iran enjoyed little bilateral trade with Russia (except arms) and was a potential future rival to export gas to Europe. Moscow had played a canny hand regarding Iran's nuclear programme as well. While it helped to dilute and delay sanctions, ultimately it accepted them in 2010, prompting anger from Ahmadinejad, who was personally disliked by Putin.[24] On the one hand Russia didn't want Iranian regime change, as it would strengthen the West, but nor did it want either a nuclear Iran or an Iranian–US détente, that could allow Tehran to become a regional hegemon at its expense.[25]

Finally, perhaps the most important regional development for Iran was negotiation with the West over its nuclear programme. Attempts to broker an impasse between Iran and the P5+1 (US, UK, France, China, Russia and Germany) had ground to a halt months before the Syria uprising, in January 2011, and were only revived in April 2012. However, a series of secret backchannel bilateral meetings did take place between lower-level US and Iranian officials in 2011 and 2012, brokered by Oman. This led to a more high-profile meeting in March 2013 when US Deputy Secretary of State William Burns and Jake Sullivan, Vice President Biden's national security adviser, met with Iranian Deputy Foreign Minister Ali Asghar Khaji in Muscat.[26] As the political climate in Iran was beginning to change, with the end of Ahmadinejad's term and the election of Hassan Rouhani in June 2013, these bilateral talks would prove vital in combining with the P5+1 talks to make progress. The extent to which the US was more cautious on Syria once these secret talks were under way, and whether this impacted Iranian thinking and audacity, is unclear.

Domestic dynamics

Regional concerns were the dominant driver of Iran's Syria policy, with a degree of consensus among the different factions of the ruling elite, but internal dynamics interacted with them. Perhaps the most important of these was the economy, which saw Iran suffer a recession at home just as it was facing limitations abroad, another sharp contrast to the success of the 2000s. Under Ahmadinejad, whose economic reforms and increase in international trade coincided with a surge in oil prices, the economy nearly tripled in size, from $192 billion in 2005 to $528 billion in 2011. Yet this boom masked widespread economic mismanagement, corruption and clientism and, according to *The Economist,* it was heading for a fall even before the UN's 2010 sanctions. Yet after enduring 'the world's most elaborate sanctions regime', the economy contracted nearly 6 per cent in 2012, and 2 per cent the year after.[27] Oil exports almost halved, from 2.5 million b/d in 2011 to 1.5 million in 2013. Inflation rose to 42 per cent at one point in 2013, the Iranian rial devalued by 80 per cent in two years and unemployment hit 18 per cent.[28]

This downturn played a major role in the election of Hassan Rouhani as President in June 2013. Rouhani was a pragmatic conservative cleric who had studied in the UK before the 1979 Revolution and then served the new regime loyally, as secretary of the Supreme National Security Council and as Iran's top nuclear negotiator 2003–05. Ideologically opposed to the Radicals dominated by the IRGC that had brought Ahmadinejad to power, Rouhani emerged as the consensus moderate candidate once his predecessor's term was up. While his political base was a mixture of the remnants of the crushed reformist Green Movement of 2009 and fellow pragmatic conservatives, votes were won on a platform of domestic and international change. By emphasising ending the sanctions regime and reordering the economy, Rouhani won a landslide victory, earning 50.8 per cent of the vote, compared to the 16.4 per cent of his nearest challenger (a Radical).[29]

However, Rouhani's election represented a nuancing of Iran's regional policy rather than a transformation, and its immediate impact on Syria was minimal. Indeed, soon after his inauguration in August 2013 Rouhani reiterated his commitment to the alliance, stating it 'will not be shaken by any force in the world'.[30] Several reasons explain this. Firstly, though he was pragmatic, Rouhani was still a conservative, an Iranian nationalist and a supporter of the Islamic Revolution and broadly accepted the strategic and symbolic value of Syria discussed above. Secondly, although polls showed declining popularity for the Syria policy, domestic pressure to change direction was low. Despite austerity at home due to sanctions, Iran was spending billions to prop up Assad – in 2015 UN special envoy Staffan de Mistura estimated it was up to $6 billion a year.[31] Even so, one poll showed that most Iranians had little interest in far off Syria, with only four in ten saying they followed the conflict, and those who did were most supportive.[32] Using foreign proxies rather than sending Iranians to fight in large numbers limited the chances of Syria becoming Iran's Vietnam or Afghanistan, despite the hopes of Tehran's enemies.[33] Thirdly, and most importantly, the structure of power in Iranian politics gave Rouhani little power over Syria policy, and foreign policy in general save for the sanctions and nuclear issue, even had he wished to change it.

Iranian domestic politics was fractious, with Khamenei more of an arbitrator when consensus among leading factions could not be found rather than an absolute dictator. The IRGC's role among these factions was particularly contentious. The force had increased its power in recent years, especially under Ahmadinejad, and controlled a large stake in the economy – at least 10 per cent in the formal economy, even more in the substantial informal one.[34] However, the IRGC was no united single body, having various hardline and pragmatic currents, often competing as much economically as politically.[35] Rouhani's election in 2013 was therefore not as unexpected as it may seem. Khamenei himself was not enthusiastic about Rouhani, but neither interfered in the election – having lost considerable political capital standing by Ahmadinejad's disputed ballot in 2009 – nor opposed the new President's re-engagement on the nuclear issue, recognising the damaging impact of sanctions.[36] Similarly, pragmatic elements within the IRGC, despite maintaining the rhetoric of resistance to the West, recognised the need for a shift. Suleimani himself defended Rouhani's Foreign Minister Mohammad Javad Zarif's engagement with the US against radicals in parliament.

At the same time as Rouhani's re-engagement on sanctions won over hardliners, the pragmatists and moderates did not contest the stout defence of Syria. Different, sometimes competing figures helped Khamenei form foreign policy – including IRGC commanders, senior clerics, and Foreign Ministry officials – but on Syria a small faction of IRGC commanders led by Suleimani enjoyed unchallenged favour.[37] They ran the day-to-day campaign and, despite being frustrated having initially been assured that the crisis would be resolved quickly, Khamenei was a strong supporter of Suleimani's approach.[38] The generally more doveish Foreign Ministry under Zarif had little influence over matters, but appeared supportive nevertheless, developing political options in favour of a negotiated settlement in parallel to the Quds Force's military operations.[39] Tehran was not naïve about the Syrian situation, especially after 2013, and few believed that Assad could regain control of the whole country militarily. However, despite the fractious nature of its politics, even after Rouhani's election all were united behind a policy of supporting the regime militarily and politically with the aim of maximising the chances of an outcome that would suit Tehran at the expense of its regional enemies.

Hezbollah's role: A dilemma for Nasrallah

A key component of Iranian support for Assad was the Lebanese Shia militia-cum-party Hezbollah (Party of God). Tehran helped create the militia in the

1980s during the Lebanese civil war and has been its principal source of funds and weapons thereafter. But Hezbollah was not simply an Iranian vassal and Secretary General Hassan Nasrallah faced a dilemma when Syria's uprising broke out.[40] On the one hand, Hezbollah faced a grave, even existential threat should Assad be toppled. Syria provided it with strategic depth, including the essential supply line to Iran, and legitimacy: the Syrian–Iranian alliance was presented as part of a wider 'Resistance' on behalf of all Muslims and Arabs against Israel and the West. Like Iran it feared a Sunni-dominated regime emerging in Damascus, but with a further domestic reason: it might shift Lebanon's delicate sectarian balance in favour of its Sunnis, at the expense of the Shia and Hezbollah. On the other hand, the costs of supporting Assad in his repression were potentially great. Regionally, Hezbollah had seen its popularity soar since it fought Israel to a standstill in the 2006 Lebanon war, and this could be compromised. Domestically, many of Lebanon's Sunnis (roughly 27 per cent of the population) instinctively sided with the mostly Sunni anti-Assad rebels and might use any Hezbollah involvement in Syria to challenge the Party of God at home.

Initially Nasrallah attempted to balance these concerns by offering Assad limited support, but publicly downplaying Hezbollah's role. As early as May 2011, before the uprising turned violent, Nasrallah publicly backed Assad – arguing in favour of his 'reforms' – but denied opposition claims that Hezbollah fighters had taken part in the crackdown.[41] As fighting intensified, the US acknowledged Hezbollah's deeper involvement in August 2012, suggesting it was facilitating the IRGC's retraining of Assad's military. In summer 2012 Ali Hussein Nassif, a senior Hezbollah commander was killed in Syria, prompting Nasrallah to admit that some of his fighters were there but, he insisted, in a private capacity.

In early 2013, however, the gloves came off. In April Nasrallah stated for the first time that Hezbollah was fighting in Syria as the militia shifted to an overt combat role.[42] Three developments caused this. Firstly, the regime's inability to repel rebel advances raised the prospect of Assad's defeat. Secondly, the rise of sectarian jihadists and Salafists among the rebels represented a force along Lebanon's border that would not just be anti-Assad, but threatened the entire Shia presence in the Levant. Finally, Iran appealed to Hezbollah for greater help. Whether this was decisive or merely confirmed Nasrallah's own conclusions is unclear, but twice in April 2013 the Secretary General flew to Tehran to meet both Khamenei and Suleimani, and soon after openly declared Hezbollah's presence in Syria.

This new approach was immediately felt at the Battle of Qusayr. A Sunni town south of Homs, Qusayr was controlled by the rebels and used to resupply the embattled rebel quarters of Homs, yet sat on the strategically valuable road used by Hezbollah to transport weapons from Syria into its Lebanese stronghold of Hermel in the Bekaa Valley. For the first time the Lebanese militia took the lead in a regime assault, sending up to 2,000 fighters into battle, capturing the city in June.[43] This helped Assad eventually recapture Homs, but also signified a new phase of the regime's war. While Hezbollah would mostly take dominant military roles in battles close to locations of essential strategic value – such as the Qalamoun region along the Lebanese border in 2014 – rebels were now frequently fighting regime forces supported by the Party of God.[44] Given Hezbollah's reputation as the most impressive military force in the Arab world, this sapped rebel morale and boosted the regime. By offering expertise that Assad lacked, such as light infantry and urban warfare expertise, training, or directing military tactics, from 2013 the Party of God became a vital component of Assad's forces and greatly shaped the conflict.[45] Curiously, despite the militia's clear interests in Syria, Western policymakers were surprised by Hezbollah's entry – another significant miscalculation in its Syria policy. As US ambassador to Syria Robert Ford later remarked, 'We did not anticipate that Hezbollah would go in in such a big way in 2013. We thought we'd get to negotiations by summer 2013 because the regime would be on its back heels, we did not see Hezbollah coming at all.'[46]

Hezbollah also greatly contributed to the war's increasingly sectarian character. As discussed, there were sectarian elements within the opposition from the beginning, and Hezbollah and Iran were often the targets of anti-Shia sentiment. In the eastern town of Al-Bukamal pictures of Nasrallah were reportedly burned in May 2011, while elsewhere some protesters chanted 'No Hezbollah, no Iran, we want a Muslim who fears God' – an anti-Shia slogan which implies that Assad, as an Alawite Shia, is not a true Muslim. Even so, seemingly the largest section of the protesters rejected sectarianism, shouting inclusive nationalist slogans, and it was the regime and the emerging radical Islamists that drove the gradual sectarianisation of the conflict.[47] But Hezbollah helped to exacerbate this trend once it entered the war. A report by the International Crisis Group in 2014 noted how it justified its role in sectarian terms. Its early involvement was based on defending Lebanese Shia near the Syrian border and the Shia shrines in Syria. Later Hezbollah cast the struggle as a pre-emptive war against 'Takfiris'. This implied that every rebel was a radical and a threat to the Shia, encouraging all Shia (or non-Sunni) in Lebanon and Syria to fear anyone supporting the rebels. At the same time, radical Islamists could point to Hezbollah's involvement as evidence of a 'Shia plot'.[48]

For Hezbollah, increased involvement came at a cost, albeit a manageable one. Regionally, its popular reputation among Sunnis was shattered. A symptom of this was the strain placed on its relationship with Hamas, especially after Hamas-style tunnels were found in Aleppo and rebel IEDs in Qusayr of a near identical type to those the Hezbollah had taught Hamas to make.[49] Domestically, Nasrallah had tried to keep Lebanon's fractious politics isolated from the chaos in Syria, in contrast to regime attempts to sow chaos by smuggling in explosives and assassinating key security figures.[50] However, as the civil war became more sectarianised – partly due to Hezbollah – confessional violence spilled over. A series of attacks on Shia areas by Sunni radical groups occurred in 2013 and early 2014, the first within a month of Hezbollah's open declaration of its Syria operations. The worst of these, a car bomb in August 2013, killed eighteen people in a Shia-dominated suburb of Beirut. A week later a far more violent attack on two Sunni mosques in the northern Lebanese city of Tripoli killed forty-seven, with many suspecting avenging militants tied to Hezbollah. Sectarian violence linked to Syria also occurred in Tripoli where Lebanese Alawis clashed with Sunnis; the Bekaa Valley where radical militants in the Sunni town of Arsal clashed with the Lebanese army and Shias from Hermel; and the southern city of Sidon, where followers of radical Sunni preacher Ahmad al-Assir fought Hezbollah supporters and the Lebanese army. Despite this disruption, Hezbollah enjoyed the tacit support of the Lebanese military, which also wished to retain the pre-2011 status quo and feared radical Sunnis. Even Sunni political leaders were fearful of such groups and reached an accommodation in April 2014 that caused the attacks to subside.[51] As such, Nasrallah contained the domestic fallout from Syria, which, though disruptive, did not gravely impact Hezbollah's support for Assad. While Hezbollah had to sacrifice its regional position to support the regime, its domestic situation was rocked but ultimately secure.

Suleimani's Syria?

'Syria is occupied by the Iranian regime,' former Syrian Prime Minister Riad Hijab told the Saudi-owned al-Arabiya news channel in February 2013, six months after his defection. 'The person who runs the country is not Bashar al-Assad but Qassem Suleimani.'[52] Similar accusations, that the thirty-year alliance had been transformed into vassalage or even military occupation became increasingly widespread as the full extent of Iranian assistance became clear.[53] Assessing the truth is difficult, given the secretive nature of the regime and the political biases of those claiming insider knowledge: it is not surprising that a defecting Prime Minister speaking to a Saudi-owned channel should wish to vilify Iran. However, the available evidence does suggest a significant shift in the dynamics of the relationship.

Qassem Suleimani and the Quds Force

Major General Qassem Suleimani was no stranger to conflict. Aged twenty-three he joined the IRGC and spent the next eight years fighting in the Iran–Iraq war. Having risen in the ranks, a decade after that brutal war finally ended he was appointed commander of the IRGC's Quds Force, Iran's extraterritorial military and intelligence force, described by one analyst as a combined CIA and special forces.[54] Despite quiet cooperation with Washington against Iran's enemy the Taleban in Afghanistan in 2001, Suleimani would make his name devising anti-US operations during the American occupation of Iraq after 2003. By sponsoring anti-US Shia militia, funding various Shia political parties, and combining accommodation with intimidation in dealing with Iraqi Kurdish leaders, Suleimani successfully helped make the US occupation untenable. When the last US troops left in December 2011, Iraq had become a solid Iranian ally, not least due to Suleimani's role in brokering Premier Nouri al-Maliki's return to office in 2010. A silver-haired smallish man, with a close-cropped beard and 'a look of intense self-containment', Suleimani's years in Iraq acquired him a fearsome reputation.[55]

Yet when he was tasked to apply his skills to Syria, the challenge proved different from the case of Iraq. In the latter, Suleimani's Quds Force had backed irregulars fighting an asymmetric war against a regular military, while in Syria the roles were reversed. In Iraq, Saddam Hussein's state had collapsed, leaving a vacuum to be filled by militia while in Syria, Hafez al-Assad's coup-proofed regime remained largely in place. Indeed, one problem was that the regime was designed to prevent any part of the military or security forces accruing too much power, which was not well suited to effectively combating an insurgency. In Iraq Suleimani had close ties with Shia and Kurdish leaders stretching back to the Iran–Iraq war and before, but in Syria Tehran had conducted relations primarily via the regime and enjoyed few deeper societal ties.

This different context prompted a divergent approach. An 'advisory mission' was sent in early 2011, including Suleimani and the former commander of the IRGC's Greater Tehran unit, Hossein Hamedani, who had led the crackdown on the 2009 Green Movement, which the Iranians wrongly believed the Syrian uprising resembled.[56] In a sign of the regime's independence from Tehran's at this point, Assad ignored the mission's advice to use only riot police, instead cracking down hard with the army, to Suleimani's reported frustration.[57] As violence grew, so did the Quds Force presence, although until 2013 Iranian leaders denied it had a combat role. IRGC commander Ali Jafari insisted in September 2012, for example, '*Sepah* [IRGC] is offering assistance in planning, as well as financial help, but does not have a military presence.'[58] However, Western officials noted in late 2012 a sharp increase in flights arriving in Damascus from Tehran, carrying weapons, ammunition and, apparently, Quds force officers.[59] This was facilitated by Iraq, which had reclaimed control of its airspace after the US withdrawal of December 2011 and had a minister of transport, Hadi al-Amiri, who was head of the Badr Corps (a pro-Iranian Shia militia) and a close ally of Suleimani. Baghdad insisted the planes contained humanitarian supplies.[60] Rumours that the Quds Force was playing an active military role seemed confirmed in January 2013 when the Assad regime released 2,130 rebel prisoners in exchange for just 48 Iranians captured by the opposition the previous August – an abnormally high military price to pay for civilians.[61]

Reorganisation: 'The Syrian Army is useless!'

By the time of the Battle of Qusayr Suleimani was directing operations. Having helped persuade Hezbollah to lead the assault, Qusayr was a major victory for him. By this point he was flying frequently to Damascus to head up a command centre comprised of the Syrian military, Hezbollah, and other Shia militia. This command centre was one of several major reorganisations he made to streamline Assad's complex web of competing security forces into an effective fighting force. The Syrian military had suffered thousands of defections, but Assad's elite units, dominated as they were by Alawis and other loyalists, remained intact, and they received an influx of new Iranian equipment and training. Regular units with a large Sunni contingent of soldiers were held back from the front line guarding checkpoints, for fear that they might desert or be less willing to fight. Suleimani was less than impressed, reportedly telling an Iraqi politician, 'The Syrian Army is useless! Give me one brigade of the Basij [Iran's paramilitary irregulars], and I could conquer the whole country.'[62]

With this in mind, Suleimani helped create the National Defence Force (NDF), a paramilitary body estimated to have 50,000 fighters in 2013 and aiming to reach 100,000, to supplement and support the beleaguered military.[63] This was not a new idea: the Ba'ath Party established several paramilitary forces on coming to power in 1963 and Hafez created citizen militias from party supporters in 1980 to defeat the Muslim Brotherhood uprising.[64] Following his father's playbook, Assad likewise looked to paramilitaries early on in the crisis. The vicious Shabiha existed before the conflict, but their numbers soon grew, drawing from a cross-sectarian pool, not just Alawis.[65] In 2012 the regime encouraged the creation of local Popular Committee militias, similar to those formed in 1980, based around neighbourhoods and often centred on the dominant sect or ethnicity (Christians, Druze, etc.). Recognising the value of these militias, Suleimani with Hezbollah's assistance first helped consolidate the most effective into the Jaysh al-Sha'bi (People's Army), but a few months later in early 2013 led their reorganisation into the NDF.

The NDF, initially tried in Homs and then extended across the country, was an umbrella organisation to formalise and professionalise various pro-Assad paramilitaries, particularly after Iranian concerns about the unreliable Shabiha.[66] The regime provided armaments, salaries and licensing, and all fighters were Syrians, but training came from the Quds Force and Hezbollah. Given Iran's weak ties with Syrian society, observers suggested that the NDF was Tehran's attempt to build a pro-Iranian proxy from scratch to act in its interests as a back-up plan should Assad fall. As one commentator noted, if Syria cannot be an Iranian ally, they won't allow it to become an enemy.[67] Michael Weiss and Hassan Hassan suggest that an IRGC officer was attached to each NDF brigade as embedded commissar and fighters were sent to train in Amir al-Momenin camp near Tehran to ensure pro-Iranian ideological discipline.[68] Though not exclusively so, NDF units were often dominated by one sect, and some Shia and Alawi brigades embraced a sectarian outlook, allegedly massacring Sunni villages on occasions.[69] However, some caution should be added here. If the NDF really had 100,000 it is unlikely that all, or even more than a handful of leaders and elite brigades, were sent to Iran for ideological indoctrination. Hezbollah, a far older and trusted Iranian ally, has an estimated strength closer to half that, and only its elite divisions trained in Iran.[70] Suleimani probably did build a loyal core within the NDF, but the umbrella organisation incorporated a wider range of militias. Some were simply locals protecting their neighbourhoods, while others were former Shabiha using the NDF as a cover for looting and extortion.[71] There were even reports of the regime buying off a rebel militia in the town of Nabq by turning it into a branch of the NDF.[72] Tehran would not be likely to see any of these as worth training and indoctrinating in Iran. The NDF did, however, transform the regime's war effort. By 2014, it had 'functionally became a branch of the regime military', manning checkpoints and taking on combat roles, while Hezbollah fighters interviewed declared they trusted the NDF far more than the regular Syrian army.[73]

Suleimani's second innovation came in his use of non-Syrian fighters. Alongside Hezbollah the Quds Force commander deployed thousands of other foreign Shia. The Institute for the Study of War estimated that in mid-2014, alongside 4–5,000 Hezbollah fighters, 3–4,000 other Shia fighters were operating in Syria.[74] The majority of these were Iraqi, drawn from Shia militia close to Suleimani from his days combating the US occupation there. In 2013 the Badr Corps stated on its Facebook page that it had 1,500 in Syria, while Kata'ib Hezbollah (KH) and Asa'ib Ahl al-Haq (AAH), Iraqi Shia groups that Suleimani helped create in the 2000s, also acknowledged their presence.[75] Many joined the Abu al-Fadl al-Abbas Brigade, formed in 2012 as a conglomerate of Syrian and foreign Shia likely ordered to Syria by Suleimani. Like Hezbollah they justified the deployment by saying that Shia shrines, particularly Sayyeda Zeynab in southern Damascus, were being defended. However, while many did fight in crucial battles around the south of the capital, they were also deployed in Homs, Hama and Aleppo.[76] With the regular Syrian military facing a serious manpower shortage these foreign fighters became increasingly important. However, as with Hezbollah, they contributed to the sectarianisation of the conflict on both sides as Shia were imported to fight Sunni, including many Shia radical sectarian jihadists.[77] In June 2014 ISIS captured Iraq's third city, Mosul, and threatened Baghdad, prompting most of the Iraqi Shia fighters in Syria to return home. To fill their place, the Quds Force recruited Afghani Hazara Shias, almost half a million of whom lived as refugees in Iran.[78] Some reports suggested Iran had even raided its jails for Hazaras to fight.[79]

Assad's eroding state: Spiralling costs, rising debt

In addition to the military presence of the Quds Force and Suleimani's Shia proxies, the gradual weakening of Assad's state, even in the rump the regime still controlled, amplified the perception of increased Iranian control. Years of war and sanctions crippled Syria's economy. For the first few years the regime proved resilient, being self-sufficient in oil and food, and utilising the financial support of pro-regime Syrian businessmen like Rami Makhlouf plus Iran and Russia. It was helped by cost-cutting measures, a drop in demand for public services due to a decreasing population, and the falling value of the Syrian lira, which allowed its foreign reserves to go further.[80] However, as the war intensified costs spiralled. Troops needed paying, including the new NDF forces, while equipment and weapons were expensive – Iran and Russia wanted Assad to win, but would not give arms away for free. The public salaries bill remained high: as part of its claim to legitimacy the regime continued providing services, even in war-torn regions and often paid public employees in rebel-controlled areas.[81] Yet from 2013 most of its oilfields and much of the agricultural land of the north and east had been lost, forcing the regime to import both oil and food crops for the first time. In 2014 Syria imported 1.5 million tonnes of wheat, while in early 2015, it was importing 60,000 b/d of oil.[82]

The regime consequently became more dependent on Iran. Firstly, it took on debt, Tehran providing two credit facilities in 2013 – $1 billion for imports of food and to prop up depleted foreign reserves and $3.6 billion for oil. As Syria's economy declined, its debt grew, almost doubling from 29 per cent of GDP in 2010, to 59 per cent in 2013.[83] Secondly, Iran's economic role was transformed from peripheral player in 2010, to key foreign actor. Bilateral trade grew from $300 million in 2010 to $1 billion in 2014, helped by a free trade agreement implemented in 2012.[84] This may only have been a tenth of the thriving Iran–Iraq trade in the same period, but still made Tehran Syria's largest trade partner. Iranian companies entered the Syrian economy as other foreign companies were leaving, with contracts agreed to rebuild Syria's damaged infrastructure. In one case, in July 2013, the regime offered substantial tax exemptions for an Iranian food export company.[85] In addition, observers noted a growth in Iranians and other foreign Shia settling permanently in south Damascus near the Sayyeda Zeynab shrine. Some speculated that Tehran's long-term plan was to carve out a loyal Shia stronghold there, akin to the Dahieh region of Beirut.

Another key source of regime funds was the World Food Programme, UN and other international agencies, which provided over $1 billion in aid for refugees and IDPs.[86] While service provision continued for political reasons, quality and reach inevitably declined. By 2016 over five million refugees had fled Syria, decreasing human and financial capital, while those that remained found taxes eventually raised and subsidies cut.[87] Fighting the war damaged the institutions of Assad's state. The military saw its command structure decentralised to fight the rebels. The new smaller mobile units were necessary to fight the war but weakened the military as a centralised body. The creation of militias, especially the NDF, exacerbated this process, with the Institute of the Study of War's Joseph Holliday remarking that, 'The distinction between Syrian Army soldiers and pro-regime paramilitaries has become increasingly irrelevant.'[88] Perhaps the most visible sign of state weakening in rump Syria was the growth of militia *outside* of the NDF structure. While some NDF acquired a fearsome repu-tation, and were permitted to loot recaptured areas if on the front lines, they were still an institution of the state. Yet the regime also tolerated and even encouraged a variety of militias allied to but outside of the NDF umbrella, such as Aleppo's Ba'ath Brigades. More than the NDF, these groups had an overt sect-based or ethnic make-up, such as the *Sootoro* –

Assyrian Christians in the eastern Hasakah region – or various different Syrian Palestinian militias.[89] In some cases, such as the Druze Jaysh al-Muwahhideen (Army of Monotheists), formed in the Druze-dominated southern city of Suwaida, or the Alawi al-Muqāwama al-Sūrīya (The Syrian Resistance) in Latakia province, militias were given considerable autonomy. As Samer Abboud has noted, this 'militiafication' inside regime territory in many way resembled the privatised, decentralised and civilianised violence seen in rebel areas.[90] Moreover, this increased the chance that ethnic identities would be strengthened at the expense of a national one and decreased the likelihood of being folded back into a centralised state after the war.

Partner or puppet?

So had Assad simply become Tehran's quisling in the Islamic Republic's 'occupation'? Insiders paint a more nuanced picture than former Premier Riad Hijab and other oppositionists. Clearly, as a result of the conflict Iran's influence in Syria penetrated deeper and wider than ever before. Qassem Suleimani played a major role in directing the war effort, recruiting foreign militias and reorganising domestic forces, while economically Syria became increasingly dependent on Iran. The general weakening of the Syrian state both territorially and institutionally further amplified Iran's increased role in what was left.

However, an increased role is not the same as either occupation or vassalage. Foreign fighters, especially Hezbollah, were essential to the regime's military in providing highly skilled and loyal fighters. However, while the exact number sent to Syria remains unknown, even the more generous accounts place the total around 20,000 in early 2016, so the overwhelming majority of soldiers in uniform on the regime's side were Syrian.[91] Oppositionists may fear that some in the NDF were brainwashed to serve Iran ahead of Syria, but the number indoctrinated in such a way is likely a minority. Iran may have built close ties to the NDF in case the regime should collapse, but this was very much a distant back-up plan. Iran had few grass-roots ties in Syria prior to 2011 so was starting from a low base when it helped build the NDF, and to rest its policy on such newly formed ties would be uncharacteristic of Suleimani. The level of investment and debt agreed with the regime did not suggest that Tehran in any way favoured the dismemberment of the Syrian state. While it may have encouraged a necessary retreat from the north and east, retaining a functioning rump state that could eventually repay its debts and benefit the Iranian economy was important.

Assad, moreover, was no puppet. It was suggested by Naame Shaam (Letter from Syria), a pro-opposition activist group, that the Quds Force was behind the assassination of Shawkat and others in July 2012. According to this account, Shawkat was critical of Iran's increasing role and, having contacted some of the Gulf states about seeking peace, he was killed in a pro-Iranian 'coup' to silence regime dissenters.[92] The truth will probably never be known and an inside job cannot be ruled out.[93] Yet even if true, such internal 'spring cleaning' of anti-Iranian elements in the regime does not make Iranian puppets of those left. In his quest for survival Assad evidently was willing to use whatever means necessary, including subordinating major military decisions to Tehran, something likely to stick in the throat of Syrian nationalists within the regime. Far from a quisling, insiders suggest that Tehran actually found Assad stubborn to deal with. Moreover, its view changed over time. In 2011, from afar, they believed the President was a disposable figurehead, but the more deeply they penetrated and understood the regime's workings, the more they saw Assad as essential.[94] As the only figure all the competing factions could agree on as leader, Assad came to be seen by Iran as the glue holding the regime together. At the popular level, many fighting for the regime genuinely believed in the 'Assad's Syria' narrative.

Western commentators frequently mooted the idea of persuading Iran to 'ditch' Assad, arranging for him to be replaced as part of a peace deal, similar to the pressure they successfully placed on their ally, Iraqi Prime Minister Nouri al-Maliki to resign in summer 2014. However, it must be questioned firstly whether Iran would ever accede to that, fearing that without Assad the regime might collapse. Secondly, it is questionable whether, despite all their assistance to the regime, they actually had the leverage to persuade Assad to go, as they lacked the deep historical ties to Syria's political elite long enjoyed in Iraq.

From the beginning of Syria's civil war, Assad's allies were willing to give more to ensure the regime's survival than those states that wished to hasten its fall. While the anti-Assad states offered the armed and political opposition money, arms and support, Russia and Iran more than matched this and were also prepared to risk their regional reputations and send their own personnel. For the first four years Iran was by far Assad's most important ally. Qassem Suleimani led a major reorganisation of the regime's forces, brought in Hezbollah and other Shia militias, and directed key aspects of military strategy. Tehran, with decades of experience, proved itself to be far more talented at proxy warfare than its rivals in Doha, Ankara and Riyadh. At the same time Iran deepened its economic and political involvement in Syria, transforming the relationship. While this did not make Assad the Iranian vassal often claimed by his opponents, it did make his regime increasingly dependent on Tehran for survival. Such deep involvement by Assad's allies greatly impacted the shape of the Syrian civil war. Financial and military support prevented the regime from collapsing under pressure, while Iran and Hezbollah's role significantly contributed to sectarianising the conflict, a price that Tehran was seemingly willing to pay.

As with so much in the conflict, Assad's enemies underestimated the lengths to which Assad's allies would go to defend the regime. In the same way that Western actors believed Russia could be persuaded to ditch Damascus, many seemingly expected Tehran to eventually cut its losses. Yet throughout, Iran showed a willingness to increase its involvement when Assad faced setbacks, not retreat. A refusal to recognise this by Assad's enemies only escalated the conflict further.

CHAPTER EIGHT

No red lines: The question of Western military intervention

I want to make it absolutely clear to Assad and those under his command. The world is watching. The use of chemical weapons is and would be totally unacceptable. And if you make the tragic mistake of using these weapons, there will be consequences, and you will be held accountable.

Barack Obama, 3 December 2012

Since the outbreak of the war, the Masnaa border crossing into Lebanon had seen a steady stream of refugees fleeing Syria's growing violence. Families waited patiently along the mountainous road in lines of packed cars and minivans to seek refuge in Syria's Western neighbour. By the summer of 2013, Lebanon had 700,000 Syrian refugees registered with the UN refugee agency (UNHCR), although the actual number was believed to be over a million. For a few weeks in late August and early September of that year, however, something changed. The numbers passing through Masnaa suddenly doubled.[1] Alongside the battered vehicles overflowing with the suitcases and bedding of poor families there appeared the glistening SUVs and Mercedes of the pro-regime elite. Even the wealthy merchants and relatives of officials were now fleeing in droves.

The prompt for this abrupt exodus was the belief that any day a Western military coalition, led by the US, would launch missile strikes on the regime. Earlier that month, up to 1,400 people had been killed in a chemical weapons attack in the Ghouta district of Damascus, which the US and its allies blamed on the Syrian government.[2] President Obama had stated repeatedly since summer 2012 that any regime deployment of its extensive chemical weapon stockpile constituted a 'red line' and, despite his long-held reluctance to intervene militarily in the civil war, he sent six destroyers to the eastern Mediterranean in late August armed with Tomahawk missiles. In preparation, Damascenes stockpiled food, taped up widows and bulk-bought candles. As one businessman crossing at Masnaa told reporters,

'My uncle is a senior officer. He is one of the decision-makers, and this week the only decision he's making is where to take shelter from the American planes.'[3] But the attack never came. After the British Parliament unexpectedly voted against UK involvement and Obama then deliberated by seeking congressional approval himself, an eleventh-hour deal mediated by Russia saw Assad peacefully surrender his chemical weapons under UN supervision. As Damascus breathed a sigh of relief, the elite slowly trickled back home, unlike many of the poorer Syrians who would remain in Lebanon indefinitely.

The 'non-strike' of late summer 2013 was something of a watershed in the Syrian civil war. Until that point some form of US-led military intervention, modelled on the actions in Libya in 2011, seemed a realistic prospect to many of the key actors and impacted their behaviour. Afterwards, while some still clung to the dream of a more limited NATO no-fly zone, most recognised that US-led military action against Assad was unlikely. While Obama did eventually authorise direct military action in Syria in September 2014 it was against ISIS, not Assad (discussed in Chapter 9). This chapter explores why the Syria conflict attracted so little direct military intervention in its early, formative years, especially by the US. The significance of the 2011 Libya conflict, which raised hopes of similar NATO intervention in Syria, will be discussed: how a misinterpretation of US actions prompted false perceptions about Obama's intent. There will also be a brief discussion of the limited direct military interventions that did occur in the first few years, from Israel and Turkey. The majority of the chapter, however, will deal with summer 2013: assessing the motives and calculations for US inaction and considering how it changed the dynamics of the conflict.

The shadow of Libya

The question of direct military intervention by a Western-led force against Assad was raised early on. Past operations in Bosnia, Sierra Leone, Kosovo, Iraq and Libya had been launched at least partly to defend civilians facing a similar onslaught, and elements of the Western and regional press, politicians and activists asked why no such intervention was forthcoming against Assad.[4] While the controversy surrounding the 2003 invasion of Iraq had damped Western enthusiasm for such adventures, the perceived success of UN1973 in Libya seemed to place intervention back on the table. However, the Libya campaign indirectly acted as a force multiplier in the Syrian civil war. It raised expectations among the opposition and the US' regional allies that were not to be met. It convinced Assad's allies that the US might be back in the business of regime change and strengthened their resolve to defend Assad. Conversely, the length and cost of the campaign, followed by the growing instability of post-war Libya, reinforced the doubts of an already cautious Obama administration and US military establishment about the far more complex Syrian case.

Western leaders recognised early on that military intervention in Syria was more problematic and less desirable than in Libya. Logistically, Assad's Russian-built air defences were stronger than Gaddafi's, while Syria was more populous, 21 million compared to 6 million, dispersed over a diverse landscape, making a more difficult operational terrain. As the crisis escalated, intervention became even less appealing. Assad showed himself to be no isolated figure like Gaddafi, receiving reinforcement from Tehran and Moscow and a clear determination by Russia to block any UN condemnation that might legalise a military strike. On top of this, the divisions within the Syrian opposition, the rise of jihadists and the increase in ethnic and sectarian violence raised the prospect that, as in Iraq, even were intervention to occur, it might bring even more chaos. These concerns grew as the apparent success story of Libya slid into anarchy in 2012, particularly after a terror attack in Benghazi in September killed US ambassador J. Christopher Stevens. If a small homogenous population in Libya couldn't stabilise after intervention, what hope for the far larger number of multi-ethnic Syrians?

Such concerns ruled out an immediate repeat of the Libya operation in Syria. In late summer 2011, for example, at a British National Security Council meeting security and intelligence chiefs told Prime Minister David Cameron, 'Syria is not Libya.'[5] Similarly, on 31 October 2011 NATO Secretary General Anders Fogh Rasmussen told reporters, 'NATO has no intention (to intervene) whatsoever. I can completely rule that out.'[6] Most importantly Obama, who had been reluctantly persuaded to back the Libya intervention, indicated early on that he did not envision something similar in Syria. This was reinforced in early 2012 when Chairman of the Joints Chiefs of Staff, General Martin Dempsey presented a slideshow in the White House situation room detailing how at least 70,000 US servicemen would be required to impose a no-fly zone over Syria, while costs would spiral far beyond the $1.6 billion of the Libya operation.[7] Though some State Department officials privately noted that these figures might have been inflated, given the Department of Defense's opposition to intervention, Obama took little persuading.[8] Individual politicians such as US Senator John McCain continued to lobby for military strikes and the

French government, the most hawkish of Western powers on Syria, urged more action, but the White House position remained firmly against. As one US official remarked, 'it's sad that Syrians are dying, but as long as it stays within Syria I don't see how that impacts upon US national security'.[9]

The difficulty, however, was that as violence increased, both the Syrian opposition and their regional backers believed that eventually US-led intervention would happen. As early as 28 October 2011, activists named a 'Friday of no fly zone', followed by a 'Friday of the Syrian Buffer Zone' on 2 December. Leading figures in the SNC such as Burhan Ghalioun and Bassma Kodmani spoke of their preference for military intervention at the beginning of 2012, as if it was a realistic possibility. As rebels formed militias, many based their strategy on taking sufficient territory not to fully defeat Assad, but to persuade the US to finish him off. As a defected general, Adnan Silu, told *Asharq al-Awsat* in July 2012, 'All we need from NATO are two air attacks on the Presidential Palace to topple the regime and we will be able to control all the Syrian cities.'[10]

Yet far from dispelling this assumption, the rebels' regional allies actively encouraged the opposition to expect US military intervention. As Kodmani later recalled, 'the regional powers were absolutely confident that intervention would happen. Again, Libya had happened, they had participated in the Libya campaign, and they were confident that they were going to participate in a campaign in Syria as well.' She went on, 'I recall very well, they were always reassuring the opposition, "it is coming, it is coming definitely, the intervention is coming."'[11] Many regional leaders, particularly Erdoğan, believed that the obstacle to US action was domestic: Obama's campaign for re-election. Turkish officials reportedly told oppositionists to be patient; that intervention would occur after the campaign finished in November 2012.[12] Intriguingly, the multiple US assurances that this was not the case were ignored, or disbelieved.[13] This shows the paradox of perceived US power in the region: regional leaders simply refused to countenance the possibility that, after decades of muscle flexing, the US would not eventually step in. This can partly be blamed on the lack of capacity and intelligence of the regional powers that misjudged Obama's intentions. At the same time, the White House did not communicate convincingly that intervention was not preferred. Perhaps it did not want to show its hand, and therefore maintain the illusion of pressure to check Assad, Iran and Russia. Alternatively, it may reflect discord within the US bureaucracy, with disillusioned members of the State Department not making Obama's position crystal clear. The result was that the war continued, with the White House convinced that direct military action was undesirable, but with the rebels and their regional allies believing the US just needed persuading. Indeed, because of Libya, many presumed there would be a tipping point where Assad's violence would become so great that intervention would become unavoidable. It was a severe misjudgement.

Military powerhouses: Turkey and Israel intervene

The reasons behind such miscalculations of US intent and their consequences will be considered below, but it is first worth noting that Western powers were not the only states willing to directly intervene against Assad. Israel and Turkey also used their own militaries but, unlike the regime's allies in Iran and, after 2015, Russia, their actions were defensive and not aimed at shifting the conflict's balance of power. These military power-houses to Syria's north and south took contrasting approaches. In the first few years, Turkey's leaders spoke frequently about the desirability of inter-vention yet ultimately took little action, preferring the proxy warfare of sponsoring the rebels. Israel, meanwhile, remained relatively silent but actually deployed its air force into Syria to achieve limited goals.

As the conflict expanded Turkey struggled to prevent violence spilling over its borders. In June 2012 a Turkish jet was downed by Syrian defences, apparently over international waters, prompting Prime Minister Erdoğan to change the Turkish military's rules of combat to regard the Syrian mili-tary as a threat. In early October this contributed to a series of clashes over the border after a stray Syrian mortar bomb killed five civilians in the Turkish town of Akçakale. More troops were deployed to the border, and Turkish airspace was closed to all Syrian planes. To deter Syrian rocket attacks, in November Turkey requested that its NATO ally deploy Patriot missile batteries, which arrived in January 2013.[14] This did not end the spillover, however, and Assad-backed groups including the PKK were blamed for a series of bomb attacks in Turkey, the largest of which killed 46 and wounded 155 in Reyhanli in May 2013.

Yet neither these bombs, the border clashes nor Erdoğan's desire to topple Assad prompted a large-scale military intervention, despite Turkey having the largest military in the Middle East. There were various reasons for this. Firstly, despite its military superiority there were doubts whether the Turkish military could achieve its objectives unilaterally. With the exception of northern Cyprus and fighting the PKK in Iraq, which were viewed as domestic issues, Turkey had long been reluctant to militarily intervene anywhere, especially in former Ottoman territories like Syria for fear of appearing irredentist.[15] After the removal of hundreds of officers in the Ergenekon and Sledgehammer scandals (see Chapter 3), morale in the military, particularly the all-important air force, was low and its effectiveness in a sizeable campaign could not be guaranteed.[16] Moreover, after a decade reducing the army's role in politics, a long-lasting war might revive its ambitions.

Secondly, the public was firmly against intervention. A Pew Research poll in May 2013 found that 65 per cent of Turks opposed sending arms to the rebels and 68 per cent were against Western military intervention.[17] A few months later, in September, a German Marshall Fund survey found that 72 per cent of Turks opposed direct military intervention.[18] Making matters worse for Erdoğan, a wave of public demonstrations against his rule broke out in summer 2013, centered on Taksim Square in Istanbul. Over ninety population centres across Turkey joined the demonstrations from May to August, swollen by outrage at police violence against protesters, representing the greatest challenge yet to Erdoğan's rule. These protests were largely unrelated to the war, although some pro-Assad Turkish Alawis in Hatay added Syria policy to their list of grievances, but they exposed Erdoğan's domestic vulnerability as never before. Even had he wished it, to launch an unpopular unilateral war against Assad, especially with a conscript army, could have been political suicide.

Turkish newspapers reported government officials mooting a Turkish-led intervention as early as August 2011, but in reality this was unlikely to happen.[19] Turkish policymakers agreed a military attack on Syria would only be launched if there was a genuine territorial threat or as part of a larger UN- or NATO-led coalition.[20] At the same time, Erdoğan believed that a Western-led military intervention (involving Turkey) was the quickest way of toppling Assad and that it would eventually happen. So Turkey found itself championing direct military intervention in both public and private, yet was never willing to act alone. Though Turkish troops did eventually unilaterally intervene in 2016, discussed in Chapter 11, it was a far more modest endeavour and, crucially, directed against the Kurds and ISIS, not Assad.

In contrast, Israel occupied a strange position in the regional landscape in the early years of the Syrian civil war. It remained disengaged from most of the pro- and anti-Assad camps' politicking, yet was the only regional state willing to deploy its air force to achieve its goals. Israel and Syria had been enemies since the former's foundation in 1948, but under the Assads Syria was a manageable foe. After Israel occupied Syria's Golan Heights in the 1967 Six Day War, and the Syrians failed to recapture them in the 1973 October War, Hafez al-Assad and Bashar after him opted to keep the border quiet, instead pressuring Israel via proxies in Lebanon and the Palestinian

Territories. Prime Minister Benjamin Netanyahu and his security chiefs therefore faced a dilemma when the civil war broke out. Assad's defeat would remove a long-standing enemy, deliver a serious blow to its regional enemy Iran and cut state sponsorship for Hezbollah and Hamas, allowing Israel to tighten its control over the occupied Golan Heights and West Bank. Yet Assad was 'the devil you know', who had done little to threaten the Golan or prevent the creeping annexation of West Bank territory. In Assad's place might come something much worse: an Islamist Sunni regime more willing to challenge Israel or jihadists like Nusra or ISIS that could attack the Golan or north-eastern Israel.

A long-lasting civil war actually served Israel's interests. Both the Assad regime and Assad's rivals were too distracted to turn their attention south. Should either side win, neither would be strong enough to pose any serious threat for years while, were the war to drag on and Syria become a failed state or partitioned, a potentially powerful neighbour would have disappeared. Israel was therefore not overly concerned with ending the war, but it did worry that Hezbollah and Iran might emerge stronger from it. It had quietly welcomed Hezbollah and Iran's distraction in Syria, but two concerns emerged as the war dragged on. Firstly, Assad's collapse might prompt a transfer of sophisticated armaments, including chemical weapons, to Hezbollah. Secondly, as Iran increased its footprint, the transformation of Syria from Iranian ally to direct proxy would give Tehran another border (alongside Lebanon) from which to harass Israel. These fears appeared confirmed when Hezbollah fighters replaced the Syrian army along parts of the Golan front line from 2013. Consequently, Israel's direct interventions in Syria were largely aimed at Hezbollah. What was believed to be its first airstrike, on 31 January 2013, was against a convoy in Rif Dimashq (the Damascus countryside) suspected of transporting anti-aircraft missiles to Hezbollah. Two further strikes in Rif Dimashq took place on 3 and 5 May 2013, also reportedly aimed at Hezbollah-bound weaponry, while an airstrike near Latakia on 5 July destroyed a stock of Russian-purchased anti-ship missiles. As was usual, Israel denied these attacks, but US military officials offered confirmation.[21]

A more local concern was to ensure that Israel remained insulated from the conflict. Since 1974 a 1,200-strong multinational UN force (UNDOF) had patrolled a thin buffer zone between the Israeli-occupied Golan and the small stretch regained by Syria after the 1973 October war. Yet as the civil war reached the Syrian Golan, UNDOF became targeted by radical rebel groups, with peacekeepers temporarily kidnapped in March 2013 and again in August 2014. The latter event, which saw Nusra hold forty Fijians for two weeks, along with the constant threat of stray shells, prompted UNDOF to retreat to the Israeli Golan that September, leaving Israel with no buffer.[22] With jihadists present on one side, and Hezbollah on the other, some commentators mooted a local Israeli invasion to establish a buffer zone in southern Syria, perhaps co-opting Syria's Druze.[23] However, having tried and failed to do something similar in Lebanon in the 1980s – an occupation that helped create Hezbollah in the first place – Israel's military was wary of repeating this. Instead, sporadic tit-for-tat shelling of regime, Hezbollah and jihadist positions became the preferred option, with one security commentator estimating there had been 12–15 Israeli retaliations by autumn 2014.[24] This was stepped up to targeted killings in January 2015 when an Israeli helicopter successfully killed six Hezbollah fighters, including two commanders, and an IRGC general, Mohammad Ali Allah-Dadi in Quneitra.[25] Similarly, another senior Hezbollah commander, Mustafa Badreddine, was killed near Damascus airport in May 2016 in what was believed to be an Israeli airstrike.[26]

The red line that wasn't

Syria's chemical weapons

Syria developed its chemical weapons programme with the help of Egypt and the USSR in the 1970s and 1980s as a deterrent to Israel's nuclear capability. By 2011, US intelligence estimated that Assad retained one of the world's largest chemical stockpiles, including VX and Sarin, with production and storage facilities near Damascus, Aleppo, Homs and Latakia.[27] As the 2011 protests descended into civil war, this stockpile became an increasing cause of international concern. As Assad lost territory, especially around Aleppo and Homs, fears grew that they might fall into radical hands for use either within Syria or in international terror attacks. Primarily, however, attention remained on the regime as reports of it moving stockpiles and allegations of chemical weapons use emerged in 2012. Israel worried about transfers to Hezbollah, while pro-opposition powers feared Assad might emulate Saddam Hussein in gassing his own citizens to hold on to power.[28] In late July 2012, as rebel advances rattled the regime, the government admitted for the first time publicly that it possessed a chemical weapons arsenal insisting, in a not so veiled threat, that it would only be used against attacking external forces, not on its own people.[29]

The regime's admission provoked a response from Washington. On 20 August, President Obama stated:

> We have been very clear to the Assad regime, but also to other players on the ground, that a red line for us is we start seeing a whole bunch of chemical weapons moving around or being utilized. That would change my calculus.[30]

While the idea of a 'red line' on chemical weapons had first been used by US military spokespeople and Hillary Clinton a few weeks before Obama's statement, the President's declaration implied a willingness to intervene in Syria should Assad go too far, after a year of seemingly ruling the possibility out. This was reiterated in December, when Obama told Assad publicly, 'The use of chemical weapons is and would be totally unacceptable.'[31] Although Israeli pressure was a factor, it was unclear exactly what prompted Obama to declare chemical weapons as a red line over Assad's other forms of slaughter. Many in his administration were surprised by Obama's sudden forcefulness.[32] Some believed that Obama, who had urged global nuclear non-proliferation on becoming President in 2009, was broadly opposed to WMD and determined to prevent their proliferation or usage as a by-product of the Syrian war. Others believed the red line was a means to check Assad, ensuring he would rein in his conventional attacks with the threat of US intervention hanging over him. Either way, the declaration shifted US engagement with the crisis to focus on chemical weapons. For Assad's local and international enemies, the prospect of the long-hoped-for US intervention prompted a determination to prove that the regime was using chemical arms.

Since the crisis began, Assad's forces had deliberately deployed ever more violent weapons incrementally to gauge international reaction before proceeding. Syria's air force, for example, remained grounded for the first year of the war, with the regime no doubt aware that it was Gaddafi's use of airpower that prompted the rush for UN1973. However, when a handful of jets bombing rebel positions in Aleppo and Rastan in July 2012 provoked no international outrage, airpower was gradually increased until it became the norm.[33] The same was seen with the use of Scud missiles, first deployed against rebels in Aleppo in December 2012, but more frequently thereafter.[34] For the regime to quietly test Obama's red line with low-level chemical weapons attacks was therefore plausible, and from late 2012 the opposition and their allies claimed this was occurring. Al-Jazeera reported that on 23 December 2012 seven people had died after a regime gas attack in the al-Bayada district of Homs.[35]

The issue moved forward on 20 March 2013 when the regime itself requested that the UN Secretary-General, Ban Ki-moon, establish a 'specialized, impartial independent mission' to investigate an alleged chemical attack by rebels on regime positions in Khan al-Asal, Aleppo province, that had killed twenty-five soldiers the day before.[36] Ban agreed to this, creating the United Nations Mission to Investigate Allegations of the Use of Chemical Weapons in the Syrian Arab Republic on 21 March. However, on the same day Britain and France insisted the team also investigate alleged regime attacks. This complicated matters, prompting the regime to postpone the UN mission's arrival for several months, as it debated modalities and on-site access. In the meantime, letters from France, Britain, Qatar and the US arrived urging investigation of more alleged regime attacks. On 18 August, having agreed its terms of operation with the regime, the mission finally arrived in Damascus intending to spend fourteen days investigating the attack in Khan al-Asal, 'credible' allegations of new regime attacks in Sheikh Maqsood (Aleppo) in April and Saraqueb (Idlib) in May, and to discuss other allegations.[37]

However, three days after its arrival, on 21 August, up to 1,400 people were killed in a chemical attack in the Ghouta area of Damascus.[38] According to the UN mission report on the attack, published a month later, 'surface-to-surface rockets containing the nerve agent sarin were used in Ein Tarma, Moadamiyah and Zamalka in the Ghouta area of Damascus'. YouTube clips of civilians choking surfaced immediately, followed by media attention and an international outcry, prompting Ban to direct the mission in Damascus to prioritise investigating events in Ghouta. Inevitably the opposition and regime blamed each other. The fact that Ghouta was a rebel-held area and it was a sophisticated rocket attack, using equipment not known to be in the rebels' arsenal, immediately put the regime under suspicion. The regime put forward what UN mission chief Åke Sellström later called 'poor theories' about the rebels having acquired chemical weapons smuggled in from Turkey or Iraq.[39] Russia leapt to Assad's defence, with Putin claiming that the attack was 'by opposition forces, to provoke intervention by their powerful foreign patrons'.[40] It was, admittedly, odd that after delaying the arrival of the UN Mission for five months the regime would launch a huge chemical weapons attack within days of their arrival barely twelve miles from the mission's Damascus headquarters. The regime, however, had a record of audaciousness, as seen in its willingness to defy the Arab Peace plan and Annan plan it had signed up to earlier in the war. While the eventual UN mission report published in September 2013 was careful not to blame either side, in line with their mandate to establish only whether chemical weapons had been used, it was highly likely that regime forces were responsible.[41] However, there was sufficient ambiguity for the regime and its Russian allies to raise doubts, impacting the international response.

Washington's response: an unstoppable course of action?

Developments since Obama had declared his 'red line' in August 2012 had placed the President in a difficult position. On the one hand, even before Ghouta US intelligence was convinced that the Assad regime had deployed chemical weapons. In April 2013 the White House wrote a letter to Congress stating it believed, with 'varying degrees of confidence', that chemical weapons had been used, and consequently urged the UN Mission to examine further. Then in June, Ben Rhodes announced that US intelligence had identified multiple regime chemical attacks since 2012, apparently impacting Obama's decision to green-light the sending of lethal aid to rebel groups discussed in Chapter 6. However, at the same time events on the ground had made direct intervention even more unappealing. Despite US endorsement, the new Syrian Opposition Coalition (SOC) and the reorganised FSA–SMC had failed to unite the rebels or stem the growth of jihadists. While toppling Assad was still official US policy, there were no guarantees that his replacement would be moderate. With Libya now unstable, the White House was ever more conscious that post-Assad Syria might become a failed state: beset by ethno-sectarian violence and a safe haven for jihadists. Some in the administration, particularly McDonough, increasingly shared Israel's view that a prolonged civil war that tied up Iran and Hezbollah might not be so bad, provided it could be contained.[42]

This approach caused tension within the US inter-agency process even before Ghouta. Since Obama had called on Assad to go in August 2011, the State Department had been the loudest advocates of doing more, but the Department of Defense and others urged caution. Officials who favoured greater action, particularly those from the State Department, have subsequently complained of a lack of strategy: that Obama's team believed aspirational rhetoric such as the 'red line' would be a sufficient deterrent to Assad.[43] Obama's allies retort, however, that those urging greater action never offered a viable alternative, hence the rejection of Petraeus and Clinton's plan to arm the rebels in 2012. One former insider noted that, unlike the groupthink of the Bush White House, Obama's team was 'incredibly deliberative', but 'the State Department *lost* the argument time and time again'.[44] The same was true when outside experts were consulted. The Brookings Institution's Shadi Hamid argues that Obama systematically ignored experts on Syria who called for greater intervention, yet Marc Lynch counters that these opinions were considered but deemed less convincing than more cautious analyses.[45] Increasingly it was Obama himself that was the loudest voice of caution, the failures in Libya helping him reject his earlier interventionism. During the 2012 re-election campaign he emphasised this cautiousness, explaining in a debate with his rival Mitt Romney his reluctance to arm the rebels or intervene directly. At the beginning of his second term the replacements he chose for the more activist Clinton and Panetta, Kerry and Hagel, were both instinctively cautious.[46] Similarly he baulked at Centcom's estimate that it would take at least 75,000 US troops to seize Assad's chemical arsenal – Obama was unwilling to risk American lives on such an indeterminable outcome.[47]

Despite these cautious instincts, the scale and media storm around the Ghouta attacks persuaded everyone in the White House, including the President, that the US needed to act. Protecting the international norm on not using chemical weapons was important, but even more important was to show that the US backed up its threats, especially with negotiations on Iran's nuclear programme coming up. While the administration made a point of not rushing to judgement, five days after the attack on 26 August Kerry announced that all the evidence strongly indicated that chemical weapons had been used.[48] He did not yet blame the Assad regime directly, but that same day four US warships, along with two British, were deployed to the eastern Mediterranean. Two days earlier, in a meeting with his national security advisers, intelligence chiefs had told Obama they believed the Ghouta rockets had been fired from regime positions. For once there seemed some consensus in the White House on Syria. Rice and Power, who had long supported humanitarian intervention, pressed for action, while the usually cautious Biden, Hagel and Kerry all agreed, although Dempsey remained conspicuously wary of any military action. The main debate was over whether to strike immediately or wait for the UN mission's report.[49] Over the next week military plans were examined, with the preferred option believed to be a forty-eight-hour campaign of cruise missile strikes against regime positions beginning on 2 September (the day after the scheduled departure of the UN mission from Damascus) – enough to punish Assad but not enough to topple him.[50]

The first questions over this seemingly unstoppable course of action appeared in Britain. Cameron, who had urged Obama several times since 2011 to do more on Syria, was keen to participate and, in accordance with a new law introduced after the 2003 Iraq war, sought parliament's endorsement on 29 August.[51] However, convinced that a US strike was imminent, Cameron's government rushed, and prepared insufficiently for the vote. Still haunted by going to war in Iraq on faulty intelligence, a large number of Cameron's own Conservative Members of Parliament opposed the motion, as did many in the opposition Labour Party, themselves wary of repeating Iraq but also eager to land a defeat on the government. After a long and heated parliamentary debate, Cameron was defeated by 285 votes to 272, and grudgingly agreed that UK forces would play no role in any coming attack.[52] Once again a largely domestic concern for one of the players had serious consequences in Syria.

Whether the vote in London caused Obama to change heart is unclear. The immediate impact seemed muted, as a fifth and a sixth US warship were dispatched on 29 and 30 August to replace the impotent British vessels, while the White House team continued to brief in favour of a strike – John Kerry describing Assad as a 'thug and murderer'.[53] Yet Obama was far from confident, and had his doubts reinforced when James Clapper, his Director of National Intelligence, had stated earlier in the week that evidence for Assad's use of sarin in Ghouta was robust, but no 'slam dunk'. Then, on the evening of 30 August the President spent an hour on the White House South Lawn with Chief of Staff Denis McDonough, purposely selecting the most anti-interventionist of his staff as a sounding board.[54] On their return, Obama told his shocked team, who all expected him to authorise force against Assad, that he too would seek Congressional approval for the strike. In theory US presidents do require Congressional support for military action, but recent presidents, including Obama himself for UN1973, had unilaterally launched limited deployments with little domestic controversy. The decision, announced by Obama on television a day later, was therefore contentious. Was the President, also haunted by the faulty intelligence of the 2003 Iraq invasion and the post-intervention meltdown of Libya, covering his back should the Syria operation go south? Alternatively, was he using the vote, set for 9 September, as a delaying tactic to find other means to avoid a strike he was still not convinced by? With Obama's Democrats controlling the Senate but not the House of Representatives, and the opposition Republicans aggressively stonewalling his domestic agenda, victory in the vote was far from assured.

Obama's critics immediately attacked the move. Not only was he giving the Assad regime time to prepare for an attack – hence the flight of the Syrian elite into Lebanon – but he was damaging the standing of his office and the US internationally.[55] As the administration scrambled in search of Congress votes US diplomats explored other routes out of the crisis. Since Kerry had become Secretary of State he had effectively taken on the Syria brief alone, and strongly favoured greater cooperation with Russia. Channels had been opened with Moscow, culminating in a joint statement from Kerry and Foreign Minister Lavrov on 7 May 2013 that a political solution to the Syrian conflict should be sought – a breakthrough great enough to dissuade UN special envoy Lakhdar Brahimi from resigning.[56]

These channels now proved vital. On 6 September, at the G20 summit in St Petersburg, in between drumming up international support for a strike on Assad, Obama had a seemingly impromptu lunch meeting with Putin for 15–30 minutes. Then, on 9 September, in a comment that State Department officials later insisted was purely 'rhetorical', Kerry quipped that if Assad wanted to stop the bombing, 'he could turn over every single bit of his chemical weapons to the international community in the next week . . . it can't be done'.[57] Lavrov leapt on the statement and within hours announced that Russia was calling on Syria to hand over its arsenal to avoid airstrikes. Syrian Foreign Minster Walid al-Muallem immediately welcomed the suggestion, possibly with some Russian prompting.[58] The same day the US Senate majority leader, Democrat Harry Reid, had to delay the proposed vote on action to avoid defeat for Obama, making Russia's negotiated route out of the crisis look increasingly appealing.

Obama later said that the idea of peaceful disarmament was discussed with Putin in St Petersburg, but Lavrov's response to Kerry's remarks gave it momentum.[59] A US team led by Kerry was immediately dispatched to Geneva to work on a deal with Russia. On the third day, 14 September, a framework to remove or destroy Syria's entire chemical weapons arsenal under international supervision was jointly announced by the two foreign ministers. Simultaneously Syria announced it was joining the Chemical Weapons Convention, the international arms treaty that outlaws the production, stockpiling and use of chemical weapons. On 27 September, the UNSC unanimously passed resolution 2118, ordering Syria to comply fully and immediately with a disarmament programme overseen by the Organisation for the Prohibition of Chemical Weapons (OPCW). US military action was therefore indefinitely postponed, though the resolution did threaten harsh 'Chapter VII measures' in the event of Syria's non-compliance. Two days later, Assad announced he would comply and the OPCW began the destruction process on 6 October, for scheduled completion by mid-2014. The threat of US-led intervention, seemingly so certain a few weeks before, was suddenly over.

Obama: Weak or wise?

Obama's decision to call off the planned strike on Assad in favour of Russia's disarmament plan appeared to be one of the most consequential decisions of his presidency and the Syrian civil war. Subsequent critics focused on two, often overlapping charges: that he damaged US interests and made the situation worse in Syria. The first charge came mostly from Obama's American opponents. Republican Senators John McCain and Lindsey Graham labelled the disarmament deal an 'act of provocative weakness', while Mike Rogers, Republican chairman of the House Intelligence Committee, called it 'a Russian plan for Russian interests'.[60] Many Beltway commentators also claimed that Obama had damaged US credibility by not militarily enforcing his red line, and emboldened enemies like Iran and Russia while betraying allies like Turkey and Saudi Arabia who were shocked when the strikes were called off.[61] Indeed, when Russia sent troops into Ukraine and annexed the Crimea in February 2014, many claimed this audacity was a direct consequence of Obama's weakness the previous summer.

However, such criticisms exaggerate the impact of US power. The massive US invasion of Iraq in 2003 did not deter Russia from invading Georgia in 2008, so to suggest a limited strike on Syria would act as a brake on Moscow in Sevastopol is tenuous.[62] Similarly the episode seemed to have had little bearing on Obama's ability to eventually strike a nuclear deal with Iran in 2015. Moreover, the loss of trust by the US' regional allies had begun long before August 2013 although, as shall be discussed below, it did catalyse more problematic policies. Ultimately, these critics disputed the President's assessment of US interests. Obama had two main priorities: to prevent the proliferation and usage of chemical weapons and to avoid being sucked into the Syrian civil war. Launching a strike against Assad would not really achieve either goal. It might have deterred Assad from using his chemical weapons again, but they would have remained in Syria possibly to be passed on to Hezbollah or captured by jihadist groups. Moreover there was no guarantee that Assad would be deterred and, having established the precedent, the US would have to attack again. This would risk Obama's other priorities: not to tip the power balance in the war, to avoid increasing US responsibility for the conflict, and not to boost its allies' call for a no-fly zone and deeper intervention.

In contrast, the Russian deal achieved all of Obama's goals. Far from being weak, from Obama's perspective it was the threat of force that had made Assad and Russia compromise, producing all the results the administration sought without having to go to war.[63] As John Kerry later remarked, 'Because President Obama threatened force, diplomacy had a chance to work . . . Military strikes couldn't get the weapons out of Syria, period.'[64] While this may have meant a short-term loss in domestic and international credibility, Obama could stomach this to achieve his goals. Indeed, the President later remarked that he was 'proud' of stepping back from the brink that summer, avoiding being pressed into military action by Washington circles. He told *The Atlantic*, 'There's a playbook in Washington that presidents are supposed to follow. It's a playbook that comes out of the foreign-policy establishment . . . But the playbook can also be a trap that can lead to bad decisions.' The same interview noted how Obama and his advisers were conscious of how many of his domestic critics in prominent think tanks were funded by Arab governments keen to instrumentalise US military power for their own ends.[65]

The second group of critics, focussing on the region, deplored the negative impact on the Syria conflict. They argued that the chemical weapons deal boosted Assad's position: de facto legitimising him until at least mid-2014 as his regime needed to survive long enough to complete the disarmament process. Moreover the regime, Iran and Russia were psychologically boosted, believing they could now attack opposition areas with conventional weapons without fearing Western attacks. In contrast, the opposition received the blow of seeing their long-hoped-for external intervention dissipate.

Some of this criticism was justified. Assad certainly appeared boosted by the chemical weapons deal, with the question of Western military intervention seemingly off the table for now. However, it should be recalled that the war was already turning more in Assad's favour by mid-2013 after Suleimani's reorganisations and the intervention of Hezbollah. With Obama's proposed strike apparently designed not to impact the balance of power on the ground, its possible impact on the course of the war, bar psychology, must be questioned. Some posited that a strike might have prompted an internal regime coup against Assad, yet this seems unlikely. Any potential coup plotters had already seen Assad lose half of the country and not acted, either still believing in the Syrian President, fearing his coup-proofed internal security network, or believing there was already too much blood on their hands to risk it. Plus Iran and Hezbollah's deeper involvement in the regime added another layer of Assad loyalists for any plotters to get through.

At the heart of much of the criticism, however, was a mistaken belief that the strike would be a prelude to a more decisive US intervention: perhaps a no-fly zone or the destruction of Assad's air power. However, even had the White House actually wanted to shift the balance of power, this was still far from guaranteed to topple the regime, end the war or even make the conflict less violent. The opposition was still fragmented and could not be relied upon to unite and defeat the remnants of Assad's forces. The jihadists were in the ascendancy and might use the removal of Assad's air force to seize more territory. While destroying Assad's airpower might have reduced the conflict's casualty rate – being a far more destructive force than his chemical weapons – it could also have spread the war wider by limiting the regime's ability to defend rump Syria. On the other hand, it was also possible that Russia would have sent its own airpower earlier to test US resolve.

Such unknowns were no doubt debated in the White House in late summer 2013. Ultimately, Obama recognised that for all the US' military superiority, direct intervention was a gamble that looked more likely to make the situation in Syria worse than to succeed and, with US interests not directly threatened, it was better to try to contain the civil war than wade into what appeared another unsolvable quagmire. This jarred with those who believed the US should try to shape the conflict, whether liberal interventionists and neo-imperialists in DC or US allies in the Middle East, but it was consistent with Obama's worldview and foreign policy priorities.[66]

Aftermath

The aftermath of the non-strike incident illustrates its importance in the development of the Syrian civil war. While the above analysis questions whether the strike would actually have tipped the balance against the regime, many of Assad's enemies believed that it would. Many rebel fighters and all three of their key regional backers, Saudi Arabia, Turkey and Qatar, had based their strategies on the assumption that eventually the US would intervene. With the chemical weapons deal seemingly removing that prospect for good, new approaches were rapidly sought. Furious with what they saw as an American betrayal, regional governments were more willing than ever to work with groups unpalatable to Washington.

Saudi Arabia had strongly supported Obama's proposed strike. John Kerry later told the House Foreign Affairs Committee that Gulf states, widely believed to be led by Saudi Arabia and Qatar, had offered to underwrite the full cost of the military operation. Saudi Arabia had also proposed putting a motion to the UN General Assembly in September endorsing the bombing to give the US legal cover that it would be denied by Russia at the Security Council. It also volunteered its air force to counter any potential Iranian retaliation in the Gulf.[67] Yet not only did Obama call off the strike, but the Saudi Arabian leadership claimed it was not informed, only discovering the news from CNN. This illustrated once more the limited capacity of Saudi Arabia, which lacked close ties with Obama's White House, to keep in the loop. It also revealed Obama's own disregard for Riyadh; showing he did not feel the need to keep Saudi Arabia informed. Even so, King Abdullah, Bandar and the Saudi Arabian leadership were outraged. Later, the BBC's Frank Gardner would suggest this was a 'seminal moment and a turning point in its [Saudi Arabia] dealings with the US', fuelling a more independent activist and militaristic regional policy.[68] This trend was already under way, as was seen by Riyadh's capture of the Syrian opposition earlier in 2013, but the non-strike betrayal catalysed it further.

The non-strike incident had already impacted the rebels. In late September, eleven Islamist, mostly northern, militia including Nusra, Tawheed and Suqour al-Sham jointly announced that they did not recognise the Syrian Opposition Coalition (SOC). They denounced it as 'unrepresentative' and called for a new opposition reorganised under 'an Islamic framework based on sharia [Islamic law]'.[69] Jihadists such as Nusra had long opposed the SOC and condemned its support for Obama's strikes. In contrast Tawheed and Suqour had been key SOC and FSA–SMC allies. Their rejection partly reflected the gradual radicalisation of the opposition. It also revealed a new lack of faith in the SOC's ability to attract Western intervention, which had been a key pragmatic justification for Islamists to cooperate. Days later one of the signatories, Liwa al-Islam, led a merger with forty-two other, mostly Damascus-based militias to form the Salafist Jaysh al-Islam (Army of Islam), with Liwa's Zahran Alloush as leader. Alloush's father was a Saudi-based Salafist preacher and the merger was brokered by Saudi intelligence to build an Islamist counterweight to the al-Qaeda-aligned Nusra and ISIS.[70] Backing a group so openly against the SOC and FSA–SMC – which it was also still supporting – represented a major departure for Riyadh, especially as it had only gained oversight of the opposition that spring. However, it illustrated the level of concern among Saudi Arabia's leaders after forlornly pinning their hopes on a moderate opposition to attract US intervention. In November, a new Islamic Front was then announced with Saudi Arabian approval, including Jaysh al-Islam, Tawheed, Suqour and Ahrar. It notably absented Nusra, with whom many had cooperated in the anti-SOC statement. The new organisation was headed by Suqour's Ahmed Issa al-Sheikh, with Alloush as military chief and Ahrar's Hassan Abboud as political bureau head. All its members dissolved their old affiliations such as the SIF and SILF, and those within the FSA–SMC withdrew. Having failed to build up a moderate force to challenge both Assad and the jihadists, Saudi Arabia became increasingly open to Salafist forces, even if it met Washington's disapproval.

Turkey similarly felt betrayed by Obama. As one Turkish official noted, 'when Obama declared a red line, we took it seriously and we were disappointed when he took no action'.[71] Of course Ankara, like Riyadh and many others, regarded 'action' purely in military terms and hadn't appreciated the possibility that this US President had a broader interpretation. Indeed,

Erdoğan had publicly said he thought Obama's limited strikes would have been insufficient, saying '24 hours of intervention is not enough, it has to be done as it was done in Kosovo'.[72] When even this did not occur, Ankara's disappointment was palpable. President Gül later remarked, 'we expected more [from the United States]. I think it is very disappointing to see the whole discussion reduced to a discussion solely on chemical weapons.'[73] Meanwhile, alarm bells were ringing in Ankara in November when the PYD unilaterally declared the Syrian territory it possessed as the autonomous region of Rojava. With the prospect of a PKK quasi-state on its southern border, Turkey turned an ever-blinder eye to the radical groups criss-crossing its border with Syria.[74] Clashes between ISIS and the PYD from autumn 2013, for example, were not wholly counter to Turkish interests. Similarly in March 2014 a joint Nusra and Ahrar attack was launched on the regime-held Syrian-Armenian village of Kassab on the Turkish border in an apparent attempt by the rebels to capture a port. Multiple witnesses claimed that Turkey, allowing them access through its territory, facilitated this assault but Ankara denied all such ties.[75]

Linking the behaviour of the regime and its allies on the ground, Iran and Hezbollah, in late 2013 to the non-strike is more difficult. Assad's forces enjoyed considerable success, including capturing key supply roads into Aleppo and the rebel-held Damascus suburbs of Sheikh Omar and Sbeineh in October and November. Obama's critics blamed this on the boost from not being attacked, but this was more likely Suleimani and Hezbollah's earlier reorganisations bearing fruit. Indeed it was only in rump Syria that these successes occurred and some ground was actually lost in peripheral Deir ez-Zor and Deraa province. The regime's successes were likely aided by the weak state of the rebels at this time partly due to the blow of the US' rejection of intervention. As the regime was advancing, some rebel groups were fighting one another, with FSA-affiliated groups in particular losing ground. Azaz in Aleppo province fell to ISIS in September, while numerous bases including FSA headquarters in Bab al-Hawa, Idlib province, fell to the new Islamic Front in December.

A final, short-lived outcome was an increase in Russian–US cooperation on Syria. Having successfully brokered the Geneva chemical weapons talks, Kerry sought to re-energise the 7 May Declaration with Lavrov. On 7 October they agreed that a peace conference based on Annan's 2012 Geneva Communiqué, dubbed 'Geneva II', should take place the next month. While Russia took a while to persuade the regime and the US its allies and the fractured opposition, eventually Ban Ki-moon announced the talks would begin on 22 January 2014. However, as shall be seen in the coming chapter, events in Ukraine and the inadequacies on both sides in the run-up to the conference ensured the abject failure of the talks and the end of US–Russian cooperation.

In the first years of the war, the question of external direct military intervention hung over the conflict and in many ways shaped it. The Turkish and Israeli militaries engaged in limited direct action, but neither fundamentally shifted the balance of power in the conflict. In contrast, the possibility of Western intervention simultaneously constrained and escalated the war. Fear of provoking the West had prompted Assad to incrementally increase his violence. Similarly the desire to encourage Western intervention had led regional powers Saudi Arabia, Turkey and Qatar to favour more moderate armed opposition groups (even if they also discreetly backed radicals too). At the same time though, Obama's unwillingness to dispel the myth that he might intervene served as a conflict escalator as rebels and regional allies pursued strategies that rested on eventual US military support. Yet once the possibility of Western intervention was removed, the Syrian civil war unquestionably worsened. Assad and his allies felt they could deploy whatever conventional weapons they liked. The US' furious regional allies increasingly shifted their sponsorship to more radical groups, while the radicals had less incentive to moderate. The number of refugees crossing into Lebanon and elsewhere accelerated. On the day of the Ghouta attack, the UNHCR had registered just under 1.8 million Syrian refugees, but that number jumped to 2.9 million a year later, and 4 million the year after that.[76] The realisation that the US was not coming to swiftly end the war may, alongside the worsening conditions of the war, have prompted even more refugees to lose hope and flee.

Obama was widely criticised for not striking Assad in summer 2013, but from a US perspective his actions made sense. The Russian plan achieved his goals of disarming Assad's chemical weapons without getting sucked into what he saw as an unwinnable war, which the proposed missile strike would not have done. From the perspective of the Syrian conflict, some argued that the regime's concessions on chemical disarmament when threatened illustrate that Obama should have used it earlier to force Assad out. Yet Assad appeared willing to compromise in 2013 primarily as a means to remain in power. Had the threat been to his leadership, he would have had no incentive to cooperate. Therefore, while it might have been possible for Obama to use the threat of force earlier in the crisis to moderate the regime's behaviour, as soon as the White House called for Assad's departure in August 2011 this possibility was effectively removed as the war became a zero sum struggle over Assad's survival. If Obama deserves criticism, then, it is for the mixed signals he sent over intervention in the run-up to summer 2013 and, afterwards, for not realising the impact the lack of action would have on the players on the ground. This again was the consequence of changing perceptions of US power in the region, and the unwillingness of regional players to believe that Washington was no longer the hegemon it had once been.

CHAPTER NINE

Descent into chaos: Stalemate and the rise of ISIS

As is so often the tragic path of revolution, it was the Montagne that triumphed over the Gironde.

Alistair Horne, *The Savage War of Peace: Algeria 1954–1962*[1]

Revolutions devour their children. The liberals that made the Tennis Court Oath in 1789 did not see the coming Terror, while leftist protesters among Tehran's 1978–79 revolutionaries did not imagine they would help bring about Khomeini's Islamic Republic. Syria's Revolution, in the lands that were freed from Assad's rule, frequently followed a similar trajectory. The street protesters of 2011 were a broad coalition, with a strong youth-led educated core, overwhelmingly peaceful and not overtly Islamist. Yet as these original protesters were killed, arrested, or fled – often deliberately targeted by Assad – radical armed groups increasingly became the dominant military and ideological forces. Conservative bodies were established to enforce strict Islamic laws in many rebel areas, such as the Islamist Sharia Authority in eastern Aleppo.[2] Some of the original protesters bemoaned the hijacking of their revolution by radicals. Nowhere was this more apparent than in the brutality meted out in the areas held by ISIS, which greatly expanded its territory in 2014. Large stretches of eastern Syria became a theocratic dictatorship that forbade music and smoking and where gruesome spectacles of violence such as public beheadings and even crucifixions were commonplace. Barely three years earlier Raqqa, which became the capital of ISIS' self-declared 'Caliphate', had seen peaceful crowds shouting 'The People want the fall of the Regime' and 'God, Syria, Freedom, that's all'. What they got was a far cry from the sentiment of 2011.

The expansion of ISIS' holdings in the summer of 2014 dramatically shifted outside views of the civil war. While the US had ultimately declined to strike Assad in 2013, a year later it assembled an international coalition to 'degrade and destroy' the newly declared 'Caliphate'. Washington regarded

ISIS as a more immediate threat than Assad, but the other players mostly saw it as a lesser priority than their other interests in Syria. This chapter will consider how and why ISIS emerged, and who was responsible – with most of the players, particularly Assad, complicit in some way. It will also examine the immediate context in which ISIS' sudden expansion came: the failure of the long-awaited Geneva II peace conference and the continued infighting among rebel groups, greatly exacerbated by the regional rivalry between Saudi Arabia and Qatar.

Geneva II

The 'Geneva II' peace talks finally began on 22 January 2014 in the Swiss resort town of Montreux. UN Special Envoy Lakhdar Brahimi would later describe the conference as 'an exercise in futility', such were the flaws in its conception and execution.[3] The meeting resulted from the previous summer's chemical weapons deal, with Moscow and Washington re-committing to Lavrov and Kerry's May 2013 agreement on seeking a peaceful solution to the war. However, the belligerents still had to be pressed. After engineering a way out of US strikes, Damascus owed Moscow and so unsurprisingly announced its intention to attend in November, although Russian diplomats claimed this had already been agreed in May.[4] Pursuing a diplomatic solution to the crisis had been Russia's stance since 2011 and the US' acceptance of this was perceived as vindication by Putin's government.[5]

Persuading the opposition was more challenging. The denunciation by eleven Islamist militias in September 2013 rocked the SOC, while the FSA saw itself undermined then attacked by former comrades in the new Islamic Front, sponsored by its own allies in Riyadh. As radical fighters became ever more dominant, the SOC struggled for relevance, and its delegates feared losing what little credibility it had by sitting down with Assad's representatives at a peace conference. The SNC, still the largest single group, threatened to withdraw from the SOC if it took part. Yet with Western and regional powers backing the talks, they were pressured to participate, first in a Friends of Syria meeting in late October, then in the Arab League in early November – when Saudi Arabia and Qatar temporarily put aside their rivalry and urged involvement. The SOC voted to attend Geneva II on 11 November but attached preconditions: relief agencies should be given access to besieged areas and all prisoners, especially women and children, had to be released.[6] These demands were later quietly dropped and the SOC delegation arrived in Montreux without any of them having been granted.[7] Yet its mandate was limited: radical militants including the Islamic Front rejected the talks, while 45 of the 120 SOC delegates abstained from the final vote to approve participation.[8]

The one concession granted the SOC was the exclusion of Iran. Tehran's invitation was controversial, as it had been absent from Annan's original 2012 Geneva gathering. William Hague and French Foreign Minister Laurent Fabius had both commented in the run-up to the conference that Iran should be party to talks while the US was more amenable now that the more moderate Rouhani was President and nuclear talks had reopened in March 2013.[9] Ban Ki-moon, Arab League Secretary General Nabil El-Araby and Brahimi all recognised the importance of Iran's presence and Ban announced an invitation days before talks began on 19 January. This prompted outrage by the SOC President Ahmad Jarba and his patron, Saudi Arabia. The US, Britain and France now insisted that Iran should attend only if it fully endorsed the Geneva Communiqué, particularly accepting the principle of a transition government, which Tehran had long rejected. With the SOC threatening to walk out, Ban had to humiliatingly rescind Iran's invitation a day later, prompting Russian disapproval. Despite the presence of representatives from forty different countries, including Australia and Indonesia, Iran, a key player, was thus excluded. It was a bad start.

It became immediately clear that the regime had no interest in negotiation. Its delegation was led by powerless diplomats rather than anyone from Assad's inner circle who might offer meaningful concessions. It appeared to have been instructed to stonewall and derail the process. On the first day the Syrian Foreign Minister, Walid al-Muallem, delivered an extraordinary opening speech that ran well over his allocated time – to the visible irritation of Ban – in which he hurled abuse at the opposition and their foreign backers. The FSA, he said, 'cannibalise human hearts and livers, barbecue heads, recruit child soldiers and rape women', their Gulf supporters were 'princes and emirs living in mud and backwardness', Erdoğan's Turkey was a 'backstabbing neighbour', and 'seated among us are representatives of countries who have blood of our people on their hands'.[10] Jarba replied in a more measured way, but clinging to the core opposition demand of Assad's departure, stating, 'Al-Assad cannot stay on his throne. We cannot have so many people dying because one man wants to stay on the throne.'

As the days progressed, things improved little. Observers noted that the SOC delegation, led by Hadi al-Bahra, gradually became more positive after prompting from their Western backers, but the regime remained uninterested, often resorting to insults. The first session in the last week of January, intended to focus on confidence-building measures like humanitarian access, ended with no serious agreements, although a local ceasefire in

Homs did eventually progress. A second round, from 10 to 15 February, was agreed upon but, despite a more successful evacuation of besieged civilians in Homs, talks broke down again. On 15 February Brahimi publicly apologised to the Syrian people for the conference's failure, stating that the regime had refused to countenance a transition government and that he would consult with the conference co-sponsors on how to move forward. However, within weeks Russia annexed the Crimea and the brief era of US–Russian cooperation after the 2013 chemical weapons deal came to a sudden end. As a reward to the SOC for attending Montreux in late January the US had already resumed sending non-lethal aid to the rebels, suspended in December after the FSA's base was raided by the Islamic Front. A month later it resumed lethal assistance too. Russia, along with China, vetoed a 65-state-sponsored resolution referring the Assad regime to the International Criminal Court on 22 May. A few weeks before, Brahimi, exasperated, had finally resigned.

So why did Geneva II prove such an 'exercise in futility'? It is difficult to avoid the conclusion that the conditions were never right for a peace conference to succeed. No side wanted to be there and both, like many of their external backers, still believed primarily in a military solution. As Brahimi had stated beforehand, the problem was getting them to accept the 'very principle of a political solution'. Academic studies of civil war concur that for negotiation to succeed, both sides need to have reached a hurting stalemate. As David Cunningham writes,

> At every point over the course of the conflict, then, each party compares the expected utility from three options: ceasing the armed struggle, agreeing to some negotiated settlement, or continuing fighting. If actors are rational and risk-neutral, they will pursue the policy that gives them the highest expected utility.[11]

Approaching Geneva II, neither side was sufficiently hurting to believe that negotiation gave them the highest expected utility. The Assad regime had survived the onslaught of 2012–13 and, with Iranian support, was fighting back. The SOC and FSA were weaker, losing ground to radical opposition fighters, but were wary of negotiation in case it should undermine their positions further. Continuing fighting, with greater Western backing, in the hope of winning back support on the ground, was still its preferred option.

The two sides attended Montreux, then, not because they saw it as a means to achieve their goals, but to appease their external allies, Russia and the US. Yet neither patron was willing or able to put sufficient pressure on their allies to change their calculations. The SOC was more pliable, due to its weaker position, but with the US offering it arms as a reward for attendance, and its other regional sponsors financing more radical groups like the Islamic Front, armed conflict was hardly being discouraged. Instead, the SOC was incentivised to be seen to engage at Geneva II, to justify receiving heavier armed support after it failed. The regime was also given no incentive to engage. Iran was not invited, leaving a key regime ally outside the tent, actively discouraging Assad from offering anything. Russia, meanwhile, seemed satisfied that Damascus was willing to send a delegation and used none of its leverage, such as withholding UNSC vetoes or weaponry, to nudge the regime further. Indeed, it must be questioned how seriously the sponsors themselves took the conference. Lavrov and Kerry both agreed to the principle of a peaceful outcome, but neither had given more ground on the Geneva Communiqué than in summer 2012. Washington and its allies saw the conference as a means to create a transition government without Assad, while Moscow saw it as a means to create one still dominated by him and his regime. This fundamental disagreement had not been resolved before Montreux, meaning that, even had the two sponsors pushed their Syrian allies harder, they still would have reached the same impasse. Emerging disagreements over Ukraine only made these tensions worse. Geneva II was therefore dead on arrival.

Regional rivalry and rebel politics

As the brief era of Russo-American detente ended, the rivalry between the opposition's regional backers was intensifying, spilling over on to Syria's battlefields. The fallout from the anti-MB coup in Egypt in July 2013 and subsequent regional developments caused a serious rupture between the anti-Assad camp's lead players of Saudi Arabia, Qatar and Turkey. Both Doha and Ankara were furious at Riyadh for sponsoring the Egyptian military's ouster of their ally Morsi, in whom they had invested considerably – over $5 billion in the case of Qatar. With Turkey insulated by its size and distance, tension centred on the Gulf where Qatar's new leader, Tamim, was pressured by Saudi Arabia and its partner in the Egyptian coup, the UAE. The Emirati Crown Prince, Mohammed bin Zayed, shared Saudi Arabia's hostility to the Muslim Brotherhood and resented Qatar's regional sponsorship of it and its affiliates, not just in Egypt but also in post-Gaddafi Libya. As the new Egyptian government violently cracked down on the MB, Qatari spokesmen and al-Jazeera programmes, especially Qaradawi's, denounced the new regime, much to Saudi Arabia and the UAE's chagrin.

Doha was believed still to be funding its persecuted allies: nine al-Jazeera journalists were put on trial in Egypt accused of aiding a terrorist organisation, as the MB was designated in September 2013. In addition Saudi Arabia was concerned that Qatar was aiding the al-Qaeda affiliate Nusra in Syria, which Doha denied.

This intra-GCC dispute boiled over in March 2014 when the UAE, Saudi Arabia and Bahrain, effectively a Saudi Arabia vassal since 2011, withdrew their ambassadors to Qatar. This was not without precedent – Saudi Arabia had done the same in 2002–08 in opposition to anti-Saudi al-Jazeera reports – but the impact was harder, coming when Tamim was still new to his throne and consolidating power. In a joint statement Qatar was accused of not complying with a commitment made in November 2013 not to support 'anyone threatening the security and stability of the GCC (Gulf Cooperation Council) whether as groups or individuals – via direct security work or through political influence, and not to support hostile media' – primarily referring to the MB.[12] Though Tamim claimed to be prioritising internal affairs, Mohammed bin Zayed and Riyadh were sceptical that Qatar's international machinations would suddenly cease, and were also confident that the new Emir was weaker and more assailable than his father. The UAE even hired an American PR consulting firm, Camstoll Group, to target Qatar in the US media and in late 2013 and early 2014 a clutch of journalists accused Qatar of supporting terrorist groups.[13] As shown in Chapter 6, Qatar was far from innocent of backing radical groups, but it was not alone. However, the media storm in the US over 2014 contributed to a backlash against Qatar's previous activism.

This intra-GCC dispute was played out in Libya, with UAE jets launching a surprise assault alongside Egypt against Qatari-backed Islamists in August 2014, and in Syria, where Riyadh's allies struggled with Doha's. Many of the groups originally sponsored by Qatar in 2012–13 had already sought support elsewhere by 2014, and the Saudi Arabian sponsorship of the Islamic Front in late 2013 had secured more rebels for Riyadh than Doha. The Battle of Yabroud in March 2014 was the starkest example of this shift in alignment, and a case of external rivalries hurting the rebel cause. Hezbollah and regime forces assaulted Yabroud as part of the Qalamoun campaign to remove rebel forces from the Lebanese border. The various rebel groups resisted for a month before the sudden loss in two days. Accounts to journalists by both sides suggested that the rebels had split, with Nusra abandoned in the town while other rebel forces retreated. Nusra sources, alleged then to be backed by Qatar, claimed that Saudi Arabia had ordered its allies to retreat and withheld reinforcements. This ensured that Yabroud would fall, weakening

Qatar's allies and preventing them from getting a foothold in Lebanon, opposed by Saudi Arabia's Lebanese Sunni allies.[14]

Yet despite success in reducing Qatar's influence, Saudi Arabia's Syria policy was not going well. Its newest ally, the Islamic Front, had more success against fellow rebels than against the regime, which was still advancing. In March 2014, barely five months after its formation, observers were noting serious fraying within the Front over relations with ISIS, which was becoming a threat. In April 2014 King Abdullah dismissed Prince Bandar from his position as head of general intelligence. Bandar had been given the Syria file partly in the hope that he could persuade Washington to increase its involvement, but this now lay in tatters after the 2013 non-strike. Since then an angry Bandar had been publicly threatening Russia and, more worryingly, criticising Obama. Though Abdullah and many Saudi Arabian leaders likely agreed in private, the prince was regarded as a loose cannon exacerbating the already strained US–Saudi relationship.[15] Bandar's strategy with the rebels was also problematic, with Saudi Arabia, Gulf and Western diplomats privately suggesting that ISIS and Nusra may have benefited from Bandar's tilt towards Salafist groups in autumn 2013.[16]

Abdullah shared the Syria file between his son, Mutaib bin Abdullah, head of the Saudi Arabian National Guard, and Minister of the Interior Prince Mohammed bin Nayef, prompting a nuanced shift in direction. Mohammed bin Nayef's appointment was an important panacea for the White House, where he was respected for leading an internal anti-terrorism campaign and for being one of the few in the next generation of Saudi Arabian princes (Ibn Saud's grandsons) to be given serious power in Riyadh – something Washington had long been urging.[17] Mohammed bin Nayef was more concerned by ISIS and Nusra than Bandar, having cracked down on al-Qaeda in Saudi Arabia in the 2000s, who targeted him for assassination in four separate attempts.[18] As a result of this, and Mohammed bin Nayef's character, the departure of Bandar coincided with a more measured Saudi Arabian approach. Attention was focused on the southern front, and in the north there was greater willingness to cooperate with Turkey and Qatar. Doha, chastened by the combined UAE–Saudi assault gradually relented, symbolically expelling several MB members from Qatar in September 2014 and delegating a lot of its leadership over the Syrian rebels to Turkey. Gradually Ankara too dropped its hostility to Saudi Arabia.[19] This cooperation wouldn't expand sufficiently to make substantial gains on the ground until early 2015, but by mid-2014 the Qatari–Saudi rivalry that had undermined the rebels for so long seemed to be turning a corner.

The Islamic State of Iraq and al-Sham

On 10 June 2014 barely 1,300 ISIS fighters captured Mosul, Iraq's third city with a population of over 600,000. At the end of the month, ISIS leader Abu Bakr al-Baghdadi (a *nom de guerre*) announced that the territory he controlled in western Iraq and eastern Syria, centred on Raqqa, were now part of a worldwide Caliphate, the 'Islamic State', which sought to unite all Muslims under its political, religious and military authority. The declaration, along with the speed of the capture of Mosul and the brutality it showed its opponents, caught the world's attention and dramatically shifted the complexion of the Syrian civil war. What had for three years appeared a binary struggle between Assad and the various rebels now included a third major actor, the Islamic State, which opposed both and concerned Western leaders far more than Assad ever had. Moreover, after ISIS stepped up its assault on Kurdish positions it became clear that Kurdish militias, dominated by the PYD, were also now effectively a fourth player in the Syrian morass. Transformative though the emergence of ISIS was, its rise took several years before 2014 and, unsurprisingly, was greatly impacted by the actions of external powers.

The rise of ISIS

ISIS had its origins in Iraq. In 2006 al-Qaeda in Iraq (AQI), which had thrived in the post-Saddam Hussein chaos, merged with other jihadists to form Islamic State in Iraq (ISI). Though its leadership was decimated by the US troop surge of 2007 and a backlash against its harsh conservatism by Iraqi Sunni tribes known as the Sahwa (Awakening) movements, the failure of the US to transform its military success into a political solution coupled with growing Sunni resentment at the sectarian politics of Shia Iraqi Prime Minister Nouri al-Maliki, opened the door for ISI's return.[20] In 2010 al-Baghdadi, an Iraqi Islamist detained in Camp Bucca by US forces before joining al-Qaeda, assumed the ISI leadership and reorganised. He recruited many of Saddam's disgruntled former army officers into his leadership and gradually rebuilt ISI power as the US drew down before leaving Iraq in December 2011.[21] Seeing advantage when the Syrian uprising turned into a civil war, as well as sending Abu-Mohammad al-Jolani to form Nusra, ISI dispatched fighters over the border. It eventually acquired sufficient supporters and territory inside Syria to rename itself the Islamic State of Iraq and al-Sham (ISIS) in April 2013. Though this prompted a split with Nusra and with al-Qaeda leader Zawahiri (described in Chapter 6) Baghdadi's organisation continued to thrive on both sides of the border.[22] From the very beginning, ISIS positioned itself as a transnational force, attracting to its ranks a large segment of the foreign jihadists that had travelled to Syria to fight Assad.

ISIS' uncompromising jihadism put it on a collision course with other rebel groups. In August 2013 it captured Raqqa, driving out Nusra and the FSA, followed by further clashes the next month in Al-Bab, Deir ez-Zor, Al-Bukamal and Azaz.[23] Alarmed, several rebel militia, including Tawheed, Suqor and Nusra, formed the first of several anti-ISIS alliances, yet made little headway. Fighting erupted more violently in January 2014 when the recently formed Islamic Front accused ISIS of torturing and murdering Hussein al-Suleiman (Abu Rayyan), a popular Ahrar commander. Encouraged by Bandar, the Islamic Front joined with the Syrian Revolutionaries Front (an FSA-dominated group of militia from Idlib) and the Jaysh al-Mujahadeen (a new Aleppo alliance composed of former FSA and MB affiliated militia) to fight ISIS directly. Within a week Nusra also joined.[24] An estimated 3,300 were killed on both sides in January and February but the campaign pushed ISIS out of Idlib and the countryside west of Aleppo. ISIS consolidated its positions around Raqqa and the east instead.[25] The fighting ended any hopes that ISIS might be reconciled with al-Qaeda. Both Nusra and Zawahiri had tried to broker truces, but ISIS refused and even assassinated the latter's special envoy, Ahrar commander Abu Khalid al-Suri.[26] On 3 February, al-Qaeda general command formally cut all links with ISIS. Some claimed that Baghdadi was too extreme even for al-Qaeda, but the split also came as Zawahiri and his allies were reassessing tactics. After failing in Iraq with the brutal top down approach now favoured by ISIS, al-Qaeda opted instead to build support from the ground up, as Nusra was attempting.[27]

In parallel with fighting rebels, ISIS faced off against Kurdish militia, primarily the PYD's YPG. After capturing Kobane from Nusra in July 2013, YPG-led Kurdish forces clashed with various Islamist rebels as it sought to expand into Syria's Kurdish-dominated north-eastern regions. ISIS engaged the YPG in a series of battles, with the latter sometimes cooperating with local Christian and Turkmen militia and Arab tribes. YPG fighters pushed ISIS out of parts of Hasakah province, including the Yaroubiyeh border crossing into Iraq in October and advanced westwards in November.[28] After declaring 'Rojava' the YPG then took advantage of rebel–ISIS fighting in early 2014 to capture Tal Abyad. By spring, however, ISIS recovered and in early April began a siege of Kobane, where the PYD had established its headquarters. By June they retook Tal Abyad and forcibly expelled a number of Kurdish and Christian residents.[29]

If ISIS' ideological differences with other rebels and the Kurds formed an important driver of conflict, another was competition for resources.

Two were particularly fought over, border crossings and oilfields, and both were found in 'Rojava'. Unlike the other rebels or the regime, neither ISIS nor the PYD were seeking to conquer the whole of Syria, but rather build autonomous regions in the east and so attached more value to these resources. Control of border crossings into Turkey and Iraq allowed the PYD to link up with Iraqi and Turkish PKK allies who supplied them with fighters, weapons and finances, and allowed ISIS to link up with their Iraqi forces (in the case of Iraqi borders), or gain access to weapons and finances from external supporters via Turkey. This also made crossings on the Turkish border valuable to non-ISIS rebel groups. All groups made considerable income from taxing anyone crossing or taking goods through their captured border posts.[30]

The oilfields similarly prompted competition. As the regime withdrew to rump Syria in 2012–13 it prioritised its western natural gas fields, which provided most of Syria's electricity, abandoning its eastern oilfields.[31] Syria's largest oilfields in Hasakah province were taken over by the PYD in 2012 and, although its leader Salih Muslim claimed the fields were not functioning, other reports suggested up to 40,000 b/d was produced for Rojava's needs and to sell on. In Deir ez-Zor and Raqqa provinces tribal actors moved in to operate the fields, constructing basic refineries and negotiating deals with the dominant rebel military groups in the area over the oil's subsequent transport and sale in Turkey or Iraq.[32] In an attempt to bolster the SOC and its allies, in April 2013 the EU lifted its embargo on the purchase of Syrian oil, permitting Europeans to buy crude if approved by the external opposition. However, FSA–SMC groups were weak in the oil-rich east and the lifting of the embargo only incentivised radical groups to secure the fields and deprive their FSA rivals of income. Initially Ahrar and Nusra dominated, but were pushed out by ISIS during clashes in 2013–14. Indeed, in a sign of the importance of resources, Nusra's last pockets of territory in eastern Syria were the large oilfields in the Euphrates valley, finally lost to ISIS in mid-2014. Using agents from clans and tribes that had sworn them loyalty, ISIS then produced up to 50,000 b/d by mid-2014, used for their own military purposes and also sold within Syria and to Turkish traders.[33]

By the time it captured Mosul, then, ISIS had a battle-hardened core that had been fighting other rebels and Kurds for well over a year, funded and fuelled by rent from oil and border posts, as well as outside supporters. It had captured and retained several cities, including Raqqa and the Iraqi city of Fallujah (gained in January 2014) and had infiltrated Mosul before its attack, winning sympathy from a Sunni population resentful of Maliki's sectarianism. Their assault was helped by the corrupt Iraqi army garrison which, though well equipped by its US allies, was low on morale.[34] Within four days, the city capitulated. Al-Baghdadi's subsequent declaration of a Caliphate came amid a massive expansion of ISIS' territory. In June the Iraqi cities of Samarra and Tikrit were captured, while pressure was placed on Kirkuk and Baghdad, prompting desperate defensive moves from the Kurdistan Regional Government (KRG) and Iraqi forces respectively. ISIS' audacity, along with its newly acquired wealth, won it many admirers and over 6,000 Syrian fighters, many former FSA, were reported to have joined in July alone.[35] Swelled by confidence, new recruits and a vast cache of US-supplied weapons looted from Iraqi army positions in Mosul, ISIS was able to attack all of its Syrian enemies simultaneously. In July Nusra was finally pushed out of the Euphrates. The new weaponry helped intensify the siege on PYD-held Kobane. Finally, it came into conflict more and more with the Assad regime, including a series of bloody clashes from June to August that gave the regime its worst casualties of the war so far. This raised questions about the regime's relationship with ISIS. Theoretically they were sworn enemies, but had not fought a great deal until now. Observers questioned whether this was simply tactical, in that they were targeting their mutual enemies in the rebels before inevitably turning on each other, or a more sinister collaboration.

ISIS and the regime

Members of the Syrian opposition and their supporters accused Damascus of complicity in ISIS' rise. Hassan and Weiss list various regime machinations. Patrick Cockburn, in contrast, claims that ISIS attacks on Assad in summer 2014 showed such conspiracies to be false.[36] Both arguments carry some weight. The regime certainly created conditions in which ISIS could thrive. Firstly, Assad sponsored al-Qaeda in Iraq (AQI) in the decade before the civil war as a means to destabilise the US presence there.[37] Despite Assad's frequent denials, many regime officials admitted this in private, and the former ambassador to Baghdad, Nawaf al-Fares, who defected in 2012, claimed that he knew several regime liaison officers who worked directly with AQI.[38] This helped scupper US attempts to militarily wipe out AQI, allowing the space for Baghdadi to reorganise in 2010 and eventually dispatch agents into Syria.[39] Moreover, the regime's flirtation with jihadism in the 2000s against the US in Iraq had created networks of Syrian jihadists that would turn on the regime in favour of ISIS and other radicals once the war began.[40] Secondly, once the war began, the regime's tactics helped radicalise the opposition, creating more space for radicals like ISIS. As described in Chapter 6, regime Shabiha deliberately mocked Sunni beliefs and targeted Sunnis for verbal, psycho-logical and sexual abuse. At the same time, renowned Islamists such as Abboud, Alloush and Issa al-Sheikh were released from prison in the hope that they would squeeze out the moderates.

Most importantly, once ISIS had declared its presence and captured Raqqa and other territory in 2013, the regime targeted it less than other rebel groups. As the regime attacked rebel positions, the ISIS strongholds in the east remained largely untouched. When Assad bombed Raqqa after the attacks of June 2014 it was the first notable regime air raid on ISIS, despite other rebel areas having been exposed to frequent strikes since 2012.[41] The opposition accused the regime of deliberately leaving ISIS alone so that it could thrive at the expense of moderate rebel forces, thereby forcing Syrians and outside powers to eventually recognise Assad as the only alternative. Such indirect collaboration looked more deliberate when it emerged that the regime was purchasing gas from ISIS-held plants in 2014.[42]

However, the extent of regime involvement should not be overstated. The rise of ISIS was broadly in its interest: strengthening the narrative that Assad was facing an Islamist-jihadist rebellion at home and abroad, and dividing the rebels further over their response to this third force. It made more sense to channel its limited military resources towards the less radical rebels, reinforcing this narrative even more. However, it was also the case that the rebels were a more immediate threat to the regime than ISIS. ISIS' goal of a state-building project irrespective of territorial borders was less immediately threatening than the rebels' national struggle. The regime was one enemy of many to ISIS, while it was *the* enemy to the other rebels. ISIS' strongholds were in the desert periphery that Assad had largely abandoned as part of Suleimani's strategy, while the rebels were threatening Assad's heartland. Direct strikes were launched, but only when ISIS began to threaten rump Syria in summer 2014 and when the regime wanted to curry favour with the West by showing that it too saw the new 'Caliphate' as an enemy.

The oil deals should also not be overstated. Before ISIS forced them from Deir ez-Zor, the regime bought gas from Nusra as well.[43] This shows a cynicism from Assad in dealing with jihadists, and it is questionable whether the regime would have bought oil had the FSA controlled the eastern fields. However, the fact that the regime was willing to buy from Nusra suggests ISIS wasn't favoured above all jihadists. This was also seen in the release of Islamist prisoners. None of the high-profile three listed above joined ISIS, instead helping to found other Islamist and Salafist groups such as Ahrar and the Jaysh al-Islam that proved powerful rebel militias. Rather than a grand plan to create ISIS, the regime wanted to see radicals defeat moderates within the rebel forces, and so used multiple tools to try to achieve this, with unpredictable results. Once ISIS emerged and the regime recognised it was the radical antagonist it was looking for, it took a hands-off approach, provided the core territory of rump Syria remained unthreatened.

The long- and short-term fallout of the summer 2014 ISIS campaign offered more indications that any regime complicity was looser than the alleged conspiracy. The regime had been enjoying its brightest successes of the war in the wake of the failed Geneva II talks. After capturing Yabroud in March, and further successes in the Qalamoun campaign, central Homs had finally been conquered in May. A deal was agreed to allow 1,200 rebel fighters to evacuate the old city in exchange for relief for besieged regime villages in Aleppo and the release of 40 rebel-held detainees, crucially including at least one Iranian. With the self-declared 'capital of the revolution' and a key strategic crossroads back in his hands, Assad defiantly stood for re-election when his seven-year presidential term expired in June.[44] The possibility that Assad would not run had been a contested point at Montreux, so his announcement to do so illustrated the extent of the conference's failure. A delegation of thirty countries including lawmakers from Iran, Russia and Venezuela, were invited to observe the poll, but no impartial international bodies were present and the US, other Western states and the opposition dismissed Assad's comfortable re-election.[45] Soon afterwards, the regime recaptured the north-western village of Kassab and, then, on 23 June, the OPCW announced the last of its chemical weapons had been handed over.

Yet any celebration was soon short-lived as the full extent of ISIS' sudden advance became clear. In the short term, ISIS violently overran regime positions in June, July and August, including the Tabqa airbase, Division 17 base in Raqqa, Regiment 121 base in Hasakah and key gas facilities in Homs and Palmyra.[46] After two weeks the regime dislodged ISIS from the key Shaer gas field in Homs province, but a fresh assault was launched in November.[47] This was significant, not just because ISIS was striking rump Syria for the first time, but because of the scale and manner of the assaults. The regime lost hundreds of troops, many gruesomely executed by ISIS, who uploaded YouTube videos of Assad soldiers' heads on spikes.[48] While the regime responded with air strikes, the psychological blow to Assad's supporters was considerable. Having characterised the opposition all as jihadists since 2011, Syrians in regime territory questioned why the government had done so little until now against this self-declared Caliphate. In an unprecedented sign of frustration, previously loyal Syrians, particularly Alawis, took to social media to complain, especially after 250 soldiers were violently executed after the fall of Tabqa. Rumours swirled that officers in some bases had been airlifted to safety, leaving the conscripted soldiers to their fate.[49]

Such grumblings were exacerbated by the long-term consequence of the ISIS expansion: the withdrawal of Iraqi Shia militias from Syria. ISIS' conquest of western Iraq is another reason to question the extent of regime conspiracy, as it weakened Iran's position there. The loss of Mosul and the threat to Baghdad prompted an internal crisis that forced Tehran, under pressure from the US, to facilitate the resignation of its ally, Maliki. Another Iranian ally from within Maliki's Dawa party, Haider al-Abadi, took over, who was believed to be less overtly sectarian than his predecessor and better placed to counter ISIS. Whether ordered by Suleimani or of their own accord, several thousand Shia Iraqi militiamen serving in Syria rapidly returned to protect their homes and the pro-Iranian government. This left Assad with an even sharper manpower shortage. Suleimani later tried to fill the gaps with Afghans and other foreign Shia, but the regime had to escalate a countrywide conscription drive already under way. In the six provinces most firmly in regime hands, young men of military age were targeted in security raids and at checkpoints to ensure they had done their compulsory military service. The Syrian Network for Human Rights (SNHR) reported an average of 170 related detentions a week in the first seven months of 2014, while decrees were passed making it harder for eligible men to leave the country or avoid service. In some instances even amnestied former rebels were conscripted.[50] Assad was already losing manpower faster than he could replace it, but the loss of the Iraqis after summer 2014 made this a more acute problem, which the regime would prove unable to solve itself.

ISIS' many parents

If the Assad regime bore considerable responsibility for ISIS, so did his many international enemies. Through a mixture of bungling, short-termism, indirect and intentional policies, the West, Turkey, Qatar and Saudi Arabia all played a role. As discussed in Chapter 1 and above, ISIS' predecessors in Iraq emerged as a direct consequence of the 2003 Iraq war and it is difficult to imagine its rise without the US and British invasion and its disastrously managed post-war reorganisations – something reluctantly conceded by former British Prime Minister Tony Blair in 2015.[51] However, Western responsibility extended further. The factors that allowed ISIS to succeed in summer 2014 owe much to the circumstances of the US withdrawal from Iraq in December 2011. Determined to fulfil Obama's election manifesto pledge to leave Iraq, his administration squandered many of the gains of the 2007–8 surge. It empowered Maliki's sectarian government without ensuring sufficient space for Sunnis after the Sahwa success, drawing many to ISIS.[52] On top of this Obama left a hastily rebuilt Iraqi military and security force to fill the void, ignoring the pleas of Iraq's own Chief of Staff that they were not ready.[53] As a consequence, when ISIS assaulted Mosul it faced an incompetent military, packed with Maliki's cronies who had boosted local support for ISIS with their sectarianism. Yet the poor quality of the Iraqi forces did not stop the US continuing to supply it with advanced military equipment – in 2014 alone the State Department approved $579 million worth of sales. This resulted in the huge cache of arms captured by ISIS in Mosul, including approximately 2,300 Humvee armoured vehicles, which instantly made it the best armed opposition group in the Syrian civil war.[54]

The US might also be accused of wilful neglect on ISIS' rise. A Defense Intelligence Agency document of 2012 noted:

> If the situation unravels [in Syria] there is the possibility of establishing a declared or undeclared Salafist principality in eastern Syria (Hasaka and Der Zor) [sic], and this is exactly what the supporting powers in the opposition want, in order to isolate the Syrian regime.[55]

The document identifies that 'Salafist, Muslim Brotherhood and AQI are the major forces driving the insurgency in Syria', acknowledges the threat that an ISIS-type organisation could pose, and recognises that the US' own regional allies were willing to entertain the idea as a counter to Assad. Of course, this was but one report among many in US intelligence circles, yet it does show that the possibility of radical groups retaining territory was considered, even if other analyses were prioritised. Even so, as discussed in Chapter 6, it was at least another year before the US started pressuring its Gulf allies to tighten the flow of private support to such radical groups, and it wasn't until after summer 2014 that it began to scrutinise Turkey's open border policy. Instead, US policy seems to have been to hope that the moderate opposition would triumph over Assad before any such principality might emerge and prove a threat to its interests in the region. Indeed, when asked about ISIS' capture of Fallujah in January 2014, Obama stated, 'If a jayvee [Junior Varsity] team puts on Lakers uniforms that doesn't make them Kobe Bryant' – implying they were no major threat.[56]

The extent to which regional powers welcomed the rise of ISIS or an equivalent warrants scrutiny. Turkey was accused by the Iraqi government and the PYD of collaborating with ISIS, with the former suspecting that Turkish intelligence helped ISIS reconstitute itself in 2011.[57] There is no direct evidence for this nor does such direct collaboration seem likely but, rather like the Syrian regime, Ankara would have seen advantages in the emergence of a counterweight to Assad, the PYD and the Iran-allied government in Baghdad. More passive collaboration or, at least, no active attempts to prevent ISIS' rise did occur. As discussed in Chapters 6 and 8, Turkey was willing to send arms and support to a variety of radical groups, with few checks in place to ensure they were not then passed on to jihadists or that the recipients did not radicalise. Similarly, Turkey's open border allowed foreign fighters drawn to ISIS to pass into Syria relatively easily. There were multiple reports of ISIS fighters crossing back into Turkey to recuperate from fighting in hospitals and safe houses, with little evidence of government crackdowns even after summer 2014.[58] Moreover, oilfields captured by ISIS in Iraq and Syria were soon made operational again, reportedly by procuring spare parts from Turkey, while oil was exported there (and Jordan) via smugglers and middlemen. Few believed Turkey was actively encouraging this but the Iraqi government argued that more could be done to shut down smuggling routes.[59] Turkey's reluctance to join the US-led coalition against ISIS in late summer 2014 only strengthened the charges of passive collaboration.

Qatar's policies similarly contributed. While Tamim stated in September 2014 that 'Qatar has never supported and will never support terrorist organizations', its scattergun approach to sending arms and finance did little to prevent radical groups, including ISIS, from benefiting.[60] Joe Biden, among others, complained about Qatar's alleged willingness to fund radical Islamists, including Nusra and al-Qaeda.[61] As noted in Chapter 6, the fluidity of allegiance to different militias early on made it perfectly possible that weapons and funds intended for Nusra and their allies could have ended up in ISIS' hands before early 2014. Similarly, the uncontrolled flow of money from the Gulf to radical groups in Syria in 2011–13 makes it highly plausible that ISIS was supported by Gulf-based backers, whatever the intentions of Doha and Riyadh. There is no evidence of direct collaboration by Qatar; however, given its closeness to Turkey on goals and ideology, a similar policy of passivity was likely pursued before summer 2014.

Saudi Arabia's role is more complex. Some have noted that Saudi Arabian support for the coup against the MB in Egypt indirectly benefited ISIS by disillusioning a generation of Islamists with the democratic process, convincing them that violent radicalism was the only route to power.[62] More directly, Cockburn argues that ISIS' ideology draws heavily on Saudi Wahhabism, drawing a link between decades of Saudi-funded religious propaganda and the appeal of radicalism in the Muslim world.[63] Similarly, some argue that Saudi-approved sectarian preaching after 2011 created space for the sectarian hatred against Shia espoused by jihadists.[64] At the same time, Saudi Arabia has long feared al-Qaeda and its equivalents. While Bandar backed Salafist groups like the Islamic Front, it was to rival ISIS and Nusra, not collaborate. As discussed, Saudi Arabia was tighter in its direct funding, preferring the moderate FSA and SNC until late 2013, although it too could have better controlled flows from private citizens, both in terms of funds and personnel. Some funds and weapons intended for more moderate forces may have ended up in ISIS' hands, but that was a feature of the fluidity of Syria's rebellion and, of the three regional powers, Riyadh appeared most intent on preventing radicals gaining arms.

It should also be noted that Assad's allies may also have played a role in ISIS' rise. The *Novaya Gazeta*, a Russian newspaper, reported in 2015 that since 2011 Russia's intelligence agency, the FSB, facilitated the movement of Dagestani Islamists into Syria. The logic of this alleged 'Green Corridor' was that it was better to have Russian Islamists fighting abroad, where ideally they would be killed, than have them cause trouble at home.[65] Charles Lister notes how a high number of the foreign jihadists fighting for ISIS were Russian speakers, though many had been living outside Russia prior to 2011.[66] Iran's, albeit indirect, role in ISIS' rise was easier to see. The Shia militia established by Suleimani himself to resist US occupation in the 2000s practised many of the sectarian policies of the Maliki government that drove some of Iraq's Sunnis into ISIS.

ISIS therefore had a variety of parents. Indigenous factors cannot be ignored, as a sense of Sunni oppression at the hands of Maliki in Iraq after 2006 (but especially after the US withdrawal in 2011) and Assad in eastern Syria after 2011 generated genuine grass-roots support. Similarly, in the context of this oppression, the sectarian propaganda emanating from elsewhere may have furthered its appeal. But the structural shifts that allowed for ISIS' rise came from the outside. The weakening of the Iraqi state after the US-led invasion of 2003 created political and physical space for ISIS' predecessors, AQI and ISI. The Syrian civil war, itself heavily shaped by external actors, created similar space for ISI to expand. The Assad regime, having facilitated AQI and ISI's activities before 2010, effectively helped the newly declared ISIS to triumph over more moderate opposition. However, the regime was far from alone, with Turkey, Qatar and Saudi Arabia in their own way culpable. Weapons and support found their way to ISIS relatively easily with no one actively trying to prevent their rise. Turkey may even have turned a blind eye to ISIS, seeing it as a counterweight to the PYD. Even the US seemed to wilfully neglect and underestimate ISIS' potential. ISIS' rise therefore came because too many actors believed it was less of a threat than other, more immediate enemies, and some, especially the regime, saw advantages to be won by its emergence. Such short-termism would come back to haunt all.

Fighting 'the Caliphate'

The sudden creation of 'the Caliphate' shocked most of the external players in the Syrian civil war, prompting a wide-ranging reaction. Moscow, fearful that such a clear success for Middle Eastern jihadists might inspire those at home, was quick to offer the embattled Iraqi government an emergency delivery of Su-25 attack aircraft in early July. Saudi Arabia was similarly alarmed. In June it strengthened border defences with Iraq, something that proved prescient when ISIS suicide bombers killed three border guards in January 2015.[67] Like Russia, Riyadh was most concerned with domestic terrorism. In November, al-Baghdadi released an audio recording urging followers to target Arabia, particularly the Shia minority in the Eastern Province. A few weeks earlier three Saudis had opened fire in a Shia mosque killing nine in Al-Dalwa, Eastern Province, and a series of similar attacks followed in 2015. Iran had potentially the most to lose with ISIS' advance in Iraq. As well as engineering Maliki's eventual departure, Tehran immediately ordered Suleimani from Damascus to Baghdad in June. With Iran determined to avoid any partition of Iraq, preferring to keep the whole state in its sphere rather than just the Shia south, the Quds Force General set about reorganising Iraq's forces to reconquer lost ground.[68] The most dramatic response, however, came from Washington, which abandoned its previous aversion to military intervention in Syria.

Obama takes action

The capture of Mosul exposed how much Obama had underestimated ISIS and he quickly reacted. The first concern was Iraq, and a small number of troops were dispatched to Baghdad to assess the threat level, while additional aircraft were sent to the region in June. In August the US launched bombing raids on ISIS positions in Iraq and by September these had been extended into Syria. Washington put together two international coalitions against ISIS, a larger group welcomed by Baghdad, and a smaller one to hit

ISIS in Syria, but without Damascus' permission to violate its sovereignty. Obama remained committed, however, to keeping substantial US troops off the ground. Instead, he offered material support to Iraqi and KRG forces in Iraq and, in late June, unexpectedly announced a $500 million DoD programme to train and equip 'moderate' Syrian rebels to fight ISIS. Unlike the support offered to rebel groups by the US since 2013, this programme was run by the Pentagon, not the CIA.

So why did Obama take action in 2014 against ISIS, when he had sought to avoid striking Assad the year before? First and foremost, ISIS' advance represented an immediate danger to US regional interests in a way that Assad did not. ISIS was dismembering a state the US had only just left, having invested time and money in rebuilding its institutions that Washington wasn't willing to write off. It also was advancing on the KRG, a key US regional ally, home to a joint operations centre with the US and Iraqi military in Erbil, and one of the Middle East's few stable entities. Secondly, attacking ISIS was consistent with Obama's declared goal since becoming President, of degrading al-Qaeda and militant jihadists.[69] While Assad posed no ideological threat to the US, jihadism, with its transnational desire to break down borders and specifically target the West, its allies and its regional interests, did. Obama hadn't believed that ISIS were equivalent to the al-Qaeda network but the Mosul takeover changed his mind.

Finally, domestic factors impacted his thinking. Obama's authorisation of airstrikes first came on 7 August after the international media had focused on 50,000 Yazidis (an ethnically Kurdish group practising an ancient religion linked to Zoroastrianism) besieged by ISIS on a mountain in Sinjar, Iraq. Addressing the nation on television, Obama cited the prevention of a Yazidi massacre as justification for military action, along with protecting US citizens in Erbil and preventing ISIS' advance on the KRG. In the coming days ISIS positions around Erbil and Sinjar were bombed, while aid was airdropped to the trapped Yazidis, most of whom eventually escaped with the help of YPG and PKK fighters who had come down to Sinjar. Public opinion also impacted Obama's decision to widen the campaign, on 3 September, announcing that the US goal was now to 'degrade, and ultimately destroy' ISIS. This followed an outcry at the videoed beheading of two US journalist prisoners by ISIS, first James Foley on 19 August and then Steven Sotloff the day before Obama's announcement. However, while the ever important need to 'do something' is likely to have entered the President's calculations, this declared objective and the subsequent forming of international anti-ISIS coalitions was consistent with Obama's long-standing anti-jihadist agenda rather than a sudden folding to public will.[70]

These solutions proved limited, however. After eighteen months of Operation Inherent Resolve, as the actions against ISIS were named, nearly 11,000 strikes had been launched, two-thirds in Iraq. The US undertook most strikes, particularly in Syria where, by mid-March 2016, 3,401 American attacks had been registered, compared to barely 225 by its coalition partners, Australia, Bahrain, Canada, France, Jordan, the Netherlands, Saudi Arabia, Turkey, the UAE and the UK.[71] US officials estimated that in this time over 22,000 ISIS targets were damaged or destroyed, including 126 tanks, 374 Humvees and 1,162 staging areas. Yet despite degrading ISIS' military capabilities, and helping to halt some advances in Iraq and Rojava (discussed below), Obama's declared goal of destroying the Caliphate proved difficult. In the first year of the operation it actually thrived, pushing deeper into western Syria to capture Palmyra from the regime and east into Iraq to gain Ramadi, both in May 2015. Via its polished multilingual propaganda ISIS released videos and publications emphasising its brutality to its enemies and its piousness to potential sympathisers, prompting up to 30,000 foreign Muslims from 86 countries, to abscond to the Caliphate by late 2015.[72] Indeed, this propaganda utilised the US-led bombings, and the civilian casualties they caused, to portray itself as yet another Muslim victim of Western imperialism. ISIS was fast replacing al-Qaeda as the worldwide beacon of jihadism; extremists in Libya, Egypt, Nigeria and elsewhere declared their loyalty.

The US was constrained by its unwillingness to deploy its own troops to the ISIS fight, insisting that local partners would do the job. In Iraq that meant the new Baghdad government and the KRG. Washington effectively cooperated with Iran in this, despite Tehran's muted protests that US strikes on ISIS in Syria (but not Iraq) were illegal.[73] In Syria, with the White House committed to Assad's fall, no such collaboration was entertained, despite impudent proposals from Damascus and some Western commentators. Instead, the 'train and equip' programme was expected to help fill the vacuum. This hastily put together plan aimed to vet non-radical rebels, and train them in camps in Turkey, Jordan, Saudi Arabia and Qatar before sending them into Syria. Importantly, they were expected to fight ISIS, not Assad. Yet the rebels saw Assad not ISIS as the primary enemy and were deterred from joining. Those that did were delayed by excruciatingly slow vetting.[74] Despite aiming for 5,400 trained troops in the first year, Defense Secretary Ash Carter admitted in July 2015 that only 60 were ready.[75]

Moreover, this handful could not match the established Islamist rebels, who were suspicious of the new US-backed forces, opposed its 'ISIS-first, Assad second' mission and coveted its weaponry. In late 2014 and early 2015, the radical rebels grew in strength, particularly Nusra and Ahrar, discussed further in Chapter 10. Nusra had already clashed with Harakat al-Hazm, a group benefiting from considerable CIA support. Hazm had been the public face of a CIA–Saudi initiative to boost FSA-aligned militia in northern Syria, receiving US-supplied TOW anti-tank weaponry from April 2014. Yet they clashed with and were defeated by Nusra on several occasions, causing many of their fighters to defect to Nusra and Ahrar, their weaponry to be seized, and, eventually, the militia to disband in March 2015.[76] Unsurprisingly the train-and-equip fighters met a similar fate. Soon after Carter's statement in July, fifty-four fighters of a Pentagon-sponsored 'New Syrian Force' (mostly from 'Division 30' of the FSA) crossed into Turkey, but within days their leader was abducted by Nusra and their weapons taken. The same happened to seventy-one further fighters in September and, soon afterwards, the train and equip programme was shelved.[77]

In the first year of the ISIS campaign, the slow progress of airstrikes and the failure of 'train and equip' can partly be attributed to strategy. Bombing alone rarely succeeds and the idea of creating a new ground force from scratch was unrealistic.[78] That said, given that the US had little more success against ISIS in Iraq where it was cooperating with the government suggests that, had Obama worked directly with Assad, he might have achieved no better results. Both governments were widely hated in ISIS-held territory whatever people's view of 'the Caliphate'. Washington's diplomatic approach created further obstacles. Regional powers joined the bombing coalition but with limited enthusiasm, as none ranked ISIS as the same level of threat as Washington. Riyadh, Doha and Ankara repeated their ongoing pleas that Assad should be dealt with first. Indeed each continued to back, whether directly or indirectly, the rebel groups that helped undermine the train and equip programme.

Turkey was particularly ambiguous toward ISIS after summer 2014. Ankara was unwilling to either join the bombing coalition or allow the US to use Turkish bases until July 2015, when a Turkish soldier was killed in an ISIS attack. This suggested either that Erdoğan underestimated the extent of the threat or, as some posited, that some kind of deal had been made with 'the Caliphate' to secure the peaceful release in September 2014 of forty-nine Turks captured in Mosul. Whatever the reason, Turkey's slowness in mobilising ensured its border into Syria remained porous, allowing foreign supporters relatively easy access. Complicating matters was Ankara's attitude to the Kurds; it saw the PKK and their Syrian affiliate the PYD as its greatest regional threat – more than Assad and certainly more than ISIS. It therefore proved problematic when the US began backing the PYD as its only viable Syrian ally against ISIS.

The Kurdish quandary

In the final days of 2012, Erdoğan had surprisingly announced that Turkey's National Intelligence Organisation (MİT) was in discussion with the imprisoned PKK leader, Abdullah Ocalan, about a possible peace process. As talks progressed, in March 2013 the PKK announced a ceasefire and a withdrawal of its forces to northern Iraq the following month. Many hoped this marked the end of the long Turkey–PKK conflict that first began in 1984. However, Erdoğan was slow to deliver the promised political and cultural reforms and some feared he was using the peace process cynically. He hoped to persuade enough Kurds to back his party to win a two-thirds 'super-majority' in parliament that was needed to change the constitution. The AKP Party's internal rules prevented Erdoğan from serving a further term as Prime Minister after August 2014 so the super-majority would allow him to transform Turkey into a presidential system with himself as a powerful head of state. Yet the wave of protests against his rule in 2013, and then a public falling out with the powerful supporters of the Turkish Islamist Fethullah Gülen derailed this plan. After deploying excessive force and autocratic means against both enemies, while also recognising that the Kurds would need real concessions that he was unwilling to give, Erdoğan changed tactics. He increasingly saw Turkey's right-wing nationalists, who strongly opposed any compromise with the PKK, as the route to his super-majority and edged away from the peace process. It helped that the PKK had not upheld its end of the bargain and retained a military presence in Turkey.

It was against this backdrop that Turkey ambivalently observed ISIS' war with the PYD. Ankara had tightened its ties to the KRG in March 2014 to counter the PYD's rise in neighbouring Syria. As well as selling Turkey 100,000 b/d of oil from Erbil, without Baghdad's authorisation, Barzani strengthened the KRG's western border to prevent KRG-based PKK operatives from supplying the PYD.[79] Then on 13 September 2014 ISIS launched a massive assault on the PYD stronghold of Kobane. Despite YPG resistance, by early October ISIS forces had reached the city centre, sending a wave of up to 200,000 Kurdish refugees over the nearby border into Turkey. As ISIS advanced, the PYD begged Turkey to allow resupply from Turkish-based PKK fighters, or even to intervene itself. Ankara refused, seemingly preferring to see the YPG crushed.

The YPG's brave stand gained global media attention, as did contrasting images of Turkish tanks perched on the border doing nothing. Consequently Ankara came under pressure from both its allies and its appalled domestic Kurdish population, who rioted and demonstrated in several cities.[80] Turkey partly relented on 29 October by allowing a small group of approved Syrian

FSA fighters into Kobane, and then a larger contingent of Barzani's Peshmerga from Iraq. The PKK, however, remained blocked, prompting several violent retaliations against the Turkish government. While the combined YPG-Peshmerga-FSA forces eventually turned the tide, pushing ISIS from Kobane by late January 2015, the damage between Ankara and its Kurds was vast. The PKK ceasefire had effectively broken down, prompting an upsurge in violence in 2015, while Kurdish nationalism had been rallied by the Kobane siege, the reverse of Erdoğan's intention.

In contrast to Turkey, the US swiftly recognised the symbolic importance of Kobane in halting ISIS' seemingly unstoppable advance and launched multiple airstrikes in support of the YPG from early October. This greatly aided the YPG's survival and also put the US in contact with the previously unknown force. The US had designated the PKK a Foreign Terrorist Organisation in 1997 in support of its NATO ally Turkey, yet now found that its Syrian affiliate was what it was looking for to counter ISIS: an effective, secular, indigenous force. In the months that followed, the Pentagon worked closely with joint forces of YPG and some FSA units, that would eventually form the Syrian Democratic Forces – a YPG-dominated military umbrella in north and eastern Syria.[81] Such was the extent of US cooperation, analyst Aron Lund half-joked that, since late 2014, 'the United States Air Force has transformed itself into something that more closely resembles the Western Kurdistan Air Force'.[82] Reinforced, the YPG and its various allies successfully pushed back against ISIS in 2015, securing Hasakah in April and capturing Tal-Abyad in July, leaving a long stretch of the Syrian side of the Turkish border under PYD control. While Washington was quietly pleased at finally rolling back ISIS, the manner of the victory and who it empowered placed considerable strain on US–Turkish ties.

Despite the dramatic events of summer 2014 and ISIS' sudden land grab, the basic structure of the Syrian civil war remained unaltered. Though territory changed hands back and forth, the conflict was essentially stalemated, and sustained as such by outside powers. The regime and the non-ISIS rebel forces both received enough support to survive, but not enough to decisively tip the conflict. Moreover, having invested so heavily in Assad's survival or demise, none of the external supporters were willing to back down, nor were hurting sufficiently from their involvement to be forced into compromise. The declaration of ISIS' 'Caliphate' did not change this, although it did ultimately exacerbate Assad's manpower shortage and shift the momentum from the regime back towards the rebels. The US' reaction and intervention against ISIS added a further layer of complexity to what was already a complex, internationalised civil war.

Obama's various actions against ISIS did not signify a return to US hegemony over the Middle East; quite the contrary. His unwillingness to consider any substantial 'boots on the ground' indicated that, on his watch at least, the days of sizeable US troop deployments in the region were over, even to deal with a clear security threat. Yet the difficulty in finding allies willing to take up the fight against ISIS showed how much the previous years' disengagement had altered the international relations of the region. Of the major powers involved in Syria, only the US saw ISIS as the number one threat, and while Washington's regional allies joined in early bombing raids and paid lip service to Obama's coalition, in reality their priorities were elsewhere. That the US couldn't persuade its long-standing ally Turkey to allow it to use Turkish airbases or even seriously regulate its border until Turkey itself was targeted was an indicator of how diminished Washington's influence had become. At the same time, regional players were far more assertive and independent than before, not just the US' traditional rivals like Iran and Russia organising their own operations against ISIS, but also allies like Saudi Arabia. The US' slow campaign against ISIS, and its difficulties in rallying sufficient regional support to successfully degrade and destroy it illustrated clearly that though the US may have remained the most powerful player in the Middle East, its days of hegemony were seemingly over. As has been shown, this trend, having already impacted the shape of the Syrian civil war, was now being strongly reinforced by it. Moreover, the extent of perceived US decline in the region was soon to be starkly exposed in late summer 2015, when Russia directly entered the war in support of Assad.

CHAPTER TEN

Enter Russia: Putin raises the stakes

There is no other solution to the Syrian crisis than strengthening the effective government structures and rendering them help in fighting terrorism, but at the same time urging them to engage in positive dialogue with the rational opposition and conduct reform.

Russian President Vladimir Putin, 24 September 2015[1]

Half an hour's drive from Latakia, Syria's major port city and an Assad stronghold, sits the Khmeimim airbase. Until summer 2015 it was an unremarkable, neglected strip of asphalt. Then, in late August, the Russians came. Cargo planes filled with military equipment and building supplies steadily arrived. Despite Foreign Minister Lavrov's insistence that this was nothing additional to Russia's pre-existing commitments to the Assad regime, satellite imagery showed an ever increasing military build-up: the runway was re-laid, a new aircraft control tower built, defences improved and new housing units constructed. Soon afterwards US officials noted that Russian aircraft and tank landing ships had been sent to Moscow's naval base in Tartous. On 14 September, a Pentagon spokesman declared that construction in Khmeimim amounted to a new Russian 'forward air operating base'.[2] It gradually dawned on the US and Assad's other enemies that this was an extraordinary move. Earlier that year the regime's overstretched and undermanned military had suffered some of its worst losses in years. The rebels had appeared resurgent, capturing Idlib in the north and pressuring Deraa in the south, ISIS had captured and ransacked the desert city of Palmyra, and some were predicting that at long last Assad was close to collapse. Now, a superpower had thrown its air force behind Damascus, deploying the Russian military outside the former Soviet Union for the first time since the end of the Cold War.

On 30 September Russian planes from Khmeimim bombed targets in Homs, Hama and Quneitra provinces.[3] Thereafter, they launched multiple attacks, with the Russian military claiming well over 6,000 sorties in the first four months.[4] While Moscow insisted it was hitting ISIS, it primarily targeted the non-ISIS rebels, with ground offensives from October coordinated with regime, Iranian, Hezbollah and other pro-regime troops to roll back rebel gains. Wrong-footed, the White House rapidly sought to revive Syria's flailing peace process. John Kerry hurriedly courted Lavrov to back what became the Vienna Process: a commitment by international actors – including Iran for the first time – to a negotiated solution. From this emerged a fragile ceasefire and a new round of peace talks, Geneva III. Yet with pro-regime forces making gains on the ground, many questioned whether Moscow, Tehran or Damascus were in any mood to make serious concessions. After five years of stalemated conflict, Russia's dramatic intervention appeared to have tipped the balance of power.

This chapter will consider why Russia suddenly raised the stakes in this way and the consequences for the Syrian civil war. It will note the importance of the rebel resurgence of spring 2015 in provoking real fears of Assad's collapse in Moscow and Tehran. Similarly the nature and scale of the intervention will be discussed, and the logic behind Putin's move. The resulting Vienna Process and accompanying ceasefire and peace talks will be also be assessed. In doing so, it will be suggested that while Russia's intervention likely prevented any prospect of sudden regime collapse, it did not immediately change the structure of the civil war or lead to an imminent decisive regime military victory. However, it did shift the balance Assad's way and created a better negotiating position for his forces.

Rebel resurgence

Russia's intervention was prompted by a series of setbacks for the regime in the first half of 2015. Assad's manpower shortage, exacerbated in 2014 by the departure of Iraqi Shia militiamen, was increasingly felt on the battlefield. Regime offensives in Aleppo and the south in February 2015 soon ran out of steam as rebels counter-attacked. Then, after the regime reduced its presence in the city, rebel forces captured Idlib on 28 March, only the second provincial capital to be lost by Assad.[5] This was the work of a new Idlib rebel coalition of seven armed groups, the Jaysh al-Fateh (Army of Conquest). Led by Ahrar and Nusra but including some local Muslim Brotherhood and FSA-aligned moderates, the formation and its success was due to both local and external factors.

Locally, the leading force was Ahrar who, according to analyst Charles Lister, initiated discussions with other rebels about the possibility of a unified coalition in the Idlib area in December 2014. Ahrar had recovered quickly from a bomb attack that killed many of its key leaders, including founder Hassan Abboud, the previous September and deployed a 'mergers and acquisitions policy' of absorbing smaller militias to become one of the largest groups. Indeed, on the eve of the Idlib assault, it merged with Ahmed Issa al-Sheikh's Suqour al-Sham, who were strong in the province.[6] Moreover, since November Ahrar had received increased logistical and military support from Turkey, which had tilted in favour of the Salafist group after the repeated failings of the moderates and when it became clear that the US was too distracted by ISIS to object. Once formed, the Jaysh al-Fateh produced what Lister calls 'a level of inter-factional coordination that had arguably not been seen before in Syria'. It possessed sophisticated weaponry, with Ahrar armed by Turkey, Nusra utilising the stock of US-supplied TOW anti-tank missiles captured from Harakat al-Hazm and several smaller FSA-aligned groups like Liwa Forsan al-Haq offering support with weapons directly supplied by the CIA.[7] Jaysh al-Fateh went on to capture Jisr al-Shughour in late April and by the end of May had secured all of Idlib province bar one airbase and two Shia villages, al-Fuah and Kafraya.

Externally, a Turkish–Saudi rapprochement facilitated the coalition. On 23 January 2015, King Abdullah of Saudi Arabia died and was succeeded surprisingly smoothly by his brother, Salman. The new king oversaw a more aggressive and activist foreign policy. On 26 March he authorised a major bombing campaign in Yemen against rebels led by former President Saleh and Houthi militants, believed to be supported by Iran, who threatened the Saudi-backed government. Much of this activism was led by the king's ambitious son, Mohammed bin Salman, appointed defence minister and, in April, second in line to the throne after Mohammed bin Nayef. Courting the new regime, Erdoğan visited Salman on 2 March, easing tensions between Saudi Arabia, Turkey and Qatar. While Riyadh played no direct role in Jaysh al-Fateh's formation, its acquiescence was important in legitimising its rebel allies' cooperation with Nusra in the coalition – previously forbidden under King Abdullah. Riyadh's endorsement was seen a month later when a key ally, Jaysh al-Islam's Zahran Alloush, travelled to Istanbul to meet with leaders of the Jaysh al-Fateh, including Ahrar.[8]

Meanwhile, the regime saw its greatest internal disruption since summer 2012, when head of the Political Security Directorate, Rustum Ghazali, was mysteriously arrested in March and then died in April. Accounts differ over whether he was planning on defecting, had challenged the regime for its increased reliance on Iran, or simply fell out with another regime insider over smuggling profits. Whatever the truth, his death hinted at discord in the higher echelons of the regime, prompting outside speculation that collapse was a step closer.[9] Piling misery on Assad, on 13 May ISIS launched a successful attack on the desert city of Palmyra (known locally as Tadmour). Taking advantage of Assad redeploying forces to the Idlib front, ISIS swept from the east to capture the city by 26 May, once again threatening the key Shaer gas field. ISIS then brutalised Palmyra, publicly beheading dozens of civilians and systematically destroying some of the city's UNESCO world heritage antiquities, including the 2,000-year-old Temple of Bel.

The rebels also advanced in the south. The 'Southern Front' had formed in February 2014 and presented itself as more moderate than the radical groups dominating the north, committing to a pluralist post-Assad Syria and consciously avoiding Islamist rhetoric.[10] Many of its fifty-four factions were still FSA, supported by the US, Saudi Arabia and Jordan via the Military Operations Center (MOC) – the Amman command room established with support from the CIA, discussed in Chapter 6. The coalition made modest gains against the regime in 2014. These helped to limit the appeal of Nusra, the largest radical group in the south, whom the Front considered its main future rival for dominance, despite several instances of collaboration.[11] On 25 March 2015 the Southern Front captured the ancient city of Bosra al-Sham, and then on 1 April, with the likely approval of the Jordanian government, the regime's last southern border post at Nassib. Thereafter, partly inspired by the advances in Idlib, but also conscious that a newly formed Jaysh al-Fateh branch in Deraa by Nusra, Ahrar and other Islamists might challenge its regional leadership, the Southern Front launched 'Southern Storm' in June.[12] Supported in the rear by Nusra and Ahrar, and partly commanded by Jaysh al-Islam's Alloush, the offensive sought to capture Deraa city. However, regime forces repelled the attack and a second, 'Operation Righteous Storm', also failed in July, halting the momentum and denting Western, Jordanian and Saudi Arabian faith in the Southern Front.[13] The assault also unexpectedly boosted the regime when rebel forces including Nusra fighters approached the environs of the southern Druze-dominated city of Suwaida in June. Druze leaders, who had stayed relatively neutral in the civil war until this point, feared Nusra after the group murdered twenty Druze in Idlib, and therefore urged their co-religionists to join the local NDF. This helped push the rebels back and kept the majority of Syria's Druze in Assad's camp.[14]

By the summer of 2015 the rebels were resurgent but further advances were far from assured, as seen by the failures in the south. Turkey, Saudi Arabia and Qatar were more united on their Syria strategy, with Riyadh seemingly endorsing Turkey's preferred allies in the north. After the successes of Jaysh al-Fateh Ankara and Doha made a concerted push to rebrand Ahrar as a viable anti-Assad partner for the international community. The new head of the SOC, the Turkmen Khaled Khoja who was close to Turkey, met regularly with Ahrar's leadership. A more doveish wing of Ahrar that favoured Western outreach battled for influence within the group. Its chief of foreign relations, Labib al-Nahhas, called for Western support in two newspaper editorials in July, prompting support from some in Washington.[15] There was also an attempt to rhetorically distance itself from its Jaysh al-Fateh partner, Nusra, although many noted their mutually dependent relationship on the ground.[16] Turkey once again mooted the possibility of a US–Turkish enforced 'safe zone' free of both ISIS and the regime in the north, supported by Ahrar and other more moderate forces, although the idea was rejected by the White House.[17] Ankara also played a role by mediating a series of local ceasefire agreements with Iran in August that eventually saw rebel fighters evacuated from the besieged town of Zabadani, in exchange for civilians being evacuated from the final regime villages in Idlib, al-Fuah and Kafraya. Importantly, the regime played no role in these negotiations and it appeared ever more in decline and peripheral.

Russian intervention

Tipping the balance: A legitimate campaign?

Russia's military intervention in September was a direct response to the rebel resurgence. On 6 May 2015, as his forces were being pushed back in Idlib province threatening the Latakia heartlands, Assad admitted for the first time that the regime's military were experiencing, 'setbacks' and 'ups and downs' on the battlefield.[18] More explicitly, in another speech on 26 July he conceded that the army faced a manpower shortage and had withdrawn from some regions to defend others considered more important.[19] With hindsight this admission was both a plea for help from his allies and a way of preparing his domestic supporters for what he likely already knew was under way: an Iranian–Russian support plan. Earlier in the summer high-level contacts in Moscow and Tehran had exchanged concern over recent rebel gains. Reuters reported that a joint military intervention was agreed in a meeting between Lavrov and Khamenei in Tehran before Suleimani was dispatched to Moscow in July to discuss specifics.[20] Soon afterwards, on 26 August, Russia and Syria signed an agreement that granted the Russian air forces use of Khmeimim free of charge for an indefinite time period.[21] In September, at least 28 planes were dispatched there, along with up to 2,000 personnel, while Russia's Black Sea fleet was sent to the eastern Mediterranean.[22]

Putin presented this as a legal and legitimate campaign against ISIS terrorism. Unlike the US-led coalition in the east, Syria's government had formally requested Russian assistance, officials noted. After Putin successfully gained unanimous authorisation to deploy the Russian Air Force from the Federation Council, Russia's second chamber, his Chief of Staff, Sergei Ivanov, reiterated that, 'The military goal of this operation is exclusively to provide air support to the Syrian government forces in their fight against ISIS.'[23] Days before, Putin had addressed the UN General Assembly, calling for an international coalition against the Islamic State. Soon afterwards he announced a Baghdad-based anti-ISIS joint information centre involving the Russian, Iranian, Syrian and Iraqi governments, with some reporting that Moscow provoca-tively invited the US, UK and Turkish governments to take part, only for the invitation to be swiftly declined. Nevertheless, barely an hour before the first planes were launched on 30 September, a Russian general entered the US' Baghdad embassy to pass on a warning to American bombers in Syria, stating, 'We launch Syria air strikes in one hour. Stay out of the way.'[24]

Yet despite the repeated emphasis on ISIS, the new campaign was primarily aimed at the non-ISIS rebels. This was seen in the accompanying ground assaults. On 7 October the regime began a campaign against rebel forces in northern Hama province, followed by attacks in Latakia, Idlib, Homs and Deraa. On 15 October up to 2,000 Iranian IRGC troops, Hezbollah and Iraqi Shia militia commanded by Suleimani combined with regime forces to advance in southern Aleppo province, fighting ISIS in the east and non-ISIS rebels in the west.[25] At first this newly reinforced pro-Assad coali-tion made only modest gains, being pushed back in Hama and making slow progress in Latakia, Idlib and Aleppo.[26] Indeed, freshly deployed Iranian troops faced particularly high casualties, with four high-ranking IRGC commanders killed in one week in October, including General Hossein Hamedani, at that point the most senior Iranian military officer to be killed in Syria.[27]

Moscow made a show of its interventions being more than just military. Russian media were invited to film Russian soldiers distributing humani-tarian aid to war-torn regime-held regions.[28] There were attempts to help broker local deals between the regime and village elders and clan leaders in some rebellious areas to bring them back within Assad's control.[29] Putin also sought to engage with what he called Assad's 'rational' opponents. This was an extension of an early policy of peeling off parts of the opposi-tion. A Moscow-based peace conference had been attempted in late 2014 and early 2015 but got nowhere after the SOC boycotted it and former leader Moaz al-Khatib, who had shown some initial interest, also declined.

This time the SOC remained unsurprisingly sceptical, but other opposition groups such as the NCB and the PYD-aligned CDS were more receptive.

Eventually Moscow's military contribution began to tell, particularly the introduction of 'signature' Russian military tactics such as frontal aviation, cauldron battles, and multiple simultaneous and successive operations, which made the pro-Assad campaigns more effective than before.[30] Moreover, the regime and its allies took advantage of the shifting diplomatic climate, making major gains in early 2016 in the run-up to and during a new round of Geneva peace talks, much to the opposition's disgust. Aided by a simultaneous advance by YPG forces from the Kurdish canton of Afrin, the regime relieved a long-lasting siege on the villages of Nubl and Zahraa in northern Aleppo, cutting the rebels off from their vital land crossing with Turkey at Bab al-Salameh. Before then, on 24 January, the last rebel stronghold in Latakia province, Rabia, had fallen, as had Sheikh Maskin in the south on 30 December, allowing the regime to tighten its hold on Deraa. In a further sign of Russia's impact, on Christmas Day airstrikes on Ghouta in Damascus had killed Zahran Alloush, Jaysh al-Islam's commander and a close Saudi Arabian ally. By the time a tentative 'cessation of hostilities' was implemented on 27 February, pro-regime forces had made major territorial gains and, as an Institute for the Study of War report noted, the intervention had 'ultimately reset the military balance in Syria'.[31]

Putin's war

What prompted such a massive military commitment from Russia? There were smaller measures that Moscow might have chosen to prop up Assad, such as providing planes for Syrian pilots, but Putin instead opted for direct intervention. In earlier chapters it was noted that the Russian President viewed the Syria crisis through three interconnected lenses: geostrategic, domestic and regional economic. Throwing his air force decisively behind Assad benefited his agenda in all three arenas, outweighing the accompanying risks.

Geostrategically, Russia's behaviour since 2011 showed its steadfast opposition to what it saw as a US victory in Syria. While this did not mean it was completely wed to the continued rule of Bashar al-Assad, whom Putin disliked, any possibility that rebel successes might force regime collapse was out of the question. If sending the air force in conjunction with an Iranian-backed offensive was the only means to ensure this, then so be it. Yet Putin was more ambitious than simply wanting to prevent Assad's defeat. While his policy in Syria since 2011 had initially been defensive, to ensure that Moscow itself would never be a target for Western-backed overthrow, as the conflict progressed and the realities of the post-American Middle East became apparent, Russia's President saw offensive advantage to be had. Carnegie's Dmitri Trenin argues that, starting with his intervention in Ukraine in 2014, Putin began breaking out of the US-dominated post-Cold-War order. His aim was to have Russia recognised as a global superpower on an equal footing with the US, not subordinate as it had been in the 1990s and 2000s. In the Middle East, this meant seeking what Trenin calls 'co-equality' with the US: presenting itself as a legitimate and viable rival superpower ally to the region's governments.[32] This partly explains the grand anti-ISIS rhetoric at the UN and the construction of a multinational Iranian–Iraqi–Syrian coalition on the eve of the intervention.

Putin saw other geostrategic gains. In the short term, the build-up in Syria forced the US to drop the diplomatic isolation it had imposed on Putin since the Ukraine crisis. At the sidelines of the UN General Assembly in September 2015 Obama and Putin held their first direct dialogue since the Ukraine dispute blew up, and soon afterwards the US was forced to consult closely with Moscow as it rapidly revived the Syria peace process. In the longer term, the military deployment gave valuable experience to Russia's recently reorganised air force. Having underperformed in the 2008 Georgia war, including, surprisingly, losing four planes, the Kremlin ordered significant military reform and investment.[33] With the expectation that potential instability in Central Asia and other parts of Russia's near abroad might prompt further military deployments in the future, combat experience was crucial.

Domestically, as discussed in Chapter 4, Putin was genuinely alarmed at the growing jihadist threat of the Syrian civil war. Were the regime to fall, Russia believed ISIS the most likely to capture Damascus. From this perspective, targeting the non-ISIS rebels was therefore justified as they were the greatest threat to the regime, and the regime was the bastion against an ISIS takeover. Yet Moscow made little distinction between the ideology of ISIS and that of the various Islamists among the rebels anyway. To Putin all Islamism was synonymous with jihadism and even if different rebel factions like Nusra, Ahrar and various Muslim Brotherhood groups were temporarily estranged from ISIS, their ideologies were so close that they would eventually converge. With 14 per cent of its population Muslim, the Russian government feared that any successes for ISIS or jihadists in Syria might embolden radicalisation and connected violence at home. Preventing any kind of Islamist victory and destroying ISIS' self-declared Caliphate thus had a strong domestic rationale. Moreover, there was a large number of Russian speakers fighting among the rebels and ISIS – known as 'Chechens' but often from various parts of the north Caucasus. These Russian speakers were among the first foreigners to flock to Syria in 2012, forming among the most effective fighting groups, and Putin was determined to kill or pin down as many as possible to prevent what he feared would be a violent homecoming.[34]

Projecting Russian power abroad also boosted Putin's domestic popularity, and nationalist policies had been well received in the past. The operations in Syria actually helped to distract from a simultaneous dialling down of the conflict in eastern Ukraine, where Putin's support for separatists against the Kiev government had struggled.[35] Pro-Putin Russian Orthodox church leaders in Moscow sought to boost this domestic support by offering the campaign religious legitimacy when a spokesman described it as a 'holy war' that would protect Syria's persecuted Christians, who were threatened by ISIS.[36] Some religious figures even blessed arms destined for Syria, while Assad himself would later emphasise this narrative, by claiming Putin was 'the sole defender of Christian civilization one can rely on.'[37]

Regional strategic and economic concerns were also at play. Russia had recently been hit by international sanctions over its intervention in Ukraine and a sharp decline in global oil prices, causing the economy to contract by 3.7 per cent in 2015. To launch a major overseas operation in Syria that cost at least $4 million a day therefore seemed unwise. However, with a $50 billion annual defence budget, the Syria campaign was affordable, provided the loss of planes and equipment was kept down – helped by the rebels' limited access to anti-aircraft weaponry.[38] Also, in the short term at least, a military campaign served as a useful domestic distraction to increased economic hardship at home. Moreover, Russian arms sales were a key pillar of the economy, worth $15.5 billion in 2015 and boosting sales might help partly offset lost jobs and income elsewhere. The very public use of Russian arms in Syria, including an audacious cruise missile strike from the Caspian Sea via Iranian and Iraqi airspace in October, acted as an advertisement to potential customers elsewhere.[39] Indeed, analysts later estimated that international customers impressed by the campaign would boost Russian arms sales by $6–7 billion.[40] Finally, the Syrian regime had been in considerable debt to Moscow since 2011; including an amount of at least $4 billion for unpaid arms contracts that would be lost were Assad defeated.[41]

Putin had previously been willing to accept short-term strains in diplomatic and economic ties with Assad's regional enemies to defend the regime. Yet as the Syria operation began, he sought to reassure, not clash. Lavrov was dispatched to the Gulf, while Israeli Premier Netanyahu was hosted in Moscow to be reassured about Russia's military build-up.[42] The one tie that was seriously damaged was with Turkey. Erdoğan was outraged when the Syria campaign began without his having being notified, despite having been in Moscow alongside Putin to witness the opening of the city's largest mosque just days before.[43] The intervention rolled back many of Turkey's rebel allies' recent gains, killed any chance of Ankara's proposed 'safe zone' and even targeted rebel and ISIS oil smuggling that was a favourable source of income.[44] Then, on 24 November, Turkey shot down a Russian Su-24, killing two servicemen, claiming it had violated Turkish airspace. Moscow, denying that the plane left Syrian territory, reacted furiously, placing economic sanctions on Turkey that one economist predicted would cost Ankara at least $10 billion.[45] Russia rattled Turkey further by increasing its ties to the PYD, allowing them to open a Moscow office in February 2016. Like the US it saw the YPG as a valuable anti-ISIS ally and hoped to woo Syria's leading Kurdish group away from Washington, something some in the PYD were receptive to, having leftist origins and stronger historical ties to Moscow. Yet this cooperation, which included Russia dispatching a small military force to Kurdish Afrin, only enraged Erdoğan further and confirmed the collapse of what had been a strong personal relationship for almost a decade.

The other regional relationship impacted was with Iran. Some noted that by placing its military alongside Iran's in Syria, Russia was effectively aligning itself with Tehran's regional agenda.[46] Yet the picture was more nuanced. Firstly, as noted, Putin was keen to maintain his other regional ties: with Iran's enemy Israel, with Riyadh's ally Egypt, with whom Moscow was growing ever closer, and with Saudi Arabia itself. Secondly, the intervention was as much about managing Iran's regional role as supporting it. In July 2015, after years of painstaking negotiation, a comprehensive deal was agreed with the P5+1 on Iran's nuclear programme, in which Tehran committed to reduce and redesign its nuclear facilities under IAEA verification in exchange for a phased end to nuclear-related Western economic sanctions. Tehran now expected economic reward, including Western investment and a resultant swelling of its regional power. While Russia previously had leverage over Tehran, being the friendliest among the P5, this was now gone and so it sought a new means to influence its southern neighbour. This was mostly friendly, including Russia's announcing it would sell S-300 air defences to Iran, but there were some concerns. In particular, Russian leaders were worried by the shape of Iranian influence in Syria, which seemingly undermined the state institutions like the military that Moscow had always worked with in favour of non-state actors like the NDF whom the IRGC alone had access to. In addition, the IRGC concentrated its efforts in the south, around Damascus airport, the Sayyeda Zeynab shrine and the mountain supply routes to Hezbollah in Lebanon, a long way from Russia's core interest of the base in Tartous that Iran looked unlikely to prioritise should Assad collapse. Russia's intervention, reinforcing the Syrian military, not militias, and in the north-west, was therefore also a means to win back some influence over Syria from Iran. This would ensure that Russia, not just a potentially rehabilitated Iran, would be the key international interlocutor in any resolution to the conflict and in post-war Syria.

Despite the short-term benefits of Putin's actions, there remained long-term risks to navigate. The greatest was over-extension and being dragged into a quagmire. Many commentators noted that Putin hoped to execute the Syria campaign like the second Chechnya war of 1999–2000 when overwhelming force led to a decisive Russian victory, despite a seeming disregard for high civilian casualties.[47] Yet the spectre of Moscow's long-lasting quagmire in Afghanistan from 1979 to 1989 also lurked uncomfortably. The first six months of the Syria campaign saw very few casualties, only five, but had these dramatically increased, the cost of the operation risen or had there been any suggestion that ground troops including conscripts might be deployed, Russian public support might have turned.[48] Likewise, by entering the war directly against ISIS and other militant Islamists, Moscow made itself a more desirable target for domestic and international terrorists. Seemingly in reaction to the intervention, ISIS claimed responsibility for a bomb that exploded on a Russian passenger jet leaving Egypt on 17 November 2015, killing all 224 on board, mainly Russian holidaymakers. While Putin responded defiantly, increasing the strikes in Syria, a sustained terror campaign targeting Russians at home or abroad might also have shifted public opinion. It was therefore imperative for Moscow to rapidly translate its military intervention into political leverage and bring about a favourable conclusion, or at least de-escalation, to the conflict before any such quagmire developed.[49]

Another peace process

Vienna

Russia's intervention coincided with a shift from the US and its Western allies towards greater compromise on Syria, and it is possible that Putin recognised this when deciding on military action. After five years of ineffectiveness, three developments shifted Western attitudes. First was the Iran nuclear deal. While Israel, Saudi Arabia and hawks in Washington and

Europe warned that Iran would take advantage of the deal to step up its regional machinations, especially in Syria, the White House and other Western governments argued that the deal had successfully prevented Iran's nuclear proliferation peacefully. Western companies, meanwhile, circled Tehran to take advantage of the end of sanctions. Though a full detente was still far off, several Western diplomats argued that Iran would now be more inclined to consolidate its regional position by helping to resolve the Syrian war. Foreign Minister Zarif, who had built a working relationship with John Kerry during the nuclear talks, had even submitted a new 'peace plan' to Assad in August, supporting this idea.

Second was the continued distraction and threat of ISIS. Europe and the US found themselves victims of ISIS terrorism, some by returning nationals who had joined the 'Caliphate' in Syria but also by citizens 'self-radicalised' by ISIS propaganda. The most violent to date occurred in Paris on 13 November 2015 when 130 people were killed by multiple coordinated attacks. Third was the sudden and unexpected migrant crisis in the summer of 2015, greatly exacerbated by a surge in Syrian refugees heading to Europe. Syrians applying for asylum in European countries leapt from a cumulative 222,156 in December 2014, to 807,337 by November 2015 – although the total number of refugees was believed to be much higher.[50] Media coverage of desperate refugees killed while crossing the Mediterranean prompted a public outcry in some quarters, and a right-wing reaction in others. Pressure mounted on Western leaders to find a resolution to the Syrian war, with some politicians and editorials urging a compromise with the 'lesser evil' of the Assad regime.[51]

With Putin then raising the stakes in September to a level that Western leaders, particularly Obama, were unwilling to match, a climbdown was required. Two pillars of western Syrian policy since summer 2011 wobbled. Firstly, Iran was invited to attend peace talks. On 23 October Kerry met with Lavrov and the foreign ministers of Turkey and Saudi Arabia in Vienna to prepare new international peace talks on Syria. At Lavrov's insistence, Iran was invited to talks on 30 October in Vienna, which even Saudi Arabia's new Foreign Minister Adel Jubair reluctantly accepted, noting he wished to 'test' if Iran could play a constructive role.[52] With this breakthrough achieved, on 14 November another meeting was convened in Vienna in which the International Syria Support Group (ISSG) was formed of the Arab League, China, Egypt, EU, France, Germany, Iran, Iraq, Italy, Jordan, Lebanon, Oman, Qatar, Russia, Saudi Arabia, Turkey, UAE, UK, UN and US. Though Syrians were notably absent from the talks, the ISSG represented a recognition for the first time in nearly five years of conflict that war in Syria required consensus from *all* the international actors involved for any resolution to occur. Secondly, after insisting for years that Assad's departure was non-negotiable, British Foreign Secretary Philip Hammond declared in early October 2015 that he might remain as titular head of state for a period of time up to three months, as long as he doesn't stand for re-election.[53] In Vienna the US and Russia continued to disagree over Assad's future, but unlike in Geneva in 2012, Lavrov and Kerry played down any disagreement in order to allow the process to begin. Indeed, in a sign of how much the perceived power balance in Syria had shifted towards Moscow, in December Kerry appeared to concede the point when stating, 'The United States and our partners are not seeking so-called regime change' – though US officials later clarified this meant Assad would not have to depart on 'Day One' of a transition.[54]

The Vienna meetings prepared the way for a renewed round of peace talks. On 30 October, those who would form the ISSG released a statement declaring, 'Syria's unity, independence, territorial integrity, and secular character are fundamental', that its state institutions must remain intact, that efforts must be made to end the war and that a 'Syrian led and Syrian owned' political process should begin.[55] On 14 November, the ISSG issued a joint statement that expanded on this, pledging: to commit to a Syrian-led political transition based on the 2012 Geneva Communiqué; to support and work to implement a nationwide ceasefire as soon as the regime and opposition took initial steps toward a transition under UN auspices; and to convene formal negotiations between regime and opposition representatives with UN Special Representative Staffan de Mistura tasked with deciding who should represent the opposition.[56] Soon afterwards on 18 December the UN Security Council, including China and Russia, unanimously adopted Resolution 2254, which endorsed the 'Vienna statements' of 30 October and 14 November. It set an ambitious target for peace talks to begin within a month, and six months after that the formation of a transitional government. It called for a new constitution and democratic elections, administered by the UN and including diaspora and refugees, to be held by July 2017. As had been noted in both Vienna statements, ISIS and Nusra were to be excluded from any talks and transition.

This prompted a flurry of diplomatic activity, but many of the dividing issues between the external actors remained unresolved. The resolution did not specify whether Assad could be involved in the transition after six months, nor whether he could stand for election in 2017. This long-standing grievance was kicked into the long grass, with many recalling that it had derailed the 2012 Geneva talks. A body to represent the opposition at any talks had been formed in Riyadh a few days before, but questions about its authority over all the opposition remained, particularly after Russia contested its make-up. Moreover, as at previous peace conferences, it remained unclear whether Assad or his allies were actually serious about the talks.

Riyadh

The tight scheduling of the Vienna Process created a sense of urgency to once again unite the opposition into a single viable body. Saudi Arabia, with considerable American encouragement, hosted a conference in Riyadh on 10–12 December 2015 with the goal of bringing together the various external political bodies alongside 'moderate' fighting groups. The result was the 34-member Higher Negotiations Committee (HNC). This was composed of: nine members from the SOC, including Khoja, the Muslim Brotherhood's Mahmoud Farouq Tayfour, the KNC's Abdel Hakim Bashar and the defected former Prime Minister Riad Hijab; five from the rival NCB group, who were more pro-Russian, with the US hoping their inclusion would placate Moscow; nine independents, including Building the Syrian State's Louay Hussein and former SOC leader Ahmed al-Jarba; and eleven representing fighting groups, including Mohammed Alloush of Jaysh al-Islam (Zahran Alloush's cousin), Labib Nahhas of Ahrar and several FSA representatives.[57] Ahrar's inclusion proved ambiguous, as its leadership publicly denounced the secular-leaning declarations of the HNC yet its representative in Riyadh, Labib Nahhas, signed up anyway, possibly acting independently. Whether this represented genuine division within Ahrar or was a tactic to allow more manoeuvrability depending on how negotiations went, remained unclear.

While the HNC was an impressive coming together of the political and armed opposition, key actors remained notably absent. Nusra was unsurprisingly not invited, having been explicitly excluded from the Vienna Process, despite its close co-operation with Ahrar and others in the Jaysh al-Fateh. Haytham Manna, who had recently split with the NCB, refused to attend, aligning himself instead with the PYD, who also were not invited. The PYD's exclusion owed much to Turkish insistence. Ankara increasingly found itself in a three-way conflict between itself, ISIS and the PKK/PYD.[58] ISIS began to launch attacks inside Turkey, generally targeting Turkish Kurds and others supportive of the PKK/PYD, such as a bomb in Suruc in July 2015 that killed thirty-two activists. Ankara couldn't tolerate attacks on its citizens, even those that supported its Kurdish enemies, and so Turkey finally joined the US anti-ISIS coalition soon afterwards. Yet, as with Russia claiming it was bombing ISIS but primarily hitting rebel positions, Turkey favoured bombing PKK positions in Iraq in its supposedly anti-ISIS campaign, prompting further PKK retaliations within Turkey. There were also domestic factors at play. In June 2015 Erdoğan's AKP had lost control of parliament after voters delivered a hung parliament in elections. In response, Erdoğan played up his nationalist credentials, emphasising the need for strong government in the face of the dual ISIS–PKK threat, a message grimly reinforced by Turkey's worst ever civilian terrorist attack in October when 102 were killed by ISIS in Ankara. The tactic worked and in a second election in November enough nationalists and right-leaning Kurds were persuaded to return a full AKP majority government. Thereafter military operations and retaliatory PKK attacks in Turkish cities increased further. In such circumstances, Erdoğan was adamant that the PKK's Syrian affiliate could be nowhere near Geneva.

Having been excluded from Riyadh, the PYD initiated its own opposition conference in the Rojava town of Derik (Al-Malikiyah in Arabic). In October 2015 the PYD created the Syrian Democratic Forces (SDF), an umbrella group that included non-Kurdish Syrian Arab fighting forces. While the PYD and its militia the YPG were still the dominant force and unquestioningly in charge, this new grouping allowed them to legitimise moving into non-Kurdish territory by claiming to be speaking for all Syrians. It also provided legal and political cover for the US to support it without officially backing the PKK, still on Washington's terrorism list.[59] The Derik conference created a political counterpart to the SDF, a 42-member Kurdish and non-Kurdish body, eventually known as the Council of Democratic Syria (CDS).[60] Manna and many of his supporters were elected, as were members of the Cairo Group, a collection of former regime officials such as Jihad Makdissi and other oppositionists reluctant to endorse the Western and Saudi-backed opposition. The Derik conference created yet another rival grouping just as the HNC had seemingly managed to pull the long-divided opposition together. The presence of only one Kurd on the HNC, the KNC's Abdel Hakim Bashar, and Turkey's steadfast refusal to allow the PYD to be included meant that, once again, the peace talks would begin in Geneva with key players excluded.

Geneva

The beginning of the Geneva III talks, as they were dubbed, echoed the run-up to their failed predecessor, Geneva II. The HNC set a list of conditions to be met before they would attend the talks, including the lifting of regime sieges on certain areas to allow humanitarian aid to reach starving inhabitants, and an end to Russian and regime airstrikes. As in early 2014, these were not met, but the HNC was sufficiently pressured by the US and Saudi Arabia to take part nonetheless. This pushed the start of talks back from early January as proposed at Vienna, as did objections by Russia over which opposition should be invited. It accused some of the HNC representatives of terrorism, notably Jaysh al-Islam's Mohammad Alloush, who was named Chief Negotiator by the head of the HNC's negotiating team, Riad Hijab. Moreover, it lobbied for both the PYD and members of the CDS to be included. While he resisted inclusion of the PYD, under Turkish pressure, Mistura eventually invited some CDS members, including Manna, to attend as consultants and advisers, but not as part of the official opposition delegation.[61] Despite Alloush remaining in place, this seemingly satisfied Russia and the regime sufficiently for talks to begin on 1 February 2016.

Mistura began with more modest goals than Lakhdar Brahimi in 2014. There were to be no face-to-face meetings as there had been at Geneva II. Instead he proposed a flexible framework that included simultaneous meetings taking place on multiple aspects of the transition process and proximity talks whereby the delegations would address intermediaries rather than the other side at first.[62] Even so, the first attempt failed rapidly, and was suspended by Mistura after just two days, on 3 February. The HNC delegates blamed the regime for disrespecting the process, launching its massive assault in Aleppo province at the same time, and refused to return until conditions on the ground improved. The regime, in turn, claimed the HNC had been ordered by Saudi Arabia, Qatar and Turkey to quit Geneva. Mistura tried to put a positive spin on the situation, insisting, 'It is not the end and it is not the failure of the talks.'[63]

The talks were salvaged when the US and Russia eventually agreed to implement the second component of the Vienna statements: a nationwide ceasefire. On 11 February, Lavrov and Kerry met once more, this time in Munich, and agreed on a 'cessation of hostilities' that eventually came into effect on 27 February – conveniently after the regime–Russian offensive in Aleppo had achieved its immediate military goals. The agreement was not termed a 'ceasefire' as it only included certain regions. Areas occupied by ISIS and Nusra remained outside of the agreement, with continued attacks on those areas by either regime, rebel, Russian, Kurdish or US forces legitimised. The great uncertainty was the Nusra-held areas as the al-Qaeda affiliate was embedded alongside other rebel groups in many places, especially Idlib. The opposition feared Russia and the regime would use this loophole to keep attacking their positions by claiming they were targeting Nusra. Given the viciousness of the recent offensives, there was deep scepticism among rebel forces that this agreement was anything more than a ploy to consolidate recent regime gains and prepare for the next attack.

The cessation of hostilities was far from perfect. The US and Russia had agreed to monitor any infringements, yet when they did occur, some rebels complained that US personnel on the hotline it had established spoke poor Arabic, impeding their task.[64] Even so, while there were reports of violations by both sides, John Kerry claimed that after two weeks there had been an 80–90 per cent decrease in violence.[65] The Syrian Observatory for Human Rights (SOHR) later stated that the month immediately after the ceasefire saw the lowest civilian casualties since November 2011.[66] Western media showed Syrians in regime-held Damascus enjoying rare moments of peace and normality. In opposition-held areas, protesters returned to the street to denounce Assad as they first had in 2011 and civil society greatly benefitted from the breathing space. Importantly though, many in rebel-held areas took advantage of the ceasefire to protest against Nusra as well, to dispel the notion that most civilians in opposition areas supported radicals.[67] Meanwhile the UN reported that it had sent 536 trucks filled with aid to nearly 240,000 people, and relief supplies to 18 besieged areas, although the regime still restricted access to several rebel-held districts.[68]

The 27 February cessation of hostilities was unique: the first time anything approaching a ceasefire had held for any significant period, despite its flaws. Like the Vienna Process as a whole, it primarily came about because of the Russian intervention. As has been noted, previous attempts at ceasefires during the Arab League plan and the Annan plan failed partly because external actors placed little pressure on their Syrian allies to abide by them, and often actively encouraged their failure. The same was true of another plan by Mistura, soon after he was appointed Brahimi's successor in July 2014, to encourage local conflict freezes. Yet Putin's intervention forced the opposition to seek compromise out of fear, while it gave Moscow real leverage to enforce compliance on the regime. Putin expended considerable international political capital to ensure the cessation was a success, personally telephoning regional leaders including Assad, King Salman, Rouhani and Netanyahu.[69]

As a result of the unexpected, but limited, success of the cessation, both sides agreed to resume talks in Geneva on 14 March. In a surprise move, Putin then announced that the military goals of his operation had been achieved and he was withdrawing 'the main part of our military group from the Syrian Arab Republic beginning tomorrow'.[70] This threw Western and regional observers as much as his initial intervention had done. Was Putin trying to maximise his leverage with Assad, showing him that Russian military intervention was finite and he needed to take talks seriously? Alternatively, was this meant to persuade the opposition and the US that Moscow was serious about the peace process? Another reading was that it was a ruse: Russia was not drawing down in truth, simply making a show to pacify international criticism for its bombing of civilian targets and downplay any talk at home of a Syrian quagmire. Similarly, was this aimed at a domestic Russian audience, with Putin trying to assuage fears of mission creep and declare a foreign policy triumph in the run-up to parliamentary elections in September? Finally, some argued Putin was hedging his bets: he was keeping the bases in Tartous and Khmeimim that could easily be re-equipped at short notice, should either the peace process fail or Assad need urgent help once more.[71] No one knew for certain the Russian President's motives, but a combination of these reasons was most likely. Indeed, soon after announcing this 'withdrawal', Russian forces were engaged in another major assault, helping regime troops recapture Palmyra from ISIS in late March. By keeping his rivals guessing, Putin likely calculated he could get the most out of the West on one side, and Assad on the other, perhaps having not yet decided which was the best means forwards for himself and Russia, but keeping as many options open as possible.

In the medium term at least, Putin's intervention served him well. Internationally, he had broken the deadlock with the US over Ukraine and boosted Russia's global and regional position. Any potential Assad collapse appeared to have been prevented and a peace process along Russia's preferred option, which included Iran and didn't necessarily call for Assad's immediate departure, had been initiated and endorsed by all sides. Putin had increased his leverage with the regime, enjoying comparable influence to Iran for the first time since the war began. Yet long-term uncertainties and threats remained. Russia had publicly invested heavily, politically and militarily, in Syria, so were Assad to still fall by a means not controlled by Moscow, any credibility gained from the intervention would be lost. Just as George Bush's optimistic 'Mission Accomplished' declaration after the Iraq invasion in 2003 proved to be hollow as the US was sucked into a doomed occupation, Putin risked similar in Syria. For all the Russian President's self-congratulations, the war in Syria had not yet ended decisively in his favour and the long-term pitfalls of mission creep, an enduring quagmire and domestic terrorist retaliations remained.

What about the impact of the intervention on the Syrian war? At the beginning of this book it was noted how in past civil wars involvement by a foreign state on one side can end a conflict by increasing the chances that its ally will win or force its enemy to negotiate. Moscow's intervention was certainly the most substantial action by a foreign power on one side since 2011, and seemingly broke with the cycle of balanced interventions until then. The Vienna Process and resulting ceasefire suggested that, indeed, the rebels and their external backers, especially the US, had been forced to negotiate. The action shook the war out of stalemate. Assad's regime was boosted and retook territory from both the rebels and ISIS. The US and Saudi Arabia were able to put together a more united opposition than had been seen before in the HNC, and accepted Iran's presence at the negotiating table for the first time. Both Assad and the rebels were induced to negotiate for longer than had been possible before, and a cessation of hostilities of record length was similarly achieved.

However, Russia's intervention should not be overstated. The Vienna Process was more favourable to Putin, but was far from a Russian diktat. Moscow proved unable to overrule Turkey's insistence that the PYD be excluded from Geneva III, and could not prevent groups it deemed terrorists being included in the HNC. The future of Assad remained debated, even if Western leaders now conceded he might last a while longer. Nor did Russian intervention lead to an immediate Assad military victory, and the regime's deep structural weaknesses of chronic manpower shortage and the inability to hold hostile territory indefinitely remained. The intervention tipped the scale more in Assad's favour, but still did not seem enough to win him the war outright. With or without the fragile Vienna Process, it still seemed unlikely that Assad would be able to regain control of all of Syria even with continued Russian help. The intervention did not make Moscow the new hegemon in Syria or the region, it simply increased its stake in the post-American Middle East. Several other players remained in Syria and they seemed unwilling to abandon their interests just yet.

CHAPTER ELEVEN

The wild card:
Syria's war in the age of Trump

The only reason President Obama wants to attack Syria is to save face over his very dumb RED LINE statement. Do NOT attack Syria, fix U.S.A.

Tweet by Donald Trump, 5 September 2013,
after alleged regime chemical weapons attack in East Ghouta[1]

These heinous actions by the Bashar al-Assad regime are a consequence of the past administration's weakness and irresolution. President Obama said in 2012 that he would establish a 'red line' against the use of chemical weapons and then did nothing.

Official statement by Donald Trump, 4 April 2017,
shortly before launching a missile strike on Assad after
alleged regime chemical weapons attack in Khan Shaikhoun, Idlib[2]

On a wet day in January 2017, the newly elected President of the United States took to the podium in front of the Capitol Building in Washington, DC and delivered his inaugural address. In his trademark red tie and coiffured blond hair, Donald J. Trump, a property mogul and reality TV star with no political experience, delivered a bleak assessment of America's place in the world. 'For many decades, we've enriched foreign industry at the expense of American industry . . . The wealth of our middle class has been ripped from their homes and then redistributed across the entire world.' He therefore promised that, 'From this moment on, it's going to be America First . . . America will start winning again, winning like never before . . . We will seek friendship and goodwill with the nations of the world – but we do so with the understanding that it is the right of all nations to put their own interests first.'

While Trump's supporters lining the Mall replied with rapturous applause, Washington's establishment figures, including members of his own Republican Party, looked on nervously. Trump was not expected to win either the Republican nomination or the presidential election against former Secretary of State Hillary Clinton. He was an outsider, prone to bellicose language, political incorrectness and U-turns, and had promised highly provocative foreign policies during his campaign, including building a wall along the Mexican border and banning all Muslims from entering the US. Historically, transitions from president to president have seen a degree of continuity in US foreign policy, but Trump's inauguration suggested a radical departure. By using the slogan 'America First', which echoed 1930s isolationists, and promising protectionist economic policies, Trump appeared to be rejecting the entire post-1945 global order and America's leading role. While many hoped that the forty-fifth president's more radical instincts might be moderated in office, it was already clear that Trump would attempt to lead the US in an international direction very different from that of Obama.

This chapter will consider the impact of the new president on the Syria conflict. It will first outline the state of the war on the eve of Trump's inauguration: the failure of Obama to halt Putin in western Syria balanced against advances over ISIS in the east. It will note how the US was increasingly marginalised in western Syria, with Russia, Iran and Turkey emerging as the leading international players, culminating in the Astana peace process after eastern Aleppo fell in late 2016. Within this context the entry of Trump will be assessed, considering whether his approach actually represented a departure. It will be suggested that although his bombastic style might have been distinctive, the end result was little different from Obama's: marginalisation in western Syria alongside further entrenchment in the post-ISIS east.

Obama's twilight

In western Syria – the areas controlled primarily by the Assad regime and the rebels – Obama's final year in office was a story of failure and decreasing influence. While 2016 began with the US and Russia negotiating to end the conflict, by the year's end Moscow appeared to have outmanoeuvred Washington diplomatically and militarily.

American diplomacy proved unable to prevent the collapse of the February 2016 cessation of hostilities, the failure of the Geneva III talks and the undermining of the Vienna Process. The cessation of hostilities did see a notable decline in fatalities, with a 35 per cent drop across Syria in the first three months.[3] Yet arguably it contained the seeds of its own demise, being only a partial ceasefire that allowed the US, Russia and the regime to continue the fight in territories controlled by ISIS and Jabhat al-Nusra. With Russia and Assad long claiming that all rebel-held territory included a jihadist presence, it didn't prove difficult for them to gradually increase their violations of the cessation. One such strike torpedoed the Geneva III talks. On 19 April regime bombers killed thirty-seven civilians in a market place in Maarat al-Nu'man. The outraged opposition HNC, which had complained more than 2,000 times since February that the regime was violating the ceasefire, walked out of Geneva in protest. Sergei Lavrov responded that he saw 'players on the outside' trying to derail the process.[4] With no talks to even pay lip service to, violations continued and the cessation broke down by May. Obama's critics argued that the whole process had been a Russian ploy to regroup.[5]

As Assad's military campaign resumed and the humanitarian situation worsened, it made Obama look even more impotent. While international law forbids targeting hospitals, between May and November regime and Russian bombers seemed to deliberately target hospitals in rebel areas, particularly eastern Aleppo. According to the Syrian Network for Human Rights, eighty medical facilities in Syria were attacked in 2016 with eighty-one medical workers killed. Assad was also accused of deliberately besieging and starving outlying rebel pockets. In one incident in June, regime forces reportedly bombed besieged Darayya immediately after a long-awaited UN food delivery was allowed in. Washington repeatedly tried to halt the carnage, but failed. It attempted once more to revive the ceasefire in September, but this collapsed within a week, not least because a US strike intended for ISIS instead struck a regime position, killing sixty-two soldiers. Western allies then twice attempted UN Security Council resolutions: a Franco–Spanish call to end the bombing of eastern Aleppo in October which Russia vetoed, and a Spanish–Egyptian–New Zealand-led appeal for a truce in the city in early December, which was similarly blocked by Russia, this time alongside China.

As Americans went to vote in November, Assad looked increasingly imperious in western Syria. Rebel-held suburbs in Damascus, Darayya and Muadamiyat agreed to evacuate to far-off Idlib in late summer. By late autumn Assad had surrounded eastern Aleppo, and its conquest appeared imminent. Obama himself said on 11 November that he was 'not optimistic about the short-term prospects in Syria', arguing that Russia and Iran's decision to back Assad in a brutal air campaign had ultimately tipped the scales.[6]

In contrast, developments in eastern Syria were more promising. Western airstrikes alongside support for SDF forces on the ground had forced ISIS to retreat. In May 2016 the SDF announced the start of a campaign to capture Raqqa, ISIS' effective capital. However, in a sign that Washington's Kurdish-dominated ally was far from a complicit proxy force, the troops for this assault were soon diverted north-west to instead capture the city of Manbij from the Caliphate. Likewise, the SDF seized Tal Rifaat near Afrin from the rebels in February, taking advantage of a Russia–Assad attack and illustrating their independent streak. The conquests of Manbij and Tal Rifaat severely irked Turkey, and would soon have greater ramifications. However, territorial gains did further squeeze out ISIS and, alongside victories for the Iraqi army in Fallujah in June and Ramadi in December, and the beginning of the siege of Mosul in October, meant that this was one area in which the administration could boast of some success.

On balance, however, the final year of Obama's presidency saw the Syrian situation worsen. While the campaign against ISIS may have turned in his favour, this was overshadowed by his perceived impotence in the face of Assad and Russia's increased advances and the humanitarian crises that came with them. Domestic critics labelled Syria 'Obama's shame', while both presidential candidates, even his former Secretary of State Hillary Clinton, were critical in different ways.[7] For many, it wasn't just that Obama had proved unable to prevent the worsening crisis, it was that he had been repeatedly outfoxed by the Kremlin.

Putin ascendant

The string of military and diplomatic successes for Putin in 2016 and Obama's inability to prevent them gave the impression that Moscow was eclipsing Washington in Syria. Of course, as has been discussed previously, the United States' influence on the conflict was always more limited than perceived, but this narrative, seized on by Obama's domestic and international critics, was also championed by Putin's supporters. Three developments in particular boosted this view: Russia's rapprochement with Turkey, Assad's recapture of eastern Aleppo and the subsequent Moscow-led peace process in Astana.

Turkey invades

On 24 August 2016, a small column of Turkish tanks supported by FSA militia rolled into the ISIS-held northern border town of Jarablus, making Turkey the first anti-Assad state to occupy Syrian territory. However, this was not the beginning of a sizeable invasion aimed at regime change, but rather a limited campaign targeting the PYD and ISIS, not Assad. It represented a significant shift in Ankara's priorities, and had come after a volte-face towards Russia and significant internal changes in Turkey.

By early 2016, the Syria war was looking grim for Turkey. The PKK and ISIS had both launched multiple terror attacks, which Ankara said had links to Syria, while Turkey's rebel allies were getting nowhere in their attempts to topple Assad. The diplomatic fallout had left Turkey isolated, sanctioned by Russia on the one hand and increasingly distant from Washington on the other. Erdoğan therefore took dramatic measures. On 5 May it was announced that Davutoğlu would be resigning as prime minister. Despite having been firm allies for over a decade, Davutoğlu was reportedly unconvinced both by Erdoğan's plans for a new executive presidency and the excessive military force now being deployed against the PKK. Yet Davutoğlu had no independent support as a politician, meaning that, after losing Erdoğan's backing, his departure was inevitable.

After appointing a new premier, the more compliant Binali Yıldırım, Erdoğan took the opportunity to reset Turkey's international position. The president's supporters were soon claiming that Ankara's foreign policy blunders such as the Syria debacle were down to Davutoğlu, glossing over Erdoğan's leading role. Diplomatic shifts followed. Officials privately briefed that regime change in Syria was no longer a priority.[8] A reconciliation agreement with Israel restoring diplomatic ties was announced on 26 June, with Israel apologising for the Mavi Marmara incident and Turkey quietly dropping its demand to fully lift the Gaza siege. Most significantly, at the end of June Erdoğan apologised to Russia for downing the Su-24 jet. This opened the way for a more general rapprochement, ultimately prompting Moscow to lift its sanctions and resume Russian tourism.

Against this backdrop, Turkey was rocked by an attempted coup d'état by sections of the military in July. Despite attempts to seize strategic places, loyal military units and public demonstrators defeated the plotters. Over 300 people were killed in the attempt and several thousand injured. In a rare moment of unity, Turks from all political backgrounds – including the opposition CHP – came together in Istanbul's Yenikapı Square to greet Erdoğan and show their support for Turkey's democracy. However, the president responded with a harsh crackdown that ultimately resembled a 'self coup', using the incident to bolster his own power. Some opponents even claimed that he had orchestrated the whole attempt as a pretext.[9]

Erdoğan pinned the blame on the Gülen movement, although Fethullah Gülen strongly denied this from his exile in the US. On 20 July the government declared a state of emergency, subsequently renewed every three months by parliament. This authorised a wave of arrests and oppression.

Even before the coup attempt, the government had cracked down on free speech, arresting hundreds of journalists and forcing the closure of several publications. Now, key public institutions were purged, with universities, the civil service, the judiciary, schools and the military all targeted. By mid-2017, 50,000 people had been arrested, including more than 10,000 soldiers, while 15,000 education staff had lost their jobs.[10] The crackdown was welcomed by Erdoğan's new domestic ally, the ultra-nationalist MHP, which in December supported the president's long-held ambition of constitutional reform by backing in parliament a plebiscite on adopting a presidential system. The vote was held in April 2017 and was narrowly won by the 'Yes' camp, with 51.4 per cent. Arguably Erdoğan now had more power than any Turkish leader since Atatürk.

With the post-purge military now dominated by loyalists, Erdoğan was able to pursue a more hawkish Syria policy. Operation Euphrates Shield was launched on 24 August with the declared goal of clearing ISIS and the PYD from Turkey's border to decrease terror attacks in Turkey and to prevent the development of a contiguous Kurdish proto-state led by the PYD. The invasion was prompted by the SDF's capture of Manbij. Alongside the PYD's capture of Tal Rifaat, this raised fears that it may soon be able to link up the Kobane and Afrin cantons. Turkey had evidently been planning an operation for months, as it had transported FSA fighters from Idlib and Syrian Turkmen militia through Turkey for the assault. The initial goal appeared to be to push ISIS out of Jarablus and nearby al-Bab, linking these areas up to a rebel pocket in Azaz and thus carving out a Turkish buffer zone. The rapprochement with Russia was absolutely key. Moscow, effectively in control of western Syrian airspace, took no action against the Turkish-rebel forces, blessing the invasion. There were also reports of significant intelligence-sharing between Russia and Turkey.[11] Moreover, while the Assad regime decried this 'blatant violation' of Syria's sovereignty, its forces did not strike Turkish troops, suggesting a degree of acceptance, most likely at Russia's behest.[12]

The operation, however, had mixed results. Ostensibly, Turkey achieved its initial goals. It swiftly captured Jarablus in August 2016, taking the symbolic village of Dabiq – after which ISIS had named its propaganda magazine – in October and al-Bab in February 2017. However, the operation took far longer than expected and at least sixty-seven Turkish troops were killed.[13] Further expansion of the buffer zone was soon prevented when regime troops conquered ISIS positions south of al-Bab, leaving Turkey and its rebel allies blocked in by Assad to the south and the PYD to the east and west. Further conquest would require attacking the allies of either Russia or the US. Given Russia's importance to the operation, attacking Assad was never an option, but with US ties strained, and even more so after Washington refused to extradite Gülen, assaults on the PYD did take place. Manbij, Afrin and their vicinities were repeatedly shelled, prompting the US to send special forces into the former in February 2017 to deter Ankara. Similarly, the next month the SDF announced that Manbij's western villages, between the town and Turkish troops, would be ceded to regime control to act as a protective buffer zone.

Outmanoeuvred, Erdoğan and Yıldırım announced the 'end' of Euphrates Shield in late March 2017. However, there were no plans to withdraw troops, and many suspected a future assault on Afrin – the one PYD stronghold without a significant US presence. Russia's withdrawal of a small military contingent from the city in June suggested Moscow might endorse this. However, any attack could leave Turkey militarily occupying a hostile Kurdish stronghold, with questions already raised over how sustainable its presence in the Jarablus–Azaz–al-Bab triangle was. As Israel discovered in south Lebanon in the 1980s and 1990s, open-ended occupations in hostile territory can prove bloody and expensive.

The fall of eastern Aleppo

The Turkey–Russia rapprochement contributed to another major victory for Putin: Assad's reconquest of rebel-held eastern Aleppo in December 2016. Reports in the Lebanese press suggested that, in exchange for permitting Turkish forces to enter the north, Erdoğan promised Putin that he would stop backing the eastern Aleppo rebels.[14] Moreover, with Euphrates Shield recruiting a contingent of Idlib rebels, this weakened the forces sent to relieve the siege of Aleppo. More significant was the sizeable increase in military support provided by Russia and Iran. In October, Moscow deployed its only aircraft carrier, the *Admiral Kuznetsov*, to the eastern Mediterranean. This added yet more airpower for the assault on Aleppo and served as a show of force to Western powers to deter any last-minute talk of intervening to save the rebel enclave.[15] Russia also bolstered its special forces and military advisers on the ground. Iran, meanwhile, increased the number of Quds Force, Hezbollah, Iraqi, Afghani and Pakistani Shia militia in Syria. Some estimated that Assad's final assault on eastern Aleppo involved more foreign Shia militiamen than Syrian army troops, with Hezbollah and Iraqi Shia leading the assaults and the Syrian army playing a supportive role.[16] That said, the Tiger Forces, an elite Syrian army special forces unit led by Suheil al-Hassan, took the lead at several key points.

The capture of eastern Aleppo came after months of gradual military advances. Alongside the brutal 'softening up' of rebel positions by targeting medical infrastructure, in July the Tiger Forces captured the strategically important Castello Road, encircling the east. In an attempt to break the siege, rebel forces – including the Jaysh al-Fateh from Idlib – launched a counter-attack. Huge piles of tyres were burnt to obscure the view of Russian and regime bombers, while multiple assaults led to a rebel breakout in the south-west in August. However, this success was short-lived, and by early September regime forces had recaptured lost ground. Several further rebel breakouts also failed, setting the stage for Assad's advance.

In late September, Russian and regime jets pounded eastern Aleppo in the harshest attacks yet. In one day over 150 airstrikes were reported, killing at least 90 people, mostly civilians.[17] In the following ground assault the regime captured the Handarat Palestinian refugee camp in the city's north and took 15 per cent of rebel territory. After a brief pause to repel another failed rebel counter-offensive, the final assault began on 15 November. After more airstrikes, in nine days regime forces captured the Hanano district, representing about a quarter of remaining rebel territory in the city and, symbolically, the first area the rebels captured in 2012. Rebel forces swiftly collapsed, with some reports suggesting that the lack of medical facilities and intense Russian bombardment had proven decisive.[18] Assad's forces continued their advance, recapturing the old city and the symbolic but badly damaged eighth-century Umayyad Mosque on 6 December. In the days that followed, the regime and Russia paused their assault, ostensibly to allow for the evacuation of up to 8,000 civilians, although people noted that troops were redeployed to Palmyra where ISIS had used the regime's distraction to successfully recapture the desert city. This setback did not ultimately change the picture in Aleppo. The remaining rebels, pushed into a tiny pocket in the south, eventually agreed to withdraw completely as part of a Russia–Turkey mediated ceasefire on 13 December.

A degree of confusion and recrimination followed. Under the terms of the ceasefire, rebel fighters and civilians were to be evacuated, but for days buses intended for the task sat motionless as negotiations continued. Eventually the evacuation commenced, in fits and starts, leading to more than 40,000 departing. Figures vary, but the International Red Cross claimed that 4,000 of these were fighters who, along with their families (around 10,000), were escorted to Idlib province. The remaining civilians stayed in western Aleppo.[19] The rebels and their Syrian and international supporters had long argued that Assad's conquest of the east would lead to massacres and unparalleled civilian slaughter. The SOHR reported that over 465 civilians were killed during the fighting, mostly by airstrikes, and 149 more in western Aleppo by rebel shelling.[20] The UN further stated it had credible evidence that Iraqi Shia militia had been responsible for the summary killing of up to eighty-two civilians in the final battle.[21] Brutal though these killings were, they were fewer than many had feared.

On 22 December the Syrian army announced it was in full control of the city for the first time since summer 2012, although the PYD retained its Kurdish enclave. West Aleppans crossed into the east to inspect the ruins of the once stunning old city, relieved that the war was finally receding from view. East Aleppans also trickled back to rebuild their destroyed neighbourhoods, some having fled only as the battle raged, others having departed in 2012. In public, those interviewed from both sides of the city praised Assad as a liberator, though some privately noted their continued fear of the regime and its new foreign Shia militia allies.[22] For the rebels, the defeat was a catastrophe. While the tide had been turning against them for years, losing their foothold in Syria's second city reduced any substantial presence in peripheral Idlib and Deraa. This diminished any claim to represent large parts of Syria and reduced their representatives' bargaining power. It may have been obvious for some time that the rebels couldn't win the war, but after Aleppo fell it looked increasingly likely they were going to lose. For Assad, in contrast, the capture was a triumph. After first regaining Homs in 2014, he now had control of all of Syria's major cities. With Russian and Iranian help 'Rump Syria' was now expanding and, while recapturing the entire east still looked daunting, eliminating the rebels in the west appeared viable for the first time. For Putin, breaking the deadlock was a major breakthrough, especially given it was his diplomatic and military moves that had facilitated the victory. He could now leverage the outcome into a new peace process that excluded the US.

Pax Russica?

The Astana peace process would not have been possible without the summer rapprochement between Turkey and Russia, and it was these states that took the lead. Building on the Aleppo ceasefire they brokered on 13 December, Putin and Erdoğan agreed that a new round of Syria talks should take place in Astana, the capital of Kazakhstan, a Russian ally. Iran endorsed this and, alongside Russia and Turkey, invoked UN Resolution 2254, passed at the beginning of the Vienna Process in 2015, as the legal justification for the new talks. True to the Vienna Process, ISIS, Jabhat al-Nusra and the PYD-aligned Syrian Democratic Council were not invited to attend, but this time Western states, including the US, were also absent. After the evacuation of Aleppo was completed, Turkey and Russia brokered a nationwide ceasefire that came into effect on 30 December. While areas controlled by ISIS and Nusra were again excluded, through Turkish pressure key rebel groups including Ahrar al-Sham and Jaysh al-Islam signed up, although they soon complained of regime violations.[23] This signified a change in how such agreements would operate and it was the fighting groups, not their political representatives like the SOC and HNC, that were invited to the first round of talks in January, although Ahrar refused to attend despite signing up to the ceasefire. Russia claimed this would prove more successful than previous talks since it involved those actually fighting, yet the shift to Astana was as much about Moscow presenting itself as the new power broker at Washington's expense.[24] Even so, the process and the ceasefire received the unanimous endorsement of the UN Security Council on 31 December.

Far from being a breakthrough, however, the process appeared, in the words of The Century Foundation's Sam Heller, 'more like a forum for its three state sponsors [Russia, Iran and Turkey] to broker deals amongst them-selves frequently at the Syrian opposition's expense'.[25] An indication of this was seen at the first gathering in January 2017, when Russia presented the opposition representatives – led by Jaysh al-Islam's Mohammad Alloush – with a new Syrian constitution. The document appeared to have involved no consultancy with Syrian representatives or the wider public. It was swiftly rejected by Alloush and then quietly cast aside, but it illustrated Moscow's top-down approach. This was seen repeatedly. At the third meeting in May Russia and Turkey announced a plan to strengthen the ceasefire with the creation of 'safe zones'. Russia, Turkey and Iran would act as external guaran-tors over four 'de-escalation' zones in western Syria, all rebel strongholds: Idlib; Rastan near Homs; East Ghouta in Damascus; and the Badia region around Deraa and the Jordanian border. The zones would effectively freeze the conflict, with regime forces forbidden from bombing or shelling them, rebels forbidden from launching attacks, and humanitarian aid allowed to pass inside. While the United States, now led by a Trump administration more open to Moscow, cautiously welcomed the idea after sending US observers to Astana for the first time, the opposition delegation was furious. Outraged that Iran, who it saw as hand in glove with Assad, was proposed as one of the guarantors, the delegation stormed out. However, in a sign of its ever-shrinking influence, the opposition, led again by Alloush, was back in Astana for the next round of talks in July.

The Astana process overshadowed the UN's efforts to broker peace, but Staffan de Mistura persisted nevertheless. The Geneva IV Process, as it was dubbed, began in February 2017 with the same indirect approach as the failed Geneva III talks. However, unlike previous efforts, these did not break down prematurely. Instead, further rounds were held in May and July. While these talks involved largely the same Syrian government delegations as attended Astana, with UN envoy Bashar al-Jaafari leading both, the opposition was still represented by the HNC rather than the armed factions. These talks avoided the acrimony of previous rounds, partly because they stuck to technical topics while avoiding the sensitive matter of Assad's future, but also because both sides knew that Astana was where the real decisions were being made.

Trump and Syria

The Donald

Into this Russian-dominated scene stepped Donald Trump, arguably the most overtly pro-Russia US president in modern history. Trump was quite unlike past presidents. He was the first to have held no prior military or government position, and was simultaneously the oldest and wealthiest ever to enter the Oval Office. He was more outspoken than his predecessors, prone to speaking, and frequently tweeting, off-script, without sticking to a recognisable line or set of policies. This combination of inexperience and indiscipline made it difficult to ascertain a clear foreign policy or 'Trump Doctrine' for the new administration. Even so, the various observers of his first year in office broadly fell into three schools of thought.

The first group anticipated a radical departure in US foreign policy. Trump's promise to put 'America First' suggested a reversion to isolationism, abdicating the US' global leadership and retreating into protectionist economics and populist nationalism.[26] The appointment of Steve Bannon, a founder of the right-wing Breitbart News website that once described itself as the platform of the alt-right, seemed to support this idea. Bannon, who opposed both free trade and US involvement in the Middle East, was made White House Chief Strategist and a member of the Principals Committee of the National Security Council.[27] The president's early statements and policies reinforced these views. Trump had questioned NATO's value, declaring it 'obsolete' on the campaign trail. Within a week of assuming office, he signed an executive order that forbade citizens of seven predominantly Muslim countries (including Syria) from entering the US, although this was ultimately delayed and amended by the courts. He also announced US withdrawal from two of Obama's landmark international deals: the Paris climate accords and the Trans-Pacific Partnership trade agreement.

However, despite these opening controversies, a second group of observers questioned how revolutionary the administration really was. They saw Trump as co-opted by the Washington and Republican establishment, ultimately following a traditional US foreign policy with a few outlandish statements along the way.[28] They noted that Trump rolled back his criticism of NATO within months, while he was no less involved in the Middle East than Obama: stepping up the campaign against ISIS; engaging, somewhat forlornly, with the Israel–Palestine peace process; and reversing his previous opposition to increasing troops in Afghanistan. There was also no rush towards a trade war with China, as some feared. Bannon and his nationalist allies were far from unchallenged and key administration positions were held by more establishment figures, mischievously labelled by some 'the adults in the room'.[29] These included James Mattis as Secretary of Defense, Rex Tillerson as Secretary of State, and H.R. McMaster as National Security Advisor after the first choice, Michael T. Flynn, was abruptly dismissed in February. As Elliott Abrams argued, 'Trump's national security team embodies "the Establishment" as much as John F. Kennedy's or Dwight Eisenhower's did.'[30] Such voices see continuity in Trump's foreign policy. He was more aggressive with Iran than Obama but continued to respect the nuclear deal, albeit begrudgingly. Moreover, as Gregory Gause noted, confrontation with Tehran was the US norm since 1979 with Obama being the anomaly.[31] A more aggressive stance towards North Korea was also viewed within the Republican foreign policy tradition and not as a sharp departure. This interpretation suggested Trump's more radical instincts were moderated over time and contained by establishment figures and the structural conditions of global politics, resulting in a more conformist foreign policy than many expected. Steve Bannon's departure from the White House in August 2017 appeared to vindicate this view.

However, a third perspective saw less logic and more chaos. Stephen Walt describes the forty-fifth president as an 'amateur' who is 'inexperienced, impulsive, and inept'.[32] Even if he was co-opted by the foreign policy establishment hoping to steer the White House towards more active global involvement, his basic incompetence and unpredictability made achieving this an impossibility. Tillerson's State Department was chronically understaffed, with key positions unfilled and huge budget cuts under way, meaning foreign policy expertise was under utilised. Commentators noted how Trump was easily swayed by individuals, not only advisers like Bannon and his son-in-law Jared Kushner, but also by foreign leaders such as Benjamin Netanyahu and Saudi Arabian Crown Prince Mohammed bin Salman. In some cases, this has led to contradictory policy. After meeting the prince in Riyadh, Trump was persuaded to publicly support a Saudi–UAE embargo of neighbouring Qatar, supposedly because of its links to funding terror. Yet this was challenged by Rex Tillerson's State Department, perhaps more aware than Trump of Qatar's strategic importance and its being home to over 11,000 US servicemen, and which stated it was 'mystified' by Saudi Arabia's actions.[33] Those subscribing to this third approach saw such confusion as inevitable given Trump's unwillingness to conform to long-term strategies and discipline. Still more of a television star than a leader, his priority was to seek short-term 'wins' that he could brag about on Twitter, even if this led to long-term difficulties.[34]

Examining Trump's actions in Syria through these three lenses, the second and third explanations fit best. Syria remained high on Trump's agenda, as can be seen in his launching of Tomahawk missiles – against Bannon's advice – in response to Assad's alleged use of chemical weapons, suggesting that isolationism was not driving policy. But US engagement with the conflict was inconsistent, partly because the administration appeared to compartmentalise the war: a determined strategy to defeat ISIS in the east on the one hand, ambiguity towards Assad, Iran and Russia in the west on the other. While the anti-ISIS campaign did not depart much from Obama's plan, suggesting a more tempered and co-opted Trump, the approach to Assad, Iran and Russia was impulsive and devoid of strategy.

'Bomb the shit' out of ISIS

On the campaign trail, Trump made much of Obama's failings regarding ISIS, suggesting he displayed unnecessary timidity. In November 2015 he declared, 'I would bomb the shit out of 'em. I would just bomb those suckers. That's right. I'd blow up the pipes . . . I'd blow up every single inch. There would be nothing left.' Accordingly, in his first week as president Trump commissioned Mattis to devise within thirty days a new plan to defeat the so-called Caliphate. The defense secretary delivered at the end of February, but the strategy that followed appeared to be a ramped-up version of Obama's approach rather than the promised radical departure. Some even claimed that Trump had ignored the recommendations.[35] Two components did shift, however. Even before Mattis delivered his report, Trump loosened control on military field commanders, allowing them to decide whether to drop bombs on areas that might have high civilian populations – something Obama had been stricter on. As a result, civilian casualties in Syria and Iraq skyrocketed. According to Airwars, a monitoring website, more civilians were killed in Trump's first seven months than Obama's entire campaign from September 2014 to January 2017, with the rate of average deaths per month rising from 80 to 380.[36]

The second shift came in May, when the White House announced that it would be arming the YPG for the first time. Knowing it would outrage

Turkey, directly arming the Kurds was avoided by Obama who instead used the SDF umbrella, which included Arab fighters, as a convenient work-around. Yet the Pentagon knew that, of the estimated 50,000 fighters in the SDF, the 27,000 in the YPG were the best and would be essential for the coming assault on Raqqa.[37] They were also sceptical of Ankara's own proposal that Operation Euphrates Shield should take Raqqa instead, especially given its poor performance capturing the much smaller al-Bab. The decision to send 'heavy machine guns, mortars, anti-tank weapons, armoured cars and engineering equipment' to the YPG in May inevitably met with anger from Ankara, even though the US insisted it would try to retrieve the weapons after the battle, and that Raqqa would subsequently be ruled by local Arabs, not Kurds.[38] While this pushed Washington and Ankara further apart, it was the logical next step in the PYD–US alliance that had grown since 2015. Indeed, the US reportedly had at least ten secret military bases on SDF-held territory at this point.[39] Obama had been able to avoid making this provoca-tive step because the SDF remained a long way from Raqqa, but his military advisers also believed the YPG was the best bet to conquer the Caliphate's capital.[40] Had Obama still been president, he may have handled the situation more diplomatically, but the outcome would likely have been similar.

Even before the new arms arrived, the SDF campaign had surged forward. After securing Manbij, the emphasis returned to Raqqa with a staged plan to capture ground around the capital. In November 2016 villages to the north were taken, followed by those to the west in December and those to the east in February 2017. A breakthrough was made in March when the Tabqa dam and airbase – scene of the notorious ISIS massacre of regime troops in 2014 – were both taken. In a sign of how closely the SDF was working with the US, its troops were airlifted alongside US special forces to assault the dam. Tabqa city itself fell in May, allowing SDF forces, led by the YPG, to move south of the city, completing an encirclement in June. In a swift vindication of the decision to arm the Kurds, a month later they had surrounded and besieged up to 4,000 ISIS fighters inside Raqqa, and were slowly advancing. At the same time, the Iraqi army's siege of ISIS-held Mosul was reaching a conclusion, with the city finally falling in mid-July. Meanwhile, in a sign that Assad might prove the major beneficiary of the US campaign, the Tiger Forces took the opportunity to mop up the last ISIS positions in Aleppo province in June. While the advance of the SDF and the empowerment of the YPG would likely lead to problems in the future, by continuing Obama's campaign against ISIS with a few adjust-ments Trump looked on the verge of the short-term 'tweetable' victory in eastern Syria and Iraq that he craved.

Struggling with Russia, Iran and Assad

Contrary to the relative clarity on ISIS in the east, the administration's approach towards Syria's west was confused. On assuming office, Trump's position on Assad and his two international allies, Russia and Iran, was ambiguous. As recently as October 2016 he had stated, 'I don't like Assad at all, but Assad is killing ISIS. Russia is killing ISIS and Iran is killing ISIS' – implying that his anti-ISIS priorities might lead him into reversing Obama's opposition to the Syrian dictator.[41] Similarly, positive statements about Putin and other strongmen such as Egypt's Abdel Fattah el-Sisi further fuelled speculation along these lines. Confusing matters, it became clear that Trump would be treating Assad's two benefactors very differently. After appointing a series of anti-Iranian figures, including Mattis, the administration adopted a hawkish line regarding Tehran. In contrast, Trump remained broadly positive about Putin, even as his embryonic administration was consumed by a scandal alleging the Kremlin's involvement in his election. These contrasting views played out in Syria, with Washington simultaneously stepping up anti-Iranian activity while softening its stance on Russia. There was even talk of attempting to peel Russia away from Iran, illustrating a misunderstanding of the extent of Iranian-Russian commitment to the conflict.

During the campaign, Trump had spoken out against Obama's 2015 nuclear agreement with Iran, calling it a 'disaster' and 'the worst deal ever negotiated', and suggesting he would seek to overturn it.[42] In office, these instincts were amplified by his association with three key, closely aligned groups. The first of these were hawkish elements of the Washington foreign policy community, disparagingly labelled 'the Blob' by Obama, who had long opposed Iran and disapproved of the nuclear deal, although they did not necessarily wish to overturn it. While many despaired of Trump's domestic rhetoric, they hoped to nudge him towards more confrontation with Tehran, over the objections of Bannon. The second was the Israeli government of Benjamin Netanyahu. Trump had made significant pro-Israel pledges on the campaign trail, including controversially moving the US embassy from Tel Aviv to Jerusalem, and his pro-Israel son-in-law Kushner was a close adviser. In power, Trump would ultimately disappoint the Israeli premier, urging an end to settlement building and sending Kushner to revive the peace process, but the Netanyahu view of Iran remained prevalent in the White House. The third factor was Saudi Arabia, which Trump visited (along with Israel) during his first foreign trip as president in May 2017. There, he and Kushner were impressed (some have argued 'played') by Mohammed bin Salman and, despite criticism of Saudi Arabia on the campaign trail, appeared to fully accept the Saudi–UAE view of Iran. At a speech in Riyadh Trump stated provocatively,

> For decades, Iran has fuelled the fires of sectarian conflict and terror. It is a government that speaks openly of mass murder, vowing the destruction of Israel, death to America, and ruin for many leaders and nations in this room. Until the Iranian regime is willing to be a partner for peace, all nations of conscience must work together to isolate Iran, deny it funding for terrorism, and pray for the day when the Iranian people have the just and righteous government they deserve.[43]

It was no coincidence that soon afterwards Saudi Arabia and the UAE launched their boycott of Qatar, with Trump's approval.[44] Mohammed bin Salman's move for power a month later, when his father named him as Crown Prince and heir to the throne, removing former Obama favourite Mohammed bin Nayef from succession, may also have resulted from a perceived endorsement by Trump. The ease with which Trump abandoned his former hostility to Riyadh and appeared to fully adopt its regional view suggested an alarming capriciousness.

Trump's anti-Iranianism influenced several confrontations in Assad's Syria. The most high-profile of these came on 7 April 2017, when the White House unilaterally launched fifty-nine Tomahawk missiles on a regime airfield for allegedly using chemical weapons. Despite Assad having given up his chemical weapons in the 2013 Russia–US agreement, opposition activists continued to accuse Damascus of launching low-level attacks using secret stockpiles. The Organisation for the Prohibition of Chemical Weapons (OPCW) investigated these allegations, claiming in February 2017 that regime forces were responsible for three chlorine attacks. Yet Russia, alongside China, vetoed an attempted UN Security Council Resolution by the US, UK and France to impose sanctions, arguing that it put the recently reconvened Geneva IV peace talks in jeopardy.[45] Partly because of this veto, the Trump administration acted unilaterally two months later. In a far more high-profile attack, on 4 April at least eighty-seven people were killed in the rebel-held town of Khan Sheikhoun by Sarin gas, confirmed months later by the OPCW. As in 2013, the White House declared Assad responsible, while the regime insisted it was the rebels. Eschewing the UN route, Trump sought a range of military options from the Pentagon, reportedly choosing the most modest: a single barrage of Tomahawks against al-Shayrat air base from which the attack was allegedly launched. Up to twenty Syrian planes were reportedly hit and several regime soldiers were killed, but the impact was negligible and the base was functioning again within days.[46]

Trump's official reason for this sudden anti-Assad strike was to protect the international norm against chemical weapons use, but it served other purposes as well. One was a shot across the bow to Iran – and it is notable that both Saudi Arabia and Israel hailed Trump for his decisiveness. Another was to boost his already flagging domestic support; the president received a burst of praise in the liberal US press after the strike, with CNN's Fareed Zakaria stating 'I think Donald Trump became president of the United States'.[47] Perhaps most importantly, however, hitting Assad allowed Trump to illustrate the contrast with his bête noir, Obama, who had famously stepped back from his own red line four years earlier. Posing as the 'anti-Obama' was the cornerstone of Trump's political brand. Aware that this was a sharp departure from his own record – Trump had lambasted Obama for even considering attacking Assad in 2013 – the president claimed that the gas attack on children in Khan Sheikhoun meant his 'attitude toward Syria and Assad has changed very much'.[48] Once again, US domestic politics were having consequences in Syria's war.

In what appeared to be a U-turn, administration officials stepped up their anti-Assad rhetoric. Nikki Haley, the US ambassador to the UN who in March had said that 'our priority is no longer to sit there and focus on getting Assad out', now stated that 'Regime change is something that we think is going to happen.'[49] Days later, on 12 April the US attempted another UN Security Council resolution to condemn the chemical attack, but it was vetoed again by Russia. Moreover, after directly attacking Assad for the first time, Washington now showed a willingness to hit conventional regime forces elsewhere. In May US jets bombed a pro-Assad Shia militia convoy, killing eight near al-Tanf, a Syrian-Iraqi border post controlled by Washington-backed rebels.[50] In June the US shot down two Iranian drones over Syrian airspace and then a regime jet near Raqqa, claiming it was attacking SDF forces. Far from reconciling himself to Assad, Trump appeared to be more and more hostile to Damascus and its Iranian allies.

However, complicating this picture was Trump's view of Russia. Notwithstanding the president's past praise of Putin, his administration was dogged by allegations of complicity with the Kremlin. Michael Flynn was forced to resign as national security adviser after only twenty-three days when it emerged he had discussed lifting US sanctions on Russia with Moscow's ambassador. Trump aroused further suspicions by firing FBI director James Comey, who had been investigating Russian interference in the 2016 election, and when the Justice Department appointed Robert Mueller to continue the inquiry afterwards, the president questioned his neutrality. Trump's son, Donald Trump Jr, was also later implicated in the scandal that looked like it would hamper the administration for some time. In this context, Trump's relative friendliness towards Russia in Syria jarred with his belligerent stance on Iran.

As well as continuing collaboration on the anti-ISIS campaign, Trump softened the US stance on Astana and Moscow's de-escalation zones. As part of this, Trump and Putin, meeting in Germany for the G20 summit in July, agreed on a ceasefire over the southern Badia region, endorsed by Israel and Jordan though rejected by some rebel groups. Russian relations remained fraught in some areas, with Moscow strongly objecting to the downing of the Syrian jet in June and to Trump's Tomahawk missile strike. However, even then, Washington had given Moscow advance warning to ensure no Russian planes or personnel were at al-Shayrat. In what appeared to be a major unilateral concession to Putin, in July the administration cancelled the CIA programme begun by Obama in 2013 supporting vetted Syrian rebel groups. The operations rooms in Jordan were scheduled to be dismantled and salaries would no longer be provided by the US. This was consistent with Trump's pre-presidency views of the rebels – on the campaign he argued 'We have no idea who these people are' – and it was also a reflection of the reality that, since the Russian intervention, the opposition looked doomed. However, the fact that the move was made unilaterally, without gaining an obvious concession from Assad, Russia or Iran in return, appeared a waste of valuable leverage, and some suspected Trump did this partly as a goodwill gesture to Moscow.[51] It also appeared wholly inconsistent with Trump's other anti-Iran and anti-Assad moves, as both would be empowered.

It also undermined his anti-extremism approach, as Jabhat al-Nusra would likely be another beneficiary. Though Nusra had officially disaffiliated itself with al-Qaeda and rebranded itself several times, first as Jabhat Fatah al-Sham and then Hayat Tahrir al-Sham (HTS), it was still viewed by the US as an Islamist terrorist organisation. Throughout 2017 its power-base grew, primarily in Idlib province, where it captured most strategic positions, including the Bab al-Hawa border crossing from Ahrar al-Sham. Indeed, Ahrar, HTS' former ally and only plausible rival, faced terminal decline after Turkish support waned and had effectively collapsed by August 2017.[52] In this context, analysts such as Charles Lister insisted that Trump's decision would inevitably empower HTS, who would mop up unemployed and underarmed rebels. Others countered that many rebels remained ideologically opposed to extremism, preventing such a process.[53] Either way, the decision likely aided Assad's aims to reconquer Idlib. If HTS did take over, he and Russia could justify a military campaign as Nusra/

HTS were excluded from any ceasefire agreements in the Geneva/Astana Process. If the remaining rebels resisted the extremists, they would be further divided, making conquest easier. Supporters of Trump's decision were correct that, regardless, this process was probably inevitable, but his critics were also right that the concession was a boost for Assad, Iran and Russia for little in return.

Battles to come

For all Trump's bluster, his arrival in the White House changed little in the immediate dynamics of the Syria conflict, but his ambiguity on Iran, Russia and Assad did raise the prospect of future confrontations. After Aleppo's fall Assad appeared secure and that trend continued into 2017 despite the Tomahawk missiles and bellicose US rhetoric. Rebel enclaves near Damascus were picked off, with evacuations agreed in Zabadani in April and in the Qaboun, Barzeh and Tishreen neighbourhoods in May. Surrendering fighters were again transported to Idlib, turning the stronghold into a convenient dumping ground before an anticipated final regime assault on the 2 million-strong province. Clearing these outliers left Assad facing just a handful of concentrated rebel areas, unlike the patchwork of 2013–14. The Russia–Turkey brokered ceasefire and Astana de-escalation zones kept these areas mostly pacified, but regime forces still frequently launched attacks, claiming they were targeting Hayat Tahrir al-Sham and others not covered by the agreement.

In March the Syrian army, with Russian support, recaptured Palmyra from ISIS for a second time, beginning an unexpected advance east towards Deir ez-Zor – the regime's last bastion in Islamic State territory. There were several reasons for this rapid assault. First and foremost was opportunity. As the SDF advanced to the north, ISIS possessions in the Syrian desert were low-hanging fruit that the regime could pick off with limited numbers while the jihadists concentrated their forces on Raqqa. This was also the first time in the conflict that Syria's west was quiet enough to free up troops to move beyond 'Rump Syria' into the strategically less important east. The second reason was to check the advance of the SDF. The YPG and its allies had advanced rapidly in the last year to the banks of the Euphrates. With American help, the regime feared they might absorb all of the former Caliphate's territory, leaving US bases and special forces stationed throughout eastern Syria. The third reason according to some Western analysts was that Tehran wanted to create a land corridor from Iran to the Mediterranean, and capturing the desert roads from Iraq into eastern Syria near Al-Bukamal would achieve this. Logistically, however, Iran already had strong air routes connecting Tehran with Damascus, Hezbollah and Lebanon, and a land route would still be prey to insurgent attacks.[54] Opening such a route may represent a symbolic success for Iran, especially given the fears raised in Washington, but was unlikely to be the primary motivator. More key was regaining key resources for the regime: the oil fields of Deir ez-Zor and the return of trade with Iraq from recapturing the border posts. Moreover, like the conquest of Aleppo, the more substantial Syrian territory Assad controlled, the more he could claim international legitimacy.

Yet this race for the east raised the prospect of new conflict. As discussed above, the PYD and the Syrian regime rarely fought, leading many in the opposition to accuse the Kurdish group of collaboration with Assad. There were, however, some clashes as the YPG grew in confidence, with an assault on regime positions in Hassakah in June 2016 resulting in Assad evacuating most army and NDF forces from the city. With Trump now directly arming the YPG and increasing his rhetoric against Iran, some forecasted that conflict would break out between Assad and the Kurds after ISIS was defeated.[55] There were some grounds for this. The US attacks on Iranian and Syrian forces in al-Tanf and Raqqa in 2017 were aimed at checking the advance eastwards, and it is possible that the unpredictable US president would want to use his Kurdish proxies as a means of scuppering Iranian regional advances. However, on the Kurdish side the PYD knew their limitations and that advancing much beyond Raqqa would prove difficult, given these are strictly Arab and traditionally hostile areas. On the regime side, Assad would want to bring Rojava back under control, either by negotiation or force. With regime enclaves remaining in Qamishli and elsewhere, he could justify an advance to liberate these areas. Yet, as ever, Assad would face logistical constraints: he would need airpower from Russia and militia provided by Iran to fight the PYD, and both had reservations. Moreover, Assad, Russia and Iran would all prioritise conquering Idlib before Rojava. However, given Trump's erraticism, an unexpected provocation might change their stance. There was also the question of how long the US would stand by the Kurds if and when ISIS was defeated. A long-term US presence would rile Assad but protect Rojava from assault, while a US withdrawal would increase the chances of an Assad reconquest, possibly with Turkish acquiescence.

Any future advances would rest on the dynamics within the Assad–Russia–Iran relationship. Although the three acted in concert, relations were not always smooth. As discussed in Chapter 8, Assad was no puppet and often exploited differences between his two patrons to maximise leverage. For example, during the assault on Aleppo in late 2016, Assad's forces sometimes broke ceasefires negotiated between Moscow and Washington with the support of Iranian commanders on the ground, forcing Russia to play catch-up. Similarly, Assad was reportedly unconvinced by Russia's de-escalation zones plan, seeing it as merely a means to buy time before attacking the last rebel strongholds. On the other side, in August 2017 Russia expressed its frustration at Damascus by refusing to authorise air support for an assault on Idlib. However, this does not mean, as some in the Trump administration hoped, that Moscow had any intention of abandoning Assad or Tehran. Russia, like Iran, showed an intention to be in Syria for the long haul, even opening up a third permanent military base, in Khirbet Ras Al-Waer south-east of Damascus, in July 2017. Both states invested in Syria's post-war reconstruction, with Iranian and Russian companies already benefiting.[56] Russia and Iran had different priorities and slightly different strategies, but for the medium term they appeared in agreement on the future direction of Syria.

Trump styled himself as anti-Obama, but his Syria policy was not the radical departure he claimed. Save for loosening restrictions on bombings, the anti-ISIS campaign stuck to the broad parameters set out by Trump's predecessor, with the decision to arm the Kurds a logical progression in a relationship built under Obama. Even in western Syria, where Trump's policies appeared more chaotic and inconsistent, the outcomes were not so different. Obama had arguably been softer on Iran and more hostile to Russia, while Trump was the reverse, but neither had much impact on preventing either state from advancing their interests. Like Obama, Trump was generally reactive rather than strategic regarding Assad, resorting to gestures such as his Tomahawk missile strike that had limited impact on the ground. This is perhaps unsurprising, as none of the structural impediments in the region that Obama faced had been removed when Trump came to office. He still had to face opposition from the American public to extensive US boots on the ground – something he had encouraged in his campaign – and the increased assertiveness of other powers such as Iran and Russia pursuing their agendas.

Where Trump differed was in style and bombast, making him far less predictable an operator than Obama. To an extent, this made little difference to western Syria given that, as outlined elsewhere in this book, the United States was not a decisive player in that conflict, unlike Iran and Russia. However, it did have two potential impacts, firstly in eastern Syria where the US emerged as the key external power due to its campaign against ISIS. While this policy has largely been left to the 'adults in the room', should Trump's chaotic character come to the fore, such as ordering a sudden withdrawal or attacking Iranian/Assad forces, it could amplify the conflict. Secondly, Trump remains the US president and, despite a relative regional retrenchment under Obama, as with his predecessor Middle Eastern powers do pay attention to his policies. This was already seen with Saudi Arabia's blockade of Qatar following apparent Trump approval. On the one hand, this increases the risks that a badly placed word could provoke negative reactions. On the other hand, with Trump known to be unpredictable, leaders may attach less importance to his comments than they did with Obama. Either way, this will likely weaken the US' regional position further – another continuation with the Obama era, ironic given Trump's claim to be his predecessor's polar opposite.

Conclusion:
The war that everyone lost

*Everybody had their agenda and the interests of the Syrian people came
second, third or not at all.*

Lakhdar Brahimi, 31 August 2015[1]

Kafranbel is a small town in Idlib province not far from Maarrat al-Nu'man.
Anti-Assad activists from the town found fame early on in the uprising for
posting photographs of their provocative and often witty protest banners,
written in English and aimed at the outside world, online. Regime forces
withdrew from the town in summer 2012 and, despite clashes with ISIS
and Nusra, it remained protected by a moderate local FSA force, enabling
the banners to remain throughout the conflict. The slogans repeatedly
emphasised Assad's brutality and urged the 'Hypocrite world!' to act.[2]
While most of the civil war's key external players – Annan, Brahimi, Kerry,
Lavrov, and especially Iran and Russia – were slated at different times, it was
Barack Obama who, after Assad, was most consistently savaged in dozens
of messages. 'Obama's Procrastination Kills Us' was one example from
December 2011, while in March 2014 they wrote, 'Obama! If you are incapable of saving the lives of Syrian children, leave the White House to a man
to act like US presidents.'[3] The activists, by writing their slogans in English,
correctly recognised from the very beginning of Syria's uprising the importance of external actors. They saw that Assad could not be defeated without
outside help and so repeatedly appealed for weapons and no-fly zones on
humanitarian grounds. Importantly, they *expected* US intervention of some
sort and attacked Obama when it was not forthcoming.

The Kafranbel activists in many ways reflected the changing international dynamics of the Middle East and their consequences. After decades
of American hegemony, it seemed natural for Assad's opponents – whether
civil society writing banners, FSA commanders or regional powers like
Qatar, Turkey and Saudi Arabia – to appeal to Washington for help. When

Obama refused, they lashed out, blaming him for allowing the regime's continued slaughter rather than questioning their own assumption that the US would eventually intervene. Their calculations were based on the old order, not the new post-American Middle East of the Obama era. It is a sad irony that when Kafranbel did finally get a reply from the outside world, it was not what it had hoped for. Russian jets, deployed to boost Assad's flagging forces, launched attacks on the town and its FSA battalions in October 2015. Riad Fares, the Kafranbel activist behind the banners and the accompanying website, wrote exasperatedly that being 'a bystander to atrocities against free people, cannot possibly be a true reflection of what the United States stands for.'[4] His amazement was sadly typical of the opposition's misreading of the US' true interests.

The war that everyone lost

Given the years of misery heaped on the Syrian people as a result of its civil war, it is difficult to speak of 'winners' and 'losers' among the external powers. Ultimately, no state has benefited from its involvement in this conflict, though some have done relatively worse than others. Referring back to the six actors' different goals and priorities outlined in Chapter 1, Turkey would appear in the worst position compared to 2011. Its ambitions for regional leadership are in tatters, with the Syrian morass now physically blocking it from the Middle East. The war has contributed to internal challenges: receiving over two million refugees and being targeted by ISIS terrorism, with some of its own citizens radicalised. Long-term destabilisation like that suffered by Pakistan as a result of the Afghanistan wars is not an unrealistic possible comparison. Turkey has maintained its alliance with NATO, although Syria continues to be a major source of disagreement, pushing it increasingly closer to Russia. The Kurdish situation has considerably worsened as a result of the Syrian war, reigniting the PKK's campaign in eastern Turkey and Ankara's violent repression of it. Unlike before, however, the PKK's Syrian ally the PYD now enjoys what was effectively a proxy state in Rojava along Turkey's border – a situation Ankara had been anxious to avoid. This has forced Turkey to invade and occupy Syrian territory for the first time, opening the prospect of direct conflict with the PYD and, at a minimum, a prolonged presence with uncertain costs in blood and treasure.

Qatar is similarly worse off. Its domestic position remains secure, as does its vital security alliance with the US, but its regional ambitions are, for now, over. While these were derailed elsewhere, notably in Egypt in 2013, Syria contributed to this. Saudi Arabia's emergence as the lead sponsor of the opposition greatly dented Doha's dual aim of projecting influence and rivalling Riyadh. The Syria conflict and Qatar's alleged ties to al-Qaeda and the Muslim Brotherhood contributed to an even greater danger in 2017 when Saudi Arabia and the UAE, alongside their allies in Bahrain and Egypt, cut diplomatic ties with Doha and imposed a trade and travel ban. Though Qatar looks likely to weather the crisis, not least due to aid from Turkey and Iran, it saw its independent international standing further reduced, illustrating clearly just how far its regional ambitions had been curtailed since the high point of 2011–12.

Saudi Arabia is in a stronger position than its Gulf rival. The Syrian war helped usher in a more activist Riyadh, emerging as a more overt regional leader than in the past. Yet, while Saudi Arabia seems to have survived the potential internal crisis that loomed towards the end of Abdullah's reign with the confident succession of Salman and his active son, Mohammed bin Salman, the rise of ISIS threatened a return to the domestic terrorism of the early 2000s. Moreover, its ambitious new crown prince is learning that it is easier to begin foreign campaigns than to end them successfully, as seen in his costly and prolonged conflict in Yemen and the high-profile but ineffective boycott of Qatar. With oil prices historically low and the prospect of related economic and social challenges following in their wake, Riyadh may yet face future difficulties. Its highest regional priority remains containing Iran and, for all of the mistakes made, this has been partially achieved in Syria. Though Assad has not been toppled, Tehran has been bogged down financially and militarily propping up Damascus and its reputation has been damaged. However, at the same time Riyadh was unable to derail the 2015 nuclear deal, which may ultimately counter any costs to Iran caused by the Syrian quagmire.

Russia's goals before the war were to ensure its domestic security from militant Islamists, to continue to expand its economic reach in the Middle East, and to boost its geopolitical position at the expense of the US. Its trade in the region was largely unaffected by its disagreements with trade partners Turkey and Saudi Arabia over Syria, with the exception of the ultimately short-lived sanctions regime on Ankara in 2015–16. Russia's geopolitical position has arguably been boosted by the Syrian war after it sent in its own jets in 2015 and increased its cooperation with Iraq and Iran against ISIS. In contrast, its domestic security may have been worsened by the war. Not only has it overseen a rise of ISIS that might inspire Russian jihadists, but Moscow's 2015 military intervention will make it even more of a target for Islamists. Since 2015 Russia has suffered several terror attacks, including the bombing of a tourist jet in Egypt and the murder of Moscow's ambassador to Turkey. Future attacks cannot be ruled out if resentment against Putin's position in Syria grows.

Iran's priorities were, similarly, seemingly satisfied by its involvement in Syria. It maintained its support for Hezbollah by securing Damascus and the Qalamoun and Bekaa delivery routes, and more recently has expanded up to the Iraqi border. It also ensured its ally, Assad, did not fall to a rebel force backed by its regional enemies, while also retaining a dominant position in Iraq. Moreover, none of this activity in Syria prevented a deal being agreed with the West over its nuclear programme. However, this all came at a severe cost to its regional reputation: Iran's support of Assad was interpreted through a sectarian lens, costing Tehran's hard-fought-for reputation on the Sunni Arab street. This may greatly impact Iran's desire to emerge as the key actor in the Middle East and Islamic world beyond Shia-dominated areas. The full financial and military cost of Iran's backing of Assad remains unknown, and may yet prove unsustainable in the long run. Iran and Russia may appear to be relatively better off than their regional rivals, having achieved their primary goal of preventing regime change, but their position is worse than it was in 2011. Even with allies secure in Damascus' Presidential Palace, it could take years before what is left of Syria proves more than a draining and unstable partner.

Washington's goals under Barack Obama at the dawn of the Arab Spring were to maintain its vital interests in the region while reducing the US physical presence, rebuilding its damaged reputation and reaching out to enemies like Iran and Russia. By resisting calls to intervene heavily in the Syrian war, Obama did reduce the US presence, arguably allowing him to focus on other foreign policy priorities such as the pivot to Asia, the nuclear deal with Iran, détente with Cuba and tackling climate change. The anti-ISIS campaign of 2014 did see a return of American jets to Iraq and also to Syria, but this was of a limited scope supporting local allies rather than the full-scale occupations of Iraq and Afghanistan. The Syria conflict has seen US relations with Tehran and Moscow fluctuate, although there have been notable moments of cooperation, such as the 2013 chemical weapons deal and the Vienna talks, and ties have generally been strained more by events outside Syria, such as Ukraine, than inside. The US' reputation has been damaged by the Syrian war, however. The sentiments of the Kafranbel protesters echo the view of many (particularly Sunnis) in the Middle East, as well as regional allies like Saudi Arabia and Turkey, that Washington has done too little. Obama seemed to calculate that it was better to accept such criticism than to be sucked into an unknown quagmire that would risk more important vital regional interests and a domestic backlash. The rise of

ISIS and the spillover from Syria may well have created an even worse and unstable Middle East than the one Obama inherited in 2008. However, from his perspective, had he waded into Syria the same result would likely have occurred, but with more American lives lost and Washington expected to take full responsibility, and possibly at the cost of his other international and domestic priorities.

Post-American chaos

This book has argued that international factors have played a key role in shaping Syria's civil war. Syria's regional environment already made it susceptible to civil war, but the six main international actors profiled did little to discourage the sides in Syria's 2011 crisis from escalating into armed conflict, and some actively encouraged it. Once under way, the same actors helped to prolong the conflict by providing balanced interventions: enough to keep their allies in the field, but not enough to win or force the other to seriously negotiate. While some commentators like to blame one government more than another for this situation, in reality all six bear some responsibility. Even before the conflict began systemic change was under way, with a post-American, more multipolar Middle East emerging after the failure of the Iraq war, the financial crisis and Obama's preference for drawdown. Russia, Iran, Saudi Arabia, Qatar and Turkey all sought to take advantage of this shift to further their influence, but many lacked the capacity to match their ambitions. Saudi Arabia, Qatar and Turkey in particular pushed headlong into encouraging a conflict in Syria that they could not end without American assistance. Russia and Iran, while more adept, proved unable to moderate their ally Assad's behaviour, but their geopolitical agendas locked them into his camp even so.

The US' role, as the declining hegemon, has been a particular focus of this study. Barack Obama was attacked at home and abroad for not doing enough on Syria. Criticism is due, though often for reasons other than those raised by his opponents. It is unknown whether, had he intervened against Assad earlier, either directly or by heavily backing the armed rebels before radicals took over, the war would have finished sooner. However, given the regional dynamics described in this study, it seems unlikely that Russia and Iran would have ceased their support for Assad and the remnants of his regime. Obama correctly identified the uncertainty of the situation, feared the possibility of another Middle Eastern entanglement for a cause not in the US' direct interest, and was unconvinced by those urging more action. Those lamenting his lack of intervention tended to favour the return of US hegemony in the Middle East and the same voices in the US foreign policy establishment have urged his successor to revert to a more dominant position in the region, especially regarding Iran. However, as this book has argued and as Obama correctly identified, structural changes in the 2000s have made any return to US regional hegemony more difficult and costly than it was after the end of the Cold War. For all his bluster, Donald Trump is also constrained by these conditions and has thus not been able to impact the course of the Syria conflict any more than Obama did. These structural shifts mean that a more selective engagement with certain regional priorities as the most powerful of several actors rather than the regional hegemon is likely Washington's most effective course for years to come. Trump may indeed pursue this policy, though more likely as a result of balancing his instinctive isolationism with the urging of a more interventionist establishment that co-opts and persuades him, rather than as a deliberate long-term strategy.

Obama should be criticised for not managing the transition into the post-American Middle East better. This book has argued that while US hegemony in the 1990s and 2000s was overstated, it was perceived to be so, creating an expectation that Obama would act. Yet despite being committed to a regional drawdown, when the Syria crisis began the US president utilised the language of a hegemon: calling for Assad to go and declaring red lines on chemical weapons. This greatly altered the behaviour of actors in the conflict. Policymakers in the Oval Office seemed not to have considered the impact of this power perception on the ground: that it might prompt overconfidence from allies like Qatar, Turkey and Saudi Arabia, and fury when expected assistance did not come. This was compounded by further misreading of the regional situation: the durability of the Assad regime, the lengths Damascus' regional allies would go to in order to preserve it, and the capacity of Washington's regional allies to pursue coherent and constructive policies in Syria. Indeed, this latter point may also have been the result of decades of reliance on the US by Turkey, Qatar and Saudi Arabia, stunting the development of their own security and intelligence institutions. A more realistic policy in line with what Washington was actually willing to commit to the Syrian conflict would have been less damaging. Rather than facilitating and even encouraging civil war, whether intentionally or indirectly, Washington would have been better served by focusing on de-escalation from the beginning, urging caution and restraint on both its allies and enemies.

The post-American Middle East was already developing before 2011 but the Syrian civil war, as well as being partly a product of this change, helped catalyse it further. Syria's collapse into a failing state battled over by competing powers has been mirrored in other states, notably Libya, Yemen and Iraq. There is a bitter irony that just as the US under Obama came to realise the limitations of force to achieve long-lasting political goals in the region, other actors increasingly emulated its earlier approach. Russia's intervention in 2015 was consciously modelled on 'US-style' anti-terrorism conflicts as an indicator of its global and regional power. Similarly, after decades of purchasing Western arms, Gulf states are increasingly flexing their muscles to launch their own military adventures. Even more states have embraced covert warfare in Syria, Libya and elsewhere. Meanwhile, the former regional master of covert warfare, Iran, has deployed its Quds forces directly in Syria and Iraq, and could emerge from the Syrian war with a formidable battle-hardened military. The growing number of failing states has created yet more space for non-state actors, notably Hezbollah, al-Qaeda, ISIS and the PKK and its allies. Alarmingly, lessons do not seem to have been learned by regional powers from their experiences in the Syrian morass. In Libya, Yemen and Iraq, regional powers are backing rival groups, intervening directly and encouraging different levels of conflict to pursue their own agendas. The voices seriously urging de-escalation and negotiation are muted, and few seem willing to sacrifice their narrow short-term goals for long-term regional stability. While some kind of update to the 1967 Khartoum Resolution in which regional states agreed to respect each other's sovereignty is sorely needed to prevent the post-American Middle East descending into a chaos of local wars and failed states, there seems little appetite from the main regional players to accept such a balanced system.

Syria's torment

For Syria's immediate neighbourhood, the near future looks uncertain. This book began by explaining how the 2003 Iraq war unleashed unexpected forces that dramatically shifted conditions for its neighbours. Studies of civil wars elsewhere have shown how it makes conflict in neighbouring states more likely, whether through access to weapons, the presence of radical armed groups or refugees.[5] Syria's war has already reopened conflicts in Iraq and Turkey, while weak neighbours like Jordan and Lebanon remain vulnerable. The chances of a renewed Hezbollah–Israel war also cannot be discounted, given Israel's concern that the Party of God will emerge from the war battle-hardened and stronger. Even were peace to come to Syria, its proximity to other regions that its war helped to destabilise could yet suck it back into conflict.

What chance is there for peace? At the time of writing the conflict between the regime and the rebels has tilted in Assad's favour. The Astana Process' 'de-escalation zones' have effectively legitimised Assad's rule in all but four pockets of western Syria. The fall of eastern Aleppo and the ending of Turkish and US support seems to have irrevocably weakened the armed rebels and removed any last hopes that they might topple the regime. However, Damascus is unlikely to accept permanent rebel enclaves and, using the heavy HTS presence as justification, will push to either co-opt or conquer the remaining hold-outs, and fighting can be expected to continue. Yet this is far from an Assad 'victory'. Large swathes of Syria are still out of his control and his regime remains reliant on Iranian and Russian support to take and hold any lost ground. Such reliance has come at a cost. While he may not be the proxy that can be dispatched at his masters' will as some Western diplomats hope, this does give Moscow and Tehran considerable leverage over Syria's future – although they may yet disagree about the direction or destination. Moreover, it remains unclear how sustainable any Assad reconquest of former rebellious western provinces could be. Having made no real concessions to the social, economic and political grievances that caused the uprising in the first place, tensions could persist and erupt afresh.

In the east, the conflict remains more active as the regime and the SDF battle ISIS and recapture its former heartlands. However, though the Islamic State looks defeated, physical destruction of the so-called Caliphate will not end the ideology of militant jihadism, nor its appeal to the socially and economically marginalized, especially if nothing is done to win over former supporters. Terror attacks in former ISIS territory and beyond could continue indefinitely, while the emergence of similar jihadist entities in Syria or other failed states should not be ruled out. As seen with the rise of ISIS, jihadism has been a useful tool wielded by foreign governments in the past and it is unlikely to cease to be so. While Assad has retaken much of central Syria as ISIS declines, the US-sponsored SDF zone in Syria's north and east could be the source of future conflict. For different reasons, neither Damascus nor Ankara will likely accept permanent autonomy for Syria's Kurds. Much will rest on the extent and longevity of protection from Washington if and when ISIS is defeated – something difficult to forecast given President Trump's unpredictability.

As has so often been the case with Syria's tragic civil war, much will depend on external actors. While Assad's international enemies have reduced support for his domestic opponents, they retain the capacity to reactivate networks if they want to pressure Damascus or its patrons. Even if Assad remains in the presidential palace, large areas are likely to remain unstable and/or out of his actual control, with external actors able to facilitate and encourage violence as they have done since 2011. As this book has shown, the absence of an international consensus on Syria played a major role in the civil war's outbreak and prolongment, and it would be wrong to assume that the seeming victory of Russia and Iran will simply be accepted by their international rivals. The battle for Syria was just one in a wider confrontation between numerous powers in the post-American Middle East that looks likely to continue for some time. Wiser heads might have sought to compartmentalise the conflict and seek a solution detached from these wider concerns, but such far-sighted statesmanship has been lacking and the Syrian people have paid the price.

Notes

Introduction

1. Patrick Seale, *The Struggle for Syria* (London: Royal Institute of International Affairs, 1965), p. 1.
2. 'Confronting fragmentation', Syrian Center for Policy Research 11/2/16, http://scpr-syria. org/publications/confronting-fragmentation/ [accessed 10/3/16]; 'Syrian regional refugee response', UNHCR, http://data.unhcr.org/syrianrefugees/regional.php [accessed 3/4/16]; 'Syria', Internal Displacement Monitoring Centre http://www.internal-displacement.org/ middle-east-and-north-africa/syria/ [accessed 3/4/16]; Oliver Holmes, 'One million people wounded, diseases spreading in Syria: WHO', Reuters, 19/12/14 http://www. reuters.com/article/2014/12/19/us-mideast-crisis-health-idUSKBN0JX0V720141219 [accessed 1/4/15]; Ben Norton, 'The shocking statistics behind Syria's humanitarian crisis', Think Progress 2/6/14, http://thinkprogress.org/world/2014/06/02/3443171/syria-crisis-stats/ [accessed 1/4/15].
3. See for example Emile Hokayem, *Syria's Uprising and the Fracturing of the Levant* (London: Routledge, 2013); David W. Lesch, *Syria: The Fall of the House of Assad* (London: Yale University Press, 2013); Samer N. Abboud, *Syria* (New York: Polity, 2015).
4. Raymond Hinnebusch, 'Structure over agency: the Arab Uprising and the regional struggle for power', in Spyridon N. Litsas and Aristotle Tziampiris (eds), *The Eastern Mediterranean in Transition: Multipolarity, Politics and Power* (London: Ashgate, 2015).
5. Christopher Layne, 'This time it's real: the end of unipolarity and the Pax Americana', *International Studies Quarterly* 56 (2012), pp. 203–213.
6. Fawaz Gerges, *Obama and the Middle East: The End of America's Moment?* (London: Palgrave, 2012); Roland Dannreuther, 'Russia and the Arab Spring: supporting the counter-revolution', *Journal of European Integration* 37.1 (2015): 77–94; Daniela Huber, 'A pragmatic actor – the US response to the Arab uprisings', *Journal of European Integration* 37.1 (2015): 57–75.
7. David Held and Kristian Coates Ulrichsen, 'The Arab Spring and the changing balance of global power', *Open Democracy* 26/2/14, https://www.opendemocracy.net/arab-awakening/david-held-kristian-coates-ulrichsen/arab-spring-and-changing-balance-of-global-power [accessed 1/5/15].
8. F. Gregory Gause, 'Beyond sectarianism: the New Middle East Cold War', Brookings Doha Center (2014); Lenore G. Martin, 'Turkey and the USA in a bipolarizing Middle East', *Journal of Balkan and Near Eastern Studies* 15.2 (2013): 175–188; Vali Nasr, *The Dispensable Nation* (London: Scribe, 2013); Curtis Ryan, 'The new Arab cold war and the struggle for Syria', *Middle East Report* 262 (2012): 28–31.
9. Nye, Joseph S. 'The twenty-first century will not be a "post-American" world', *International Studies Quarterly* 56.1 (2012): 215–217; Stephen Brooks, G. John Ikenberry and William Wohlforth, 'Don't come home, America: the case against retrenchment', *International Security* 37.3 (Winter 2012–2013): 7–51.

10. Stephen Walt, 'Double diss', *Foreign Policy* 13/8/14, http://foreignpolicy.com/2014/08/13/double-diss/ [accessed 2/6/15].

11. Lieber, Robert, 'Rhetoric or reality? American grand strategy and the contemporary Middle East', Prepared for delivery at the 2014 Annual Meeting of the American Political Science Association Washington, DC, 28–31 August 2014; Kenneth Pollack in 'Symposium: U.S. foreign policy and the future of the Middle East', *Middle East Policy* 21.3 (Fall 2014), 1–30, Kenneth Pollack, Paul R. Pillar, Amin Tarzi and Chas W. Freeman Jr.

12. Thomas Juneau, 'U.S. Power in the Middle East: not declining', *Middle East Policy* 1.2 (Summer 2014), 40–52.

13. Stephen Walt, 'Lax Americana', *Foreign Policy* 23/10/15; Steven Simon and Jonathan Stevenson, 'The end of Pax Americana', *Foreign Affairs* November/December 2015; Marc Lynch, 'Obama and the Middle East', *Foreign Affairs* September/October 2015.

14. Gideon Rose, 'The post American Middle East', *Foreign Affairs* November/December 2015; Fareed Zakaria, *The post-American World* (New York: W.W. Norton, 2008).

15. Nazih Ayubi, *Overstating the Arab State, Politics and Society in the Middle East* (London: I.B. Tauris, 1995).

16. There have been several excellent studies of the Syrian civil war published to date, many utilised in this work. Hokayem (2013), Lesch (2013), Abboud (2015) and Yassin-Kassab and Al-Shami (2016) offer overviews of the conflict while others focus on specific aspects notably jihadism (Cockburn, 2015; Hassan and Weiss, 2015; Lister, 2015), the Alawis (Goldsmith, 2015) or the Kurds (Allsop, 2014). There are also many detailed memoirs and first-hand accounts from Syrians and foreign journalists including Starr, 2012; Ehrlich, 2014; Sahner, 2014; Darke, 2014; Yazbek, 2015 and al-Sabouni, 2016. The international dimension of the conflict is mostly secondary in these works, with the most detailed accounts Hokayem (2013), Lesch (2013) and Abboud (2015) offering one or two chapters on the subject.

17. Seale, *Struggle*, p. 3.

18. Kristian Skrede Gleditsch and Kyle Beardsley 'Nosy neighbors: third-party actors in Central American conflicts', *Journal of Conflict Resolution* 48.3 (2004): 379–402; Patrick Regan, 'Third party interventions and the duration of intrastate conflicts', *Journal of Conflict Resolution* 46.1 (2002): 55–73; Alan Kuperman and Timothy Crawford (eds), *Gambling on Humanitarian Intervention: Moral Hazard, Rebellion, and Internal War* (New York: Routledge, 2006).

19. Kristian Skrede Gleditsch, 'Transnational dimensions of civil war', *Journal of Peace Research* 44.3 (2007): 293–309.

20. Dylan Balch-Lindsay and Andrew Enterline, 'Killing time: the world politics of civil war duration, 1820–1992', *International Studies Quarterly* 44.4 (2000): 615–642.

21. David E. Cunningham, Kristian Skrede Gleditsch and Idean Salehyan, 'It takes two: a dyadic analysis of civil war duration and outcome', *Journal of Conflict Resolution* 53.4 (2009): 570–597.

22. Patrick Cockburn, *The Rise of Islamic State: ISIS and the New Sunni Revolution* (London: Verso Books, 2015). [Kindle edition] L1203–1295.

Chapter 1: Syria and the Middle East on the eve of civil war

1. Adam Hochschild, *To End All Wars: a Story of Loyalty and Rebellion, 1914–1918* (London: Houghton Mifflin Harcourt, 2011).

2. Hanna Batatu, *Syria's Peasantry, the Descendants of its Lesser Rural Notables, and their Politics* (Princeton: Princeton University Press, 1999), pp. 10–29.

3. Raymond Hinnebusch, 'Syria–Iraq relations: state construction and deconstruction and the Mena states system', *LSE Middle East Centre Series 04* (2014), http://www.lse.ac.uk/middleEastCentre/publications/Paper-Series/SyriaIraqRelations.aspx [accessed 1/5/15].

4. Samer Abboud, *Syria (Hotspots in Global Politics)*, (London: Polity, 2015). [Kindle edition] L669.

5. Abboud, *Syria* [Kindle edition]. L761.

6. Richard W. Murphy, 'Why Washington didn't intervene in Syria last time', *Foreign Affairs* 20 March 2012.

7. Alan George, *Syria: Neither Bread nor Freedom* (London: Zed Books, 2003).

8. Andrew Tabler, *In the Lion's Den: an Eyewitness Account of Washington's Battle with Syria* (Chicago: Lawrence Hill, 2011), pp. xvi–xx.

9. Michael Weiss and Hassan Hassan, *Isis: Inside the Army of Terror* (New York: Regan Arts, 2015). [Kindle edition] L1533–1546.

10. H.R. 1828 (108th): Syria Accountability and Lebanese Sovereignty Restoration Act of 2003, https://www.govtrack.us/congress/bills/108/hr1828 [accessed 20/4/15].

11. Orla Guerin, 'Syria sidesteps Lebanon demands', BBC, 6/3/05, http://news.bbc.co.uk/1/hi/world/middle_east/4322477.stm [accessed 21/4/15].

12. Flynt Leverett, *Inheriting Syria: Bashar's Trial by Fire* (New York: Brookings Institution Press, 2005).

13. Nader Habibi, 'A decade of growing U.S. trade with the Middle East', *Global Insight*, http://www.mefacts.com/cache/html/us-israel/11079.htm [accessed 1/5/15].

14. Yezid Sayigh and Avi Shlaim (eds), *The Cold War and the Middle East* (Oxford: Clarendon Press, 1997).

15. Buzan, Barry and Ole Waever, *Regions and Powers: the Structure of International Security*, vol. 91 (Cambridge University Press, 2003), p. 200.

16. Fred Halliday, *The Middle East in International Relations. Power, Politics and Ideology* (Cambridge: Cambridge University Press, 2005).

17. William C. Wohlforth, 'Unipolarity, status competition, and great power war', *World Politics* 61.01 (2009): 28–57; Christopher Layne, 'The unipolar illusion: why new great powers will rise', *International Security* (1993): 5–51.

18. Fawaz Gerges, *Obama and the Middle East* (London: Palgrave, 2012), pp.19–24.

19. Michael Hudson, 'The United States in the Middle East', in Louise Fawcett (ed.), *International Relations of the Middle East* (Oxford: Oxford University Press, 2005).

20. Robert Lieber, 'Rhetoric or reality? American grand strategy and the contemporary Middle East'. Paper prepared for delivery at the 2014 Annual Meeting of the American Political Science Association Washington, DC, 28–31 August 2014.

21. World Bank data via tradingeconomics.com http://www.tradingeconomics.com/iran/gdp [accessed 12/5/14].

22. F. Gregory Gause, 'Beyond sectarianism: the New Middle East Cold War', Brookings Doha Center (2014).

23. Morton Valbjørn and Andre Bank, 'The new Arab Cold War: rediscovering the Arab dimension of Middle East regional politics', *Review of International Studies* 38:1 (2012), 3–24; Gause, 'Beyond Sectarianism' (2014).

24. Salah Nasrawi, 'Saudis reportedly funding Iraqi Sunnis', AP for *Washington Post* 8/12/06.

25. Definition by Haddad in F. Haddad, *Sectarianism in Iraq: Antagonistic Visions of Unity* (New York: Columbia University Press, 2011), p. 31.

26. For example see Paul Valley, 'The vicious schism between Sunni and Shia has been poisoning Islam for 1,400 years – and it's getting worse', *Independent* 19/2/14.

27. Haddad, *Sectarianism in Iraq*, pp.1–6.

28. Toby Dodge, 'State collapse and the rise of identity politics', in Markus Bouillon, David Malone and Ben Rowsell (eds), *Iraq: Preventing Another Generation of Conflict* (Boulder: Lynne Rienner Publishers, 2007).

29. Simon Mabon, *Saudi Arabia and Iran: Soft Power Rivalry in the Middle East* (London: I.B. Tauris, 2013), p. 123.

30. Shibley Telhami, *2008 Arab Public Opinion Poll* (University of Maryland, 2008).

31. Fawaz Gerges, *The Far Enemy: Why Jihad Went Global* (Cambridge: Cambridge University Press, 2009); Jason Burke, *Al-Qaeda: the True Story of Radical Islam* (London: I.B. Tauris, 2004).

32. Weiss and Hassan, *Isis*.

33. 'Views of Middle East unchanged by recent events', Pew Research Center 10/6/11, http://www.people-press.org/2011/06/10/views-of-middle-east-unchanged-by-recent-events/ [accessed 14/6/15]; Gerges, *Obama and the Middle East* (2012), 7–10.

34. Pollack in 'Symposium: U.S. Foreign Policy and the Future of the Middle East', *Middle East Policy* 21.3 (Fall 2014), 1–30, Kenneth Pollack, Paul R. Pillar, Amin Tarzi and Chas W. Freeman Jr.

35. Stephen Brooks, G. John Ikenberry and William Wohlforth, 'Don't come home, America: the case against retrenchment', *International Security* 37.3 (Winter 2012–2013), 7–51; Bret Stephens, *America in Retreat: The New Isolationism and the Coming Global Disorder* (New York: Sentinel, 2014); Robert Kagan, *the World America Made* (New York: Vintage, 2013).

36. Christopher Layne, 'This time it's real: the end of unipolarity and the Pax Americana', *International Studies Quarterly* 56 (2012), 203–213.

37. David Held and Kristian Coates Ulrichsen, 'The Arab Spring and the changing balance of global power', *Open Democracy* essay, 26 February 2014.

38. Gerges, *Obama and the Middle East*, p. 15.

39. Ryan Lizza, 'The consequentialist: how the Arab Spring remade Obama's foreign policy', *New Yorker* 2 May 2011.

40. Ibid.

41. Daniela Huber, 'A pragmatic actor – the US response to the Arab uprisings', *Journal of European Integration* 37.1 (2015), 57–75.

42. Gerges, *Obama and the Middle East*, p. 91.

43. 'Obama – the Vox conversation', *Vox* 8 February 2015, http://www.vox.com/a/barack-obama-interview-vox-conversation/obama-foreign-policy-transcript [accessed 10/10/15].

44. Gerges, *Obama and the Middle East*, p. 103; Tarzi in 'Symposium: U.S. foreign policy', *Middle East Policy* (2014).

45. Vali Nasr, *The Dispensable Nation* (London: Scribe, 2013) p. 163.

46. Lizza, 'The consequentialist'.

47. Interviews with US officials, Washington, August 2014 and May 2015.

48. Bruce Crumley, 'France's fling with Syria', *Time* 4/9/08; Christian Chesnot and Georges Malbrunot, *Les Chemins de Damas: Le dossier noir de la relation franco-syrienne* (Paris: Robert Lafront, 2014). [Kindle edition].

49. 'Foreign Secretary William Hague visits Syria' BBC, 26/01/11 http://www.bbc.co.uk/news/uk-politics-12293205 [accessed 10/9/15]; Interview with British Diplomat, March 2015.

50. Andrew C. Kuchins and Igor A. Zevelev, 'Russian foreign policy: continuity in change', *Washington Quarterly* 35.1 (2012), 147–161.

51. Talal Nizameddin, *Putin's New Order in the Middle East* (London: Hurst, 2013).

52. Nick Paton Walsh and Ewen MacAskill, 'Putin lashes out at "wolf-like" America', *Guardian* 11/5/06.

53. Roland Dannreuther, 'Russia and the Middle East: a Cold War Paradigm?' *Europe-Asia Studies* 64.3 (2012): 543–556.

54. Stephen J. Flanagan, 'The Turkey–Russia–Iran nexus: Eurasian power dynamics', *Washington Quarterly* 36.1 (2013), 163–178.

55. Nizameddin, *Putin's New Order*.

56. Dannreuther, 'Russia and the Middle East'.

57. Dmitri Trenin, 'The mythical alliance: Russia's Syria policy', Carnegie Moscow Centre, February 2013, http://carnegieendowment.org/files/mythical_alliance.pdf [accessed 6/11/14]; Nizameddin, *Putin's New Order*.

58. Karim Sadjadpour, 'The supreme leader', *The Iran Primer,* United States Institute of Peace http://iranprimer.usip.org/resource/supreme-leader [accessed 1/5/15].

59. Mahmood Monshipouri and Manochehr Dorraj, 'Iran's foreign policy: a shifting strategic landscape', *Middle East Policy*, 20.4 (Winter 2013), 133–147.

60. Frederic Wehrey, Jerrold D. Green, Brian Nichiporuk, Alireza Nader, Lydia Hansell, Rasool Nafisi and S. R. Bohandy, *The Rise of Pasrdaran: Assessing the Domestic Roles of Iran's Islamic Revolutionary Guards Corps* (Washington, DC: Rand Corps, 2009).

61. Ibid.

62. J. Goodarzi, 'Iran: Syria as the first line of defense', in *The Regional Struggle for Syria* (London: European Council on Foreign Relations, 2013).

63. 'Imports and Exports by country 2006–2011', *Syrian Central Bureau of Statistics* http://www.cbssyr.sy/trade/Foreign-Trade/2011/Trade-State2.htm [accessed 19/3/16].

64. Majid Rafizadeh, 'Iran's Economic Stake in Syria', *Foreign Policy* 4/1/13.

65. 'Assad and Ahmadinejad – "There is no separating Iran and Syria"', *Syria Comment*, 26/2/10 http://www.joshualandis.com/blog/assad-and-ahmadinejad-there-is-no-separating-iran-and-syria/ [accessed 22/4/15].

66. Simon Henderson, 'Good riddance', *Foreign Policy* 18/6/12.

67. 'Saudi Arabia,' *CIA World Factbook* https://www.cia.gov/library/publications/the-world-factbook/geos/sa.html [accessed 13/7/15].

68. Robert Mason, 'Back to realism for an enduring U.S.–Saudi relationship', *Middle East Policy* 21. 4 (Winter 2014), 32–44.

69. Joost R. Hiltermann, 'Disorder on the border: Saudi Arabia's war inside Yemen', *Foreign Affairs* 16 (2009).

70. Ross 'Colvin, "Cut off head of snake" Saudis told U.S. on Iran', Reuters 29/11/10, http://www.reuters.com/article/us-wikileaks-iran-saudis-idUSTRE6AS02B20101129 [accessed 12/5/15].

71. Nasr, *Dispensable Nation*, p. 161.

72. Interview with former Saudi official, Riyadh, March 2015.

73. Hassan Hassan, 'Syria the view from the Gulf states', European Council of Foreign Relations, June 2013, http://www.ecfr.eu/article/commentary_syria_the_view_from_the_gulf_states135 [accessed 10/10/14]; J. Al-Saadi, 'Saudi–Syrian relations: a historic divide', *al-akhbar* 4/2/12, http://english.al-akhbar.com/node/3906 [accessed 12/3/14].

74. Philip Robbins, *Suits and Uniforms: Turkish Foreign Policy since the Cold War* (London: Hurst, 2003), p. 99.

75. In reality, Assad's effectiveness in aiding Turkish goals was mixed. On the one hand Syria facilitated the spread of jihadist fighters into Iraq that prolonged Iraq's civil wars, creating destabilisation. On the other hand, Assad provided diplomatic support for Turkey's operations in Iraqi Kurdistan, notably the PKK crisis of 2007–8. See William Hale, *Turkish Foreign Policy, 1774–2000* (London: Routledge, 2002), p. 169.

76. Günter Seufert, 'Internal driving forces for Turkey's Middle East policy', *Südosteuropa Mitteilungen* 01 (2013): 79–84.

77. Şaban Kardaş, 'From zero problems to leading the change: making sense of transformation in Turkey's regional policy', *TEPAV Turkish Policy Brief Series*, no. 5 (2012).

78. 'What lies beneath Ankara's new foreign policy', leaked memo from James Jeffrey, 26/1/10, *Wikileaks* https://www.wikileaks.ch/cable/2010/01/10ANKARA87.html [accessed 10/12/15].

79. Meliha Benli Altunışık. 'The Middle East in Turkey–USA relations: managing the alliance', *Journal of Balkan and Near Eastern Studies*, 15:2 (2013), 157–173.

80. Philip Robins, 'Turkey's "double gravity" predicament: the foreign policy of a newly activist power', *International Affairs* 89.2 (2013), 381–397.

81. Interview with Şaban Kardaş, Assistant Professor, TOBB University, Ankara, 17 July 2012.

82. Turkish Statistical Institute, The Syria Report, 31 January 2011, http://www.turkstat.gov.tr/VeriBilgi.do?alt_id=12.

83. Interview with Turkish officials, Ankara, July 2012.

84. World Bank data at tradingeconomics.com http://www.tradingeconomics.com/qatar/gdp [accessed 4/6/15].

85. Kristian Coates Ulrichsen, *Qatar and the Arab Spring* (London: Hurst, 2014), p. 4.

86. Hugh Miles, al-Jazeera, (London: Abacus, 2005).

87. Bernard Haykel, 'Qatar and Islamism', *NOREF Paper* February 2013. http://www.peace-building.no/var/ezflow_site/storage/original/application/ac81941df1be874ccb-da35e747218abf.pdf [accessed 4/4/14].

88. Ulrichsen, *Qatar*.

89. Lina Khatib, 'Qatar's foreign policy: the limits of pragmatism', *International Affairs* 89.2 (2013), 417–431.

90. Ulrichsen, *Qatar*, p. 109.

91. Giorgio Cafiero and Daniel Wagner, 'Turkey and Qatar: close allies, sharing a doomed Syria policy', *The National Interest* 9/11/15 http://nationalinterest.org/feature/turkey-qatar-close-allies-sharing-doomed-syria-policy-14283?page=2 [accessed 10/3/16].

Chapter 2: The Arab Spring comes to Syria

1. 'Interview with Syrian President Bashar al-Assad', *Wall Street Journal* 31/1/11.
2. Stephen Walt, 'Why the Tunisian Revolution won't spread', *Foreign Policy* 16/1/11.
3. Christopher Phillips, *Everyday Arab Identity: the Daily Reproduction of the Arab World* (London: Routledge, 2013); David Lesch, *The New Lion of Damascus* (New York: Yale University Press, 2005).
4. David Lesch, *Syria: The Fall of the House of Assad* (New York: Yale University Press, 2013); Carsten Wieland, *Syria at Bay: Secularism, Islamism, and 'Pax Americana'* (Hurst & Co., London 2005), p. 159.
5. Emile Hokayem, *Syria's Uprising and the Fracturing of the Levant* (London: Routledge, 2013), p. 26.
6. Lesch, *Syria*, p. 59.
7. Economist Intelligence Unit – http://www.eiu.com/index.asp?layout=displayIssue&publication_id=250000825 [accessed 12/5/15].
8. Raymond Hinnebusch, *Syria: Revolution from Above* (Routledge, London 2001), p. 63.
9. Raymond Hinnebusch, 'Syria: from "authoritarian upgrading" to revolution?' *International Affairs* 88:1 (2012), 95–113.
10. Robert G. Rabil, *Syria, the United States, and the War on Terror in the Middle East*, (Praeger Security International, 2006), p. 187.
11. Lesch, *Syria*, p. 115.
12. Wieland, *Syria at Bay*, p. 165.
13. Lesch, *Syria*, p. 71.
14. Marwān Iskandarm, *Rafiq Hariri and the Fate of Lebanon* (London: Saqi, 2006), p. 201.
15. Philip Droz-Vincent, ' "State of Barbary" (Take Two): from the Arab Spring to the return of violence in Syria', *Middle East Journal* 68.1 (2014), 33–58.
16. Hinnebusch, 'Syria: from authoritarian upgrading' (2012),
17. Francesca De Châtel, 'The role of drought and climate change in the Syrian uprising: untangling the triggers of the revolution', *Middle Eastern Studies* 50.4 (2014), 521–535.
18. Employment stats from Economist Intelligence Unit; *Syria's Uprising*, p. 25.
19. 'Unemployment rate in Syria increased to 14.90 percent', Syrian Economic Forum, 28/11/12 http://www.syrianef.org/En/?p=418 [accessed 15/5/15]; Lesch, *Syria*, p. 62.
20. Lesch, *Syria*, p. 62.
21. De Châtel, 'The role of drought and climate change'; David Butter, *Syria's Economy: Picking up the Pieces*, Chatham House Research Paper, June 2015.
22. Abboud, *Syria* [Kindle edition] L878.
23. Hokayem, *Syria's Uprising*.
24. Droz-Vincent, "State of Barbary", although this figure is disputed and some say as few as 250,000 migrated due to drought. See Jan Selby and Mike Hulme, 'Is climate change really to blame for Syria's civil war?' *Guardian* 29/11/15.
25. Abboud, *Syria* [Kindle edition] L905.
26. De Châtel, 'The role of drought and climate change'.
27. Lesch, *Syria*, p. 63.
28. Shamel Azmeh, *The Uprising of the Marginalised: A Socio-Economic Perspective of the Syrian Uprising*, LSE Middle East Centre Paper Series 06 (2014).
29. Bassam Haddad, *The Syrian Regime's Business Backbone*, Middle East Report 42.262 (2012).
30. Hokayem, *Syria's Uprising*, p. 29.
31. Peter Harling and Sarah Birke, *The Syrian Heartbreak*, Middle East Report (2013).
32. For a further discussion of Salafism, see Chapter 6.
33. Thomas Pierret, 'Sunni clergy politics in the cities of Ba'athi Syria', in Fred Lawson (ed.), *Demystifying Syria* (London: Saqi, 2009), pp. 70–84; L.R. De Elvira and T. Zintl, 'The end

of the Ba'thist social contract in Bashar Al-Assad's Syria: reading sociopolitical transformations through charities and broader benevolent activism', *International Journal of Middle East Studies* 46.2 (2014), 329–349.

34. Christopher Phillips, 'The Arabism debate and the Arab uprisings', *Mediterranean Politics* 19.1 (2014), 141–144.

35. Jonathan Allen and Amie Parnes, *HRC* (New York: Crown Publishers, 2014), p. 471.

36. Lesch, *Syria*, p. 56; Phil Sands, Justin Vela and Suha Maayeh, 'Blood ties: the shadowy member of the Assad clan who ignited the Syrian conflict', *The National* 20/3/14,http://www.thenational.ae/world/middle-east/blood-ties-the-shadowy-member-of-the-assad-clan-who-ignited-the-syrian-conflict [accessed 15/5/15].

37. Abboud, *Syria* [Kindle edition] L1202.

38. Droz-Vincent, ' "State of Barbary" '.

39. Aron Lund, 'The political geography of Syria's war: an interview with Fabrice Balanche', *Syria in Crisis* for Carnegie 30/1/15, http://carnegieendowment.org/syriaincrisis/?fa=58875 [accessed 12/5/15].

40. Wieland, *Syria at Bay*, p. 22.

41. Dawn Chatty, 'Syria's bedouin enter the fray: how tribes could keep Syria together', *Foreign Affairs*, 13 November. (2013).

42. Interviews with Syrians, Lebanon, July 2013.

43. Eliza Griswold, 'Is this the end of Christianity in the Middle East?' *New York Times* 22/7/15.

44. Lisa Wedeen, *Ambiguities of Domination: Politics, Rhetoric, and Symbols in Contemporary Syria* (Chicago: University of Chicago Press, 1999).

45. James T. Quinlivan, 'Coup-proofing: its practice and consequences in the Middle East', *International Security* 24.2 (1999), 131–165.

46. Droz-Vincent, ' "State of Barbary" '.

47. Nicholas Blanford, *Killing Mr Lebanon: the Assassination of Rafik Hariri and its Impact on the Middle East* (London: I.B. Tauris, 2006).

48. Violations Documentation Center in Syria. http://www.vdc-sy.info/index.php/en/ [accessed 14/12/14]; Droz-Vincent, ' "State of Barbary" '.

49. Abboud, *Syria* [Kindle edition] L1357.

50. Michael Weiss and Hassan Hassan, *Isis: Inside the Army of Terror* (New York: Regan Arts, 2015). [Kindle edition] L1965.

51. Lesch, *Syria*, pp.177–178.

52. Anthony Shadid, 'Syria arrests scores in house-to-house roundup', *New York Times* 5/5/11.

53. 'Assad emails: "We should be in control of all public spaces" – translation', *Guardian* 14/3/12.

54. Hokayem, *Syria's Uprising*, pp. 51–55.

55. Lesch, *Syria*, p. 84.

56. Harriet Allsopp, *The Kurds of Syria* (London: I.B. Tauris, 2014), p. 199.

57. Interview with former Syrian regime official, January 2015.

58. Ariel Zirulnick, 'Government forces open fire on protesters in Syria's third-largest city, Homs', *Christian Science Monitor* 19/4/11, http://www.csmonitor.com/World/terrorism-security/2011/0419/Government-forces-open-fire-on-protesters-in-Syria-s-third-largest-city-Homs [accessed 10/9/15].

59. Christopher Phillips, 'Sectarianism and conflict in Syria', *Third World Quarterly* 36.2 (2015), 357–376; 'Syria: the crisis and its implications', Hearing before the Committee on Foreign Relations, United States Senate, 1/2/12 S. HRG. 112–472, https://www.gpo.gov/fdsys/pkg/CHRG-112shrg75019/pdf/CHRG-112shrg75019.pdf [accessed 2/2/15].

60. Abboud, *Syria* [Kindle edition] L1612.

61. Lesch, *Syria*, p. 74.

62. Interview with former Syrian regime officials, January 2015.

63. David Lesch, 'Assad's fateful choice', *Syria Comment* 9/4/16, http://www.joshualandis.com/blog/ [accessed 11/4/16].

64. Jeremy Bowen, 'Assad is firm in defending his actions in BBC interview', BBC 10/2/15, http://www.bbc.com/news/world-middle-east-31311896 [accessed 1/5/15].

65. Interview with British diplomat, March 2015; Joshua Landis, 'Regime's top Sunni defects – General Manaf Mustafa Tlass flees to Turkey', *Syria Comment* 5/7/12, http://www.joshualandis.com/blog/regimes-top-sunni-defects-general-manaf-mustafa-tlass-flees-to-turkey/ [accessed 1/6/15].

66. Lesch, *Syria*, p. 75.

67. Lesch, *Syria*, p. 74.

68. Interview with British diplomat, March 2015.

69. Lesch, *Syria*, p. 49; interview with former Syrian regime official, January 2015.

70. Lesch, *Syria*, p. 241.

71. 'Assad emails: "Rubbish laws of parties, elections, media . . ."' *Guardian* 14/3/12.

72. Hokayem, *Syria's Uprising*, pp. 40–41.

Chapter 3: Assad must stand aside? The international community's ambivalent response

1. 'President Obama: "The future of Syria must be determined by its people, but President Bashar al-Assad is standing in their way"', The White House 18/8/11, https://www.whitehouse.gov/blog/2011/08/18/president-obama-future-syria-must-be-determined-its-people-president-bashar-al-assad [accessed 3/6/15].

2. 'Turkish PM praises growing ties with Syria', AFP for Ahram online 6/2/11, http://english.ahram.org.eg/NewsContent/2/8/5096/Index.aspx [accessed 3/6/15].

3. Construction on the dam was abandoned in June 2011.

4. Kim Ghattas, *The Secretary: A Journey with Hillary Clinton from Beirut to the Heart of American Power* (London: Macmillan, 2013). [Kindle edition] L3972.

5. Vali Nasr, *The Dispensable Nation* (London: Scribe, 2013), p. 166.

6. Ghattas, *The Secretary*, p. 238.

7. Christopher Davidson, *After the Sheikhs: the Coming Collapse of the Gulf Oil Monarchies* (London: Hurst, 2012), p. 202.

8. Davidson, *After the Sheikhs*, p. 232.

9. Hillary Rodham Clinton, *Hard Choices: A Memoir* (New York: Simon and Schuster, 2014), pp. 331–362.

10. Mehran Kamrava, 'The Arab Spring and the Saudi-led counterrevolution', *Orbis* 56.1 (2012), pp. 96–104.

11. Ghattas, *The Secretary*, p. 260.

12. 'Libya protests: defiant Gaddafi refuses to quit', BBC 22/2/11, http://www.bbc.com/news/world-middle-east-12544624 [accessed 20/5/15].

13. Evan Osnos, 'The Biden agenda', *New Yorker* 28/7/14.

14. Ghattas, *The Secretary*, p. 269.

15. Nasr, *The Dispensable Nation*, p. 178; Ghattas, *The Secretary*, p. 259.

16. Ghattas, *The Secretary*, p. 254.

17. Guido Steinberg, 'Qatar and the Arab Spring: support for Islamists and new anti-Syria policy', German Institute for International and Security Affairs, *SWP commentary* 7/2/12, http://www.swp-berlin.org/fileadmin/contents/products/comments/2012C07_sbg.pdf [accessed 12/6/15].

18. Kristian Coates Ulrichsen, *Qatar and the Arab Spring* (London: Hurst, 2014), p. 124.

19. Interview with British official, London, December 2014.

20. Interview with US official, Washington, August 2014.

21. Interview with British official, October 2014.

22. Interview with al-Jazeera journalists, Doha, February 2015.

23. 'Saudi king expresses support to Syrian president', Xinhua 29/3/11, http://news.xinhuanet.com/english2010/world/2011-03/29/c_13802184.htm [accessed 1/6/15].

24. 'The general and the particular in the ongoing Syrian popular uprising', Arab Center for Research and Policy Studies May 2011, http://english.dohainstitute.org/file/get/324a0bcf-cdd1-4932-b1bf-454761a5d792.pdf [accessed 1/5/15].

25. 'A Statement by President Obama on Syria', White House 22/4/11, https://www.whitehouse.gov/blog/2011/04/22/statement-president-obama-syria [accessed 1/6/15].

26. Interview with Western officials, March 2015; 'Council of the European Union Foreign Affairs Press Release' 11/4/11 8741/1/11 REV 1, https://www.consilium.europa.eu/uedocs/cms_data/docs/pressdata/EN/foraff/121506.pdf [accessed 1/6/15].

27. Multiple private interviews with Syrians, 2011–15.

28. Violations Documentation Center in Syria, http://www.vdc-sy.info/index.php/en/ [accessed 1/5/15].

29. Ibid.

30. Alistair Good, 'Syrian protest song that killed its writer', *Telegraph* 10/7/11.

31. Anthony Shadid, 'Thousands turn out for Assad', *New York Times* 21/6/11.

32. Interview with Western officials, March 2015; Interview with Robert Ford, Washington, 15/6/15.

33. Jubin Goodarzi, 'Iran: Syria as the first line of defense', in *The Regional Struggle for Syria* (London: European Council on Foreign Relations, 2013).

34. Khalid Ali, 'Iran calls on Syrian President to consider protesters' demands', *Independent* 29/8/11.

35. Deborah Amos, 'Pro-Assad "Army" wages cyberwar in Syria', *NPR*, 25/9/11 – http://www.npr.org/2011/09/25/140746510/pro-assad-army-wages-cyberwar-in-syria [accessed 20/5/13]; Robert Booth, Mona Mahmood and Luke Harding, 'Exclusive: secret Assad emails lift lid on life of leader's inner circle', *Guardian* 14/3/12; 'Assad emails: "Suggestions for the president's speech" – translation', *Guardian* 14/3/12; 'Assad emails: "Blaming Al-Qaida is not in our interest" – translation', *Guardian* 14/3/12; Interview with former Syrian regime insider, January 2015.

36. Interview with Saudi official, Riyadh, March 2015.

37. A. Blomfield, 'Syria unrest: Saudi Arabia calls on "killing machine" to stop', *Telegraph* 8/8/11.

38. Lina Khatib, 'Qatar's foreign policy: the limits of pragmatism', *International Affairs* 89 (2012), 417–431.

39. Allegedly stated by Hamad to Syrian Foreign Minister Walid al-Muallem in Doha, 31 October 2011. Interview with former regime officials, January 2015.

40. Private interview with HH Sheikh Tamim, to journalists in London on Thursday, 30 October 2014.

41. Philip Robins, *Suits and Uniforms: Turkish Foreign Policy since the Cold War* (London: Hurst, 2003), p. 69.

42. Ahmet Davutoğlu (1994) *Alternative Paradigms: The Impact of Islamic and Western Weltanschauungs on Political Theory* (Lanham–New York–London: University Press of America), p. 5.

43. Interview with Soli Ozel, Istanbul, August 2012.

44. Christopher Phillips, *Into the Quagmire: Turkey's Frustrated Syria Policy*, Chatham House Briefing Paper (2012), p. 5.

45. UK Diptel from Damascus to FCO, 'Syria: Opposition Meeting in Exile' 7/6/11.

46. UK Diptel from Ankara to FCO, 'TURKEY/SYRIA: TURKEY TALKS TOUGH' 17/6/11.

47. Interview with Turkish official, Ankara, July 2012.

48. Interview with former Syrian insider, January 2015.

49. Philip Robins, 'Turkey's "double gravity" predicament: the foreign policy of a newly activist power', *International Affairs* 89.2 (2013), 381–397.

50. *Turkey's Power Capacity in the Middle East*, USAK Center for Middle Eastern and African Studies Report no. 12–04, June 2012, p. 2, http://www.usak.org.tr/dosyalar/rapor/ctZTC1gAenLx7HaF8Gi7oip20CoDVX.pdf [accessed 4/6/15].

51. Interviews with various Turkish commentators, Ankara and Istanbul, July–August 2012.

52. Interview with Soli Özel, 10 July 2012.

53. Economist Intelligence Unit, 'Syria Country Report', March 2011; interview with official from Gaziantep Chamber of Commerce, Gaziantep, 30 July 2012.

54. Robins, 'Turkey's "double gravity"' (2013).

55. Elif Shafak, 'On Turkey's turmoil: "Intimidation and paranoia dominates the land"', *Guardian* 1/3/16.

56. Bilgin Ayata, 'Turkish foreign policy in a changing Arab world: rise and fall of a regional actor?' *Journal of European Integration* 37.1 (2015).
57. Günter Seufert, 'Internal driving forces for Turkey's Middle East policy', *Südosteuropa Mitteilungen* 01 (2013), 79–84.
58. Henri J. Barkey, 'Erdogan's foreign policy is in ruins', *Foreign Policy* 4/2/16.
59. Phillips, *Into the Quagmire*.
60. İlhan Uzgel, 'New Middle East: Turkey from being a playmaker to seclusion in the new Middle East', *Centre for Policy and Research on Turkey* 4.1 (2015), pp. 47–55.
61. Robins, 'Turkey's "double gravity" ' (2013).
62. Interview with US officials, Washington, August 2014; interview with Robert Ford, Washington, 15/6/15.
63. Nasr, *The Dispensable Nation*, p. 2.
64. Kilic Bugra Kanat, *A Tale of Four Augusts: Obama's Syria Policy* (Washington, DC: SETA, 2015).
65. Nasr, *The Dispensable Nation*.
66. Interview with Western official, October 2014.
67. 'Consolidated list of financial sanctions targets in the UK's HM Treasury', http://www.hmtreasury.gov.uk/d/syria.htm [accessed 14/5/13]
68. Lesch, *Syria*, p. 153.
69. Interview with Robert Ford, Washington, 15/6/15.
70. UK Diptel from Damascus to FCO, 'Syria – Homs', 27/5/11.
71. Lesch, *Syria*, p. 135.
72. UK Diptel from Damascus to FCO, 'Syria: the pace quickens' 19/7/11.
73. Christian Chesnot and Georges Malbrunot, *Les Chemins de Dama : Le dossier noir de la relation franco-syrienne* (Paris: Robert Lafront, 2014) [Kindle edition].
74. Interview with Robert Ford, Washington, 15/6/15.
75. *Les Chemins*, [Kindle edition] L3819.
76. Interview with Western diplomat, March 2015.
77. 'President Obama: "The future of Syria must be determined by its people, but President Bashar al-Assad is standing in their way" ', White House, https://www.whitehouse.gov/blog/2011/08/18/president-obama-future-syria-must-be-determined-its-people-president-bashar-al-assad [accessed 15/5/15].
78. Chris McGreal and Martin Chulov, 'Syria: Assad must resign, says Obama', *Guardian* 19/8/15.
79. Kanat, *A Tale of Four Augusts*, p. 81.
80. Quoted ibid. pp. 82–83.
81. Lesch, *Syria*, p. 157.
82. Interview with Alistair Burt, London, 18/11/14.
83. Interview with British officials, London, July 2014.
84. Interview with Fred Hof, Washington, 30/7/14.
85. Interview with former US official, July 2014.
86. McGreal, Chris and Martin Chulov, 'Syria: Assad must resign, says Obama', *Guardian* 19/8/11
87. Interview with British diplomat, March 2015.

Chapter 4: International institutions and the slide to war

1. Abboud, *Syria* [Kindle edition] L318.
2. It is unclear how many of the 500 listed regime fatalities were killed by the regime for refusing orders, as has been alleged. See 'Latest Regime Fatalities', Violations Documentation Center in Syria. Despite being an opposition site this is the most accurate accumulator of data on verified regime and opposition deaths. http://www.vdc-sy.info/index.php/en/ [accessed 14/12/14].
3. The agendas of those running these online forums will be discussed in Chapter 5. See Chapter 5, note 4.

4. Matthew Barber, 'The names of the Revolution,' *Syria Comment* 14/12/13, http://www.joshualandis.com/blog/names-of-the-revolution/ [accessed 14/12/14].

5. George Baghdadi, 'Syrians march in support of Assad', *CBS News* 13/11/11, http://www.cbsnews.com/news/syrians-march-in-support-of-assad/ [accessed 14/12/14].

6. David W. Lesch, *Syria: The Fall of the House of Assad* (London: Yale University Press, 2013), p. 103.

7. Aron Lund, 'The Free Syria Army doesn't exist', *Syria Comment* 16/3/13, http://www.joshualandis.com/blog/the-free-syrian-army-doesnt-exist/ [accessed 1/2/15].

8. The numbers are disputed. The regime claims 13, SANA (http://www.sana.sy/eng/337/2011/10/01/372492.htm), while the FSA claims 80 – Al-Arabiya (http://english.alarabiya.net/articles/2011/09/29/169224.html) 29/9/11 [both accessed 14/12/14].

9. See map on 'Homs, Syria, Capital of the Revolution', https://syriamap.files.wordpress.com/2011/11/homs_final_1111081.jpg [accessed 2/4/15].

10. Interviews with Syrian refugees from Homs, Jordan, August 2012.

11. Jonathan Littell, *Syrian Notebooks: Inside the Homs Uprising* (London: Verso Books, 2015). [Kindle edition] L977.

12. Violations Documentation Center in Syria, http://www.vdc-sy.info/index.php/en/ [accessed 14/12/14].

13. Rabie Nasser, 'Socioeconomic roots and impact of the Syria crisis', Syria Center for Policy Research, January 2013, p. 62, http://scpr-syria.org/att/1360464324_Tf75J.pdf [accessed 2/2/15].

14. Lesch, *Syria* p. 188.

15. David Butter, *Syria's Economy: Picking up the Pieces*, Chatham House Research Paper, June (2015).

16. Nasser, 'Socioeconomic roots', p. 64.

17. Abboud, *Syria* [Kindle edition] L2289.

18. C. Drury, 'Revisiting economic sanctions reconsidered', *Journal of Peace Research* 35.4 (1998), 497–509. Cited in Nasser, 'Socioeconomic roots'; Lee Jones, *Societies under Siege: Exploring how international economic sanctions (do not) work.* (Oxford: Oxford University Press, 2015)

19. Interview with US official, Washington, August 2014.

20. UK Diptel from Damascus to FCO, 'Syrian economy: Assad's weak spot, and what more we can do to squeeze it', 23/10/11

21. James Denselow, 'Panama Papers: how the Seychelles saved Syria', al-Jazeera 9/4/16, http://www.aljazeera.com/indepth/opinion/2016/04/seychelles-saved-syria-160407085452247.html [accessed 12/4/16].

22. Nasser, 'Socioeconomic roots', p. 64.

23. 'Syria: the crisis and its implications', Hearing before the Committee on Foreign Relations, United States Senate, 1/2/12 S. HRG. 112–472, https://www.gpo.gov/fdsys/pkg/CHRG-112shrg75019/pdf/CHRG-112shrg75019.pdf [accessed 2/2/15].

24. Paul Danahar, *The New Middle East: the World after the Arab Spring* (London: Bloomsbury Publishing, 2013), pp. 237–238.

25. Kristian Coates Ulrichsen, *Qatar and the Arab Spring* (London: Hurst, 2014), pp. 134–135.

26. Moscow had already vetoed an anti-Assad resolution at the UNSC in October 2011 and wanted to avoid having to do so again so soon, fearing the Arab League would refer to New York if Damascus continued to stonewall. See Lesch, *Syria*, p. 188.

27. Richard Gowan cited in Lesch, *Syria*, p. 189.

28. Littell, *Syrian Notebooks* [Kindle edition] L1050.

29. Ironically, Dabi's time as Sudan's ambassador to Qatar made the regime suspicious of him too.

30. 'Ex-Arab-League monitor labels Syria mission "a farce"', BBC 11/1/12, http://www.bbc.co.uk/news/world-middle-east-16507805 [accessed 3/10/15].

31. Lesch, *Syria*, p.182, note 38.

32. Emile Hokayem, *Syria's Uprising and the Fracturing of the Levant* (London: Routledge, 2013), p. 160.

33. Hassan Hassan, 'Syria: the view from the Gulf states', *ECFR*, June 2013, http://www.ecfr. eu/article/commentary_syria_the_view_from_the_gulf_states135 [accessed 10/10/14].

34. Previous no-fly zones over Iraq in 1991 had no explicit UN authorisation, even though the US and UK used UN688 as justification.

35. 'Outcome Document of World Summit', UN General Assembly A/60/L.1, 15/9/05, http://responsibilitytoprotect.org/world%20summit%20outcome%20doc%202005(1). pdf [accessed 12/5/13].

36. Aiden Hehir, *The Responsibility to Protect* (London: Palgrave Macmillan, 2012), p. 52.

37. Justin Morris, 'Libya and Syria: R2P and the spectre of the swinging pendulum', *International Affairs* 89.5 (2013), 1265–1283.

38. Hillary Rodham Clinton, *Hard Choices: A Memoir* (New York: Simon and Schuster, 2014), pp. 447–470.

39. Interview with Russian official, Moscow, November 2014; Lesch, *Syria*, p. 183.

40. Interview with Alistair Burt, London, 18/11/14.

41. Clinton, *Hard Choices*, pp. 447–470.

42. Mark N. Katz, 'Russia and the conflict in Syria: four myths', *Middle East Policy* 20.2 (2013), 38–46.

43. Roy Allison, 'Russia and Syria: explaining alignment with a regime in crisis', *International Affairs* 89.4 (2013), 795–823.

44. Dmitri Trenin, 'The mythical alliance: Russia's Syria policy', Carnegie Moscow Centre February 2013, http://carnegieendowment.org/files/mythical_alliance.pdf [accessed 6/11/14].

45. 'Syria unrest: Medvedev urges Assad to reform or go', BBC 7/10/11, http://www.bbc. com/news/world-middle-east-15218727 [accessed 6/11/14].

46. Ivanov, M. and D. Kozlov, 'Resolution is ripe for Russia', Kommersant 22/3/11 in Roland Dannreuther, 'Russia and the Arab Spring: supporting the counter-revolution', *Journal of European Integration* 37.1 (2015), 77–94.

47. Dannreuther, 'Russia and the Arab Spring'.

48. Interview with Russian official, Moscow, November 2014.

49. Interview with various Russian officials and former officials, Moscow, November 2014.

50. Dannreuther, 'Russia and the Arab Spring'.

51. Ibid.

52. 'Russia will not allow Libya-style military intervention in Syria', Middle East Online, 1/11/11, http://www.middle-east-online.com/english/?id=48833 (accessed 10/5/13).

53. Samuel Charap, 'Russia, Syria and the doctrine of intervention', *Survival* 55.1 (February– March 2013), 35–41.

54. Interview with former Russian official, Moscow, November 2014.

55. Trenin, 'The mythical alliance'.

56. Dannreuther, 'Russia and the Arab Spring'; interview with Russian official, Moscow, November 2014.

57. Trenin, 'The mythical alliance'.

58. Interview with Alexey Maleshenko, Moscow, 27/11/14; interview with Ramazan Duarov, Moscow, 24/11/14.

59. Dannreuther, 'Russia and the Arab Spring'.

60. Trenin, 'The mythical alliance'; Katz, 'Russia and the conflict in Syria'.

61. Katz, 'Russia and the conflict in Syria'.

62. Vitaly Naumkin, 'Russia's Middle East policy after the G-20 summit', *Al-Monitor* 24/11/14, http://www.al-monitor.com/pulse/originals/2014/11/russia-middle-east-policy-after-g20.html#ixzz3uTctmzmI [accessed 12/4/15]; Dmitri Trenin, 'Putin's Syria gambit aims at something bigger than Syria', *Tablet* 13/10/15, http://www.tabletmag.com/ jewish-news-and-politics/194109/putin-syria-trenin [accessed 10/3/16].

63. Trenin, 'The mythical alliance'.

64. Dannreuther, 'Russia and the Arab Spring'.

65. Interview with Vitaly Naumkin, Moscow, 25 November 2014

66. 'UNSMIS Background', *United Nations*, http://www.un.org/en/peacekeeping/missions/ past/unsmis/background.shtml [accessed 10/5/15].

67. Richard Gowan, 'Kofi Annan, Syria and the uses of uncertainty in mediation', *Stability: International Journal of Security and Development* 2.1 (2013), 8.

68. 'UNSMIS Background', *United Nations*.

69. In August a report by the UN Human Rights Commission would confirm regime involvement.

70. 'UN calls for investigation into Houla killings in Syria', BBC 1/6/12, http://www.bbc.com/news/world-middle-east-18295291 [accessed 1/6/15].

71. Hokayem, *Syria's Uprising*, p. 161.

72. Gowan, 'Kofi Annan'.

73. 'Mission impossible: why Kofi Annan's peace plan for Syria failed', ABC 16/9/12, http://www.abc.net.au/radionational/programs/rearvision/kofi-annan27s-peace-plan/4242708#transcript [accessed 4/5/15].

74. 'Action Group for Syria: Final Communiqué', 30/6/12, http://www.un.org/News/dh/infocus/Syria/FinalCommuniqueActionGroupforSyria.pdf [accessed 3/5/15].

75. Clinton, *Hard Choices*, pp. 447–470.

76. 'Kofi Annan on Syria, hard choices of peacekeeping', NPR, 27/8/12, http://www.npr.org/2012/09/01/160135085/kofi-annan-on-the-difficult-choices-of-a-peacekeeper.

77. Ian Black, 'Kofi Annan resigns as Syria envoy', *Guardian* 2/8/12. http://www.theguardian.com/world/2012/aug/02/kofi-annan-resigns-syria-envoy [accessed 22/5/15].

78. J. Michael Greig, 'Intractable Syria – insights from the scholarly literature on the failure of mediation', *Penn State Journal of Law and International Affairs* 2 (2013), p. 48.

79. According to the Violations Documentation Center in Syria in the 59 days before UN peacekeepers arrived but after the departure of the AL monitors (17 Feb.–15 April) there were 4,290 recorded fatalities. For the 59 days when the UN peacekeepers were deployed (16 April–14 June) there was a slight drop, to 3,991; 59 days after UN peacekeepers ended operations (14 June–12 Aug.) there was a huge increase, to 9,251. http://www.vdc-sy.info/index.php/en/ [accessed 14/12/14].

80. Lesch, *Syria*, p. 187.

Chapter 5: A legitimate representative? Supporting and subverting Syria's political opposition

1. 'Moaz al-Khatib: the priority is to save Syria', al-Jazeera 11/5/13, http://www.aljazeera.com/programmes/talktojazeera/2013/05/2013510141112681380.html [accessed 2/7/15].

2. Robin Yassin-Kassab and Leila Al-Shami, *Burning Country: Syrians in Revolution and War* (London: Pluto, 2016), p. 37.

3. Reinoud Leenders and Steven Heydemann, 'Popular mobilisation in Syria: opportunity and threat, and the social networks of the early risers', *Mediterranean Politics* 17.2 (2012), 139–159.

4. For Friday titles see Matthew Barber, 'The names of the Revolution', 14/12/13, http://www.joshualandis.com/blog/names-of-the-revolution/ [accessed 14/12/14]; however, Littell notes there were rival forums and websites, sometimes leading to different names on the same day: see Jonathan Littell, *Syrian Notebooks: Inside the Homs Uprising* (London: Verso Books, 2015). [Kindle edition] L1072.

5. Interview with Bassma Kodmani, Paris, 31/8/15.

6. 'National Coordination Body for Democratic Change' Carnegie Syria resources 15/1/12, http://carnegie-mec.org/publications/?fa=48369 [accessed 12/7/15]; Yezid Sayigh, 'The Syrian Opposition's leadership problem', *Carnegie Papers*, 3/4/13, http://carnegieendowment.org/2013/04/03/syrian-opposition-s-leadership-problem/fx6v# [accessed 10/5/13].

7. 'Building the Syrian state', Carnegie Syria resources 28/9/12, http://carnegie-mec.org/publications/?fa=49517 [accessed 12/7/15].

8. Interview with Western diplomat, March 2015.

9. Interview with Western diplomat, February 2015.

10. 'Chairman's Conclusions of Friends of Syria meeting', Foreign and Commonwealth Office 27/2/12, https://www.gov.uk/government/news/chairmans-conclusions-of-friends-of-syria-meeting [accessed 12/7/15].

11. Interview with Bassma Kodmani, Paris, 31/8/15.
12. Emile Hokayem, *Syria's Uprising and the Fracturing of the Levant* (London: Routledge, 2013), p. 72.
13. Interview with Robert Ford, Washington, 15/6/15.
14. Interviews with US officials, Washington, July and August 2014; interviews with Western officials based in Turkey, Ankara and Gaziantep, July 2012 and August 2013.
15. Abboud, *Syria* [Kindle edition] L1393.
16. Raphaël Lefèvre, *Ashes of Hama: The Muslim Brotherhood in Syria* (Oxford: Oxford University Press, 2013), pp. 191–192.
17. Reinoud Leenders and Steven Heydemann, 'Popular mobilisation in Syria'; Reinoud Leenders, 'Collective action and mobilization in Dar'a: an anatomy of the onset of Syria's popular uprising', *Mobilisation*,17.4 (2012), 419–434.
18. Joshua Landis, 'The man behind "Syria Revolution Facebook Page" speaks out', *Syria Comment* 24/4/11, http://www.joshualandis.com/blog/the-man-behind-syria-revolution-2011-facebook-page-speaks-out/ [accessed 3/6/15]; Uri Freedman, 'How Syrian activists name their Friday protests', *The Wire* 16/9/11, http://www.thewire.com/global/2011/09/how-syrian-activists-name-their-friday-protests/42586/ [accessed 3/6/15].
19. Lefèvre, *Ashes of Hama*, p. 188.
20. David Roberts, 'Qatar: domestic quietism, elite adventuring', in F. Ayub (ed.), *What Does the Gulf Think about the Arab Awakening?* (London: ECFR, 2013), http://www.ecfr.eu/page/-/ECFR75_GULF_ANALYSIS_AW.pdf [accessed 3/4/14].
21. Interview with Qatar officials, Doha, February 2015.
22. Jeremy Shapiro, 'The Qatar problem', *Foreign Policy* 28/8/13.
23. Lefèvre, *Ashes of Hama*, p. 189.
24. Interview with Bassma Kodmani, Paris, 31/8/15.
25. Lefèvre, *Ashes of Hama*, p. 190.
26. Interview with Western diplomat, February 2015.
27. Hokayem, *Syria's Uprising*, p. 75.
28. Borzou Daragahi, 'Libya helps bankroll Syrian opposition', *Financial Times* 5/11/12.
29. Shapiro, 'The Qatar problem'.
30. Carsten Wieland, *Syria at Bay: Secularism, Islamism, and 'Pax Americana'* (London: Hurst, 2005).
31. Harriet Allsopp, *The Kurds of Syria* (London: I.B. Tauris, 2014), p. 288.
32. Ibid., p. 196.
33. The PYD insists it is independent of the PKK, although it is openly a member of the Union of Kurdistan Communities (KCK), the umbrella body for groups supportive of PKK ideology and goals. Robert Lowe and Cengiz Gunes, *The Impact of the Syrian War on Kurdish Politics across the Middle East*, Chatham House Research Paper, July 2015.
34. Allsopp, *The Kurds of Syria*, pp. 196–205.
35. Ibid., p. 205.
36. Ibid., pp. 198–200.
37. Ibid., p. 207.
38. Interview with Turkish official, Ankara, 2013.
39. Interview with Abdul Hakim Bashar, KNC chairman, London, 18/1/12.
40. Allsopp, *The Kurds of Syria*, p. 214.
41. UK Diptel from Damascus to FCO, 'Syria: Opposition Meeting in Exile' 7/6/11.
42. Interview with Robert Ford, Washington, 15/6/15; interview with Western diplomat, March 2015
43. Robert Marquand, 'Syria's opposition concerned about independent armed rebel groups', *Christian Science Monitor*, 27/1/12, http://www.csmonitor.com/World/Europe/2012/0127/Syria-s-opposition-concerned-about-independent-armed-rebel-groups [accessed 7/7/15].
44. Interview with Bassma Kodmani, Paris, 31/8/15; interviews with member of the SNC, October 2014.
45. Abboud, *Syria* [Kindle edition] L1534.

46. 'Syria opposition chiefs at odds over military body', Reuters 1/3/12, http://uk.reuters. com/article/2012/03/01/us-syria-opposition-idUSTRE8200SA20120301.

47. Interview with Bassma Kodmani, Paris, 31/8/15.

48. Hokayem, *Syria's Uprising* p. 43.

49. Interview with Jon Wilks, Muscat, 3/2/15.

50. Meliha Benli Altunışık, 'The Middle East in Turkey–USA relations: managing the alliance', *Journal of Balkan and Near Eastern Studies* 15.2 (2013), 157–173.

51. 'KNC: A Statement on Joining the National Coalition of Syrian Opposition Forces', Carnegie 12/12/12 http://carnegieendowment.org/syriaincrisis/?fa=50350 [accessed 13/10/15].

52. Ibrahim Hemeidi, 'Syria's Kurds formally join opposition coalition', *Al-Monitor* 28/8/13, http://www.al-monitor.com/pulse/politics/2013/08/syria-kurds-join-national-coalition.html#; Interview with US official, Washington, May 2015.

53. Interview with Robert Ford, Washington, 15/6/15.

54. Interview with US official, Washington, May 2015.

55. Ibid.

56. Christian Chesnot and Georges Malbrunot, *Les Chemins de Damas: Le dossier noir de la relation franco-syrienne* (Paris: Robert Lafront, 2014) [Kindle edition].

57. J. Goodarzi, 'Iran: Syria as the first line of defense', in *The Regional Struggle for Syria* (London: European Council on Foreign Relations, 2013).

58. Yezid Sayigh, 'The Syrian opposition's very provisional government', Carnegie 28/3/13, http://carnegie-mec.org/2013/03/28/syrian-opposition-s-very-provisional-government [accessed 3/7/15].

59. 'Moaz al-Khatib: the priority is to save Syria', al-Jazeera.

60. A report released by the International Monetary Fund in September 2012 said that Saudi Arabia pledged $17.9 billion in aid to the region between 2011 and 2012 but that only $3.7 billion of these pledges had been disbursed. Ahmed Al Omran, 'Saudi Arabia: a new mobilisation', in F. Ayub (ed.), *What Does the Gulf Think about the Arab Awakening?* (London: ECFR, 2013).

61. Christopher Davidson, *After the Sheikhs: the Coming Collapse of the Gulf Oil Monarchies* (London: Hurst, 2012), pp. 214–215; Mehran Kamrava, 'The Arab Spring and the Saudi-led counterrevolution', *Orbis* 56.1 (2012), 96–104.

62. Hassan Hassan, 'Syria: the view from the Gulf states', ECFR, June 2013, http://www.ecfr. eu/article/commentary_syria_the_view_from_the_gulf_states135 [accessed 10/10/14].

63. Frederic Wehrey, *The Forgotten Uprising in Eastern Saudi Arabia* (Carnegie Endowment for International Peace, 2013).

64. Vali Nasr, *The Dispensable Nation* (London: Scribe, 2013), p. 213.

65. Robert Lacey, *Inside the Kingdom* (London: Random House, 2011).

66. Madawi Al-Rasheed, 'Saudi Arabia: local and regional challenges', *Contemporary Arab Affairs* 6:1 (2013), 28–40.

67. Stephane Lacroix, *Saudi Islamists and the Arab Spring*, Kuwait Programme on Development, Governance and Globalisation in the Gulf States, Research Paper 36, May 2014, http://eprints.lse.ac.uk/56725/1/Lacroix_Saudi-Islamists-and-theArab-Spring_2014.pdf [accessed 12/8/15].

68. Al Omran, 'Saudi Arabia: A new mobilisation'.

69. Daniela Huber, 'A pragmatic actor – the US response to the Arab uprisings', *Journal of European Integration* 37.1 (2015), 57–75.

70. Mark Heartsgaard, 'Secret tapes of the 2013 Egypt coup plot pose a problem for Obama', *Daily Beast* 5/10/15, http://www.thedailybeast.com/articles/2015/05/10/secret-tapes-of-the-2013-egypt-coup-plot-pose-a-problem-for-obama.html [accessed 10/11/15].

71. Huber, 'A pragmatic actor'.

72. Simon Henderson, 'The Saudi problem and the head of the snake', *Foreign Policy*, 28/3/14, http://foreignpolicy.com/2014/03/28/the-saudi-problem-and-the-head-of-the-snake/ [accessed 10/11/15].

73. Robert Mason, 'Back to realism for an enduring U.S.–Saudi relationship', *Middle East Policy* 21.4 (Winter 2014), 32–44.

74. Ibid.
75. Hassan, 'Syria: the view from the Gulf states'; Al-Rasheed, 'Saudi Arabia'.
76. Wehrey, F. 'Saudi Arabia reins in its clerics on Syria', Carnegie Endowment for International Peace, July 2012, http://carnegieendowment.org/2012/06/14/saudi-arabia-reins-in-its-clerics-on-syria/bu10. [accessed 12/3/14].
77. S. Kerr, 'Saudi cracks down on youths travelling to Syria', Financial Times 4/2/14, http://www.ft.com/cms/s/0/c98efe4e-8d88–11e3-bbe7–00144feab7de.html#axzz2wJCikVoa [accessed 12/3/14]; Wehrey, 'Saudi Arabia reins in its clerics on Syria'.
78. Simon Henderson, 'The prince and the revolution', Foreign Policy 24/7/12.
79. Al-Rasheed, 'Saudi Arabia'.
80. Interview with Saudi official, Riyadh, March 2015.
81. Michael Stephens, 'The underestimated Prince Nayef', Foreign Policy 18/6/12.
82. Hassan, 'Syria: the view from the Gulf states'.
83. Interview with Saudi official, Riyadh, March 2015.
84. Craig Unger, House of Bush, House of Saud: The Secret Relationship between the World's Two Most Powerful Dynasties (New York: Gibson Square Books, 2007).
85. David Ottaway, The King's Messenger: Prince Bandar bin Sultan and America's Tangled Relationship with Saudi Arabia (New York: Walker, 2008); Dam Entous, Nour Malas and Margaret Coker, 'A veteran Saudi power player works to build support to topple Assad', Wall Street Journal 23/8/13.
86. See Chapter 6.
87. Hassan Hassan, 'Saudis overtaking Qatar in sponsoring Syrian rebels', The National 15/5/13.
88. 'The latest expansion of the Syrian coalition', The National Coalition of Syrian Revolution and Opposition Forces 31/5/13, http://en.etilaf.org/press/the-latest-expansion-of-the-syrian-coalition.html [accessed 12/11/15].
89. Hassan Hassan, 'Syria is now Saudi Arabia's problem', Foreign Policy, 6/6/13.
90. Raphael Lefevre, 'Saudi and Syrian Muslim Brotherhood', Middle East Institute 27/9/13, http://www.mei.edu/content/saudi-arabia-and-syrian-brotherhood [accessed 2/5/15].

Chapter 6: 'Arm the rebels!' Backing the armed opposition

1. 'The 8th IISS Regional Security Summit: the Manama Dialogue, second plenary session' 8/12/12, https://www.iiss.org//media/Documents/Events/Manama%20Dialogue/MD2012/Plenary%202%20QA.pdf [accessed 12/10/15].
2. 'Syrian army colonel defects forms Free Syrian Army', Asharq al-Awsat 1/8/15.
3. Abboud, Syria, L1726.
4. Interview with US officials, Washington, July 2014; Abboud, Syria [Kindle edition] L1800.
5. Aron Lund, 'The Free Syria Army doesn't exist', Syria Comment,16/3/13, http://www.joshualandis.com/blog/the-free-syrian-army-doesnt-exist/ [accessed 1/2/15].
6. Emile Hokayem, Syria's Uprising and the Fracturing of the Levant (London: Routledge, 2013), p. 85.
7. Ibid., p. 83.
8. Jonathan Littell, Syrian Notebooks: Inside the Homs Uprising (London: Verso Books, 2015), [Kindle edition], L1064; interview with Robert Ford, Washington, 15/6/15.
9. Abboud, Syria [Kindle edition] L1738.
10. Hokayem Syria's Uprising, pp. 88–89.
11. David Butter, Syria's Economy: Picking up the Pieces, Chatham House Research Paper June (2015).
12. The perpetrators of this attack remain unknown. Some have questioned how rebel forces could have infiltrated such a secure location, when they proved unable to repeat the feat thereafter. This has prompted some to speculate that the assassination may have been an inside job against Shawkat. Shawkat was a possible rival to Assad, with strong ties in the security establishment and the Alawi community. He also had long-standing ties with French intelligence. Some have speculated the IRGC were behind the attack, targeting Shawkat for opposing increased Iranian involvement in Syria. Alternatively,

there was a history of bad blood between Shawkat and Assad's younger brother and enforcer Maher. In the past, regime insiders had been found dead in suspicious circumstances at times of great convenience to Damascus, such as the suicide of former head of Syria's security apparatus in Lebanon, Gazi Kannan in October 2005, just as he was allegedly about to pass to the UN evidence linking the regime to the assassination of Rafik Hariri.

13. Hokayem, *Syria's Uprising*, p. 91.
14. Abboud, *Syria* [Kindle edition] L1776.
15. Joshua Landis, 'Islamic Education in Syria: Undoing Secularism'. Unpublished paper prepared for 'Constructs of Inclusion and Exclusion: Religion and Identity Formation in Middle Eastern School Curricula', Watson Institute for International Studies, Brown University, November 2003. https://faculty-staff.ou.edu/L/Joshua.M.Landis-1/Islamic%20Education%20in%20Syria.htm [accessed 20/2/15]
16. Lister, *The Syria Jihad* (London: Hurst, 2015), pp. 31–47.
17. The border posts were Bab al-Hawa, Bab al-Salameh, Jarablus on the Turkish border, and Al-Bukamal on the Iraqi. Ibid., pp.1 and 77.
18. Christian Chesnot and Georges Malbrunot, *Les Chemins de Damas: Le dossier noir de la relation franco-syrienne* (Paris: Robert Lafront, 2014) [Kindle edition].
19. Michael Weiss and Hassan Hassan, *Isis: Inside the Army of Terror* (New York: Regan Arts, 2015) [Kindle edition] L2104.
20. Ibid., L2135; Lister, *The Syria Jihad* (London: Hurst, 2015,) p. 55.
21. Hokayem, *Syria's Uprising*, p. 97.
22. Raphaël Lefèvre, *Ashes of Hama: The Muslim Brotherhood in Syria* (Oxford: Oxford University Press, 2013), p. 193; 'Guide to Syrian rebels', BBC 13/12/13, http://www.bbc.co.uk/news/world-middle-east-24403003 [accessed 12/4/15].
23. Sam Heller and Aaron Stein, 'The problem with Turkey's favourite Syrian Islamists', *War on the Rocks* 18/8/15, http://warontherocks.com/2015/08/the-trouble-with-turkeys-favorite-syrian-islamists/ [accessed 10/10/15].
24. Rania Abouzeid, 'Meet the Islamist militants fighting alongside Syria's rebels', *Time*, 26/7/12; Herve Bar, 'Ahrar al-Sham jihadists emerge from shadows in north Syria', *Daily Star* 13/2/13 http://www.dailystar.com.lb/News/Middle-East/2013/Feb-13/206284-ahrar-al-sham-jihadists-emerge-from-shadows-in-north-syria.ashx [accessed 10/10/15]. [shorten?]
25. 'Syria: mapping militant organisations', Stanford University, http://web.stanford.edu/group/mappingmilitants/cgi-bin/maps/view/syria [accessed 16/12/15].
26. Lister, *The Syria Jihad*, pp. 99–100.
27. 'Syria Document: founding declaration of the Islamic Front',*EA Worldview* 2/12/13, http://eaworldview.com/2013/12/syria-document-founding-declaration-islamic-front/ [accessed 16/12/15].
28. Weiss and Hassan, *Isis* [Kindle edition] L2208; Lister, *The Syrian Jihad*, pp. 56–57.
29. Lister, *The Syrian Jihad*, p. 58.
30. Ibid., p. 85.
31. Interview with Robert Ford, Washington, 15/6/15.
32. Lister, *The Syrian Jihad*, pp. 7–8.
33. Danny Gold, 'Meet the YPG, the Kurdish militia that doesn't want help from anyone', *Vice* 31/10/12, http://www.vice.com/read/meet-the-ypg [accessed 16/12/15.]
34. Harriet Allsopp, *The Kurds of Syria* (London: I.B. Tauris, 2014), p. 211.
35. Ibid., p. 214.
36. Wladimir van Wilgenburg, 'Syrian Kurds agree to disagree', *Al-Monitor* 30/12/13, http://www.al-monitor.com/pulse/originals/2013/12/syria-kurds-geneva-opposition-delegation-peace.html# [accessed 16/10/15].
37. Kheder Khaddour, *The Assad Regime's hold on the Syrian State*, Carnegie Research Paper 8/7/15, http://carnegie-mec.org/2015/07/08/assad-regime-s-hold-on-syrian-state/id3k [accessed 5/9/15].
38. Lister, *The Syrian Jihad*, p. 96.
39. Allsopp, *The Kurds of Syria*.

40. Khaled Hroub, 'Qatar and the Arab Spring', *Heinrich Böll Stiftung* 2013, http://lb.boell. org/en/2014/03/03/qatar-and-arab-spring-conflict-intl-politics [accessed 5/5/15]; Madawi al-Rasheed 'Saudi Arabia: local and regional challenges', *Contemporary Arab Affairs*, 6:1 (2013): 28–40; Kristian Coates Ulrichsen, *Qatar and the Arab Spring* (London: Hurst, 2014), p. 136.

41. Ulrichsen, *Qatar*, p. 112.

42. 'Assad emails: "I'm sure you have many places to turn to, including Doha"', *Guardian* 14/3/12.

43. Various Qatar officials and experts, Doha, February 2015.

44. Christopher M. Blanchard, *Qatar: Background and US Relations*, Congressional Research Service paper, 4/11/14, http://www.fas.org/sgp/crs/mideast/RL31718.pdf [accessed 6/5/15].

45. Ulrichsen, *Qatar*, p. 114.

46. Various Qatar officials and experts, Doha, February 2015.

47. Lina Khatib, 'Qatar's foreign policy: the limits of pragmatism', *International Affairs* 89.2 (2013): 417–431.

48. 'Article 7', *Qatar's Constitution of 2003*, https://www.constituteproject.org/constitution/ Qatar_2003.pdf [accessed 10/8/15].

49. Nonnemann in Ulrichsen, *Qatar*, p. 70.

50. Nour Malas, 'Syria rebels plead for ammunition', *Wall Street Journal* 3/3/12 http:// on.wsj.com/1y3D2dq [accessed 5/5/15].

51. Hokayem, *Syria's Uprising*, p. 86.

52. Ruth Sherlock, 'Libya to arm rebels in Syria', *Telegraph* 27/11/11.

53. J. Vela, 'Rebel forces armed by wealthy exiles'. *Independent* 23/2/12.

54. Lister, *The Syrian Jihad*, p. 76.

55. Ulrichsen, *Qatar*, p. 136.

56. 'Final report of the Panel of Experts established pursuant to resolution 1973 (2011) concerning Libya', *United Nations Security Council* S /2014/106 19/2/14, p. 47, http:// www.securitycouncilreport.org/atf/cf/%7B65BFCF9B-6D27-4E9C-8CD3- CF6E4FF96FF9%7D/s_2014_106.pdf [accessed 14/7/15].

57. Interviews with Turkish officials, July 2012, September 2013, January 2015.

58. Multiple interviews with Western officials 2012–15; C. J. Chivers and Eric Schmitt, 'Arms Airlift to Syria Rebels Expands, with Aid from C.I.A.', *New York Times* 24/3/13.

59. 'Final report of the Panel of Experts', p. 48.

60. C. J. Chivers and Eric Schmitt, 'Saudis step up help for rebels in Syria with Croatian arms', *New York Times* 25/2/13.

61. Lister, *The Syrian Jihad*, pp. 99–100.

62. Interview with Qatar-based Western officials, Doha, February 2015.

63. Phil Sands and Suha Maayeh, 'Syrian rebels get arms and advice through secret command centre in Amman', *The National* 28/12/13, http://www.thenational.ae/world/ middle-east/syrian-rebels-get-arms-and-advice-through-secret-command-centre-in- amman [accessed 5/5/15].

64. In a meeting with Kerry in Istanbul April 2013, all three agree to channel all weapons via the FSA–SMC. See Karen DeYoung, Anne Gearan and Scott Wilson, 'Decision to arm Syrian rebels was reached weeks ago, U.S. officials say', *Washington Post* 14/6/13 reached-weeks-

65. The 8th IISS Regional Security Summit', 8/12/12.

66. Shapiro, 'The Qatar Problem', *Foreign Policy* 28/8/13.

67. Interview with Saudi official, Riyadh, March 2015.

68. Rania Abouzeid, 'Syria's secular and Islamist rebels: who are the Saudis and the Qatars arming?' *Time* 18/9/12.

69. Hokayem, *Syria's Uprising*, pp. 121–123.

70. Interview with US official, Washington, July 2014.

71. Interviews with Jordanian officials, Amman, April 2014.

72. Hassan Hassan, 'Syria is now Saudi Arabia's problem', *Foreign Policy* 6/6/13.

73. Interview with Western officials in Turkey, Ankara, July 2012.

74. Correspondence with former Tawheed fighters, 2016.
75. Raymond Hinnebusch, 'Back to enmity: Turkey–Syria relations since the Syrian uprising', *Orient, Journal of German Orient Institute* (2015).
76. Interview with Turkish officials, January 2015.
77. William McCants, 'Gulf charities and Syrian sectarianism', *Foreign Policy* 30/9/13; Elizabeth Dickinson, 'Follow the money: how Syrian Salafis are funded from the Gulf', *Carnegie Endowment for International Peace*, 23/12/13, http://carnegieendowment. org/syriaincrisis/?fa=54011 [accessed 17/3/14].
78. McCants, 'Gulf charities'.
79. Stephane Lacroix, *Saudi Islamists and the Arab Spring*, Kuwait Programme on Development, Governance and Globalisation in the Gulf States, Research Paper 36, May 2014 http://eprints.lse.ac.uk/56725/1/Lacroix_Saudi-Islamists-and-theArab-Spring_2014.pdf [accessed 12/8/15].
80. Dickinson, 'Follow the money'.
81. Elizabeth Dickinson, 'The Syrian war's private donors lose faith', *New Yorker* 16/1/14.
82. Hokayem, *Syria's Uprising*, p. 96; 'The charm of telesalafism', *Economist* 20/10/12.
83. 'Syria conflict: Cleric Qaradawi urges Sunnis to join rebels', BBC, 13/1/13, http://www. bbc.co.uk/news/world-middle-east-22741588 (accessed 12/3/14).
84. Alexander Kühn, Christoph Reuter and Gregor Peter Schmitz, 'After the Arab Spring: Al-Jazeera Losing Battle for Independence' *Spiegel Online International* 15/2/13 http:// www.spiegel.de/international/world/al-jazeera-criticized-for-lack-of-independence-after-arab-spring-a-883343.html [accessed 10/5/14]
85. F. Wehrey, 'Saudi Arabia reins in its clerics on Syria', *Carnegie Endowment for International Peace*, July 2012. http://carnegieendowment.org/2012/06/14/saudi-arabia-reins-in-its-clerics-on-syria/bu10. [accessed 12/3/14].
86. Dickinson, 'Follow the money'.
87. 'ICSR Insight: Up to 11,000 foreign fighters in Syria; steep rise among Western Europeans', International Centre for the Study of Radicalisation and Political Violence 17/12/2013 http://icsr.info/2013/12/icsr-insight-11000-foreign-fighters-syria-steep-rise-among-western-europeans/ [accessed 12/6/15]; Lister, *The Syrian Jihad*, p. 1.
88. Elizabeth Dickinson, 'The Syrian war's private donors lose faith'; Rania Abouzeid, 'Syria's secular and Islamist rebels'.
89. Weiss and Hassan, *Isis* [Kindle edition] L2613.
90. Hokayem, *Syria's Uprising*.
91. Interviews with US official, Washington, May 2015; interview with Alistair Burt, London, 18/11/14.
92. Interviews with US official, Washington, May 2015.
93. Hillary Rodham Clinton, *Hard Choices: A Memoir* (New York: Simon and Schuster, 2014), pp. 447–470.
94. 'Syrian rebels get influx of arms with Gulf neighbours' money, US cooperation', *Washington Post* 15/5/12.
95. 'Syrian rebels get influx of arms', *Washington Post;* Eric Schmitt, 'C.I.A. said to aid in steering arms to Syrian opposition', *New York Times* 21/6/12; interview with Western official, March 2015; interview with British official, October 2014.
96. Clinton, *Hard Choices*, pp. 447–470.
97. Clinton, *Hard Choices*, pp. 447–470; Kim Ghattas, *The Secretary: A Journey with Hillary Clinton from Beirut to the Heart of American Power* (London: Macmillan, 2013), p. 336.
98. Anne Gearan and Karen DeYoung, 'Obama unlikely to reconsider arming Syrian rebels despite views of security staff', *Washington Post* 8/2/13.
99. DeYoung, Gearan and Wilson, 'Decision to arm Syrian rebels'.
100. 'US and UK suspend non-lethal aid for Syria rebels' BBC 11/12/13.
101. Interview with Alistair Burt, London, 18/11/14; interview with British official, London, October 2014.
102. 'US says it will give military aid to Syria rebels' BBC 14/6/13; Faysal Itani, 'The End of American Support for Syrian Rebels Was Inevitable', *Atlantic* 21/7/17 https://www. theatlantic.com/international/archive/2017/07/trump-syria-assad-rebels-putin-cia/ 534540/ [accessed 01/08/17].

103. Charles Lister, for example, argues that the failure for the international community to support the fledgling FSA in mid-2011 contributed to its ultimate weakness and the rise of radicals. Lister, *The Syrian Jihad*, p. 390.

104. Mark Mazzetti, 'C.I.A. study of covert aid fueled skepticism about helping Syrian rebels', *New York Times* 14/10/14.

105. Lister, *The Syrian Jihad*, p. 107.

106. Hokayem, *Syria's Uprising*, p. 123.

Chapter 7: To the hilt: Assad's allies dig in

1. 'Iran's new president Hassan Rouhani vows to support Syrian regime as President Assad vows to crush rebels with "iron fist"', *Independent* 5/8/13.

2. 'Mapping the conflict in Aleppo, Syria', *Caerus*, February 2014. Basel Dayoub, 'Bustan al-Qasr crossing in Aleppo: daily humiliation and nonsensical rules', *Al-Akhbar* 27/3/14 http://english.al-akhbar.com/node/19177 [accessed 10/9/15].

3. 'Are the Islamic courts in Aleppo run by al-Nusra? Aron Lund answers', *Syria Comment* 18/9/13 http://www.joshualandis.com/blog/newly-founded-islamic-courts-aleppo-run-al-qaida-ask-expert-aron-lund/ [accessed 10/9/15].

4. Edward Dark, 'Syrian Baath militia commander goes rags-to-riches', *Al-Monitor* 20/11/13 http://www.al-monitor.com/pulse/originals/2013/11/baath-party-brigade-syria-war-aleppo.html# [accessed 10/9/15].

5. 'Syrian regime loses last credible ally among the Sunni ulema. By Thomas Pierret', *Syria Comment* 22/3/13, http://www.joshualandis.com/blog/syrian-regime-loses-last-credible-ally-among-the-sunni-ulama-by-thomas-pierret/ [accessed 24/5/15].

6. David W. Lesch, 'The golden runaway', *Foreign Policy* 12/7/12.

7. David Butter, *Syria's Economy: Picking up the Pieces*, Chatham House Research Paper June (2015).

8. Kheder Khaddour, *The Assad Regime's hold on the Syrian State*, Carnegie Research Paper 8/7/15, http://carnegie-mec.org/2015/07/08/assad-regime-s-hold-on-syrian-state/id3k [accessed 5/9/15].

9. Shaun Walker, 'Plane loads of cash: flight records reveal Russia flew 30 tonnes of bank notes to Syrian regime', *Independent* 26/11/12.

10. Vivienne Walt, 'Syria's air-defense arsenal: the Russian missiles keeping Assad in power', *Time* 3/6/13.

11. Roy Allison, 'Russia and Syria: explaining alignment with a regime in crisis', *International Affairs* 89.4 (2013), 795–823; 'Assad: Russia is supplying weapons to Syria under contracts finalized since the conflict began', *Reuters* 30/5/15, http://uk.businessinsider.com/r-syria-gets-russian-arms-under-deals-signed-since-conflict-began-assad—2015–3?r=US&IR=T [accessed 10/11/15].

12. Vitaly Naumkin, 'Russia's Middle East policy after the G-20 summit', *Al-Monitor* 24/11/14, http://www.al-monitor.com/pulse/originals/2014/11/russia-middle-east-policy-after-g20.html#ixzz3uTctmzmI [accessed 12/4/15].

13. 'Who is supplying weapons to the warring sides in Syria?' BBC 14/6/13, http://www.bbc.co.uk/news/world-middle-east-22906965 [accessed 12/4/15]; Louis Charbonneau, 'Exclusive: Iran steps up weapons lifeline to Assad', *Reuters* 14/3/13 http://www.reuters.com/article/2013/03/14/us-syria-crisis-iran-idUSBRE92D05U20130314 [accessed 12/4/15].

14. 'Evidence of Iranian arms provided to Syria in the past 18 months', Brown Moses Blog 20/5/13, http://brown-moses.blogspot.co.uk/2013/05/evidence-of-iranian-arms-provided-to.html [accessed 12/4/15]; 'More evidence of sanction busting Iranian munitions deliveries to Syria', Brown Moses Blog 26/5/13, http://brown-moses.blogspot.co.uk/2013/05/more-evidence-of-sanction-busting.html [accessed 12/4/15].

15. Dmitri Trenin, 'The mythical alliance: Russia's Syria policy', Carnegie Moscow Centre, February 2013, http://carnegieendowment.org/files/mythical_alliance.pdf [accessed 6/11/14].

16. Miriam Elder and Ian Black, 'Russia withdraws its remaining personnel from Syria', *Guardian* 26/6/13.

17. Aram Nerguizian, 'The military balance in a shattered Levant', Centre for Strategic and International Studies, 15/6/15, p. 113; http://csis.org/files/publication/150615_Nerguizian_Levant_Mil_Bal_Report_w_cover_v2.pdf [accessed 10/8/15].

18. J. Goodarzi, 'Iran: Syria as the first line of defense', in *The Regional Struggle for Syria* (London: European Council on Foreign Relations, 2013).

19. Yossi Melman and Sof Hashavua, 'In depth: how Iranian weapons reach Hezbollah', *Jerusalem Post* 25/5/13, http://www.jpost.com/Defense/In-Depth-How-Iranian-weapons-go-through-Syria-to-Hezbollah-314313 [accessed 1/5/15]; Sara Bazoobandi, 'Iran's regional policy: interests, challenges and ambitions', *ISPI Analysis* November 2014, http://www.ispionline.it/sites/default/files/pubblicazioni/analysis_275__2014_0.pdf [accessed 15/2/16].

20. Simon Mabon, *Saudi Arabia and Iran: Soft Power Rivalry in the Middle East* (London: I.B. Tauris 2013), p. 200.

21. Paul Danahar, *The New Middle East: the World after the Arab Spring* (London: Bloomsbury Publishing, 2013), pp. 269–270.

22. Jonathan Schanzer, 'The anatomy of Turkey's "Gas-For Gold" scheme with Iran', Foundation for the Defense of Democracies 14/3/14, http://www.defenddemocracy.org/media-hit/the-anatomy-of-turkeys-gas-for-gold-scheme-with-iran/ [accessed 23/7/15]; Asli Kandemir, 'Turkey to Iran gold trade wiped out by new U.S. sanction', *Reuters* 15/2/13, http://www.reuters.com/article/2013/02/15/us-iran-turkey-sanctions-idUSBRE91E0IN20130215 [accessed 23/7/15].

23. Nasr, *Dispensable Nation*, p. 207.

24. Stephen J. Flanagan, 'The Turkey–Russia–Iran nexus: Eurasian power dynamics'. *Washington Quarterly* 36.1 (2013), 163–178.

25. Thomas Juneau, 'Iran under Rouhani: still alone in the world', *Middle East Policy* 21.4 (Winter 2014), 92–104.

26. Laura Rozen, 'Three days in March: new details on how US, Iran opened direct talks', *The Backchannel* 8/1/14, http://backchannel.al-monitor.com/index.php/2014/01/7484/three-days-in-march-new-details-on-the-u-s-iran-backchannel/ [accessed 23/7/15].

27. 'Shackled: The story of the world's most elaborate sanctions regime', *Economist* 1/11/14; 'Melons for everyone', *Economist* 27/10/14.

28. Mahmood Monshipouri and Manochehr Dorraj, 'Iran's foreign policy: a shifting strategic landscape', *Middle East Policy* 20.4 (Winter 2013), pp. 133–14.

29. Juneau, 'Iran under Rouhani'.

30. Alireza Nader, 'Iran & Region III: goals in Syria', *The Iran Primer* 26/1/15. http://iranprimer.usip.org/blog/2015/jan/26/iran-region-iii-goals-syria [accessed 10/10/15].

31. Eli Lake, 'Iran spends billions to prop up Assad', *Bloomberg View* 9/6/15, http://www.bloombergview.com/articles/2015-06-09/iran-spends-billions-to-prop-up-assad [accessed 10/12/15].

32. According a Gallup poll, in December 2012 52 per cent of Iranians polled backed economic support for Assad, 41 per cent military support and 51 per cent political support, while these numbers dropped to 45 per cent, 37 per cent and 48 per cent respectively by June 2013. Jay Loshky, 'Iranians support for Syria softens', *Gallup* 15/11/13, http://www.gallup.com/poll/165878/iranians-support-syria-softens.aspx [accessed 12/12/14].

33. Thanassis Cambanis, 'How do you say quagmire in Farsi?' *Foreign Policy* 13/5/13.

34. 'Melons for everyone', *Economist*; Kazem Alamdari, 'Power structure of the Islamic Republic of Iran: transition from populism to clientelism, and militarization of the government', *Third World Quarterly*, 2:8 (2005), 1285–1301.

35. Frederic Wehrey, Jerrold D. Green, Brian Nichiporuk, Alireza Nader, Lydia Hansell, Rasool Nafisi and S. R. Bohandy, *The Rise of Pasrdaran: Assessing the Domestic Roles of Iran's Islamic Revolutionary Guards Corps* (Washington, DC: Rand Corps, 2009).

36. Monshipouri and Dorraj, 'Iran's foreign policy'.

37. Dexter Filkins, 'The shadow commander', *New Yorker* 30/9/13.

38. Goodarzi, 'Iran: Syria as the first line of defense'.

39. Ibid.

40. Hokayem, *Syria's uprising.*

41. Marisa Sullivan, 'Hezbollah in Syria', Institute for the Study of War, April 2014, p. 11, http://www.understandingwar.org/report/hezbollah-syria [accessed 12/5/15]; Abboud, *Syria*, L2156.

42. Ibid., p. 12.

43. Jeffrey White, 'The Qusayr rules: the Syrian regime's changing way of war', Washington Institute, 31/5/13, http://www.washingtoninstitute.org/policy-analysis/view/the-qusayr-rules-the-syrian-regimes-changing-way-of-war [accessed 20/1/16].

44. Alex Rowell, 'Mapping Hezbollah's Syria war since 2011', *Now Lebanon* 12/8/15, https://mobile.mmedia.me/lb/en/reportsfeatures/565725-mapping-hezbollahs-syria-war-since-2011 [accessed 3/9/15].

45. Sullivan, 'Hezbollah in Syria', p. 9.

46. Interview with Robert Ford, Washington, 15/6/15.

47. Christopher Phillips, 'Sectarianism and conflict in Syria', *Third World Quarterly*, 36:2 (2015), 357–376.

48. *Hezbollah Turns Eastward to Syria* International Crisis Group Middle East Report no.153, 27/5/14, http://www.crisisgroup.org/en/regions/middle-east-north-africa/egypt-syria-lebanon/lebanon/153-lebanon-s-hizbollah-turns-eastward-to-syria.aspx [accessed 3/5/15].

49. Sullivan, 'Hezbollah in Syria'.

50. Martin Chulov, 'Lebanon's great divide exposed by assassination of security chief', *Guardian* 19/10/12.

51. *Hezbollah Turns Eastward to Syria*, p. 10.

52. Michael Weiss and Hassan Hassan, *Isis: Inside the Army of Terror* (New York: Regan Arts, 2015) [Kindle edition] L2068.

53. See for example Naame Shaam, 'Iran in Syria from an ally of the regime to an occupying force' (September 2014), http://www.naameshaam.org/report-iran-in-syria/ [accessed 2/3/15].

54. Filkins, 'The shadow commander'.

55. Ibid.

56. Naame Shaam, 'Iran in Syria'.

57. Joseph Holliday, *Syria's Maturing Insurgency*, Institute for the Study of War, June 2012, http://www.understandingwar.org/report/syrias-maturing-insurgency [accessed 7/7/15]; Joseph Holliday, *The Assad Regime: From Counter-insurgency to Civil War*, Institute for the Study of War, March 2013, http://www.understandingwar.org/report/assad-regime [accessed 7/7/15]; interview with former Damascus-based Western diplomat, March 2015.

58. Naame Shaam, 'Iran in Syria', p. 16.

59. Filkins, 'The shadow commander'.

60. Hassan and Weiss, *Isis* [Kindle edition] L2074.

61. Ibid., L2062; the regime relied on its special forces and elite units as mobile offensive forces. See Christopher Kozak, ' "An army in all corners" Assad's campaign strategy in Syria', Institute for the Study of War, April 2015, p. 13, http://www.understandingwar.org/sites/default/files/An%20Army%20in%20All%20Corners%20by%20Chris%20Kozak%201.pdf [accessed 7/7/15]

62. Filkins, 'The shadow commander'.

63. Lister, *The Syrian Jihad*, p. 128.

64. Patrick Seale, *Asad of Syria: the Struggle for the Middle East* (University of California Press, 1990), p. 327; Holliday, 'The Assad regime'.

65. Kheder Khaddour, 'Securing the Syrian regime', *Sada*, Carnegie Endowment for International Peace 3/6/14.

66. Will Fulton, Joseph Holliday and Sam Wyer, 'Iranian Strategy in Syria' May 2013, http://www.understandingwar.org/sites/default/files/IranianStrategyinSyria-1MAY.pdf [accessed 13/7/15]; Abboud, *Syria*, L2105.

67. Goodarzi, 'Iran: Syria as the first line of defense'.

68. Weiss and Hassan, *Isis* [Kindle edition] L2044.

69. Ibid.

70. Nicholas Blanford, *Warriors of God: Inside Hezbollah's Thirty-year Struggle against Israel* (London: Random House, 2011); discussion with Dr Filippo Dionigi, London School of Economics, July 2015.

71. Interviews with Syrians, Lebanon, August 2013, January–February 2015.

72. Patrick Cockburn, *The Rise of Islamic State: ISIS and the New Sunni Revolution* (London: Verso Books, 2015). [Kindle edition].

73. Kozak, '"An army in all corners"'.

74. Ibid., p. 16.

75. Weiss and Hassan, *Isis* [Kindle edition] L2092; Fulton, Holliday and Wyer, 'Iranian strategy in Syria', p. 24.

76. Mona Mahmood and Martin Chulov, 'Syrian war widens Sunni–Shia schism as foreign jihadis join fight for shrines', *Guardian* 4/6/13.

77. Lister, *Syrian Jihad*, p. 386.

78. Philip Smyth, 'Iran's Afghan Shiite fighters in Syria', *Washington Institute* 3/6/14, http://www.washingtoninstitute.org/policy-analysis/view/irans-afghan-shiite-fighters-in-syria [accessed 5/7/15].

79. Christopher Reuter, 'Syria's mercenaries: the Afghans fighting Assad's war', *Spiegel Online* 11/5/15, http://www.spiegel.de/international/world/afghan-mercenaries-fighting-for-assad-and-stuck-in-syria-a-1032869.html [accessed 7/8/15].

80. Jihad Yazigi, 'Syria's war economy', *ECFR*, April 2014 http://www.ecfr.eu/page/-/ECFR97_SYRIA_BRIEF_AW.pdf [accessed 4/12/14].

81. Khaddour, 'The Assad regime's hold on the Syrian state'.

82. Butter, 'Syria's economy'.

83. 'Syria', *CIA World Factbook*, https://www.cia.gov/library/publications/resources/the-world-factbook/geos/sy.html [accessed 7/8/14].

84. Salam al-Saadi, 'Iran's stake in Syria's economy', *Sada for Carnegie* 2/6/15, http://carnegieendowment.org/sada/2015/06/02/iran-s-stakes-in-syria-s-economy/i9cj [accessed 2/8/15].

85. Ibid.

86. Butter, 'Syria's economy'; Yazigi, 'Syria's war economy'.

87. Christopher Phillips, 'What is left of Assad's state is eroding from within', *Chatham House* 9/3/15, http://www.chathamhouse.org/expert/comment/17113 [accessed 24/8/15]; 'Syrian regional refugee response', UNHCR http://data.unhcr.org/syrianrefugees/regional.php [accessed 26/03/16].

88. Holliday, 'The Assad regime'.

89. Kozak, '"An army in all corners"'.

90. Abboud, *Syria*, L2066.

91. Sam Dagher, 'Iran's Foreign Legion leads battle in Syria's north', *Wall Street Journal* 17/2/16.

92. Naame Shaam, 'Iran in Syria'.

93. Discussed further in Chapter 6, note 12.

94. Interview with various parties to track II discussions with Iranian officials, 2014–16.

Chapter 8: No red lines: The question of Western military intervention

1. Fernande van Tets, 'Exodus: terrified Syrians dash to flee air strikes', *Independent* 1/9/13.

2. The White House's preliminary estimation of 1,429 was the highest made by non-Syrian sources; British and French estimations were lower. 'Government assessment of the Syrian government's use of chemical weapons on August 21, 2013', White House 30/8/13, https://www.whitehouse.gov/the-press-office/2013/08/30/government-assessment-syrian-government-s-use-chemical-weapons-august-21 [accessed 9/12/15].

3. Martin Chulov and Mona Mahmood, 'Syria's elite join compatriots to flee country fearing Western air strike', *Guardian* 27/8/13.

4. See, for example, Haroon Siddiqui, 'Bomb Assad's palaces and army barracks', *Toronto Star* 2/6/12.

5. Interview with senior British official, October 2014.

6. 'NATO rules out Syria intervention', al-Jazeera 1/11/11, http://www.aljazeera.com/news/middleeast/2011/11/201111103948699103.html [accessed 9/4/15].

7. Mark Mazzetti, Robert F. Worth and Michael R. Gordon, 'Obama's uncertain path amid Syria bloodshed', *New York Times* 22/10/13; Christopher Phillips, 'Intervention and non-intervention in the Syria crisis', in F. Kühn and M. Turner (eds), *The Politics of International Intervention* (London: Routledge, 2016).

8. Interviews with US officials, Washington, July 2014.

9. Kim Ghattas, *The Secretary: A Journey with Hillary Clinton from Beirut to the Heart of American Power* (London: Macmillan, 2013), p. 317.

10. 'Syrian army defector urges limited NATO intervention', *Atlantic Council* 16/7/12, http://www.atlanticcouncil.org/blogs/natosource/syrian-army-defector-urges-limited-nato-intervention [accessed 10/11/15].

11. Interview with Bassma Kodmani, Paris, 31/8/15.

12. Interview with Bassma Kodmani, Paris, 31/8/15; interview with Turkish official, Ankara, July 2012; interview with US official, Washington, May 2015.

13. Interview with Robert Ford, Washington, 15/6/15.

14. Bilgin Ayata, 'Turkish foreign policy in a changing Arab world: rise and fall of a regional actor?' *Journal of European Integration* 37.1 (2015).

15. Philip Robins, *Suits and Uniforms: Turkish Foreign Policy since the Cold War* (London: Hurst, 2003), pp. 45–48.

16. Jeremy Shapiro, 'The Qatar problem', *Foreign Policy* 28/8/13 – http://mideastafrica.foreignpolicy.com/posts/2013/08/28/the_qatar_problem [accessed 3/4/14].

17. Ibid.

18. 'Majority of Turks against Syria intervention: survey', *Hurriyet* 6/9/13, http://www.hurriyetdailynews.com/majority-of-turks-against-syria-intervention-survey.aspx?pageID=238&nID=53995&NewsCatID=34 [accessed 12/12/15].

19. Murat Yetkin, 'Syria intervention not off table', *Hurriyet* 12/8/11, http://www.hurriyetdailynews.com/default.aspx?pageid=438&n=syria-intervention-not-off-table-2011-08-12#.TkaR7iNMDA8.blogger [accessed 12/12/15].

20. Interview with Turkish official, Ankara, July 2012.

21. Michael R. Gordon, 'Israel airstrike targeted advanced missiles that Russia sold to Syria, U.S. says', *New York Times* 13/7/13.

22. 'UN peacekeepers withdraw from Syria-controlled sector of Golan Heights', *Middle East Eye* 15/9/14, http://www.middleeasteye.net/news/un-peacekeepers-withdrawn-syria-controlled-sector-golan-heights-819345932 [accessed 24/11/15].

23. Caroline Mortimer, 'Israel on verge of sending troops into Syria over increased threat of terrorist attack', *Independent* 17/8/15.

24. 'UN peacekeepers withdraw', *Middle East Eye*.

25. 'Iran general died in "Israeli strike" in Syrian Golan', BBC 19/1/15, http://www.bbc.co.uk/news/world-middle-east-30882935 [accessed 1/2/16].

26. Martin Chulov and Kareem Shaheen, 'Leading Hezbollah commander and key Israel target killed in Syria' *The Guardian* 13/5/16, http://www.theguardian.com/world/2016/may/13/hezbollah-commander-killed-israel-mustafa-badreddine [accessed 13/5/16]

27. Jay Solomon, 'U.S., Israel monitor suspected Syrian WMD', *Wall Street Journal*, 27/8/11; Mary Beth D. Nikitin, 'Syria's chemical weapons: issues for Congress', Congressional Research Service 30/9/13, http://www.fas.org/sgp/crs/nuke/R42848.pdf [accessed 24/11/15].

28. In March 1988 in the final days of the Iran–Iraq war, Saddam Hussein's forces dropped chemical weapons on the Iranian-occupied Iraqi-Kurdish town of Halabja, killing up to 5,000 civilians.

29. Ian Black, 'Syria insists chemical weapons would only be used against outside forces', *Guardian*, 24/7/12.

30. Kilic Bugra Kanat, *A Tale of Four Augusts: Obama's Syria Policy* (Washington, DC: SETA, 2015), p. 99.

31. Ibid., p. 103.

32. Interview with US official, Washington, August 2014; Kanat, *A Tale of Four Augusts*, p. 102.

33. 'Amateur footage emerges of Syrian jets deployed against rebels', *Telegraph* 25/7/12.

34. Some noted that this may have been the unintended consequence of Obama's red line comment – that Assad viewed all weapons below this as 'fair game'. See Michael R. Gordon and Eric Schmitt, 'Syria uses Scud missiles in new effort to push back rebels', *New York Time*,12/12/12.

35. 'Gas used in Homs leaves seven people dead and scores affected, activists say', al-Jazeera 24/12/12, http://blogs.aljazeera.com/topic/syria/gas-used-homs-leaves-seven-people-dead-and-scores-affected-activists-say [accessed 5/7/15].

36. *United Nations Mission to Investigate Allegations of the Use of Chemical Weapons in the Syrian Arab Republic Final Report*, United Nations, https://unoda-web.s3.amazonaws.com/wp-content/uploads/2013/12/report.pdf [accessed 5/7/15].

37. Ibid., p. 7.

38. See note Chapter 8, note 2.

39. 'Modern warfare', *CBRNe World* February 2014, http://www.cbrneworld.com/_uploads/download_magazines/Sellstrom_Feb_2014_v2.pdf [accessed 5/7/15].

40. Vladimir V. Putin, 'A plea for caution from Russia', *New York Times* 11/9/13.

41. *Report of the United Nations Mission to Investigate Allegations of the Use of Chemical Weapons in the Syrian Arab Republic on the alleged use of chemical weapons in the Ghouta area of Damascus on 21 August 2013*, United Nations, 16/9/13, A /67/997-S /2013/553 https://disarmament-library.un.org/UNODA/Library.nsf/780cfafd472b0477 85257b1000501037/e4d4477c9b67de9085257bf800694bd2/$FILE/A%2067% 20997-S%202013%20553.pdf [accessed 5/9/15].

42. Matezzi et al. in Kanat, *A Tale of Four Augusts*, p. 120.

43. Interview with Fred Hof, Washington, 30/7/14; Kanat, *A Tale of Four Augusts*, p. 102.

44. Interviews with US officials, Washington July–August 2014.

45. Shadi Hamid, 'Why doesn't Obama seem to listen to Syria experts?' *Brookings* 10/2/16, http://www.brookings.edu/blogs/markaz/posts/2016/02/10-obama-syria-policy-experts-hamid [accessed 1/4/16]; Marc Lynch, 'After the political science relevance revolution', *Washington Post*, 23/3/16.

46. Kanat, *A Tale of Four Augusts*, p. 104.

47. David E. Sanger and Eric Schmitt, 'Pentagon says 75,000 troops might be needed to seize Syria chemical arms', *New York Times* 15/11/12

48. John Kerry, 'Remarks on Syria', US Department of State 26/8/13, http://www.state.gov/secretary/remarks/2013/08/213503.htm [accessed 14/5/15].

49. Kanat, *A Tale of Four Augusts*, p. 122; Nina Burleigh, 'Obama vs the Hawks', *Rolling Stone* 1/4/14.

50. For a full account of the White House's deliberations see Burleigh, 'Obama vs the Hawks'.

51. Interview with UK official, February 2015.

52. For a full account see 'The Syria vote: one day in August', BBC Radio 4, 10/11/14, http://www.bbc.co.uk/programmes/b04nrqsk [accessed 14/5/15].

53. Kanat, *A Tale of Four Augusts*, p. 124.

54. Jeffrey Goldberg, 'The Obama doctrine', *Atlantic*, April 2016.

55. David Rothkopf, 'The gamble', *Foreign Policy* 31/8/13.

56. Interview with Lahkdar Brahimi, Paris, 31/8/15.

57. Arshad Mohammed, 'Kerry: Syrian surrender of chemical arms could stop U.S. attack', Reuters 9/9/13 http://www.reuters.com/article/us-syria-crisis-kerry-idUSBRE9880BV20130909 [accessed 14/6/15].

58. Julian Borger and Patrick Wintour, 'Russia calls on Syria to hand over chemical weapons', *Guardian*, 9/9/13; interview with US officials, Washington, July 2014.

59. Goldberg, 'The Obama doctrine', *Atlantic*.

60. Carlo Munoz, 'McCain, Graham: Syria deal an "act of weakness" by White House', *The Hill* 14/9/13 http://thehill.com/policy/defense/322281-syria-deal-an-act-of-weakness-by-white-house-say-senate-republicans [accessed 4/8/15]; Richard Spencer, 'Barack Obama rejects accusations of American weakness over Syria', *Telegraph* 15/9/13.

61. Burleigh, 'Obama vs the Hawks'.

62. Ibid.

63. Thomas Juneau, 'U.S. power in the Middle East: not declining', *Middle East Policy*, 21.2 (Summer 2014), 40–52; interview with various Russian officials and former officials, Moscow, November 2014.
64. Burleigh, 'Obama vs the Hawks'.
65. Goldberg, 'The Obama doctrine', *Atlantic*.
66. Ibid.
67. Colum Lynch, 'Saudis to push General Assembly vote on Syria intervention', *Foreign Policy*, 6/9/13; interview with Saudi official, Riyadh, March 2015.
68. Frank Gardner, 'Saudi Arabia flexing its muscles in Middle East', BBC 8/8/15 http://www.bbc.co.uk/news/world-middle-east-33825064 [accessed 13/10/15].
69. Richard Hall, 'Syria crisis: coalition of powerful rebel groups rejects Western-backed opposition', *Independent* 25/9/15.
70. Khaled Yacoub Oweis, 'Insight: Saudi Arabia boosts Salafist rivals to al Qaeda in Syria', Reuters 1/10/13, http://www.reuters.com/article/2013/10/01/us-syria-crisis-jihadists-insight-idUSBRE9900RO20131001 [accessed 13/10/15].
71. Interview with Turkish official, January 2015.
72. İlhan Uzgel, 'New Middle East: Turkey from being a playmaker to seclusion in the New Middle East', *Centre for Policy and Research on Turkey*, IV.1 (2015), 47–55.
73. Jeremy Shapiro, 'The Qatar problem', *Foreign Policy* 28/8/13 – http://mideastafrica.foreignpolicy.com/posts/2013/08/28/the_qatar_problem [accessed 3/4/14].
74. Bayram Balci, 'Turkey's flirtation with Syrian Jihadism', *Carnegie* 7/11/13, http://carnegieendowment.org/syriaincrisis/?fa=53532 [accessed 3/4/14].
75. Dominic Evans, 'Rebels battle for Syria border post near Mediterranean', Reuters 22/3/14, http://www.reuters.com/article/2014/03/23/us-syria-crisis-idUSBREA2L0G020140323 [accessed 24/11/15].
76. 'Syrian Regional Refugee Response', UNHCR http://data.unhcr.org/syrianrefugees/regional.php [accessed 17/12/15] [italicise if report title]

Chapter 9: Descent into chaos: Stalemate and the rise of ISIS

1. Alistair Horne, *The Savage War of Peace: Algeria 1954–1962* (New York: New York Review Book Classics, 2006 [1977]), p. 518.
2. 'The boy killed for an off-hand remark about Muhammad – Sharia spreads in Syria', BBC 2/7/13 http://www.bbc.co.uk/news/world-middle-east-23139784 [accessed 14/1/15].
3. Interview with Lahkdar Brahimi, Paris, 31/8/15.
4. Richard Spencer, 'Syria: Bashar al-Assad agrees "in principle" to head to peace conference', *Telegraph* 24/5/13.
5. Roland Dannreuther, 'Russia and the Arab Spring: supporting the counter-revolution', *Journal of European Integration* 37.1 (2015), 77–94.
6. 'Syrian National Coalition agrees Geneva talks position', BBC 11/11/13, http://www.bbc.co.uk/news/world-middle-east-24894536 [accessed 22/6/15].
7. Interview with Robert Ford, Washington, 15/6/15.
8. 'Islamist rebels reject "hollow" Syria peace talks', *Daily Star* 20/1/14.
9. Mahmood Monshipouri and Manochehr Dorraj, 'Iran's foreign policy: a shifting strategic landscape', *Middle East Policy*, 20.4 (Winter 2013), 133–147.
10. Kim Sengupta, 'Syria peace talks: John Kerry leads calls for removal of President Bashar al-Assad', *Independent* 22/1/14 http://www.independent.co.uk/news/world/middle-east/syria-un-peace-talks-syrian-foreign-minister-calls-opposition-fighters-traitors-9076574.html [accessed 30/8/15]. [check: online title different]
11. David E. Cunningham, 'Blocking resolution: how external states can prolong civil wars', *Journal of Peace Research* 47.2 (2010), 115–127.
12. 'Gulf ambassadors pulled from Qatar over "interference"', BBC 5/3/14 http://www.bbc.co.uk/news/world-middle-east-26447914 [accessed 12/7/15].
13. Glen Greenwald, 'How former Treasury officials and the UAE are manipulating American journalists', *The Intercept* 25/9/14 https://theintercept.com/2014/09/25/uae-qatar-camstoll-group/.

14. Erika Solomon 'Betrayal and disarray behind Syrian rebel rout in Yabroud', *Financial Times* 21/3/14.

15. Robert Mason, 'Back to realism for an enduring U.S.–Saudi relationship', *Middle East Policy* 21.4 (Winter 2014), 32–44.

16. Numerous conversations with Western and regional officials.

17. David B. Ottoway, 'The struggle for power in Saudi Arabia', *Foreign Policy* 19/6/13; Mason, 'Back to realism'.

18. Simon Mabon, *Saudi Arabia and Iran: Soft Power Rivalry in the Middle East* (London: I..B Tauris, 2013), p. 129.

19. David D. Kirkpatrick, 'Muslim Brotherhood says Qatar ousted its members', *New York Times* 13/9/14, http://www.nytimes.com/2014/09/14/world/middleeast/bowing-to-pressure-qatar-asks-some-muslim-brotherhood-leaders-to-leave.html?_r=2 [accessed 20/5/15].

20. Abboud, *Syria* [Kindle edition] L2001.

21. Liz Sly, 'How Saddam Hussein's former military officers and spies are controlling Isis', *Independent* 5/4/15.

22. Patrick Cockburn, *The Rise of Islamic State: ISIS and the New Sunni Revolution* (London: Verso Books, 2015) [Kindle edition] L536.

23. Fred Lawson, 'Implications of the 2011–13 Syrian uprising for the Middle Eastern Regional Security Complex', *Georgetown Papers,* 2014.

24. Michael Weiss and Hassan Hassan, *Isis: Inside the Army of Terror* (New York: Regan Arts, 2015) [Kindle edition] L2824.

25. Estimates by the Syrian Observatory of Human Rights.

26. Weiss and Hassan, *Isis* [Kindle edition] L2680.

27. Daveed Gartenstein-Ross, 'Islamic State vs. Al-Qaeda', Foundation for the Defence of Democracies 4/12/15, http://www.defenddemocracy.org/media-hit/gartenstein-ross-daveed-islamic-state-vs-al-qaeda/ [accessed 17/12/15].

28. Fred H. Lawson, 'Syria's mutating civil war and its impact on Turkey, Iraq and Iran', *International Affairs* 90.6. 2014, 1351–1365.

29. Ibid.

30. Rim Turkmani, 'Countering the logic of the war economy in Syria; evidence from three local areas', *Security in Transition Report for the London School of Economics* 30/7/15, http://www.securityintransition.org/wp-content/uploads/2015/08/Countering-war-economy-Syria2.pdf [accessed 12/11/15],

31. Ben Hubbard, Clifford Kraus and Eric Schmitt, 'Rebels in Syria claim control of resources', *New York Times* 28/1/14.

32. David Butter, *Syria's Economy: Picking up the Pieces*, Chatham House Research Paper, June (2015).

33. Ibid.

34. Cockburn, *The Rise of Islamic State* [Kindle edition] L235.

35. Lauren Williams, 'Syrians adjust to life under ISIS rule', *Daily Star* 30/8/14.

36. Cockburn, *The Rise of Islamic State* [Kindle edition] L431.

37. Lister, *The Syrian Jihad*, p. 34.

38. Ruth Sherlock, 'Exclusive interview: why I defected from Bashar al-Assad's regime, by former diplomat Nawaf Fares', *Telegraph* 14/7/12.

39. Weiss and Hassan, *Isis* [Kindle edition] L1521.

40. Lister, *The Syrian Jihad*, pp. 32–47.

41. Ibid., L3178.

42. Butter, 'Syria's economy'.

43. Ruth Sherlock and Richard Spencer, 'Syria's Assad accused of boosting al-Qaeda with secret oil deals', *Telegraph* 20/1/14.

44. Discussed in Chapter 7, see p. 151

45. 'Bashar al-Assad wins re-election in Syria as uprising against him rages on', *Guardian* 4/6/14.

46. Weiss and Hassan, *Isis* [Kindle edition] L3159.

47. Butter, 'Syria's economy'.

48. Cockburn, *The Rise of Islamic State* [Kindle edition] L374.

49. Lauren Williams, 'Syria's Alawites not deserting Assad yet, despite crackdown', *Middle East Eye* 11/9/14, http://www.middleeasteye.net/in-depth/features/syrias-alawites-not-deserting-assad-yet-despite-crackdown-526622504 [accessed 12/4/15].

50. Christopher Kozak, '"An army in all corners": Assad's campaign strategy in Syria'. *Institute for the Study of War*, April 2015, p. 13, http://www.understandingwar.org/sites/default/files/An%20Army%20in%20All%20Corners%20by%20Chris%20Kozak%201.pdf [accessed 7/7/15].

51. Nicholas Watt, 'Tony Blair makes qualified apology for Iraq war ahead of Chilcot report', *Guardian* 25/10/15, http://www.theguardian.com/uk-news/2015/oct/25/tony-blair-sorry-iraq-war-mistakes-admits-conflict-role-in-rise-of-isis [accessed 4/8/15].

52. Emma Sky, *The Unraveling* (New York: Public Affairs, 2015), pp. 329–344.

53. Toby Dodge, *Iraq: From War to a New Authoritarianism* (London: Routledge, 2013), p. 116.

54. 'Isis captured 2,300 Humvee armoured vehicles from Iraqi forces in Mosul', *Guardian* 1/6/15.

55. 'Department of Defense Information Report, Not Finally Evaluated Intelligence – Iraq' 3/7/12 http://www.judicialwatch.org/wp-content/uploads/2015/05/Pg.-291-Pgs.-287-293-JW-v-DOD-and-State-14-812-DOD-Release-2015-04-10-final-version11.pdf [accessed 4/8/15].

56. Steve Contorno, 'What Obama said about Islamic State as a "JV" team', *Politifact* 7/9/14, http://www.politifact.com/truth-o-meter/statements/2014/sep/07/barack-obama/what-obama-said-about-islamic-state-jv-team/ [accessed 14/10/15].

57. Cockburn, *The Rise of Islamic State* [Kindle edition] L755.

58. Janice Dickson, 'Turkey turns blind eye to ISIS fighters using its hospitals: sources', *Ipolitics* 27/5/15, http://ipolitics.ca/2015/07/27/turkey-turns-blind-eye-to-isis-fighters-using-its-hospitals-sources/ accessed 14/10/15].

59. Fazel Hawramy and Luke Harding, 'Inside Islamic State's oil empire: how captured oilfields fuel Isis insurgency', *Guardian* 19/11/14 http://www.theguardian.com/world/2014/nov/19/-sp-islamic-state-oil-empire-iraq-isis [accessed 14/2/15]; Butter, 'Syria's economy'.

60. Christopher M. Blanchard, *Qatar: Background and US Relations*, Congressional Research Service paper, 4/11/14, http://www.fas.org/sgp/crs/mideast/RL31718.pdf [accessed 6/5/15].

61. Cockburn, *The Rise of Islamic State* [Kindle edition] L137; Evan Osnos, The Biden agenda', *New Yorker* 28/7/14.

62. Ewan Stein, 'Modalities of Jihadist activism in the Middle East and North Africa', *IEMed Mediterranean Yearbook 2015*, http://www.iemed.org/observatori/arees-danalisi/arxius-adjunts/anuari/med.2015/IEMed%20Yearbook%202015_JihadismMENA_EwanStein.pdf [accessed 12/12/15].

63. Cockburn, *The Rise of Islamic State* [Kindle edition] L181.

64. Stephane Lacroix, *Saudi Islamists and the Arab Spring*, Kuwait Programme on Development, Governance and Globalisation in the Gulf States, Research Paper 36, May 2014, http://eprints.lse.ac.uk/56725/1/Lacroix_Saudi-Islamists-and-theArab-Spring_2014.pdf [accessed 12/8/15].

65. Michael Weiss, 'Russia is sending Jihadis to join ISIS', *Daily Beast* 23/8/15, http://www.thedailybeast.com/articles/2015/08/23/russia-s-playing-a-double-game-with-islamic-terror0.html [accessed 2/3/16].

66. Lister, *The Syrian Jihad*.

67. Mason, 'Back to realism'.

68. Dina Esfandiary and Ariane Tabatabai, 'Iran's ISIS policy', *International Affairs* 91.1 (2015), 1–15.

69. Marc Lynch, 'Obama and the Middle East', *Foreign Affairs* September/October 2015,.

70. Ibid.

71. 'Strikes in Syria and Iraq', *Operation Inherent Resolve – US Department of Defense* http://www.defense.gov/News/Special-Reports/0814_Inherent-Resolve [accessed 28/3/15].

72. 'Foreign fighters: an updated assessment of the flow of foreign fighters into Syria and Iraq', *The Soufan group* 8/12/15 http://soufangroup.com/foreign-fighters/ [accessed 12/12/15].

73. Alireza Nader, 'Iran & Region III: goals in Syria', *The Iran Primer* 26/1/15, http://iranprimer.usip.org/blog/2015/jan/26/iran-region-iii-goals-syria [accessed 10/10/15]; İlhan Uzgel, 'New Middle East: Turkey from being a playmaker to seclusion in the new Middle East', *Centre for Policy and Research on Turkey*, IV.1 (2015), 47–55.

74. Interview with US official, Washington, May 2015.

75. Austin Wright and Philip Ewing, 'Carter's unwelcome news: only 60 Syrian rebels fit for training', *Politico* 7/7/15, http://www.politico.com/story/2015/07/ash-carter-syrian-rebel-training-119812 [accessed 23/11/15].

76. Lister, *The Syrian Jihad*, pp. 322–338.

77. Ibid., p. 382.

78. Frederic Hof, Bassma Kodmani and Jeffery White, 'Setting the stage for peace in Syria: the case for a Syrian National Stabilization Force', *Atlantic Council*, 14/4/15.

79. Fred Lawson, 'Implications of the 2011–13 Syrian uprising for the Middle Eastern Regional Security Complex', *Georgetown Papers*, 2014.

80. Thomas McGee 'Mapping action and identity in the Kobani crisis response', *Kurdish Studies Journal*, 4.1 (2016): 51–77.

81. Interview with US official, Washington, May 2015.

82. Aron Lund, 'The ten most important developments in Syria in 2015', *Syria Comment* 3/1/16, http://www.joshualandis.com/blog/ten-most-important-developments-syria-2015/ [accessed 12/3/16].

Chapter 10: Enter Russia: Putin raises the stakes

1. 'Vladimir Putin: supporting Syrian regime only way to end war', *Telegraph* 25/9/16.

2. 'BBC inside airbase where Russia carries out Syria airstrikes', BBC 11/11/15, http://www.bbc.co.uk/news/world-europe-34790153 [accessed 20/1/16]; 'Russia 'plans forward air operating base in Syria – US' BBC 14/9/15, http://www.bbc.co.uk/news/world-middle-east-34252810 [accessed 10/3/16].

3. Ed Payne, Barbara Starr and Susannah Cullinane, 'Russia launches first airstrikes in Syria', CNN 1/10/15, http://edition.cnn.com/2015/09/30/politics/russia-syria-airstrikes-isis/index.html [accessed 10/3/16].

4. 'Inside Russian airbase launching Syria strikes', BBC 20/1/16, http://www.bbc.co.uk/news/world-europe-35365747 [accessed 10/2/16].

5. Lister, *The Syrian Jihad*, p. 338.

6. Ibid., pp. 339–342.

7. Ibid., p. 349.

8. Ibid., p. 344.

9. Aron Lund, 'The death of Rustum Ghazaleh', *Syria in Crisis* for Carnegie Endowment for International Peace http://carnegieendowment.org/syriaincrisis/?fa=59953 [accessed 10/3/16].

10. *New Approach in Southern Syria*, International Crisis Group Middle East Report no. 163, 2 September 2015, http://www.crisisgroup.org/~/media/Files/Middle%20East%20North%20Africa/Iraq%20Syria%20Lebanon/Syria/163-new-approach-in-southern-syria.pdf [accessed 15/3/16].

11. Ibid.

12. Haid Haid, 'The Southern Front: allies without a strategy', *Heinrich Böll Stiftung*, 21/8/15, http://lb.boell.org/en/2015/08/21/southern-front-allies-without-strategy [accessed 10/3/16].

13. Aron Lund, 'The ten most important developments in Syria in 2015', *Syria Comment* 3/1/16, http://www.joshualandis.com/blog/ten-most-important-developments-syria-2015/ [accessed 12/3/16].

14. Lister, *The Syrian Jihad*, pp. 360–363.

15. Robert S. Ford and Ali El Yassir, 'Yes, talk with Syria's Ahrar al-Sham', *Middle East Institute* 15/7/15, http://www.mei.edu/content/at/yes-talk-syria%E2%80%99s-ahrar-al-sham [accessed 10/2/16].

16. Lister, *The Syrian Jihad*, p. 343; Fabrice Balanche, 'How to prevent al-Qaeda from Seizing a Safe Zone in Northwestern Syria', *The Washington Institute* 7/3/16, http://www. washingtoninstitute.org/policy-analysis/view/how-to-prevent-al-qaeda-from-seizing-a-safe-zone-in-northwestern-syria#.Vt4AZPz_zRA.twitter [accessed 15/3/16]

17. Lister, *The Syrian Jihad*, p. 372; Josh Rogin, 'U.S. shoots down idea of Syria Safe Zone', *Bloomberg View* 28/7/15, http://www.bloombergview.com/articles/2015–07–28/u-s-shoots-down-idea-of-syria-safe-zone [accessed 10/3/16].

18. 'Assad admits "setbacks" in war against Syrian rebels', al-Jazeera, 6/5/15, http://www. aljazeera.com/news/2015/05/150506185408811.html [accessed 10/2/16].

19. Maher Samaan and Anne Barnard, 'Assad, in rare admission, says Syria's army lacks manpower', *New York Times* 26/7/15.

20. Laila Bassam and Tom Perry, 'How Iranian general plotted out Syrian assault in Moscow', Reuters 6/10/15, http://www.reuters.com/article/us-mideast-crisis-syria-soleimani-insigh-idUSKCN0S02BV20151006 [accessed 11/2/16].

21. 'Russo-Syrian agreement allows permanent stationing of Russian airbase on Syrian soil', *Info News* 14/1/16, http://info-news.eu/russo-syrian-agreement-allows-permanent-stationing-of-russian-air-base-on-syrian-soil/ [accessed 10/3/16].

22. Lizzie Dearden, 'Russia joins fight against Isis: parliament approves Vladimir Putin's request for military intervention', *Independent*, 30/9/15. parliament-approves-vladimir-putins-request-for-military-a6673091.html [accessed 15/3/16]

23. Kathrin Hille, Geoff Dyer, Demetri Sevastopulo and Erika Solomon, 'Russian air strikes on Syrian targets raise "grave concerns" in US', *Financial Times* 30/9/15.

24. Roland Oliphant, Harriet Alexander and David Blair, 'Russian general tells US diplomats: "We launch Syria air strikes in one hour. Stay out of the way"', *Telegraph* 30/9/15

25. Chris Kozak, 'Regime and Iranian forces launch multip offensive in Aleppo', Institute for the Study of War, 22/10/15 http://understandingwar.org/map/regime-and-iranian-forces-launch-multi-pronged-offensive-aleppo#sthash.p4mP44mf.dpuf [accessed 11/3/16].

26. Lund, 'The ten most important developments', *Syria Comment*.

27. Hossein Bastani, 'Iran quietly deepens involvement in Syria's war', BBC 20/10/15, http:// www.bbc.co.uk/news/world-middle-east-34572756 [accessed 11/3/16].

28. 'Russia delivers humanitarian aid to Syria', *RT* 24/2/16, https://www.rt.com/ in-motion/333520-russia-syria-humanitarian-aid/ [accessed 10/3/16].

29. Aron Lund, 'After Palmyra, where next for Assad?' *Syria in Crisis* for Carnegie Endowment for International Peace 31/3/16, http://carnegieendowment.org/syriaincrisis/?fa=63201 [accessed 1/4/16].

30. Genevieve Casagrande, Christopher Kozak and Jennifer Cafarella, 'Syria 90 day forecast: the Assad regime and Allies in northern Syria', Institute for the Study of War 24/2/16, http://understandingwar.org/sites/default/files/Syria%2090%20Day%20 Forecast%2024%20FEB%202016(1).pdf [accessed 11/3/16].

31. Ibid.

32. Dimitri Trenin, 'Putin's Syria gambit aims at something bigger than Syria', *Tablet* 13/10/15, http://www.tabletmag.com/jewish-news-and-politics/194109/putin-syria-trenin [accessed 24/2/16].

33. Fred Weir, 'In Georgia, Russia saw its army's shortcomings', *Christian Science Monitor* 10/10/08, http://www.csmonitor.com/World/Europe/2008/1010/p01s01-woeu. html [accessed 10/2/16].

34. Lister, *The Syrian Jihad*, pp. 3 and 75; Trenin, 'Putin's Syria gambit', *Tablet*.

35. Ibid.

36. Hazel Torres, 'Russian Orthodox Church supports Putin's "holy war" in Syria to protect Christians', *Christian Today* 2/10/15,http://www.christiantoday.com/article/russian. orthodox.church.supports.putins.holy.war.in.syria.to.protect.christians/66312.htm [accessed 10/2/16].

37. Trenin, 'Putin's Syria gambit', *Tablet*; Ray Nothstine, 'Syrian President Assad: Putin is the only world leader protecting Christians', *Christian Post* 20/11/15, http://www.christianpost.com/news/syria-assad-putin-only-world-leader-protecting-christians-150472/ [accessed 10/2/16].

38. Peter Hobson, 'Calculating the cost of Russia's war in Syria', *Moscow Times* 20/10/15,http://www.themoscowtimes.com/business/article/calculating-the-cost-of-russias-war-in-syria/540015.html [accessed 10/3/16].

39. Ibid.

40. Alec Luhn, 'Russia's campaign in Syria leads to arms sale windfall', *Guardian* 29/3/16.

41. James O'Toole, 'Billions at stake as Russia backs Syria', CNN, 10/2/12, http://money.cnn.com/2012/02/09/news/international/russia_syria/ [accessed 10/3/16].

42. Peter Beaumont, 'Netanyahu meets Putin to discuss concerns over Russian activity in Syria', *Guardian* 21/9/15.

43. Trenin, 'Putin's Syria gambit', *Tablet*.

44. Dmitri Trenin, 'Turkish-Russian war of words goes beyond downed plane', al-Jazeera America 9/12/15, http://america.aljazeera.com/articles/2015/12/9/turkey-russian-relationship-felled-by-more-than-a-downed-jet.html [accessed 10/3/16].

45. Selin Girit, 'Turkey faces big losses as Russia sanctions bite', *BBC* 2/1/16, http://www.bbc.co.uk/news/world-europe-35209987 [accessed 10/3/16].

46. Trenin, 'Putin's Syria gambit', *Tablet*.

47. Noah Bonsey, 'More Chechnya, less Afghanistan', *Foreign Policy*, 12/10/15.

48. Trenin, 'Putin's Syria gambit', *Tablet*.

49. Ibid.

50. 'Europe: Syrian asylum applications', *UNHCR Syrian Regional Refugees Response* http://data.unhcr.org/syrianrefugees/asylum.php [accessed 15/12/15].

51. 'Engaging with Assad a "lesser evil", Spain says after Paris attacks', *Daily Star* 18/11/15.

52. Laura Rozen, 'On eve of Syria peace talks, Saudi Arabia questions Russian, Iranian intentions', *Al-Monitor* 28/10/15, http://www.al-monitor.com/pulse/originals/2015/10/us-welcome-iran-syria-peace-talks.html# [accessed 12/3/16].

53. Louisa Loveluck, 'Assad can stay in power "three months or longer", says Hammond', *Telegraph* 4/10/15.

54. Matthew Lee and Bradley Klapper, 'Assad can stay, for now: Kerry accepts Russian stance', Associated Press 15/12/15, http://news.yahoo.com/kerry-moscow-talks-syria-ukraine-081842398.html [accessed 10/2/16].

55. 'Final declaration on the results of the Syria talks in Vienna as agreed by participants', *European Union External Action* 30/10/15, http://eeas.europa.eu/statements-eeas/2015/151030_06.htm [accessed 10/2/16].

56. 'Statement of the International Syria Support Group', US Department of State 14/11/15, http://www.state.gov/r/pa/prs/ps/2015/11/249511.htm [accessed 10/3/16].

57. Aron Lund, 'Syria's opposition conferences: results and expectations', *Syria in Crisis* for Carnegie Endowment for International Peace 11/12/15,http://carnegieendowment.org/syriaincrisis/?fa=62263 [accessed 10/3/16].

58. Aaron Stein, 'Turkey's two-front war', *The American Interest* 4/2/16, http://www.the-american-interest.com/2016/02/04/turkeys-two-front-war/ [accessed 10/3/16].

59. Aron Lund, 'Syria's Kurds at the center of America's anti-Jihadi strategy', *Syria in Crisis* for Carnegie Endowment for International Peace 2/12/15, http://carnegieendowment.org/syriaincrisis/?fa=62158 [accessed 10/3/16].

60. Lund, 'Syria's opposition conferences'.

61. Aron Lund, 'The road to Geneva: the who, when, and how of Syria's peace talks', *Syria in Crisis* for Carnegie Endowment for International Peace 29/1/16, http://carnegieendowment.org/syriaincrisis/?fa=62631[accessed 10/3/16].

62. Ibid.

63. 'Syria conflict: UN suspends peace talks in Geneva', BBC 3/2/16, http://www.bbc.co.uk/news/world-middle-east-35488073 [accessed 10/3/16].

64. Tim Walker, 'Syria civil war: staff manning US ceasefire hotline "can't speak Arabic"', *Independent* 3/3/16

65. 'Syria war: John Kerry says violence drastically reduced', al-Jazeera 12/3/16, http://www.aljazeera.com/news/2016/03/syria-war-john-kerry-violence-drastically-reduced-160312082042884.html [accessed 10/3/16].

66. 'Civilian deaths drop to four-year low after Syria truce: monitor', AFP 27/3/16, http://news.yahoo.com/civilian-deaths-drop-four-low-syria-truce-monitor-182900708.html [accessed 29/3/16].

67. Thanassis Cambanis, 'The Syrian revolution against al Qaeda', Foreign Policy 29/3/16 http://foreignpolicy.com/2016/03/29/the-syrian-revolution-against-al-qaeda-jabhat-al-nusra-fsa/ [accessed 31/3/16].

68. 'Syria war: John Kerry says violence drastically reduced', al-Jazeera.

69. 'Putin discusses Syria ceasefire with world leaders by phone', RT 24/2/16,https://www.rt.com/news/333481-putin-assad-syria-ceasefire/ [accessed 10/3/16].

70. 'Putin orders start of Russian military withdrawal from Syria, says "objectives achieved"', RT 14/3/16, https://www.rt.com/news/335554-putin-orders-syria-withdrawal/ [accessed 31/3/16].

71. Aron Lund, 'Interpreting the Russian withdrawal from Syria', Syria in Crisis for Carnegie Endowment for International Peace, http://carnegieendowment.org/syriaincrisis/?fa=63042 [accessed 25/3/16].

Chapter 11: The Wild Card: Syria's war in the age of Trump

1. Nicholas Fandos, 'Trump's View of Syria: How It Evolved, in 19 Tweets', New York Times 7/4/17.

2. Julian Borger, 'Donald Trump's response to Syria gas attack: blame Obama', Guardian 5/4/17, https://www.theguardian.com/world/2017/apr/04/syria-gas-attack-trump-us-foreign-policy [accessed 1/8/17].

3. According to the Violations Documentation Center in Syria, in the month before the cessation there were 1,635 recorded fatalities; this dropped to 868 for 26 February–26 March 2016, then rose to 1,250 the month afterwards, and 1,271 the month after that. http://www.vdc-sy.info/index.php/en/martyrs [accessed 12/8/17].

4. DW, 'Syrian opposition walks out of Geneva peace talks', DW 20/4/16, http://www.dw.com/en/syrian-opposition-walks-out-of-geneva-peace-talks/a-19200135 [accessed 10/8/17].

5. Dave Boyer, 'Problems mount for Obama in Syria, Iraq', Washington Times, 21/4/16, http://www.washingtontimes.com/news/2016/apr/21/problems-mount-obama-syria-iraq/ [accessed 12/8/17].

6. The White House, 'Press Conference by President Obama in Lima, Peru', The White House Office of the Press Secretary 20/11/16, https://obamawhitehouse.archives.gov/the-press-office/2016/11/20/press-conference-president-obama-lima-peru [accessed 10/8/17].

7. Kristina Wong, 'Ex-NATO supreme commander: Obama will look back in 'shame' on Syria', The Hill 14/14/16, http://thehill.com/policy/defense/310343-ex-nato-supreme-commander-obama-will-look-back-in-some-shame-on-syria [accessed 15/7/17]; Natalie Nougayrède, 'The devastation of Syria will be Obama's legacy', Guardian 22/9/16, https://www.theguardian.com/commentisfree/2016/sep/22/syria-obama-us-president-putin-russia [accessed 20/7/17].

8. Discussions with Turkish officials in Ankara and Istanbul, June 2016; Leela Jacinto, 'Turkey's Post-Coup Purge and Erdogan's Private Army', Foreign Policy 13/7/17, http://foreignpolicy.com/2017/07/13/turkeys-post-coup-purge-and-erdogans-private-army-sadat-perincek-gulen/ [accessed 10/8/17].

9. Amana Fontanella-Khan, 'Fethullah Gülen: Turkey coup may have been 'staged' by Erdoğan regime', Guardian 16/7/16, https://www.theguardian.com/world/2016/jul/16/fethullah-gulen-turkey-coup-erdogan [accessed 10/8/17].

10. Kareem Shaheen, 'One year after the failed coup in Turkey, the crackdown continues', Guardian 14/7/17, https://www.theguardian.com/world/2017/jul/14/one-year-after-the-failed-coup-in-turkey-the-crackdown-continues [accessed 15/8/17].

11. Haid Haid, 'Did Turkey abandon Aleppo to fight Syrian Kurds?' *Now* 4/10/16, https://now.mmedia.me/lb/en/commentaryanalysis/567401-did-turkey-abandon-aleppo-to-fight-the-syrian-kurds [accessed 10/8/17].

12. RT, '"Blatant violation of sovereignty": Damascus condemns Turkish operation in Jarablus', *RT* 24/8/16 https://www.rt.com/news/357060-syria-condemn-turkey-operation/ [accessed 5/8/17].

13. al-Jazeera, 'Erdogan: Turkish army will press on to ISIL-held Raqqa', *al-Jazeera* 12/2/17, http://www.aljazeera.com/news/2017/02/erdogan-turkish-troops-isil-bastion-al-bab-170212115151375.html [accessed 10/8/17].

14. Haid, 'Did Turkey abandon Aleppo'.

15. Patrick Wintour, 'Russian aircraft carrier is more a show of force than "start of world war"', *Guardian* 20/10/16, https://www.theguardian.com/world/2016/oct/20/russian-fleet-aircraft-carrier-admiral-kuznetsov-syria [accessed 10/8/17].

16. Martin Chulov, 'Pro-Assad forces seize third of east Aleppo in rapid advance', *Guardian* 28/11/16, https://www.theguardian.com/world/2016/nov/28/pro-assad-forces-seize-third-of-east-aleppo-in-rapid-advance-syria [accessed 15/8/17].

17. al-Jazeera, 'Scores killed as Syrian jets pound rebel-held Aleppo', *al-Jazeera* 23/9/16, http://www.aljazeera.com/news/2016/09/scores-killed-syrian-jets-pound-rebel-held-aleppo-160923134637232.html [accessed 15/8/17].

18. Lisa Barrington and Tom Perry, 'Syrian army captures part of rebel-held east Aleppo', *Reuters* 26/11/16, https://www.reuters.com/article/us-mideast-crisis-syria-aleppo-idUSKBN13L0KR [accessed 10/8/15].

19. Reuters Staff, '4,000 fighters have left Aleppo in latest stage, thousands await evacuation: Red Cross', *Reuters* 22/12/16, https://www.reuters.com/article/us-mideast-crisis-syria-aleppo-redcross-idUSKBN14B14O [accessed 10/8/17]; Reuters Staff, 'U.N. Syria envoy says rebel city Idlib risks Aleppo fate if no peace talks', *Reuters* 15/12/16, https://www.reuters.com/article/us-mideast-crisis-syria-demistura-idUSKBN1442N1 [accessed 10/8/17].

20. AFP, 'Hundreds of civilians, rebels evacuated from Aleppo', *AFP* 16/12/16, https://www.dawn.com/news/1302622/hundreds-of-civilians-rebels-evacuated-from-aleppo [accessed 15/8/17].

21. BBC, 'Aleppo battle ends as Syria rebel deal reached', *BBC* 13/12/16, http://www.bbc.co.uk/news/world-middle-east-38308883 [accessed 7/8/17].

22. Erika Solomon, 'Syria: a tale of three cities', *Financial Times* 3/8/17, https://www.ft.com/content/6710ab2a-7716-11e7-90c0-90a9d1bc9691 [accessed 10/8/17].

23. BBC, 'Syria conflict: Clashes reported despite truce', *BBC* 30/12/16, http://www.bbc.co.uk/news/world-middle-east-38463021 [accessed 10/8/17].

24. Patrick Wintour, 'Russia in power-broking role as Syria peace talks begin in Astana', *Guardian* 23/1/17, https://www.theguardian.com/world/2017/jan/22/russia-syria-talks-astana-kazakhstan- [accessed 6/8/17].

25. Sam Heller, 'Geneva Peace Talks Won't Solve Syria—So Why Have Them?' The Century Foundation 30/6/17, https://tcf.org/content/report/geneva-peace-talks-wont-solve-syria/ [accessed 6/8/17].

26. Stephen Sestanovich, 'The Brilliant Incoherence of Trump's Foreign Policy', *Atlantic* May 2017, https://www.theatlantic.com/magazine/archive/2017/05/the-brilliant-incoherence-of-trumps-foreign-policy/521430/ [accessed 1/8/17]; Bret Stephens, 'Trump's Foreign Policy: The Conservatives' Report Card', *The New York Times* 21/7/17, https://www.nytimes.com/2017/07/21/opinion/trumps-foreign-policy-the-conservatives-report-card.html [accessed 4/8/17].

27. Elliott Abrams, 'Trump the Traditionalist', *Foreign Affairs* 96:4 July/August 2017: 10–16.

28. Ibid.

29. David Frum, 'The Death Knell for America's Global Leadership', *Atlantic* 31/5/17, https://www.theatlantic.com/international/archive/2017/05/mcmaster-cohn-trump/528609/ [accessed 12/8/17].

30. Abrams, 'Trump the Traditionalist'.

31. F. Gregory Gause, 'The Trump Administration and the Middle East', *The International Security Studies Forum* 14/8/17, https://issforum.org/roundtables/policy/1-5AV-Middle East [accessed 20/8/17].

32. Stephen Walt, 'This Isn't Realpolitik. This Is Amateur Hour', *Foreign Policy* 3/5/17, http://foreignpolicy.com/2017/05/03/this-isnt-realpolitik-this-is-amateur-hour/ [accessed 20/8/17].

33. Julian Borger, 'US rebukes Saudi Arabia over Qatar embargo in reversal after Trump comments', *Guardian* 20/6/17, https://www.theguardian.com/world/2017/jun/20/us-saudi-arabia-qatar-embargo-trump [accessed 10/8/17].

34. Rebecca Friedman Lissner and Micah Zenko, 'There Is No Trump Doctrine, and There Will Never Be One', *Foreign Policy* 21/7/17, http://foreignpolicy.com/2017/07/21/there-is-no-trump-doctrine-and-there-will-never-be-one-grand-strategy/ [accessed 15/8/17].

35. Fred Kaplan, 'Whatever Happened to the Plan to Defeat ISIS?' *Slate* 8/5/17, http://www.slate.com/articles/news_and_politics/war_stories/2017/05/trump_has_been_given_a_plan_to_defeat_isis_why_isn_t_he_acting_on_it.html [accessed 15/8/17].

36. Caroline Mortimer, 'Donald Trump's campaign against Isis results in nearly as many civilian deaths as during Obama's entire administration', *The Independent* 17/7/17, http://www.independent.co.uk/news/world/middle-east/donald-trump-syria-death-toll-campaign-military-operations-barack-obama-administration-a7844526.html [accessed 17/8/17]; Airwars, 'Civilian and "friendly fire" casualties', *Airwars*, https://airwars.org/civilian-casualty-claims/ [accessed 10/8/17].

37. David Kenner and Molly O'Toole, 'The Race to Raqqa Could Cost Trump Turkey', *Foreign Policy* 21/3/17, http://foreignpolicy.com/2017/03/21/the-race-to-raqqa-could-cost-trump-turkey/ [accessed 2/8/17].

38. Michael R. Gordon and Eric Schmitt, 'Trump to Arm Syrian Kurds, Even as Turkey Strongly Objects', *New York Times* 9/5/17, https://www.nytimes.com/2017/05/09/us/politics/trump-kurds-syria-army.html [accessed 5/8/17].

39. Ragip Soylu, 'Turkish officials say they didn't reveal secret US bases in Syria', *Daily Sabah* 21/7/17, https://www.dailysabah.com/war-on-terror/2017/07/21/turkish-officials-say-they-didnt-reveal-secret-us-bases-in-syria [accessed 5/8/17].

40. Interviews with US officials, Washington DC, February 2017; Eric Schmitt, 'Obama Administration Considers Arming Syrian Kurds Against ISIS', *New York Times* 21/9/17, https://www.nytimes.com/2016/09/22/world/middleeast/obama-syria-kurds-isis-turkey-military-commandos.html?mcubz=0 [accessed 16/8/17].

41. Michael Crowley, 'Trump's praise of Russia, Iran and Assad regime riles GOP experts', *Politico* 10/10/16, http://www.politico.com/story/2016/10/trump-praise-russia-iran-assad-criticism-229546 [accessed 16/8/17].

42. Reuters, 'Benjamin Netanyahu to discuss "bad" Iran nuclear deal with Donald Trump', *Guardian* 4/12/16, https://www.theguardian.com/world/2016/dec/04/benjamin-netan-yahu-donald-trump-iran-nuclear-deal [accessed 1/8/17].

43. Telegraph reporters, 'Donald Trump's Saudi Arabia speech: eight key points', *The Telegraph* 21/5/17, http://www.telegraph.co.uk/news/2017/05/21/donald-trumps-saudi-arabia-speech-eight-key-points/ [accessed 15/8/17].

44. Richard Wolffe, 'How Trump's foreign policy threatens to make America weak again', *Guardian* 2/7/17, https://www.theguardian.com/us-news/2017/jul/02/donald-trump-foreign-policy-diplomacy [accessed 1/8/17].

45. Reuters, 'Russia and China veto UN resolution to impose sanctions on Syria', *Guardian* 1/3/17, https://www.theguardian.com/world/2017/mar/01/russia-and-china-veto-un-resolution-to-impose-sanctions-on-syria [accessed 15/8/17].

46. Andrew Buncombe, 'Trump orders missile strike on Syria after chemical weapon attack on civilians', *The Independent* 7/4/17, http://www.independent.co.uk/news/world/americas/us-tomahawk-missiles-syria-reports-latest-donald-trump-homs-bashar-al-assad-russia-a7671411.html [accessed 15/8/17].

47. CNN, 'Zakaria: Trump just became president', *CNN Politics* 7/4/17, http://edition.cnn.com/videos/politics/2017/04/07/fareed-zakaria-trump-became-president-syria-newday.cnn [accessed 15/8/17].

48. Julian Borger, David Smith and Jennifer Rankin, 'Syria chemical attack has changed my view of Assad, says Trump', *Guardian* 6/4/17, https://www.theguardian.com/us-news/2017/apr/05/syria-chemical-gas-attack-donald-trump-nikki-haley-assad [accessed 5/8/17].

49. Guardian, 'No peace in Syria until Assad is ousted, says Nikki Haley', *Guardian* 9/4/17, https://www.theguardian.com/world/2017/apr/09/no-peace-in-syria-until-assad-is-ousted-says-nikki-haley [accessed 5/8/17].

50. al-Jazeera, 'US-led coalition hits pro-Assad fighters' convoy', *al-Jazeera* 19/5/17, http://www.aljazeera.com/news/2017/05/civilians-die-isil-attacks-aleppo-homs-170518151433809.html [accessed 10/8/17].

51. Faysal Itani, 'The end of American support for Syrian rebels was inevitable', *Atlantic* 21/7/17, https://www.theatlantic.com/international/archive/2017/07/trump-syria-assad-rebels-putin-cia/534540/ [accessed 15/8/17]; Euan McKirdy and Laura Smith-Spark, 'CIA no longer arming anti-Assad rebels, Washington Post reports', *CNN* 20/7/17, http://edition.cnn.com/2017/07/20/politics/cia-syria-anti-assad-rebels/index.html [accessed 15/8/17].

52. Aron Lund, 'Black flags over Idlib: The jihadi power grab in northwestern Syria', *IRIN news* 9/8/17, https://www.irinnews.org/analysis/2017/08/09/black-flags-over-idlib-jihadi-power-grab-northwestern-syria [accessed 20/8/17]; Alex MacDonald, 'ANALYSIS: Ahrar al-Sham's fall hands Syrian rebellion to al-Qaeda', *Middle East Eye* 18/8/17, http://www.middleeasteye.net/news/destruction-major-rebel-group-leaves-syrian-opposition-hands-hts-1909379351 [accessed 20/8/17].

53. Sam Heller, 'A Deadly Delusion: Were Syria's Rebels ever going to defeat the Jihadists?' *War on the Rocks* 10/8/17, https://warontherocks.com/2017/08/a-deadly-delusion-were-syrias-rebels-ever-going-to-defeat-the-jihadists/ [accessed 28/8/17]; MEE Staff, '"Putin won in Syria": Trump ends CIA weapons, training for Syria rebels', *Middle East Eye* 19/7/18, http://www.middleeasteye.net/news/putin-won-syria-trump-ends-cia-weapons-training-syria-rebels-587124117 [accessed 28/8/17].

54. Aymenn Jawad Al-Tamimi, 'The Iranian Land Route to the Mediterranean: Myth or Reality?' *American Spectator* 22/8/17, http://www.aymennjawad.org/20190/the-iranian-land-route-to-the-mediterranean-myth [accessed 30/8/17].

55. Mohamad Bazzi, 'The Growing U.S.–Iran Proxy Fight in Syria', *Atlantic* 20/6/17, https://www.theatlantic.com/international/archive/2017/06/iran-syria-trump-saudi-arabia-escalation-isis/530844/ [accessed 15/8/17].

56. Tom O'Connor, 'Russia, Iran, other Assad allies and enemies cash in on success in Syria, but US left out', *Newsweek* 17/8/17, http://www.newsweek.com/russia-iran-assad-ally-enemy-syria-war-us-651953 [accessed 20/8/17].

Conclusion: The war that everyone lost

1. Interview with Lahkdar Brahimi, Paris, 31/8/15.

2. 'Banners' 31/1/15, *Occupied Liberated Kafranbel*, http://www.occupiedkafranbel.com/banners [accessed 15/12/15].

3. Ibid. 16/12/11 and 15/3/14.

4. Raed Fares, 'Why is Russia bombing my town?' *Washington Post* 6/11/15.

5. Kristian Skrede Gleditsch, 'Transnational dimensions of civil war', *Journal of Peace Research* 44.3 (2007), 293–309.

Bibliography

Abboud, Samer N., *Syria (Hotspots in Global Politics)*, (New York: Polity, 2015).

ABC, 'Mission impossible: why Kofi Annan's peace plan for Syria failed', ABC 16/9/12.

Abouzeid, Rania, 'Meet the Islamist militants fighting alongside Syria's rebels', *Time*, 26/7/12.

Abouzeid, Rania, 'Syria's secular and Islamist rebels: who are the Saudis and the Qatars arming?' *Time*, 18/9/12.

Abrams, Elliott, 'Trump the Traditionalist', *Foreign Affairs* 96:4 July/August 2017, 10–16.

AFP, 'Turkish PM praises growing ties with Syria' AFP for *Ahram online* 6/2/11, http://english.ahram.org.eg/NewsContent/2/8/5096/Index.aspx [accessed 3/6/15].

AFP, 'Civilian deaths drop to four-year low after Syria truce: monitor', *AFP* 27/3/16, http://news.yahoo.com/civilian-deaths-drop-four-low-syria-truce-monitor-182900708.html [accessed 29/3/16].

AFP, 'Hundreds of civilians, rebels evacuated from Aleppo', *AFP* 16/12/16, https://www.dawn.com/news/1302622/hundreds-of-civilians-rebels-evacuated-from-aleppo [accessed 15/8/17].

Airwars, 'Civilian and "friendly fire" casualties', *Airwars*, https://airwars.org/civilian-casualty-claims/ [accessed 10/8/17].

Alamdari, Kazem, 'Power structure of the Islamic Republic of Iran: transition from populism to clientelism, and militarization of the government', *Third World Quarterly*, 26: 8 (2005), 1285–1301.

Ali, Khalid, 'Iran calls on Syrian President to consider protesters' demands', *Independent* 29/8/11.

al-Jazeera, 'NATO rules out Syria intervention', *al-Jazeera* 1/11/11, http://www.aljazeera.com/news/middleeast/2011/11/201111103948699103.html [accessed 9/4/15].

al-Jazeera, 'Moaz al-Khatib: the priority is to save Syria', *al-Jazeera* 11/5/13, http://www.aljazeera.com/programmes/talktojazeera/2013/05/2013510141112681380.html [accessed 2/7/15].

al-Jazeera, 'Gas used in Homs leaves seven people dead and scores affected, activists say', *al-Jazeera* 24/12/12, http://blogs.aljazeera.com/topic/syria/gas-used-homs-leaves-seven-people-dead-and-scores-affected-activists-say [accessed 5/7/15].

al-Jazeera, 'Assad admits "setbacks" in war against Syrian rebels', *al-Jazeera* 6/5/15, http://www.aljazeera.com/news/2015/05/150506185408811.html [accessed 10/2/16].

al-Jazeera, 'Syria war: John Kerry says violence drastically reduced', *al-Jazeera* 12/3/16, http://www.aljazeera.com/news/2016/03/syria-war-john-kerry-violence-drastically-reduced-160312082042884.html [accessed 10/3/16].

al-Jazeera, 'Scores killed as Syrian jets pound rebel-held Aleppo', *al-Jazeera* 23/9/16, http://www.aljazeera.com/news/2016/09/scores-killed-syrian-jets-pound-rebel-heldaleppo-160923134637232.html [accessed 15/8/17].

al-Jazeera, 'Erdogan: Turkish army will press on to ISIL-held Raqqa', *al-Jazeera* 12/2/17, http://www.aljazeera.com/news/2017/02/erdogan-turkish-troops-isil-bastion-al-bab-170212115151375.html [accessed 10/8/17].

al-Jazeera, 'US-led coalition hits pro-Assad fighters' convoy', *al-Jazeera* 19/5/17, http://www.aljazeera.com/news/2017/05/civilians-die-isil-attacks-aleppo-homs-170518151433809.html [accessed 10/8/17].

Allen, Jonathan and Amie Parnes, *HRC* (New York: Crown Publishers, 2014).

Allison, Roy, 'Russia and Syria: explaining alignment with a regime in crisis', *International Affairs*, 89: 4 (2013), 795–823.

Allsopp, Harriet, *The Kurds of Syria* (London: I.B. Tauris, 2014).

Al-Omran, Ahmed, in F. Ayub (ed.), *What Does the Gulf Think about the Arab Awakening?* (London: ECFR, 2013).

Al-Rasheed, Madawi, 'Saudi Arabia: local and regional challenges', *Contemporary Arab Affairs*, 6: 1 (2013), 28–40.

Al-Saadi, J., 'Saudi–Syrian relations: a historic divide', *al-akhbar* 4/2/12, http://english.al-akhbar.com/node/3906 [accessed 12/3/14].

Al-Saadi, Salam, 'Iran's stake in Syria's economy', *Sada for Carnegie* 2/6/15, http://carnegieendowment.org/sada/2015/06/02/iran-s-stakes-in-syria-s-economy/i9cj [accessed 2/8/15].

Al-Sabouni, Marwa, *The Battle for Home: Memoir of a Syrian Architect* (London: Thames and Hudson, 2016).

Al-Tamimi, Aymenn Jawad, 'The Iranian Land Route to the Mediterranean: Myth or Reality?' *American Spectator* 22/8/17, http://www.aymennjawad.org/20190/theiranian-land-route-to-the-mediterranean-myth [accessed 30/8/17].

Altunışık, Meliha Benli 'The Middle East in Turkey–USA relations: managing the alliance', *Journal of Balkan and Near Eastern Studies*, 15: 2 (2013), 157–73.

Amos, Deborah, 'Pro-Assad "Army" wages cyberwar in Syria', *NPR* 25/9/11, http://www.npr.org/2011/09/25/140746510/pro-assad-army-wages-cyberwar-in-syria [accessed 20/5/13].

Arab Center for Research and Policy Studies, 'The general and the particular in the ongoing Syrian popular uprising', *Arab Center for Research and Policy Studies* May 2011, http://english.dohainstitute.org/file/get/324a0bcf-cdd1-4932-b1bf-454761a5d792.pdf [accessed 1/5/15].

Asharq al-Awsat, 'Syrian Army colonel defects forms Free Syrian Army', *Asharq al-Awsat* 1/8/15 http://www.aawsat.net/2011/08/article55245595/syrian-army-colonel-defects-forms-free-syrian-army [accessed 10/10/15].

Ayata, Bilgin, 'Turkish foreign policy in a changing Arab world: rise and fall of a regional actor?' *Journal of European Integration*, 37: 1 (2015), 95–112.

Ayubi, Nazih, *Overstating the Arab State, Politics and Society in the Middle East* (London: I.B, Tauris, 1995).

Azmeh, Shamel, *The Uprising of the Marginalised: A Socio-Economic Perspective of the Syrian Uprising*, LSE Middle East Centre Paper Series 06 (2014).

Baghdadi, George, 'Syrians march in support of Assad,' *CBS News* 13/11/11, http://www.cbsnews.com/news/syrians-march-in-support-of-assad/ [accessed 14/12/14].

Balanche, Fabrice, 'How to prevent al-Qaeda from seizing a safe zone in northwestern Syria', *The Washington Institute* 7/3/16, http://www.washingtoninstitute.org/policy-analysis/view/how-to-prevent-al-qaeda-from-seizing-a-safe-zone-in-northwestern-syria#.Vt4AZPz_zRA.twitter [accessed 15/3/16].

Balch-Lindsay, Dylan and Andrew Enterline, 'Killing time: the world politics of civil war duration, 1820–1992', *International Studies Quarterly*, 44: 4 (2000), 615–42.

Balci, Bayram, 'Turkey's flirtation with Syrian jihadism', *Carnegie* 7/11/13, http://carnegieendowment.org/syriaincrisis/?fa=53532 [accessed 3/4/14].

Bar, Herve, 'Ahrar al-Sham jihadists emerge from shadows in north Syria', *Daily Star* 13/2/13.

Barber, Matthew, 'The names of the Revolution', *Syria Comment* 14/12/13, http://www.joshualandis.com/blog/names-of-the-revolution/ [accessed 14/12/14].

Barkey, Henri J., 'Erdoğan's foreign policy is in ruins', *Foreign Policy* 4/2/16.

Barrington, Lisa and Tom Perry, 'Syrian army captures part of rebel-held east Aleppo', *Reuters* 26/11/16, https://www.reuters.com/article/us-mideast-crisis-syria-aleppoidUSKBN 13L0KR [accessed 10/8/15].

Bassam, Laila and Tom Perry, 'How Iranian general plotted out Syrian assault in Moscow', *Reuters* 6/10/15 http://www.reuters.com/article/us-mideast-crisis-syria-soleimani-insigh-idUSKCN0S02BV20151006 [accessed 11/2/16].

Bastani, Hossein, 'Iran quietly deepens involvement in Syria's war', BBC 20/10/15, http://www.bbc.co.uk/news/world-middle-east-34572756 [accessed 11/3/16].

Batatu, Hanna, *Syria's Peasantry, the Descendants of its Lesser Rural Notables, and their Politics* (Princeton: Princeton University Press, 1999).

Bazoobandi, Sara, 'Iran's regional policy: interests, challenges and ambitions', *ISPI Analysis* November 2014, http://www.ispionline.it/sites/default/files/pubblicazioni/analysis_275__2014_0.pdf [accessed 15/2/16].

Bazzi, Mohamad, 'The Growing U.S.-Iran Proxy Fight in Syria', *The Atlantic* 20/6/17, https://www.theatlantic.com/international/archive/2017/06/iran-syria-trump-saudiarabia-escalation-isis/530844/ [accessed 15/8/17].

BBC, 'Foreign Secretary William Hague visits Syria', BBC 26/01/11, http://www.bbc.co.uk/news/uk-politics-12293205 [accessed 10/9/15].

BBC, 'Libya protests: defiant Gaddafi refuses to quit', BBC 22/2/11, http://www.bbc.com/news/world-middle-east-12544624 [accessed 20/5/15].

BBC, 'Syria unrest: Medvedev urges Assad to reform or go', BBC 7/10/11, http://www.bbc.com/news/world-middle-east-15218727 [accessed 6/11/14].

BBC, 'Ex-Arab League monitor labels Syria mission "a farce"', BBC 11/1/12, http://www.bbc.co.uk/news/world-middle-east-16507805 [accessed 3/10/15].

BBC, 'UN calls for investigation into Houla killings in Syria', BBC 1/6/12, http://www.bbc.com/news/world-middle-east-18295291 [accessed 1/6/15].

BBC, 'Syria conflict: Cleric Qaradawi urges Sunnis to join rebels', BBC 13/1/13, http://www.bbc.co.uk/news/world-middle-east-22741588 [accessed 12/3/14].

BBC, 'US says it will give military aid to Syria rebels', BBC 14/6/13, http://www.bbc.co.uk/news/world-us-canada-22899289 [accessed 4/7/15].

BBC, 'Who is supplying weapons to the warring sides in Syria?' BBC 14/6/13, http://www.bbc.co.uk/news/world-middle-east-22906965 [accessed 12/4/15].

BBC, 'The boy killed for an off-hand remark about Muhammad – Sharia spreads in Syria', BBC 2/7/13, http://www.bbc.co.uk/news/world-middle-east-23139784 [accessed 14/1/15].

BBC, 'Syrian National Coalition agrees Geneva talks position', BBC 11/11/13, http://www.bbc.co.uk/news/world-middle-east-24894536 [accessed 22/6/15].

BBC, 'US and UK suspend non-lethal aid for Syria rebels', BBC 11/12/13, http://www.bbc.co.uk/news/world-middle-east-25331241 [accessed 4/7/15].

BBC, 'Guide to Syrian rebels', BBC 13/12/13, http://www.bbc.co.uk/news/world-middle-east-24403003 [accessed 12/4/15].

BBC, 'Gulf ambassadors pulled from Qatar over "interference"', BBC 5/3/14, http://www.bbc.co.uk/news/world-middle-east-26447914 [accessed 12/7/15].

BBC, 'Iran general died in "Israeli strike" in Syrian Golan', BBC 19/1/15, http://www.bbc.co.uk/news/world-middle-east-30882935 [accessed 1/2/16].

BBC, 'Russia "plans forward air operating base" in Syria – US', BBC 14/9/15, http://www.bbc.co.uk/news/world-middle-east-34252810 [accessed 10/3/16].

BBC, 'BBC inside airbase where Russia carries out Syria airstrikes', BBC 11/11/15, http://www.bbc.co.uk/news/world-europe-34790153 [accessed 20/1/16].

BBC, 'Inside Russian airbase launching Syria strikes', BBC 20/1/16, http://www.bbc.co.uk/news/world-europe-35365747 [accessed 10/2/16].

BBC, 'Syria conflict: UN suspends peace talks in Geneva', BBC 3/2/16, http://www.bbc.co.uk/news/world-middle-east-35488073 [accessed 10/3/16].

BBC, 'Aleppo battle ends as Syria rebel deal reached', *BBC* 13/12/16, http://www.bbc.co.uk/news/world-middle-east-38308883 [accessed 7/8/17].

BBC, 'Syria conflict: Clashes reported despite truce', *BBC* 30/12/16, http://www.bbc.co.uk/news/world-middle-east-38463021 [accessed 10/8/17].

Beaumont, Peter, 'Netanyahu meets Putin to discuss concerns over Russian activity in Syria', *Guardian* 21/9/15.

Black, Ian, 'Kofi Annan resigns as Syria envoy', *Guardian* 2/8/12.

Black, Ian, 'Syria insists chemical weapons would only be used against outside forces', *Guardian* 24/7/12 http://www.theguardian.com/world/2012/jul/23/syria-chemical-weapons-own-goal [accessed 17/12/15].

Blanchard, Christopher M., *Qatar: background and US relations*, Congressional Research Service paper, 4/11/14, http://www.fas.org/sgp/crs/mideast/RL31718.pdf [accessed 6/5/15].

Blanford, Nicholas, *Killing Mr Lebanon: the Assassination of Rafik Hariri and its Impact on the Middle East* (London: I.B. Tauris, 2006).

Blanford, Nicholas, *Warriors of God: Inside Hezbollah's Thirty-year Struggle against Israel*. (London: Random House, 2011).

Blomfield, A., 'Syria unrest: Saudi Arabia calls on "killing machine" to stop', *Telegraph* 8/8/11.

Bonsey, Noah, 'More Chechnya, less Afghanistan', *Foreign Policy* 12/10/15.

Booth, Robert, Mona Mahmood and Luke Harding, 'Exclusive: secret Assad emails lift lid on life of leader's inner circle', *Guardian* 14/3/12.

Borger, Julian and Patrick Wintour, 'Russia calls on Syria to hand over chemical weapons', *Guardian* 9/9/13.

Borger, Julian, 'Donald Trump's response to Syria gas attack: blame Obama', *Guardian* 5/4/17, https://www.theguardian.com/world/2017/apr/04/syria-gas-attacktrump-us-foreign-policy [accessed 1/8/17].

Borger, Julian, David Smith and Jennifer Rankin, 'Syria chemical attack has changed my view of Assad, says Trump', *Guardian* 6/4/17, https://www.theguardian.com/us-news/2017/apr/05/syria-chemical-gas-attack-donald-trump-nikki-haley-assad [accessed 5/8/17].

Borger, Julian, 'US rebukes Saudi Arabia over Qatar embargo in reversal after Trump comments', *Guardian* 20/6/17, https://www.theguardian.com/world/2017/jun/20/us-saudi-arabia-qatar-embargo-trump [accessed 10/8/17].

Bowen, Jeremy, 'Assad is firm in defending his actions in BBC interview', BBC 10/2/15, http://www.bbc.com/news/world-middle-east-31311896 [accessed 1/5/15].

Boyer, Dave, 'Problems mount for Obama in Syria, Iraq', *Washington Times* 21/4/16, http://www.washingtontimes.com/news/2016/apr/21/problems-mount-obama-syria-iraq/ [accessed 12/8/17]

Brooks, Stephen, G. John Ikenberry and William Wohlforth, 'Don't come home, America: the case against retrenchment', *International Security*, 37: 3 (Winter 2012–2013), 7–51.

Brown Moses, 'Evidence of Iranian arms provided to Syria in the past 18 months', *Brown Moses* 20/5/13, http://brown-moses.blogspot.co.uk/2013/05/evidence-of-iranian-arms-provided-to.html [accessed 12/4/15].

Brown Moses, 'More evidence of sanction busting Iranian munitions deliveries to Syria', *Brown Moses* 26/5/13, http://brown-moses.blogspot.co.uk/2013/05/more-evidence-of-sanction-busting.html [accessed 12/4/15].

Buncombe, Andrew, 'Trump orders missile strike on Syria after chemical weapon attack on civilians', *The Independent* 7/4/17, http://www.independent.co.uk/news/world/americas/us-tomahawk-missiles-syria-reports-latest-donald-trump-homs-bashar-alassad-russia-a7671411.html [accessed 15/8/17].

Burke, Jason, *Al-Qaeda: the True Story of Radical Islam* (London: I.B. Tauris, 2004).

Burleigh, Nina, 'Obama vs the hawks', *Rolling Stone*, 1/4/14 [accessed 14/5/15].

Butter, David, *Syria's Economy: Picking up the Pieces*, Chatham House Research Paper, June 2015.

Buzan, Barry, and Ole Waever, *Regions and Powers: the Structure of International Security*, vol. 91. (Cambridge: Cambridge University Press, 2003).

Caerus, 'Mapping the conflict in Aleppo, Syria', *Caerus*, February 2014, https://s3.amazonaws.com/fmg_static/aleppo/Caerus_AleppoMappingProject_SecurityConditions.pdf [accessed 10/9/15].

Cafiero, Giorgio and Daniel Wagner, 'Turkey and Qatar: close allies, sharing a doomed Syria policy', *The National Interest* 9/11/15, http://nationalinterest.org/feature/turkey-qatar-close-allies-sharing-doomed-syria-policy-14283?page=2 [accessed 10/3/16].

Cambanis, Thanassis, 'How do you say quagmire in Farsi?' *Foreign Policy* 13/5/13.

Cambanis, Thanassis, 'The Syrian revolution against al Qaeda', *Foreign Policy* 29/3/16.

Casagrande, Genevieve, Christopher Kozak and Jennifer Cafarella, 'Syria 90 day forecast: the Assad regime and allies in northern Syria', Institute for the Study of War 24/2/16, http://understandingwar.org/sites/default/files/Syria%2090%20Day%20Forecast%2024%20FEB%202016(1).pdf [accessed 11/3/16].

Charap, Samuel, 'Russia, Syria and the doctrine of intervention', *Survival*, 55: 1 (February–March 2013), pp. 35–41.

Charbonneau, Louis, 'Exclusive: Iran steps up weapons lifeline to Assad', *Reuters* 14/3/13, http://www.reuters.com/article/2013/03/14/us-syria-crisis-iran-idUSBRE92D05U20130314 [accessed 12/4/15].

Chatty, Dawn, 'Syria's bedouin enter the fray: how tribes could keep Syria together', *Foreign Affairs*, November (2013).

Chesnot, Christian and Georges Malbrunot, *Les Chemins de Dama : Le dossier noir de la relation franco-syrienne* (Paris: Robert Lafront, 2014) [Kindle edition].

Chivers, C. J. and Eric Schmitt, 'Arms airlift to Syria rebels expands, with aid from C.I.A.', *New York Times* 24/3/13.

Chulov, Martin, 'Lebanon's great divide exposed by assassination of security chief', *Guardian* 19/10/12.

Chulov, Martin and Mona Mahmood, 'Syria's elite join compatriots to flee country fearing western air strike', *Guardian* 27/8/13.

Chulov, Martin, 'Pro-Assad forces seize third of east Aleppo in rapid advance', *Guardian* 28/11/16, https://www.theguardian.com/world/2016/nov/28/pro-assad-forcesseize-third-of-east-aleppo-in-rapid-advance-syria [accessed 15/8/17].

Clinton, Hillary Rodham, *Hard Choices: A Memoir* (New York: Simon and Schuster, 2014).

CNN, 'Zakaria: Trump just became president', *CNN Politics* 7/4/17, http://edition.cnn.com/videos/politics/2017/04/07/fareed-zakaria-trump-became-president-syrianewday.cnn [accessed 15/8/17].

Cockburn, Patrick, *The Rise of Islamic State: ISIS and the New Sunni Revolution* (London: Verso Books, 2015) [Kindle edition].

Colvin, Ross, ' "Cut off head of snake" Saudis told U.S. on Iran', Reuters 29/11/10, http://www.reuters.com/article/us-wikileaks-iran-saudis-idUSTRE6AS02B20101129 [accessed 12/5/15].

Contorno, Steve, 'What Obama said about Islamic State as a "JV" team', *Politifact* 7/9/14 http://www.politifact.com/truth-o-meter/statements/2014/sep/07/barack-obama/what-obama-said-about-islamic-state-jv-team/ [accessed 14/10/15].

Crowley, Michael, 'Trump's praise of Russia, Iran and Assad regime riles GOP experts', *Politico* 10/10/16, http://www.politico.com/story/2016/10/trump-praise-russia-iran-assad-criticism-229546 [accessed 16/8/17].

Crumley, Bruce, 'France's fling with Syria', *Time* 4/9/08.

Cunningham, David E., Kristian Skrede Gleditsch and Idean Salehyan, 'It takes two: a dyadic analysis of civil war duration and outcome', *Journal of Conflict Resolution*, 53: 4 (2009), 570–97.

Cunningham, David E. 'Blocking resolution: how external states can prolong civil wars', *Journal of Peace Research*, 47: 2 (2010), 115–27.

Dagher, Sam, 'Iran's Foreign Legion leads battle in Syria's north', *Wall Street Journal* 17/2/16.

Danahar, Paul, *The New Middle East: the World after the Arab Spring* (London: Bloomsbury Publishing, 2013).

Dannreuther, Roland. 'Russia and the Middle East: A Cold War Paradigm?' *Europe–Asia Studies*, 64: 3 (2012), 543–56.

Dannreuther, Roland, 'Russia and the Arab Spring: supporting the counter-revolution', *Journal of European Integration*, 37: 1 (2015), 77–94.

Daragahi, Borzou, 'Libya helps bankroll Syrian opposition', *Financial Times*, 5 /11/12.

Dark, Edward, 'Syrian Baath militia commander goes rags-to-riches', *Al- Monitor* 20/11/13. http://www.al-monitor.com/pulse/originals/2013/11/baath-party-brigade-syria-war-aleppo.html# [accessed 10/9/15].

Darke, Diana, *My House in Damascus: An Inside View of the Syrian Revolution*, (London: Haus, 2014).

Dayoub, Basel, 'Bustan al-Qasr crossing in Aleppo: daily humiliation and nonsensical rules', *Al-Akhbar* 27/3/14 http://english.al-akhbar.com/node/19177 [accessed 10/9/15].

Davidson, Christopher, *After the Sheikhs: the Coming Collapse of the Gulf Oil Monarchies* (London: Hurst, 2012).

Davutoğlu, Ahmet, *Alternative Paradigms: the Impact of Islamic and Western Weltanschauungs on Political Theory* (Lanham–New York–London: University Press of America, 1994).

Dearden, Lizzie, 'Russia joins fight against Isis: parliament approves Vladimir Putin's request for military intervention', *Independent* 30/9/15.

De Châtel, Francesca, 'The role of drought and climate change in the Syrian uprising: untangling the triggers of the revolution', *Middle Eastern Studies* 50: 4 (2014), 521–35.

De Elvira, L. R. and T. Zintl, 'The end of the Ba'thist social contract in Bashar al-Assad's Syria: reading sociopolitical transformations through charities and broader benevolent activism', *International Journal of Middle East Studies* 46: 2 (2014), 329–49.

Denselow, James, 'Panama Papers: how the Seychelles saved Syria', *al-Jazeera* 9/4/16, http://www.aljazeera.com/indepth/opinion/2016/04/seychelles-saved-syria-160407085452247.html [accessed 12/4/16].

DeYoung, Karen, Anne Gearan and Scott Wilson, 'Decision to arm Syrian rebels was reached weeks ago, U.S. officials say', *Washington Post* 14/6/13.

De Young, Karen and Liz Sly, 'Syrian rebels get influx of arms with Gulf neighbours' money, US cooperation', *Washington Post* 15/5/12.

Dickinson, Elizabeth, 'Follow the money: how Syrian Salafis are funded from the Gulf', Carnegie Endowment for International Peace, 23/12/13, http://carnegieendowment.org/syriaincrisis/?fa=54011 [accessed 17/3/14].

Dickinson, Elizabeth, 'The Syrian war's private donors lose faith', *New Yorker* 16/1/14.

Dickson, Janice, 'Turkey turns blind eye to ISIS fighters using its hospitals: sources', *Ipolitics* 27/5/15, http://ipolitics.ca/2015/07/27/turkey-turns-blind-eye-to-isis-fighters-using-its-hospitals-sources/ [accessed 14/10/15].

Dinçer, Osman Bahadır and Mustafa Kutlay, 'Turkey's power capacity in the Middle East', *USAK Center for Middle Eastern and African Studies Report* no. 12–04 (June 2012), http://www.usak.org.tr/dosyalar/rapor/ctZTC1gAenLx7HaF8Gi7oip20CoDVX.pdf [accessed 4/6/15].

Dodge, Toby, 'State collapse and the rise of identity politics', in Markus Bouillon, David Malone and Ben Rowsell (eds), *Iraq: Preventing Another Generation of Conflict* (Boulder: Lynne Rienner Publishers, 2007).

Dodge, Toby, *Iraq: From War to a New Authoritarianism* (London: Routledge, 2013).

DPA, 'Syrian army defector urges limited NATO intervention', Atlantic Council 16/7/12, http://www.atlanticcouncil.org/blogs/natosource/syrian-army-defector-urges-limited-nato-intervention [accessed 10/11/15].

Droz-Vincent, Philip, ' "State of Barbary" (Take Two): from the Arab Spring to the return of violence in Syria', *Middle East Journal*, 68:1 (2014), 33–58.

Drury, C., 'Revisiting economic sanctions reconsidered', *Journal of Peace Research*, 35:4 (1998), 497–509.

DW, 'Syrian opposition walks out of Geneva peace talks', *DW* 20/4/16, http://www.dw.com/en/syrian-opposition-walks-out-of-geneva-peace-talks/a-19200135 [accessed 10/8/17].

Elder, Miriam and Ian Black, 'Russia withdraws its remaining personnel from Syria', *Guardian* 26/6/13.

Entous, Dam, Nour Malas and Margaret Coker, 'A veteran Saudi power player works to build support to topple Assad', *Wall Street Journal* 23/8/13.

Erlich, Reese, *Inside Syria: The Backstory of their Civil War and What the World Can Expect* (New York: Prometheus, 2014).

Esfandiary, Dina and Ariane Tabatabai, 'Iran's ISIS policy', *International Affairs*, 91:1 (2015), 1–15.

Evans, Dominic, 'Rebels battle for Syria border post near Mediterranean', *Reuters* 22/3/14, http://www.reuters.com/article/2014/03/23/us-syria-crisis-idUSBREA2L0G020140323 [accessed 24/11/15].

Fandos, Nicholas, 'Trump's View of Syria: How it Evolved, in 19 Tweets', *New York Times* 7/4/17.

Fares, Raed, 'Why is Russia bombing my town?' *Washington Post* 6/11/15.

Filkins, Dexter, 'The shadow commander', *New Yorker* 30/9/13.

Flanagan, Stephen J., 'The Turkey–Russia–Iran nexus: Eurasian power dynamics', *Washington Quarterly*, 36:1 (2013), 163–78.

Fontanella-Khan, Amana, 'Fethullah Gülen: Turkey coup may have been 'staged' by Erdoğan regime', *Guardian* 16/7/16, https://www.theguardian.com/world/2016/jul/16/fethullah-gulen-turkey-coup-erdogan [accessed 10/8/17].

Ford, Robert S. and Ali El Yassir, 'Yes, talk with Syria's Ahrar al-Sham', Middle East Institute 15/7/15, http://www.mei.edu/content/at/yes-talk-syria%E2%80%99s-ahrar-al-sham [accessed 10/2/16].

Freedman, Uri, 'How Syrian activists name their Friday protests', *The Wire* 16/9/11.

Friedman Lissner, Rebecca and Micah Zenko, 'There Is No Trump Doctrine, and There Will Never Be One', *Foreign Policy* 21/7/17, http://foreignpolicy.com/2017/07/21/thereis-no-trump-doctrine-and-there-will-never-be-one-grand-strategy/ [accessed 15/8/17].

Frum, David, 'The Death Knell for America's Global Leadership', *The Atlantic* 31/5/17, https://www.theatlantic.com/international/archive/2017/05/mcmaster-cohn-trump/528609/ [accessed 12/8/17].

Fulton, Will, Joseph Holliday and Sam Wyer, 'Iranian strategy in Syria', May 2013 http://www.understandingwar.org/sites/default/files/IranianStrategyinSyria-1MAY.pdf [accessed 13/7/15].

Gardner, Frank, 'Saudi Arabia flexing its muscles in Middle East', BBC 8/8/15, http://www.bbc.co.uk/news/world-middle-east-33825064 [accessed 13/10/15].

Gartenstein-Ross, Daveed, 'Islamic State vs. Al-Qaeda', *Foundation for the Defence of Democracies* 4/12/15, http://www.defenddemocracy.org/media-hit/gartenstein-ross-daveed-islamic-state-vs-al-qaeda/ [accessed 17/12/15].

Gause, F. Gregory, 'Beyond sectarianism: the new Middle East Cold War', The Brookings Doha Center 11 (2014).

Gause, F. Gregory, 'The Trump Administration and the Middle East', *The International Security Studies Forum* 14/8/17, https://issforum.org/roundtables/policy/1-5AV-MiddleEast [accessed 20/8/17].

Gearan, Anne and Karen DeYoung, 'Obama unlikely to reconsider arming Syrian rebels despite views of security staff', *Washington Post* 8/2/13.

George, Alan, *Syria: Neither Bread nor Freedom* (London: Zed Books, 2003).

Gerges, Fawaz, *The Far Enemy: Why Jihad Went Global* (Cambridge: Cambridge University Press, 2009).

Gerges, Fawaz, *Obama and the Middle East: The End of America's Moment?* (London: Palgrave, 2012).

Ghattas, Kim, *The Secretary: A Journey with Hillary Clinton from Beirut to the Heart of American Power* (London: Macmillan, 2013). [Kindle edition]

Girit, Selin, 'Turkey faces big losses as Russia sanctions bite', BBC 2/1/16, http://www.bbc.co.uk/news/world-europe-35209987 [accessed 10/3/16].

Gleditsch, Kristian Skrede, 'Transnational dimensions of civil war', *Journal of Peace Research*, 44:3 (2007), 293–309.

Gleditsch, Kristian Skrede and Kyle Beardsley, 'Nosy neighbors: third-party actors in Central American conflicts', *Journal of Conflict Resolution*, 48.3 (2004), 379–402.

Gold, Danny, 'Meet the YPG, the Kurdish militia that doesn't want help from anyone', *Vice* 31/10/12.

Goldberg, Jeffrey, 'The Obama doctrine', *The Atlantic*, April 2016.

Goldsmith, Leon T., *Cycle of Fear: Syria's Alawites in War and Peace* (London: Hurst, 2015).

Good, Alistair, 'Syrian protest song that killed its writer', *Telegraph* 10/7/11.

Goodarzi, Jubin, 'Iran: Syria as the first line of defense', in Julien Barnes-Dacey and Daniel Levy (eds) *The Regional Struggle for Syria* (London: European Council on Foreign Relations, 2013).

Gordon, Michael R. and Eric Schmitt, 'Syria uses Scud missiles in new effort to push back rebels', *New York Times* 12/12/12.

Gordon, Michael R., 'Israel airstrike targeted advanced missiles that Russia sold to Syria, U.S. says', *New York Times* 13/7/13.

Gordon, Michael R. and Eric Schmitt, 'Trump to Arm Syrian Kurds, Even as Turkey Strongly Objects', *New York Times* 9/5/17, https://www.nytimes.com/2017/05/09/us/politics/trump-kurds-syria-army.html [accessed 5/8/17].

Gowan, Richard, 'Kofi Annan, Syria and the uses of uncertainty in mediation', *Stability: International Journal of Security and Development*, 2:1 (2013), 8.

Greenwald, Glen, 'How former Treasury officials and the UAE are manipulating American journalists', *The Intercept* 25/9/14, https://theintercept.com/2014/09/25/uae-qatar-camstoll-group/.

Greig, J. Michael, 'Intractable Syria – insights from the scholarly literature on the failure of mediation'. *Penn State Journal of Law and International Affairs* 2 (2013), 48–56.

Griswold, Eliza, 'Is this the end of Christianity in the Middle East?' *New York Times* 22/7/15.

Guardian, 'Assad emails: "We should be in control of all public spaces" – translation', *Guardian* 14/3/12.

Guardian, 'Assad emails: "Rubbish laws of parties, elections, media . . ."', *Guardian* 14/3/12.

Guardian, 'Assad emails: "Suggestions for the president's speech" – translation', *Guardian* 14/3/12.

Guardian, 'Assad emails: "Blaming Al-Qaida is not in our interest" – translation', *Guardian* 14/3/12.

Guardian, 'Assad emails: "I'm sure you have many places to turn to, including Doha"', *Guardian* 14/3/12.

Guardian, 'Bashar al-Assad wins re-election in Syria as uprising against him rages on', *Guardian* 14/6/14.

Guardian, 'Isis captured 2,300 Humvee armoured vehicles from Iraqi forces in Mosul', *Guardian* 1/6/15.

Guardian, 'No peace in Syria until Assad is ousted, says Nikki Haley', *Guardian* 9/4/17, https://www.theguardian.com/world/2017/apr/09/no-peace-in-syria-until-assadis-ousted-says-nikki-haley [accessed 5/8/17].

Guerin, Orla, 'Syria sidesteps Lebanon demands', *BBC* 6/3/05, http://news.bbc.co.uk/1/hi/world/middle_east/4322477.stm [accessed 21/4/15].

Habibi, Nader, 'A decade of growing U.S. trade with the Middle East', *Global Insight*, http://www.mefacts.com/cache/html/us-israel/11079.htm [accessed 1/5/15].

Haddad, Bassam, 'The Syrian regime's business backbone', *Middle East Report*, 42.262 (2012).

Haddad, Fanar, *Sectarianism in Iraq: Antagonistic Visions of Unity* (New York: Columbia University Press, 2011).

Haid, Haid, 'The Southern Front: allies without a strategy', *Heinrich Böll Stiftung* 21/8/15. http://lb.boell.org/en/2015/08/21/southern-front-allies-without-strategy [accessed 10/3/16].

Haid, Haid, 'Did Turkey abandon Aleppo to fight Syrian Kurds?' *Now* 4/10/16, https://now.mmedia.me/lb/en/commentaryanalysis/567401-did-turkey-abandon-aleppo-tofight-the-syrian-kurds [accessed 10/8/17].

Hale, William, *Turkish Foreign Policy, 1774–2000* (London: Routledge, 2002).

Hall, Richard, 'Syria crisis: coalition of powerful rebel groups rejects Western-backed opposition', *Independent* 25/9/15.

Halliday, Fred, *The Middle East in International Relations: Power, Politics and Ideology* (Cambridge: Cambridge University Press, 2005).

Hamid, Shadi, 'Why doesn't Obama seem to listen to Syria experts?' *Brookings* 10/2/16, http://www.brookings.edu/blogs/markaz/posts/2016/02/10-obama-syria-policy-experts-hamid [accessed 1/4/16].

Harling, Peter and Sarah Birke, 'The Syrian heartbreak', *Middle East Report* (2013).

Hassan, Hassan, 'Saudis overtaking Qatar in sponsoring Syrian rebels', *The National* 15/5/13, http://www.thenational.ae/thenationalconversation/comment/saudis-overtaking-qatar-in-sponsoring-syrian-rebels [accessed 12/11/15].

Hassan, Hassan, 'Syria the view from the Gulf states', *European Council of Foreign Relations*, June 2013 http://www.ecfr.eu/article/commentary_syria_the_view_from_the_gulf_states135 [accessed 10/10/14]

Hassan, Hassan, 'Syria is now Saudi Arabia's problem', *Foreign Policy* 6/6/13.

Hawramy, Fazel and Luke Harding, 'Inside Islamic State's oil empire: how captured oilfields fuel Isis insurgency', *Guardian* 19/11/14.

Haykel, Bernard, 'Qatar and Islamism', *NOREF Paper* February 2013, http://www.peacebuilding.no/var/ezflow_site/storage/original/application/ac81941df1be874ccb-da35e747218abf.pdf [accessed 4/4/14].

Heartsgaard, Mark, 'Secret tapes of the 2013 Egypt coup plot pose a problem for Obama', *The Daily Beast* 5/10/15, http://www.thedailybeast.com/articles/2015/05/10/secret-tapes-of-the-2013–egypt-coup-plot-pose-a-problem-for-obama.html [accessed 10/11/15].

Hehir, Aiden, *The Responsibility to Protect* (London: Palgrave Macmillan, 2012).

Held, David and Kristian Coates Ulrichsen, 'The Arab Spring and the changing balance of global power', *Open Democracy* 26/2/14, https://www.opendemocracy.net/arab-awakening/david-held-kristian-coates-ulrichsen/arab-spring-and-changing-balance-of-global-power [accessed 1/5/15].

Heller, Sam and Aaron Stein, 'The problem with Turkey's favourite Syrian Islamists', *War on the Rocks* 18/8/15, http://warontherocks.com/2015/08/the-trouble-with-turkeys-favorite-syrian-islamists/ [accessed 10/10/15].

Heller, Sam, 'Geneva Peace Talks Won't Solve Syria—So Why Have Them?' The Century Foundation 30/6/17, https://tcf.org/content/report/geneva-peace-talks-wont-solve-syria/ [accessed 6/8/17].

Heller, Sam, 'A Deadly Delusion: Were Syria's Rebels ever going to defeat the Jihadists?' *War on the Rocks* 10/8/17, https://warontherocks.com/2017/08/a-deadly-delusion-were-syrias-rebels-ever-going-to-defeat-the-jihadists/ [accessed 28/8/17].

Hemeidi, Ibrahim, 'Syria's Kurds formally join opposition coalition', *Al-Monitor* 28/8/13, http://www.al-monitor.com/pulse/politics/2013/08/syria-kurds-join-national-coalition.html.

Henderson, Simon, 'Good riddance', *Foreign Policy* 18/6/12

Henderson, Simon, 'The prince and the revolution', *Foreign Policy* 24/7/12.

Henderson, Simon, 'The Saudi problem and the head of the snake', *Foreign Policy* 28/3/14.

Hille, Kathrin, Geoff Dyer, Demetri Sevastopulo and Erika Solomon, 'Russian air strikes on Syrian targets raise "grave concerns" in US', *Financial Times* 30/9/15.

Hiltermann, Joost R. 'Disorder on the border: Saudi Arabia's war inside Yemen', *Foreign Affairs*, 16 (2009).

Hinnebusch, Raymond, *Syria: Revolution from Above* (Routledge, London 2001).

Hinnebusch, Raymond, 'Syria: from "authoritarian upgrading" to revolution?' *International Affairs* 88:1 (2012), 95–113.

Hinnebusch, Raymond, *Syria–Iraq Relations: State Construction and Deconstruction and the Mena States System*, LSE Middle East Centre Series 04 (2014).

Hinnebusch, Raymond, 'Back to enmity: Turkey–Syria relations since the Syrian uprising', *Orient, Journal of German Orient Institute* (2015).

Hinnebusch, Raymond, 'Structure over agency: the Arab uprising and the regional struggle for power', in Spyridon N. Litsas and Aristotle Tziampiris (eds), *The Eastern Mediterranean in Transition: Multipolarity, Politics and Power* (London: Ashgate, 2015).

Hobson, Peter, 'Calculating the cost of Russia's war in Syria', *Moscow Times* 20/10/15.

Hochschild, Adam, *To End All Wars: A Story of Loyalty and Rebellion, 1914–1918* (London: Houghton Mifflin Harcourt, 2011).

Hof, Frederic, Bassma Kodmani and Jeffery White, 'Setting the stage for peace in Syria: the case for a Syrian National Stabilization Force', *Atlantic Council*, 14/4/15.

Hokayem, Emile, *Syria's Uprising and the Fracturing of the Levant* (London: Routledge, 2013).

Holmes, Oliver, 'One million people wounded, diseases spreading in Syria: WHO', Reuters 19/12/14, http://www.reuters.com/article/2014/12/19/us-mideast-crisis-health-idUSKBN0JX0V720141219 [accessed 1/4/15].

Holliday, Joseph, *Syria's Maturing Insurgency*, Institute for the Study of War, June 2012, http://www.understandingwar.org/report/syrias-maturing-insurgency [accessed 7/7/15].

Holliday, Joseph, *The Assad Regime: From Counter-insurgency to Civil War*, Institute for the Study of War, March 2013, http://www.understandingwar.org/report/assad-regime [accessed 7/7/15].

Horne, Alistair, *The Savage War of Peace: Algeria 1954–1962* (New York: New York Review Book Classics, 2006 [1977]).

Hroub, Khaled, 'Qatar and the Arab Spring', *Heinrich Boll Stiftung*, 2013, http://lb.boell.org/en/2014/03/03/qatar-and-arab-spring-conflict-intl-politics [accessed 5/5/15].

Hubbard, Ben, Clifford Kraus and Eric Schmitt, 'Rebels in Syria claim control of resources', *New York Times* 28/1/14.

Huber, Daniela, 'A pragmatic actor – the US response to the Arab uprisings', *Journal of European Integration*, 37:1 (2015), 57–75.

Hudson, Michael, 'The United States in the Middle East', in Louise Fawcett (ed.), *International Relations of the Middle East* (Oxford: Oxford University Press, 2005).

Hurriyet, 'Majority of Turks against Syria intervention: Survey', *Hurriyet* 6/9/13, http://www.hurriyetdailynews.com/majority-of-turks-against-syria-intervention-survey.aspx?pageID=238&nID=53995&NewsCatID=34 [accessed 12/12/15].

International Crisis Group, *Hezbollah Turns Eastward to Syria*, International Crisis Group Middle East Report no.153 27/5/14, http://www.crisisgroup.org/en/regions/middle-east-north-africa/egypt-syria-lebanon/lebanon/153-lebanon-s-hizbollah-turns-eastward-to-syria.aspx [accessed 3/5/15].

International Crisis Group, *New Approach in Southern Syria*, International Crisis Group Middle East Report no. 163, 2/9/15, http://www.crisisgroup.org/~/media/Files/Middle%20East%20North%20Africa/Iraq%20Syria%20Lebanon/Syria/163–new-approach-in-southern-syria.pdf [accessed 15/3/16].

Iskandarm, Marwān, *Rafiq Hariri and the Fate of Lebanon* (London: Saqi, 2006).

Itani, Faysal, 'The End of American Support for Syrian Rebels Was Inevitable', *The Atlantic* 21/7/17, https://www.theatlantic.com/international/archive/2017/07/trumpsyria-assad-rebels-putin-cia/534540/ [accessed 15/8/17].

Jacinto, Leela, 'Turkey's Post-Coup Purge and Erdogan's Private Army', *Foreign Policy* 13/7/17, http://foreignpolicy.com/2017/07/13/turkeys-post-coup-purge-and-erdogans-private-armysadat-perincek-gulen/ [accessed 10/8/17].

Jones, Lee, *Societies under Siege: Exploring how international economic sanctions (do not) work* (Oxford: Oxford University Press, 2015).

Juneau, Thomas, 'U.S. power in the Middle East: not declining', *Middle East Policy*, 21: 2 (Summer 2014), 40–52.

Juneau, Thomas, 'Iran under Rouhani: still alone in the world', *Middle East Policy*, 21: 4 (Winter 2014), 92–104.

Kagan, Robert, *The World America Made* (New York: Vintage, 2013).

Kamrava, Mehran, 'The Arab Spring and the Saudi-led counterrevolution', *Orbis*, 56: 1 (2012), 96–104.

Kanat, Kilic Bugra, *A Tale of Four Augusts: Obama's Syria Policy* (Washington, DC: SETA, 2015).

Kaplan, Fred, 'Whatever Happened to the Plan to Defeat ISIS?' *Slate* 8/5/17, http://www.slate.com/articles/news_and_politics/war_stories/2017/05/trump_has_been_given_a_plan_to_defeat_isis_why_isn_t_he_acting_on_it.html [accessed 15/8/17].

Kandemir, Asli, 'Turkey to Iran gold trade wiped out by new U.S. sanction', *Reuters* 15/2/13, http://www.reuters.com/article/2013/02/15/us-iran-turkey-sanctions-idUSBRE91E0IN20130215 [accessed 23/7/15].

Kardaş, Şaban, *From Zero Problems to Leading the Change: Making Sense of Transformation in Turkey's Regional Policy*, TEPAV Turkish Policy Brief Series, no. 5 (2012).

Katz, Mark N., 'Russia and the conflict in Syria: four myths', *Middle East Policy*, 20: 2 (2013), 38–46.

Kenner, David and Molly O'Toole, 'The Race to Raqqa Could Cost Trump Turkey', *Foreign Policy* 21/3/17, http://foreignpolicy.com/2017/03/21/the-race-to-raqqa-couldcost-trump-turkey/ [accessed 2/8/17].

Kerr, S., 'Saudi cracks down on youths travelling to Syria', *Financial Times* 4/2/14.

Khaddour, Kheder, 'Securing the Syrian regime', *Sada*, Carnegie Endowment for International Peace 3/6/14, http://carnegieendowment.org/sada/?fa=55783 [accessed 10/12/15].

Khaddour, Kheder, *The Assad Regime's Hold on the Syrian State*, Carnegie Research Paper 8/7/15, http://carnegie-mec.org/2015/07/08/assad-regime-s-hold-on-syrian-state/id3k [accessed 5/9/15].

Khatib, Lina, 'Qatar's foreign policy: the limits of pragmatism', *International Affairs*, 89: 2 (2013), 417–431.

Kirkpatrick, David D., 'Muslim Brotherhood says Qatar ousted its members', *New York Times* 13/9/14.

Kozak, Christopher, ' "An army in all corners": Assad's campaign strategy in Syria', Institute for the Study of War, April 2015, http://www.understandingwar.org/sites/default/files/An%20Army%20in%20All%20Corners%20by%20Chris%20Kozak%201.pdf [accessed 7/7/15].

Kozak, Christopher, 'Regime and Iranian forces launch multi-pronged offensive in Aleppo', Institute for the Study of War, 22/10/15, http://understandingwar.org/map/regime-and-iranian-forces-launch-multi-pronged-offensive-aleppo#sthash.p4mP44mf.dpuf [accessed 11/3/16].

Kuchins, Andrew C. and Igor A. Zevelev, 'Russian foreign policy: continuity in change', *Washington Quarterly*, 35: 1 (2012), 147–161.

Kühn, Alexander, Christoph Reuter and Gregor Peter Schmitz, 'After the Arab Spring: Al-Jazeera Losing Battle for Independence', *Spiegel Online International* 15/2/13, http://www.spiegel.de/international/world/al-jazeera-criticized-for-lack-of-independence-after-arab-spring-a-883343.html [accessed 10/5/14].

Kuperman, Alan and Timothy Crawford (eds), *Gambling on Humanitarian Intervention: Moral Hazard, Rebellion, and Internal War* (New York: Routledge, 2006).

Lacey, Robert, *Inside the Kingdom* (London: Random House, 2011).

Lacroix, Stephane, *Saudi Islamists and the Arab Spring*, Kuwait Programme on Development, Governance and Globalisation in the Gulf States, Research Paper 36, May 2014, http://eprints.lse.ac.uk/56725/1/Lacroix_Saudi-Islamists-and-theArab-Spring_2014.pdf [accessed 12/8/15].

Lake, Eli, 'Iran spends billions to prop up Assad', *Bloomberg View* 9/6/15, http://www.bloombergview.com/articles/2015-06-09/iran-spends-billions-to-prop-up-assad [accessed 10/12/15].

Landis, Joshua, 'Islamic education in Syria: undoing secularism'. Unpublished paper prepared for *Constructs of Inclusion and Exclusion: Religion and Identity Formation in Middle Eastern School Curricula*, Watson Institute for International Studies, Brown University, November 2003. https://faculty-staff.ou.edu/L/Joshua.M.Landis-1/Islamic%20Education%20in%20Syria.htm [accessed 20/2/15].

Landis, Joshua, 'Assad and Ahmadinejad – "There is no separating Iran and Syria" ', *Syria Comment* 26/2/10, http://www.joshualandis.com/blog/assad-and-ahmadinejad-there-is-no-separating-iran-and-syria/ [accessed 22/4/15].

Landis, Joshua, 'The man behind "Syria Revolution Facebook Page" speaks out', *Syria Comment* 24/4/11, http://www.joshualandis.com/blog/the-man-behind-syria-revolution-2011-facebook-page-speaks-out/ [accessed 3/6/15].

Landis, Joshua, 'Regime's top Sunni defects – General Manaf Mustafa Tlass flees to Turkey', *Syria Comment* 5/7/12, http://www.joshualandis.com/blog/regimes-top-sunni-defects-general-manaf-mustafa-tlass-flees-to-turkey/ [accessed 1/6/15].

Lawson, Fred H., 'Implications of the 2011–13 Syrian uprising for the Middle Eastern Regional Security Complex', *Georgetown Papers* 2014.

Lawson, Fred H., 'Syria's mutating civil war and its impact on Turkey, Iraq and Iran', *International Affairs*, 90.6 (2014), 1351–65.

Layne, Christopher, 'The unipolar illusion: why new great powers will rise', *International Security* (1993), 5–51.

Layne, Christopher, 'This time it's real: the end of unipolarity and the Pax Americana', *International Studies Quarterly*, 56 (2012), 203–13.

Lee, Matthew and Bradley Klapper, 'Assad can stay, for now: Kerry accepts Russian stance', Associated Press 15/12/15, http://news.yahoo.com/kerry-moscow-talks-syria-ukraine-081842398.html [accessed 10/2/16].

Leenders, Reinoud and Steven Heydemann, 'Popular mobilisation in Syria: opportunity and threat, and the social networks of the early risers', *Mediterranean Politics*, 17: 2 (2012), 139–59.

Leenders, Reinoud, 'Collective action and mobilization in Dar'a: an anatomy of the onset of Syria's popular uprising', *Mobilisation*, 17: 4 (2012), 419–34.

Lefèvre, Raphaël, *Ashes of Hama: The Muslim Brotherhood in Syria* (Oxford: Oxford University Press, 2013).

Lefèvre, Raphaël, 'Saudi and Syrian Muslim Brotherhood', *Middle East Institute* 27/9/13, http://www.mei.edu/content/saudi-arabia-and-syrian-brotherhood [accessed 2/5/15].

Lesch, David W., *The New Lion of Damascus* (New York: Yale University Press, 2005).

Lesch, David W., *Syria: The Fall of the House of Assad* (London: Yale University Press, 2013).

Lesch, David W., 'The Golden Runaway', *Foreign Policy*, 12/7/12.

Lesch, David W., 'Assad's fateful choice', *Syria Comment* 9/4/16, http://www.joshualandis.com/blog/ [accessed 11/4/16].

Leverett, Flynt, *Inheriting Syria: Bashar's Trial by Fire* (New York: Brookings Institution Press, 2005).

Lieber, Robert, 'Rhetoric or reality? American grand strategy and the contemporary Middle East', paper prepared for delivery at the 2014 Annual Meeting of the American Political Science Association Washington, DC, 28–31 August 2014.

Lister, Charles, *The Syria Jihad* (London: Hurst, 2015).

Littell, Jonathan, *Syrian Notebooks: Inside the Homs Uprising* (London: Verso Books, 2015) [Kindle edition].

Lizza, Ryan, 'The consequentialist: how the Arab Spring remade Obama's foreign policy', *New Yorker* 2/15/2011.

Loshky, Jay, 'Iranians' support for Syria softens', *Gallup* 15/11/13, http://www.gallup.com/poll/165878/iranians-support-syria-softens.aspx [accessed 12/12/14].

Loveluck, Louisa, 'Assad can stay in power "three months or longer", says Hammond', *Telegraph* 4/10/15.

Lowe, Robert and Cengiz Gunes, *The Impact of the Syrian War on Kurdish Politics across the Middle East,* Chatham House Research Paper, July 2015.

Luhn, Alec, 'Russia's campaign in Syria leads to arms sale windfall', *Guardian* 29/3/16.

Lund, Aron, 'The Free Syrian Army doesn't exist', *Syria Comment* 16/3/13, http://www.joshualandis.com/blog/the-free-syrian-army-doesnt-exist/ [accessed 1/2/15].

Lund, Aron, 'The political geography of Syria's war: an interview with Fabrice Balanche', *Syria in Crisis* for Carnegie Endowment for International Peace 30/1/15, http://carnegieendowment.org/syriaincrisis/?fa=58875 [accessed 12/5/15].

Lund, Aron, 'The death of Rustum Ghazaleh', *Syria in Crisis* for Carnegie Endowment for International Peace 30/4/15, http://carnegieendowment.org/syriaincrisis/?fa=59953 [accessed 10/3/16].

Lund, Aron, 'Syria's Kurds at the center of America's anti-Jihadi strategy', *Syria in Crisis* for Carnegie Endowment for International Peace 2/12/15, http://carnegieendowment.org/syriaincrisis/?fa=62158 [accessed 10/3/16].

Lund, Aron, 'Syria's opposition conferences: results and expectations', *Syria in Crisis* for Carnegie Endowment for International Peace 11/12/15, http://carnegieendowment.org/syriaincrisis/?fa=62263 [accessed 10/3/16].

Lund, Aron, 'The ten most important developments in Syria in 2015', *Syria Comment* 3/1/16, http://www.joshualandis.com/blog/ten-most-important-developments-syria-2015/ [accessed 12/3/16].

Lund, Aron, 'The road to Geneva: the who, when, and how of Syria's peace talks', *Syria in Crisis* for Carnegie Endowment for International Peace 29/1/16, http://carnegieendowment.org/syriaincrisis/?fa=62631[accessed 10/3/16].

Lund, Aron, 'Interpreting the Russian withdrawal from Syria', *Syria in Crisis* for Carnegie Endowment for International Peace 15/3/16, http://carnegieendowment.org/syriaincrisis/?fa=63042 [accessed 25/3/16].

Lund, Aron, 'After Palmyra, where next for Assad?' *Syria in Crisis* for Carnegie Endowment for International Peace 31/3/16, http://carnegieendowment.org/syriaincrisis/?fa=63201 [accessed 1/4/16].

Lund, Aron, 'Black flags over Idlib: The jihadi power grab in northwestern Syria', *IRIN news* 9/8/17, https://www.irinnews.org/analysis/2017/08/09/black-flags-over-idlibjihadi-power-grab-northwestern-syria [accessed 20/8/17].

Lynch, Colum, 'Saudis to push General Assembly vote on Syria intervention', *Foreign Policy*, 6/9/13.

Lynch, Marc, 'Obama and the Middle East', *Foreign Affairs* September/October 2015.

Lynch, Marc, 'After the political science relevance revolution', *Washington Post*, 23/3/16.

Mabon, Simon, *Saudi Arabia and Iran: Soft Power Rivalry in the Middle East* (London: I.B. Tauris, 2013).

MacDonald, Alex, 'ANALYSIS: Ahrar al-Sham's fall hands Syrian rebellion to al-Qaeda', *Middle East Eye* 18/8/17, http://www.middleeasteye.net/news/destruction-major-rebel-group-leaves-syrian-oppositionhands-hts-1909379351 [accessed 20/8/17].

Mahmood, Mona and Martin Chulov, 'Syrian war widens Sunni–Shia schism as foreign jihadis join fight for shrines', *Guardian* 4/6/13.

Malas, Nour, 'Syria rebels plead for ammunition', *Wall Street Journal* 3/3/12.

Marquand, Robert, 'Syria's opposition concerned about independent armed rebel groups', *Christian Science Monitor*, 27/1/12, http://www.csmonitor.com/World/Europe/2012/0127/Syria-s-opposition-concerned-about-independent-armed-rebel-groups [accessed 7/7/15].

Martin, Lenore G., 'Turkey and the USA in a bipolarizing Middle East', *Journal of Balkan and Near Eastern Studies* 15: 2 (2013), 175–188.

Mason, Robert, 'Back to realism for an enduring U.S.–Saudi relationship', *Middle East Policy*, 21: 4 (Winter 2014), 32–44.

Mazzetti, Mark, 'C.I.A. study of covert aid fueled skepticism about helping Syrian rebels', *New York Times* 14/10/14.

Mazzetti, Mark, Robert F. Worth and Michael R. Gordon, 'Obama's uncertain path amid Syria bloodshed', *New York Times* 22/10/13.

McCants, William. 'Gulf charities and Syrian sectarianism', *Foreign Policy* 30/9/13.

McGee Thomas, 'Mapping action and identity in the Kobani crisis response', *Kurdish Studies Journal*, 4: 1 (2016), 51–77.

McGreal, Chris and Martin Chulov, 'Syria: Assad must resign, says Obama', *Guardian* 19/8/15.

MEE Staff, '"Putin won in Syria": Trump ends CIA weapons, training for Syria rebels', *Middle East Eye* 19/7/18, http://www.middleeasteye.net/news/putin-won-syria-trump-ends-cia-weaponstraining-syria-rebels-587124117 [accessed 28/8/17].

McKirdy, Euan and Laura Smith-Spark, 'CIA no longer arming anti-Assad rebels, Washington Post reports', *CNN* 20/7/17, http://edition.cnn.com/2017/07/20/politics/cia-syria-anti-assad-rebels/index.html [accessed 15/8/17].

Melman Yossi and Sof Hashavua, 'In depth: how Iranian weapons reach Hezbollah', *Jerusalem Post* 25/5/13.

Middle East Eye, 'UN peacekeepers withdraw from Syria-controlled sector of Golan Heights', *Middle East Eye* 15/9/14, http://www.middleeasteye.net/news/un-peacekeepers-withdrawn-syria-controlled-sector-golan-heights-819345932 [accessed 24/11/15].

Middle East Online, 'Russia will not allow Libya-style military intervention in Syria', *Middle East Online*, 1/11/11, http://www.middle-east-online.com/english/?id=48833 [accessed 10/5/13].

Miles, Hugh, *al-Jazeera* (London: Abacus, 2005).

Mohammed, Arshad, 'Kerry: Syrian surrender of chemical arms could stop U.S. attack', *Reuters* 9/9/13, http://www.reuters.com/article/us-syria-crisis-kerry-idUSBRE9880BV20130909 [accessed 14/6/15].

Monshipouri, Mahmood and Manochehr Dorraj, 'Iran's foreign policy: a shifting strategic landscape', *Middle East Policy*, 20: 4 (Winter 2013), pp. 133–47.

Morris, Justin, 'Libya and Syria: R2P and the spectre of the swinging pendulum', *International Affairs*, 89: 5 (2013), 1265–83.

Mortimer, Caroline, 'Israel on verge of sending troops into Syria over increased threat of terrorist attack', *Independent* 17/8/15.

Mortimer, Caroline, 'Donald Trump's campaign against Isis results in nearly as many civilian deaths as during Obama's entire administration', *Independent* 17/7/17, http://www.independent.co.uk/news/world/middle-east/donald-trump-syria-death-tollcampaign-military-operations-barack-obama-administration-a7844526.html [accessed 17/8/17].

Munoz, Carlo, 'McCain, Graham: Syria deal an "act of weakness" by White House', *The Hill* 14/9/13, http://thehill.com/policy/defense/322281–syria-deal-an-act-of-weakness-by-white-house-say-senate-republicans [accessed 4/8/15].

Murphy, Richard W., 'Why Washington didn't intervene in Syria last time', *Foreign Affairs*, 20 March 2012.

Naame Shaam, *Iran in Syria: From an Ally of the Regime to an Occupying Force*, September 2014, http://www.naameshaam.org/report-iran-in-syria/ [accessed 2/3/15].

Nader, Alireza, 'Iran & Region III: goals in Syria', *The Iran Primer* 26/1/15, http://iranprimer.usip.org/blog/2015/jan/26/iran-region-iii-goals-syria [accessed 10/10/15].

Nasr, Vali, *The Dispensable Nation* (London: Scribe, 2013).

Nasrawi, Salah, 'Saudis reportedly funding Iraqi Sunnis', AP for *Washington Post* 8/12/06.

Nasser, Rabie, 'Socioeconomic roots and impact of the Syria crisis', Syria Center for Policy Research, January 2013, http://scpr-syria.org/att/1360464324_Tf75J.pdf [accessed 2/2/15].

Naumkin, Vitaly, 'Russia's Middle East policy after the G-20 summit', *Al-Monitor* 24/11/14, http://www.al-monitor.com/pulse/originals/2014/11/russia-middle-east-policy-after-g20.html#ixzz3uTctmzmI [accessed 12/4/15].

Nerguizian, Aram, 'The military balance in a shattered Levant', Centre for Strategic and International Studies, 15/6/15 p. 113, http://csis.org/files/publication/150615_Nerguizian_Levant_Mil_Bal_Report_w_cover_v2.pdf [accessed 10/8/15].

Nizameddin, Talal, *Putin's New Order in the Middle East* (London: Hurst, 2013)

Norton, Ben, 'The shocking statistics behind Syria's humanitarian crisis', *Think Progress* 2/6/14 http://thinkprogress.org/world/2014/06/02/3443171/syria-crisis-stats/ [accessed 1/4/15].

Nothstine, Ray, 'Syrian President Assad: Putin is the only world leader protecting Christians', *Christian Post* 20/11/15.

Nougayrède, Natalie, 'The devastation of Syria will be Obama's legacy', *Guardian* 22/9/16, https://www.theguardian.com/commentisfree/2016/sep/22/syria-obama-us-president-putin-russia [accessed 20/7/17].

NPR, 'Kofi Annan on Syria, hard choices of peacekeeping', *NPR*, 27/8/12, http://www.npr.org/2012/09/01/160135085/kofi-annan-on-the-difficult-choices-of-a-peacekeeper. [accessed 10/8/15]

Nye, Joseph S. 'The twenty-first century will not be a "post-American" World', *International Studies Quarterly*, 56: 1 (2012), 215–17.

Occupied Liberated Kafranbel, http://www.occupiedkafranbel.com/banners [accessed 15/12/15].

O'Connor, Tom, 'Russia, Iran, other Assad allies and enemies cash in on success in Syria, but US left out', *Newsweek* 17/8/17, http://www.newsweek.com/russia-iran-assad-allyenemy-syria-war-us-651953 [accessed 20/8/17].

Osnos, Evan, 'The Biden agenda', *New Yorker* 28/7/14.

O'Toole, James, 'Billions at stake as Russia backs Syria', *CNN* 10/2/12, http://money.cnn.com/2012/02/09/news/international/russia_syria/ [accessed 10/3/16]

Ottaway, David,. *The King's Messenger: Prince Bandar bin Sultan and America's Tangled Relationship with Saudi Arabia* (New York: Walker, 2008).

Ottaway, David, 'The struggle for power in Saudi Arabia', *Foreign Policy* 19/6/13.

Oweis, Khaled Yacoub, 'Insight: Saudi Arabia boosts Salafist rivals to al Qaeda in Syria' *Reuters* 1/10/13, http://www.reuters.com/article/2013/10/01/us-syria-crisis-jihadists-insight-idUSBRE9900RO20131001 [accessed 13/10/15].

Paton Walsh, Nick and Ewen MacAskill, 'Putin lashes out at "wolf-like" America', *Guardian* 11/5/06.

Payne, Ed, Barbara Starr and Susannah Cullinane, 'Russia launches first airstrikes in Syria', *CNN* 1/10/15, http://edition.cnn.com/2015/09/30/politics/russia-syria-airstrikes-isis/index.html [accessed 10/3/16].

Pew Research Center, 'Views of Middle East unchanged by recent events', Pew Research Center 10/6/11, http://www.people-press.org/2011/06/10/views-of-middle-east-unchanged-by-recent-events/ [accessed 14/6/15].

Phillips, Christopher, *Into the Quagmire: Turkey's Frustrated Syria Policy*, Chatham House Briefing Paper (2012), 5.

Phillips, Christopher, *Everyday Arab Identity: The Daily Reproduction of the Arab World* (London: Routledge, 2013).

Phillips, Christopher, 'The Arabism debate and the Arab uprisings', *Mediterranean Politics*, 19: 1 (2014), 141–4.

Phillips, Christopher, 'Sectarianism and Conflict in Syria', *Third World Quarterly*, 36: 2 (2015), 357–76.

Phillips, Christopher, 'What is left of Assad's state is eroding from within', *Chatham House* 9/3/15, http://www.chathamhouse.org/expert/comment/17113 [accessed 24/8/15].

Phillips, Christopher, 'Intervention and non-intervention in the Syria crisis', in F. Kühn and M. Turner (eds), *The Politics of International Intervention* (London: Routledge, 2016)

Pierret, Thomas, 'Sunni clergy politics in the cities of Ba'athi Syria', in Fred Lawson (ed.), *Demystifying Syria* (London: Saqi, 2009), 70–84.

Pierret, Thomas, '"Syrian regime loses last credible ally among the Sunni ulema", by Thomas Pierret', *Syria Comment*, 22/3/13, http://www.joshualandis.com/blog/syrian-regime-loses-last-credible-ally-among-the-sunni-ulama-by-thomas-pierret/ [accessed 24/5/15].

Pollack, Kenneth, Paul R. Pillar, Amin Tarzi and Chas W. Freeman Jr., 'Symposium: U.S. foreign policy and the future of the Middle East', *Middle East Policy*, 21: 3 (Fall 2014), 1–30.

Putin, Vladimir V., 'A plea for caution from Russia', *New York Times* 11/9/13.

Quinlivan, James T., 'Coup-proofing: its practice and consequences in the Middle East', *International Security*, 24: 2 (1999), 131–65.

Rabil, Robert G. *Syria, the United States, and the War on Terror in the Middle East* (Praeger Security International, 2006).

Rafizadeh, Majid, 'Iran's economic stake in Syria', *Foreign Policy* 4/1/13.

Regan, Patrick, 'Third party interventions and the duration of intrastate conflicts', *Journal of Conflict Resolution*, 46: 1 (2002), 55–73.

Reuter, Christopher, 'Syria's mercenaries: the Afghans fighting Assad's war', *Spiegel Online* 11/5/15, http://www.spiegel.de/international/world/afghan-mercenaries-fighting-for-assad-and-stuck-in-syria-a-1032869.html [accessed 7/8/15].

Reuters, 'Syria opposition chiefs at odds over military body', *Reuters* 1/3/12, http://uk.reuters.com/article/2012/03/01/us-syria-opposition-idUSTRE8200SA20120301.

Reuters, 'Assad: Russia is supplying weapons to Syria under contracts finalized since the conflict began', *Reuters* 30/5/15, http://uk.businessinsider.com/r-syria-gets-russian-arms-under-deals-signed-since-conflict-began-assad—2015–3?r=US&IR=T [accessed 10/11/15].

Reuters, 'Benjamin Netanyahu to discuss "bad" Iran nuclear deal with Donald Trump', *Guardian* 4/12/16, https://www.theguardian.com/world/2016/dec/04/benjaminnetan-yahu-donald-trump-iran-nuclear-deal [accessed 1/8/17].

Reuters, 'U.N. Syria envoy says rebel city Idlib risks Aleppo fate if no peace talks', *Reuters* 15/12/16, https://www.reuters.com/article/us-mideast-crisis-syria-demistura-idUSKBN1442N1 [accessed 10/8/17].

Reuters, '4,000 fighters have left Aleppo in latest stage, thousands await evacuation: Red Cross', *Reuters* 22/12/16, https://www.reuters.com/article/us-mideast-crisis-syria-aleppo-redcross-idUSKBN14B14O [accessed 10/8/17].

Reuters, 'Russia and China veto UN resolution to impose sanctions on Syria', *Guardian* 1/3/17, https://www.theguardian.com/world/2017/mar/01/russia-and-chinaveto-un-resolution-to-impose-sanctions-on-syria [accessed 15/8/17].

Roberts, David, 'Qatar: domestic quietism, elite adventuring', in F. Ayub (ed.), *What Does the Gulf Think about the Arab Awakening?* (London: ECFR, 2013), http://www.ecfr.eu/page/-/ECFR75_GULF_ANALYSIS_AW.pdf [accessed 3/4/14].

Robins, Philip, *Suits and Uniforms: Turkish Foreign Policy since the Cold War* (London: Hurst, 2003).

Robins, Philip, 'Turkey's "double gravity" predicament: the foreign policy of a newly activist power', *International Affairs*, 89: 2 (2013), 381–97.

Rogin, Josh, 'U.S. shoots down idea of Syria Safe Zone', *Bloomberg View* 28/7/15, http://www.bloombergview.com/articles/2015–07–28/u-s-shoots-down-idea-of-syria-safe-zone [accessed 10/3/16].

Rose, Gideon, 'The post-American Middle East', *Foreign Affairs* November/December 2015.

Rothkopf, David, 'The Gamble', *Foreign Policy* 31/8/13.

Rowell, Alex, 'Mapping Hezbollah's Syria war since 2011', *Now Lebanon* 12/8/15, https://mobile.mmedia.me/lb/en/reportsfeatures/565725–mapping-hezbollahs-syria-war-since-2011 [accessed 3/9/15].

Rozen, Laura, 'Three days in March: New details on how US, Iran opened direct talks', *The Backchannel* 8/1/14, http://backchannel.al-monitor.com/index.php/2014/01/7484/three-days-in-march-new-details-on-the-u-s-iran-backchannel/ [accessed 23/7/15].

Rozen, Laura, 'On eve of Syria peace talks, Saudi Arabia questions Russian, Iranian Intentions', *Al-Monitor* 28/10/15, http://www.al-monitor.com/pulse/originals/2015/10/us-welcome-iran-syria-peace-talks.html# [accessed 12/3/16].

RT, 'Russia delivers humanitarian aid to Syria', *RT* 24/2/16, https://www.rt.com/in-motion/333520–russia-syria-humanitarian-aid/ [accessed 10/3/16].

RT, 'Putin discusses Syria ceasefire with world leaders by phone', *RT* 24/2/16, https://www.rt.com/news/333481–putin-assad-syria-ceasefire/ [accessed 10/3/16].

RT, 'Putin orders start of Russian military withdrawal from Syria, says "objectives achieved"', *RT* 14/3/16, https://www.rt.com/news/335554–putin-orders-syria-withdrawal/ [accessed 31/3/16].

RT, '"Blatant violation of sovereignty": Damascus condemns Turkish operation in Jarablus', *RT* 24/8/16, https://www.rt.com/news/357060-syria-condemn-turkey-operation/ [accessed 5/8/17].

Ryan, Curtis, 'The new Arab cold war and the struggle for Syria', *Middle East Report* 262 (2012), 28–31.

Sadjadpour, Karim, 'The supreme leader', *The Iran Primer, United States Institute of Peace*, http://iranprimer.usip.org/resource/supreme-leader [accessed 1/5/15].

Sahner, Christian, *Among the Ruins: Syria Past and Present* (London: Hurst, 2014).

Samaan, Maher and Anne Barnard, 'Assad, in rare admission, says Syria's army lacks manpower', *New York Times* 26/7/15.

Sands, Phil, and Suha Maayeh, 'Syrian rebels get arms and advice through secret command centre in Amman', *The National* 28/12/13, http://www.thenational.ae/world/middle-east/syrian-rebels-get-arms-and-advice-through-secret-command-centre-in-amman [accessed 5/5/15].

Sands, Phil, Justin Vela and Suha Maayeh, 'Blood ties: the shadowy member of the Assad clan who ignited the Syrian conflict', *The National* 20/3/14, http://www.thenational.ae/world/middle-east/blood-ties-the-shadowy-member-of-the-assad-clan-who-ignited-the-syrian-conflict [accessed 15/5/15].

Sanger, David E. and Eric Schmitt, 'Pentagon says 75,000 troops might be needed to seize Syria chemical arms', *New York Times* 15/11/12.

Sayigh, Yezid, 'The Syrian opposition's very provisional government', *Carnegie* 28/3/13, http://carnegie-mec.org/2013/03/28/syrian-opposition-s-very-provisional-government [accessed 3/7/15].

Sayigh, Yezid, 'The Syrian opposition's leadership problem', *Carnegie Papers* 3/4/13, http://carnegieendowment.org/2013/04/03/syrian-opposition-s-leadership-problem/fx6v# [accessed 10/5/13].

Sayigh, Yezid and Avi Shlaim (eds), *The Cold War and the Middle East* (Oxford: Clarendon Press, 1997).

Schanzer, Jonathan, 'The anatomy of Turkey's "Gas-For Gold" scheme with Iran', *Foundation for the Defense of Democracies* 14/3/14, http://www.defenddemocracy.org/media-hit/the-anatomy-of-turkeys-gas-for-gold-scheme-with-iran/ [accessed 23/7/15].

Schmitt, Eric, 'C.I.A. said to aid in steering arms to Syrian opposition', *New York Times* 21/6/12.

Schmitt, Eric, 'Obama Administration Considers Arming Syrian Kurds Against ISIS', *New York Times* 21/9/17, https://www.nytimes.com/2016/09/22/world/middleeast/obama-syria-kurds-isisturkey-military-commandos.html?mcubz=0 [accessed 16/8/17].

Seale, Patrick, *The Struggle for Syria* (London: The Royal Institute of International Affairs, 1965).

Seale, Patrick, *Asad of Syria: The Struggle for the Middle East* (University of California Press, 1990).

Selby, Jan and Mike Hulme, 'Is climate change really to blame for Syria's civil war?' *Guardian* 29/11/15.

Sestanovich, Stephen, 'The Brilliant Incoherence of Trump's Foreign Policy', *The Atlantic* May 2017, https://www.theatlantic.com/magazine/archive/2017/05/the-brilliantincoherence-of-trumps-foreign-policy/521430/ [accessed 1/8/17].

Sengupta, Kim, 'Syria peace talks: John Kerry leads calls for removal of President Bashar al-Assad', *Independent* 22/1/14.

Seufert, Günter, 'Internal driving forces for Turkey's Middle East policy', *Südosteuropa Mitteilungen*, 01 (2013), 79–84.

Shadid, Anthony, 'Syria arrests scores in house-to-house roundup', *New York Times* 5/5/11.

Shadid, Anthony, 'Thousands turn out for Assad', *New York Times* 21/6/11.

Shafak, Elif, 'On Turkey's turmoil: "Intimidation and paranoia dominates the land"', *Guardian* 1/3/16.

Shaheen, Kareem, 'One year after the failed coup in Turkey, the crackdown continues', *Guardian* 14/7/17, https://www.theguardian.com/world/2017/jul/14/one-yearafter-the-failed-coup-in-turkey-the-crackdown-continues [accessed 15/8/17]

Shapiro, Jeremy, 'The Qatar problem', *Foreign Policy* 28/8/13.

Sherlock, Ruth, 'Libya to arm rebels in Syria', *Telegraph* 27/11/11.

Sherlock, Ruth, 'Exclusive interview: why I defected from Bashar al-Assad's regime, by former diplomat Nawaf Fares', *Telegraph* 14/7/12 [accessed 14/7/15].

Sherlock, Ruth and Richard Spencer, 'Syria's Assad accused of boosting al-Qaeda with secret oil deals', *Telegraph* 20/1/14.

Siddiqui, Haroon, 'Bomb Assad's palaces and army barracks', *Toronto Star* 2/6/12.

Simon, Steven and Jonathan Stevenson, 'The end of Pax Americana', *Foreign Affairs* November/December 2015,

Sky, Emma, *The Unraveling* (New York: Public Affairs, 2015).

Sly, Liz, 'How Saddam Hussein's former military officers and spies are controlling Isis', *Independent* 5/4/15.

Smyth, Philip, 'Iran's Afghan Shiite fighters in Syria', Washington Institute 3/6/14, http://www.washingtoninstitute.org/policy-analysis/view/irans-afghan-shiite-fighters-in-syria [accessed 5/7/15].

Solomon, Erika, 'Betrayal and disarray behind Syrian rebel rout in Yabroud', *Financial Times* 21/3/14.

Solomon, Erika, 'Syria: a tale of three cities', *Financial Times* 3/8/17, https://www.ft.com/content/6710ab2a-7716-11e7-90c0-90a9d1bc9691 [accessed 10/8/17].

Solomon, Jay, 'U.S., Israel monitor suspected Syrian WMD', *Wall Street Journal* 27/8/11.

Soylu, Ragip, 'Turkish officials say they didn't reveal secret US bases in Syria', *Daily Sabah* 21/7/17, https://www.dailysabah.com/war-on-terror/2017/07/21/turkish-officialssay-they-didnt-reveal-secret-us-bases-in-syria [accessed 5/8/17].

Spencer, Richard, 'Barack Obama rejects accusations of American weakness over Syria', *Telegraph* 15/9/13.

Spencer, Richard, 'Syria: Bashar al-Assad agrees "in principle" to head to peace conference', *Telegraph* 24/5/13.

Starr, Stephen, *Revolt in Syria: Eye-witness to the Uprising* (London: Hurst, 2012).

Stein, Aaron, 'Turkey's two-front war', *The American Interest* 4/2/16.

Stein, Ewan, 'Modalities of Jihadist activism in the Middle East and North Africa', *IEMed Mediterranean Yearbook 2015* http://www.iemed.org/observatori/arees-danalisi/arxius-adjunts/anuari/med.2015/IEMed%20Yearbook%202015_JihadismMENA_EwanStein.pdf [accessed 12/12/15].

Steinberg, Guido, 'Qatar and the Arab Spring: support for Islamists and new anti-Syria policy', German Institute for International and Security Affairs, *SWP commentary* 7/2/12, http://www.swp-berlin.org/fileadmin/contents/products/comments/2012C07_sbg.pdf [accessed 12/6/15].

Stephens, Bret, *America in Retreat: The New Isolationism and the Coming Global Disorder* (New York: Sentinel, 2014).

Stephens, Bret, 'Trump's Foreign Policy: The Conservatives' Report Card', *New York Times* 21/7/17, https://www.nytimes.com/2017/07/21/opinion/trumps-foreign-policy-the-conservatives-reportcard.html [accessed 4/8/17].

Stephens, Michael, 'The underestimated Prince Nayef', *Foreign Policy* 18/6/12.

Sullivan, Marisa, 'Hezbollah in Syria', Institute for the Study of War April 2014, http://www.understandingwar.org/report/hezbollah-syria [accessed 12/5/15].

Syrian Center for Policy Research, *Confronting Fragmentation* 11/2/16, http://scpr-syria.org/publications/confronting-fragmentation/ [accessed 10/3/16].

Tabler, Andrew, *In the Lion's Den: An Eyewitness Account of Washington's Battle with Syria* (Chicago: Lawrence Hill, 2011).

Telhami, Shibley, *2008 Arab Public Opinion Poll* (University of Maryland, 2008).

The Daily Star, 'Islamist rebels reject "hollow" Syria peace talks', *Daily Star* 20/1/14.

The Daily Star, 'Engaging with Assad a "lesser evil", Spain says after Paris attacks', *Daily Star* 18/11/15.

The Economist, 'The charm of telesalafism', *Economist* 20/10/12.

The Economist, 'Shackled: the story of the world's most elaborate sanctions regime', *Economist* 1/11/14.

The Economist, 'Melons for everyone', *Economist* 27/10/14.

The Telegraph, 'Amateur footage emerges of Syrian jets deployed against rebels', *Telegraph* 25/7/12.

The Telegraph, 'Vladimir Putin: supporting Syrian regime only way to end war', *Telegraph* 25/9/16.

The Telegraph, 'Donald Trump's Saudi Arabia speech: eight key points', *The Telegraph* 21/5/17, http://www.telegraph.co.uk/news/2017/05/21/donald-trumps-saudi-arabia-speech-eight-key-points/

The White House, 'Press Conference by President Obama in Lima, Peru', The White House Office of the Press Secretary 20/11/16, https://obamawhitehouse.archives.gov/the-press-office/2016/11/20/press-conference-president-obama-lima-peru [accessed 10/8/17].

Torres, Hazel, 'Russian Orthodox Church supports Putin's "holy war" in Syria to protect Christians', *Christian Today* 2/10/15, http://www.christiantoday.com/article/russian.orthodox.church.supports.putins.holy.war.in.syria.to.protect.christians/66312.htm [accessed 10/2/16].

Trenin, Dmitri, 'The mythical alliance: Russia's Syria policy', Carnegie Moscow Centre, February 2013, http://carnegieendowment.org/files/mythical_alliance.pdf [accessed 6/11/14].

Trenin, Dmitri, 'Putin's Syria gambit aims at something bigger than Syria', *Tablet* 13/10/15.

Trenin, Dmitri, 'Turkish–Russian war of words goes beyond downed plane', al-Jazeera America 9/12/15, http://america.aljazeera.com/articles/2015/12/9/turkey-russian-relationship-felled-by-more-than-a-downed-jet.html [accessed 10/3/16].

Turkmani, Rim, 'Countering the logic of the war economy in Syria: evidence from three local areas', Security in Transition Report for the London School of Economics 30/7/15 http://www.securityintransition.org/wp-content/uploads/2015/08/Countering-war-economy-Syria2.pdf [accessed 12/11/15].

Ulrichsen, Kristian Coates, *Qatar and the Arab Spring* (London: Hurst, 2014).

Unger, Craig, *House of Bush, House of Saud: The Secret Relationship between the World's Two Most Powerful Dynasties* (New York: Gibson Square Books, 2007).

Uzgel, İlhan, 'New Middle East: Turkey from being a playmaker to seclusion in the new Middle East', *Centre for Policy and Research on Turkey*, 4: 1 (2015), 47–55.

Valbjørn, Morton and Andre Bank, 'The new Arab Cold War: rediscovering the Arab dimension of Middle East regional politics', *Review of International Studies*, 38: 1 (2012), 3–24.

Valley, Paul, 'The vicious schism between Sunni and Shia has been poisoning Islam for 1,400 years – and it's getting worse', *Independent* 19/2/14.

van Tets, Fernande, 'Exodus: terrified Syrians dash to flee air strikes', *Independent* 1/9/13.

van Wilgenburg, Wladimir, 'Syrian Kurds agree to disagree', *Al-Monitor* 30/12/13, http://www.al-monitor.com/pulse/originals/2013/12/syria-kurds-geneva-opposition-delegation-peace.html# [accessed 16/10/15].

Vela, J. 'Rebel forces armed by wealthy exiles', *Independent* 23/2/12.

Violence Documentation Center in Syria, http://vdc-sy.net/en/ [accessed 12/8/17].

Walker, Shaun, 'Plane loads of cash: flight records reveal Russia flew 30 tonnes of bank notes to Syrian regime', *Independent* 26/11/12.

Walker, Tim, 'Syria civil war: staff manning US ceasefire hotline "can't speak Arabic"', *Independent* 3/3/16.

Wall Street Journal, 'Interview with Syrian President Bashar al-Assad', *Wall Street Journal* 31/1/11.

Walt, Stephen, 'Why the Tunisian Revolution won't spread', *Foreign Policy* 16/1/11.

Walt, Stephen, 'Double Diss', *Foreign Policy* 13/8/14.

Walt, Stephen, 'Lax Americana', *Foreign Policy* 23/10/15.

Walt, Stephen, 'This Isn't Realpolitik. This Is Amateur Hour', *Foreign Policy* 3/5/17, http://foreignpolicy.com/2017/05/03/this-isnt-realpolitik-this-is-amateur-hour/ [accessed 20/8/17].

Walt, Vivienne, 'Syria's air-defense arsenal: the Russian missiles keeping Assad in power', *Time* 3/6/13.

Watt, Nicholas, 'Tony Blair makes qualified apology for Iraq war ahead of Chilcot report', *Guardian* 25/10/15.

Wedeen, Lisa, *Ambiguities of Domination: Politics, Rhetoric, and Symbols in Contemporary Syria* (Chicago: University of Chicago Press, 1999).

Wehrey, Frederic, 'Saudi Arabia reins in its clerics on Syria', Carnegie Endowment for International Peace, July 2012, http://carnegieendowment.org/2012/06/14/saudi-arabia-reins-in-its-clerics-on-syria/bu10. [accessed 12/3/14].

Wehrey, Frederic, *The Forgotten Uprising in Eastern Saudi Arabia*, Carnegie Endowment for International Peace, 2013.

Wehrey, Frederic, Jerrold D. Green, Brian Nichiporuk, Alireza Nader, Lydia Hansell, Rasool Nafisi and S.R. Bohandy, *The Rise of Pasrdaran: Assessing the Domestic Roles of Iran's Islamic Revolutionary Guards Corps* (Washington: Rand Corps, 2009).

Weir, Fred. 'In Georgia, Russia saw its Army's shortcomings', *Christian Science Monitor* 10/10/08 http://www.csmonitor.com/World/Europe/2008/1010/p01s01–woeu.html [accessed 10/2/16].

Weiss, Michael and Hassan Hassan, *Isis: Inside the Army of Terror* (New York: Regan Arts, 2015) [Kindle edition].

Weiss, Michael, 'Russia is sending jihadis to join ISIS', *Daily Beast*, 23/8/15, http://www.thedailybeast.com/articles/2015/08/23/russia-s-playing-a-double-game-with-islamic-terror0.html [accessed 2/3/16].

White, Jeffrey, 'The Qusayr rules: the Syrian regime's changing way of war', The Washington Institute 31/5/13, http://www.washingtoninstitute.org/policy-analysis/view/the-qusayr-rules-the-syrian-regimes-changing-way-of-war [accessed 20/1/16].

Wieland, Carsten, *Syria at Bay: Secularism, Islamism, and 'Pax Americana'* (London-Hurst 2005).

Wikileaks, 'What lies beneath Ankara's new foreign policy', leaked memo from James Jeffrey, 26/1/10, Wikileaks https://www.wikileaks.ch/cable/2010/01/10ANKARA87.html [accessed 10/12/15].

Williams, Lauren, 'Syrians adjust to life under ISIS rule', *Daily Star* 30/8/14.

Williams, Lauren, 'Syria's Alawites not deserting Assad yet, despite crackdown', *Middle East Eye* 11/9/14, http://www.middleeasteye.net/in-depth/features/syrias-alawites-not-deserting-assad-yet-despite-crackdown-526622504 [accessed 12/4/15].

Wintour, Patrick, 'Russia in power-broking role as Syria peace talks begin in Astana', *Guardian* 32/1/17, https://www.theguardian.com/world/2017/jan/22/russia-syria-talks-astana-kazakhstan- [accessed 6/8/17].

Wintour, Patrick, 'Russian aircraft carrier is more a show of force than "start of world war"', *Guardian* 20/10/16, https://www.theguardian.com/world/2016/oct/20/russian-fleet-aircraft-carrier-admiral-kuznetsov-syria [accessed 10/8/17].

Wohlforth, William C., 'Unipolarity, status competition, and great power war', *World Politics*, 61:01 (2009), 28–57.

Wolffe, Richard, 'How Trump's foreign policy threatens to make America weak again', *The Guardian* 2/7/17, https://www.theguardian.com/us-news/2017/jul/02/donald-trump-foreign-policy-diplomacy [accessed 1/8/17].

Wong, Kristina, 'Ex-NATO supreme commander: Obama will look back in "shame" on Syria', *The Hill* 14/14/16, http://thehill.com/policy/defense/310343-ex-nato-supreme-commander-obama-will-look-back-in-some-shame-on-syria [accessed 15/7/17].

Wright, Austin and Philip Ewing, 'Carter's unwelcome news: only 60 Syrian rebels fit for training', *Politico* 7/7/15, http://www.politico.com/story/2015/07/ash-carter-syrian-rebel-training-119812 [accessed 23/11/15].

Xinhua, 'Saudi king expresses support to Syrian president', *Xinhua* 29/3/11, http://news.xinhuanet.com/english2010/world/2011–03/29/c_13802184.htm [accessed 1/6/15].

Yassin-Kassab, Robin and Leila Al-Shami, *Burning Country: Syrians in Revolution and War* (London: Pluto, 2016).

Yazbek, Samar, *The Crossing: My Journey to the Shattered Heart of Syria* (London: Rider, 2015).

Yazigi, Jihad. 'Syria's war economy', ECFR April 2014, http://www.ecfr.eu/page/-/ECFR97_SYRIA_BRIEF_AW.pdf [accessed 4/12/14].

Yetkin, Murat, 'Syria intervention not off table', *Hurriyet* 12/8/11, http://www.hurriyetdaily-news.com/default.aspx?pageid=438&n=syria-intervention-not-off-table-2011–08–12#.TkaR7iNMDA8.blogger [accessed 12/12/15].

Yglesias, Matthew, 'Obama – The Vox Conversation', *Vox* 8/2/15, http://www.vox.com/a/barack-obama-interview-vox-conversation/obama-foreign-policy-transcript [accessed 10/10/15].

Zakaria, Fareed, *The Post-American World* (New York: W.W. Norton, 2008).

Zirulnick, Ariel, 'Government forces open fire on protesters in Syria's third-largest city, Homs', *Christian Science Monitor* 19/4/11, http://www.csmonitor.com/World/terrorism-security/2011/0419/Government-forces-open-fire-on-protesters-in-Syria-s-third-largest-city-Homs [accessed 10/9/15].

Index